An Astrological Diary of the
Seventeenth Century

An Astrological Diary of the Seventeenth Century

Samuel Jeake of Rye
1652–1699

EDITED WITH AN INTRODUCTION
BY MICHAEL HUNTER AND
ANNABEL GREGORY

CLARENDON PRESS · OXFORD

1988

Oxford University Press, Walton Street, Oxford OX2 6DP

Oxford New York Toronto
Delhi Bombay Calcutta Madras Karachi
Petaling Jaya Singapore Hong Kong Tokyo
Nairobi Dar es Salaam Cape Town
Melbourne Auckland

and associated companies in
Beirut Berlin Ibadan Nicosia

Oxford is a trade mark of Oxford University Press

Published in the United States
by Oxford University Press, New York

British Library Cataloguing in Publication Data
Jeake, Samuel
An astrological diary of the seventeenth
century: Samuel Jeake of Rye, 1652–1699.
1. Astrology
I. Title   II. Hunter, Michael
III. Gregory, Annabel
133.5   BF1708.1
ISBN 0-19-822962-3

Library of Congress Cataloging in Publication Data
Jeake, Samuel, 1652–1699.
An Astrological diary of the seventeenth century.
Bibliography: p.
Includes index.
1. Horoscopes—History—17th century. 2. Astrology—
History—17th century. 3. Jeake, Samuel, 1652–1699—
Diaries. I. Hunter, Michael. II. Gregory, Annabel.
BF1728.A2J43 1987   133.5   87-12269
ISBN 0-19-822962 3

Set by Eta Services (Typesetters) Ltd, Beccles, Suffolk
Printed and bound in Great Britain by
Biddles Ltd, Guildford and King's Lynn

PREFACE

THIS book is the principal fruit of a search by Michael Hunter for manuscripts which might throw fresh light on the history of English astrology in its seventeenth-century heyday. Much has been written about astrology in early modern England, particularly in Keith Thomas' *Religion and the Decline of Magic* (London, 1971) and Bernard Capp's *Astrology and the Popular Press* (London, 1979). Both books give excellent accounts of astrological practice and its context but both are pitched at a general level, and it seemed worth while to try to probe more deeply into individual cases of astrological enthusiasm to see what could be learnt from these about the uses to which people put the art in their lives, and about the relationship of astrology to other developments at the time.

Jeake's diary came to light in 1981 while the search was being pursued at the William Andrews Clark Memorial Library, University of California, Los Angeles. Its significance for the history of astrology was immediately apparent, as was its quality as a source in its own right, despite the fact that Jeake's name was at that time as unfamiliar to Michael Hunter as it will be to most readers of this book. On his return to England, however, he enquired further of his colleague, Annabel Gregory, who had worked extensively on the history of early modern Rye, and learnt that Jeake was indeed well known to historians of Rye, who had been searching for his apparently lost diary for years.

Subsequent investigation revealed that not only the diary but a profusion of manuscripts associated with Jeake survive. One major holding is at the East Sussex County Record Office at Lewes, which has two Jeake items in the Rye municipal archive, an eighteenth-century copy of a map of the town made by Jeake in 1667 and his ledger for 1680–8, which was presented to the Corporation by a local estate agent in 1916, presumably after being found in a house in the town. In addition, the Record Office has extensive holdings of the correspondence of both Jeake and his father—in the case of the younger man, mostly business correspondence, though including some letters to and from his father and his wife. These letters are on deposit at Lewes as part of the Frewen family archive; the Jeakes became linked to the Frewens through the marriage to Dr Thomas Frewen of Philadelphia, daughter of the diarist's widow, Elizabeth, by her second husband, Joseph Tucker.

v

More remarkable, however, is the collection of Jeake manuscripts now housed at Rye Museum, the majority of them on deposit by their owners, the Selmes family. These also descended to the Frewens, but in the mid-nineteenth century they were lent and subsequently given to Dr Wake Smart, a local doctor and antiquary who developed an interest in the Jeakes. Like the diary, they then disappeared from sight for nearly a century, coming to light only in 1959, and they have been very little known since. Among them are a full series of Jeake's school-books and early calligraphic exercises; his accounts for the 1670s; the shorthand diary for 1699 which has been included in this edition; and, above all, an extensive series of manuscripts dealing with astrology. Indeed, with the diary and *Astrological Experiments Exemplified*, another astrological work which was acquired by the William Andrews Clark Memorial Library at the same time as that, Jeake's astrological writings survive almost complete.

In the course of our Introduction and apparatus a good deal will be said about these works and about the relationship between astrology and Jeake's other interests and activities. Astrology figures prominently in sections 2 and 9 of the Introduction and more briefly in sections 6 and 7, and we hope that the account we have given of Jeake's aspirations for improving the art and the uses to which he put it will be of interest to all concerned with the history of astrology.

But we have also been encouraged by our publishers to take advantage of the profuse survival of Jeake's accounts, letters, and other non-astrological manuscripts to fill in the background to the diary's other prominent themes. The result is a lengthy account of Jeake which we hope will help to rescue him from the unjust neglect that he has suffered; it should also underline the diary's significance as a source for the intellectual, political, social, and economic history of its day.

Responsibility for this book has been shared as follows. Annabel Gregory has transcribed the diary text and transliterated the passages in Jeake's shorthand, of which she has made a special study. Michael Hunter has written the Introduction. The annotation of the text and the preparation of the apparatus has been the joint work of both authors.

While preparing this volume we have incurred many debts, and various people must be singled out for special thanks. At Rye, Mr Geoffrey Bagley, Honorary Curator of Rye Museum, has long been a champion of the Jeakes, 'Rye's most remarkable family', as he has put it in his *Book of Rye* (Buckingham, 1982). He has been enthusiastic about our project since first learning of our discovery of the diary, and has been most co-operative in providing access to and making copies of the Jeake manuscripts in Rye Museum, including the 1699 diary published as Appendix 1, permission to print which has been given by its owner, Mr Nicholas Selmes. Christopher Whittick of East Sussex County Record Office has been a constant source of encouragement, remaining indefatigable to the last in making suggestions and providing information. At the Clark Library, Carol Reid Briggs has been most attentive in answering queries, facilitating access to the manuscript, and arranging for items to be photographed, while in London Geoffrey Cornelius has spent many hours in helping to unravel the diary's astrological mysteries.

The following have read all or part of our work in typescript and have made helpful suggestions for improving it: David Bebbington, Lucinda Beier, Colin Brent, Barry Coward, J. C. Eade, Kaspar von Greyerz, Ralph Houlbrooke, Neil Keeble, Milo Keynes, Peter Le Fevre, Margaret Pelling, Isabel Rivers, Ronald Sawyer, David Vaisey, and Margaret Whittick. Other have kindly answered specific queries or assisted in more miscellaneous ways: Jennifer Bray, Judith Brent, Patrick Curry, Liz Doff, Janet Dudley, Jill Eddison, Moti Feingold, Lady Frewen, Henry Gillett, Maggie Hanbury, David Harley, Cynthia Herrup, Tim Hudson, Maggie Hyde, Graham Mayhew, Mary Parsons, James Robertson, J. W. Steedman, David Sulkin, Eric Tappe, and Keith Thomas. John Andrews gave us permission to cite his unpublished thesis. Work on the final stages of the project was facilitated by the award to Michael Hunter of a short-term Fellowship at the Clark Library in March–April 1987. A generous grant from the Wolfson Foundation has paid for various expenses that we have incurred in our work, and this has been supplemented by a Research Grant from Birkbeck College. To everyone in this list we extend our warm thanks, and we hope that they will feel satisfied with the finished work.

M.H.
A.G.

CONTENTS

LIST OF ILLUSTRATIONS

List of Illustrations

SYMBOLS AND ABBREVIATIONS

☉	Sunday
☽	Monday
♂	Tuesday
☿	Wednesday
♃	Thursday
♀	Friday
♄	Saturday

For elucidation of the symbols used in Jeake's horoscopes see Appendix 2 (ii).

AEE	Samuel Jeake, *Astrological Experiments Exemplified*, William Andrews Clark Memorial Library, University of California, Los Angeles, MS J43M3/A859.
AMS	ESRO Additional Manuscripts.
Berry	William Berry (ed.), *County Genealogies . . . of the County of Kent* (London, 1830).
Burchall	M. J. Burchall, 'Inhabitants of Rye in 1660', *Sussex Genealogist and Local Historian*, 4 (1982), 97–108.
Cowper	J. M. Cowper (ed.), *Canterbury Marriage Licenses: 4th series, 1677–1700* (Canterbury, 1898).
CSP Dom.	*Calendar of State Papers, Domestic.*
DNB	*Dictionary of National Biography.*
ESRO	East Sussex County Record Office.
Foster	Joseph Foster (ed.), *Alumni Oxonienses, 1500–1714* (4 vols., Oxford, 1891–2).
FRE	ESRO Frewen Archive.
Henning	B. D. Henning, *The House of Commons, 1660–1690* (3 vols., London, 1983).
Holloway	William Holloway, *The History and Antiquities of the Town and Port of Rye* (London, 1847).
Hull	Felix Hull (ed.), *A Calendar of the White and Black Books of the Cinque Ports* (Kent Records, 19, 1966).
Jeake MS(S)	Jeake manuscript(s) at Rye Museum from the Deacon and other bequests.
KAO	Kent Archives Office.
LAWR	ESRO Lewes Archdeaconry Wills Register.
PAB	ESRO Paine and Brettell (Grebble and Lamb of Rye) Archive.
PCC	Prerogative Court of Canterbury Wills (references in the footnotes are to the relevant microfilm reels at the PRO).

PRO   Public Record Office.
RYE   ESRO Rye Corporation Archives.
SAC   *Sussex Archaeological Collections.*
SAU   ESRO St Audries (Fuller of Catsfield) Archive.
Selmes MS(S) Rye Museum Selmes Manuscript(s).
Smart   T. W. W. Smart, 'A Biographical Sketch of Samuel Jeake, senior,
            of Rye', *SAC*, 13 (1861), 57–79.
SP   State Papers.
Venn   John and J. A. Venn, *Alumni Cantabrigienses: Part 1, to 1751*
            (4 vols., Cambridge, 1922–7).
Vidler   L. A. Vidler, *A New History of Rye* (Hove, 1934).
Wing   Donald Wing, *Short-Title Catalogue of Books Printed in England*
            ... 1641–1700 (vols. 1–2, 2nd edn., New York, 1972–82, vol. 3, 1st
            edn., New York, 1951).
Woodhead   J. R. Woodhead, *The Rulers of London, 1660–1689* (London, 1965).
WSRO   West Sussex County Record Office.

INTRODUCTION

I. THE DIARY AND ITS AUTHOR

THE diary of Samuel Jeake (1652–99), which is here published for the first time, represents a quite novel addition to the autobiographical literature that has come down to us from seventeenth-century England. Until recently, historians might have been forgiven for presuming that Jeake's diary, though extant in the nineteenth century, had since been lost. Extensive quotations were made from the work by William Holloway in his *History and Antiquities of the Town and Port of Rye* (1847), while the manuscript was the subject of a brief correspondence in *Notes and Queries* in 1893.[1] But then it disappeared from sight until 1959, when it was purchased from an English bookseller by the William Andrews Clark Memorial Library, University of California, Los Angeles. Though its presence at the Clark has not been widely known, those who have had the opportunity of reading the manuscript have been immediately struck by its quality,[2] and it is by courtesy of its present owners that this unusual and intriguing document now appears in print in full.

Though relatively brief, and lacking in the frankness of such contemporary diaries as that of Samuel Pepys, Jeake's has a number of features which make it remarkable. In its initial conception, the diary's roots are to be found in the tradition of autobiographical writing associated with the Puritans in seventeenth-century England, and it shares various characteristics with works of this kind, including a preoccupation with the dispensations of God's providence. But it diverges from this tradition in quite significant ways, while it has a number of other components which are highly noteworthy.

Most immediately striking is its author's interest in astrology, for one of Jeake's motives in compiling the diary was to subject the events of his life to

---

[1] Holloway, esp. pp. 344–5, 550–76, 605–7; *Notes and Queries*, 8th ser. 4 (1893), 147, 277–8, 374. See also W. D. Cooper, 'Monetary Affairs after the Revolution of 1688', *Gentleman's Magazine*, 37 (1852), 567–8 (where Jeake's name is unfortunately spelt 'Leake').

[2] See e.g. an unpublished letter from H. G. Dick to L. C. Powell, 27 Feb. 1959, at the Clark Library. The only published reference to the manuscript since it has been at the Clark is in Thomas Shelton, *A Tutor to Tachygraphy* and *Tachygraphy*, ed. William Matthews (Augustan Reprint Society, Nos. 145–6, 1970), p. ii.

astrological analysis. Perhaps the work's strangest feature is a sequence of thirty-six horoscopes concerning critical moments in his life, while astrological comments are scattered through the text, and an astrological rationale clearly partially dictated its content. Autobiographical writings for astrological purposes—though relatively unusual—comprise a significant genre in seventeenth-century England which has hitherto been entirely overlooked: Jeake's is perhaps the most remarkable specimen of its type.

In addition, the diary provides a very full view of Jeake's intellectual development, not least through the numbered list it gives of books that he had read. This is virtually without parallel, as is the obsessive catalogue of attacks of 'ague' that Jeake included, part of a very detailed medical history which is again of considerable interest.

The diary also provides unusually extensive information on the life of a provincial merchant. Personal writings by merchants and tradesmen are rare, and even those that exist often take the form of spiritual autobiographies to which the author's source of livelihood was incidental.[3] But Jeake's gives a detailed view of his commercial activity in and around Rye over some twenty years, at times on a virtually day-to-day basis. Moreover, whereas as a record of local economic life Jeake's account may be paralleled by others—such as the autobiography of William Stout of Lancaster—in its latter stages the diary reaches a climax with its narrative of Jeake's encounter with the London money-market and the newly founded Bank of England, and here again his diary is unique. Jeake's is the only known journal of the Financial Revolution then in progress written from the point of view of one of the hundreds of small investors who helped to make it possible.

Lastly, the diary is notable for the way in which its different components are juxtaposed. In view of our expectations about the forces making for change in early modern England, we may initially be surprised to find a merchant who invested in the Bank of England casting a horoscope for the moment at which he did so. The relationship between Jeake's religious views and his astrology is also of considerable interest, as is his eclectic mixture of magic and science. It is not least for its combination of the predictable and the unpredictable that the diary is worthy of a place in the autobiographical literature of its day.

Samuel Jeake was born and lived all his life in the ancient port of Rye in Sus-

---

[3] See e.g. W. Orme (ed.), *Remarkable Passages in the Life of William Kiffin* (London, 1823). On the rarity of such writings by merchants see J. D. Marshall (ed.), *The Autobiography of William Stout of Lancaster, 1665–1752* (Manchester, 1967), 1, 14–16. For listings of diaries and autobiographies of the period see William Matthews, *British Diaries* (Berkeley and Los Angeles, 1950) and *British Autobiographies* (Berkeley and Los Angeles, 1955).

sex. The Jeakes were probably of Huguenot extraction: 'Jeake' is evidently a bizarre Sussex variant of 'Jacques'. The earliest member of the family of whom we hear is William Jeake, who appears to have been a merchant in the late sixteenth century, and who was probably father of the diarist's grand-father, Henry Jeake, a baker in the town.[4] Though little is known of Henry Jeake himself beyond the fact that he was reasonably well off, more informa-tion is available about his wife, Anne Peerson, and the diarist's mother, Frances Hartridge. Both came from a strongly Puritan background, as is illustrated by a series of letters which survive because they were incorpor-ated into a letterbook compiled by the diarist's father, also Samuel Jeake, which has been used to paint a telling picture of godly circles in Sussex in the early seventeenth century.[5]

This elder Samuel Jeake (1623–90) was a committed evangelist and a leading figure in Rye affairs throughout the mid and late seventeenth cen-tury. His upbringing and education remain frustratingly obscure; but already in the early 1640s, when only in his teens, he was involved in heated religious debates in the town. Later in that decade he penned a petition to Lord General Fairfax in the aftermath of the Civil War, hailing Fairfax as the nation's saviour and urging him to take the opportunity to realize the programme of retribution and reform to which Jeake and his circle were committed.[6] In the 1650s Jeake remained active as a religious leader and preacher, as is documented by surviving sermons and letters of godly exhor-tation.[7] He also acted as registrar of births, deaths, and marriages under the Cromwellian Marriage Act, and as town clerk, a job for which he was fitted by the legal career which he had by this time adopted in the interstices between his religious activities.

After the Restoration Jeake lost his position as town clerk, but he con-tinued to lead the nonconformist congregation in Rye, combining this with a flourishing legal practice in the neighbourhood until the 1680s, when he was forced to flee to London by the persecution which is described in the younger Jeake's diary and will be considered more fully later in this intro-duction. Indeed the virulence with which he was attacked at that point itself testifies to his dominant role in the town: 'I should be glad to see you at

---

[4] Smart, p. 57; R. F. Dell (ed.), *Rye Shipping Records, 1566–90* (Sussex Record Society, 64, 1965–6), 26–7; Vidler, p. 76.

[5] FRE 4223; Anthony Fletcher, *A County Community in Peace and War: Sussex, 1600–1660* (London, 1975), esp. ch. 3, and 'Puritanism in Seventeenth Century Sussex', in M. J. Kitch (ed.), *Studies in Sussex Church History* (London, 1981), 141–55.

[6] Fletcher, *County Community* (see n. 5 above), 292–3; see also ibid., ch. 6.

[7] Selmes MS 4; FRE 4223. See also Holloway, p. 554.

home for me thinkes Rye is naked without you', complained a friend when Jeake was briefly in London in 1664.[8]

The elder Jeake was no inconsiderable intellectual, the author of two scholarly books published after his death and of other works which remain in manuscript. His Λογιστικηλογία or *Arithmetick Surveighed and Reviewed* was published in 1696 by his son in a typical gesture of filial piety, the early stages of which are described in the diary;[9] his *Charters of the Cinque Ports* followed in 1728. Moreover, Jeake's letters and papers—many of which survive—were made the subject of an important study by the nineteenth-century doctor and antiquary T. W. W. Smart.[10] He also owned a remarkable library and a collection of rarities, which he gave to his son in 1672 (6.5.72).

By comparison, the younger Jeake is less well known, and it is hoped that the present work will attract more attention to him. He never published a book of his own, and he has hitherto been overshadowed by his father, whom he outlived by less than a decade. Clearly the father and son had a very intense relationship, which the diary documents, not least in its moving description of the older man's last illness and death (3.10.90). The diarist's mother and his only brother and sister had all died by the time he was four years old, and thereafter he and his father lived alone together until his own marriage and the older man's exile in the 1680s. In addition, the elder Jeake was solely responsible for his son's education, since the boy attended school only for a few months (21.4, 6.7.56).

As a career, the younger man chose that of a merchant, thereby exemplifying a trend among Restoration nonconformists that has often been commented on, and contrasting with the professional and administrative calling of his father.[11] Nevertheless, it is clear that his father's influence explains much about the younger man, and not least the extent of his intellectual activities, unusual for a merchant.[12] Even the diarist's passionate interest in astrology was initially learnt from his father, who had indulged in such pursuits since the late 1640s.[13]

But the younger Jeake was no pale reflection of the older. Though the two

---

[8] Richard Hartshorne to Jeake, 20 Oct. 1664, FRE 4387. For other letters from Hartshorne to Jeake, see FRE 4412, 4481, 4765.

[9] 15, 21.6, 11.8.93; 18.4.94. Here and herinafter, references in this form in both the notes and the text denote entries in the diary: i.e., the day followed by the month followed by the year.

[10] Smart. See also 18.9.91 and, on the library, below, sect. 6.

[11] See e.g. R. H. Tawney, *Religion and the Rise of Capitalism* (London, 1926), 252–3, Charles Wilson, *England's Apprenticeship* (2nd edn., London, 1985), 137, 340–2.

[12] Cf. Michael Hunter, *Science and Society in Restoration England* (Cambridge, 1981), 74.

[13] See Smart, pp. 71–5; Selmes MS 2 (an analysis of his nativity of 1648).

shared an interest in astrology, it should be stressed that for the father this was one out of a number of scholarly concerns, whereas the son pursued astrology with a single-mindedness amounting almost to obsession.

Indeed, though unknown in this connection since none of his writings has hitherto been published, Jeake was a prolific astrological author. His various writings on this topic, including the diary, illustrate astrology's marked intellectual vitality in his day, and the seriousness with which its study might be pursued. The importance that Jeake attached to his activity in this field is illustrated by an autobiographical sketch of 1687, in which he placed 'His Studies Astrological' before 'His Imployment Merchandize'.[14]

Quite apart from his commitment to astrology and his career as a merchant, the younger Jeake also deserves to be better known for the portrait of himself which—as might be expected from a good diary—emerges from the text that follows. At one point he actually describes his appearance almost as if looking at himself in a mirror, itemizing his 'Face pale & lean, Forehead high; Eyes grey, Nose large, Teeth bad & distorted' (4.7.71).

Cumulatively the piecemeal entries provide a telling picture of Jeake's priorities and preoccupations and his attitude to the world. The diary gives a sense of an earnest, self-preoccupied figure, conscientious, hard-working, and ever keen to better himself. One is also struck by Jeake's enquiring, empirical frame of mind, his precise and methodical approach to all facets of his life, and his engrained pessimism and cautiousness, which at times verges on the ridiculous. For all his formality, there is an endearing quality about Jeake which the reader soon comes to appreciate, while the comments that he makes in passing often have a disarming candour from which much can be learnt.

2. RELIGION, ASTROLOGY, AND THE MAKING OF THE DIARY

What made Jeake wish to record the 'Actions & Accidents' of his life in such detail? To some extent, he partook of the obsessive quality which makes a diarist, the proclivity to compile lists and to arrange things neatly that is so much in evidence in diary-keeping contemporaries like Samuel Pepys or Oliver Heywood.[1] Jeake's notes on his height at annual intervals during his

---

[14] *AEE*, p. 7.

[1] Cf. R. C. Latham and William Matthews (eds.), *The Diary of Samuel Pepys* (11 vols., London, 1970–83), i. xxviii and *passim*; J. H. Turner (ed.), *The Rev. Oliver Heywood, BA, 1630–1702: His Autobiography, Diaries, Anecdote, and Event Books* (4 vols., Brighouse and Bingley, 1881–5). For Jeake's records of his height see 4.7.55, 4.7.66, 4.7.68, 4.7.69, 4.7.70.

youth make sense in this context, for instance, as do some of the more miscellaneous and trivial details which he included later in life.

Another motive may have been to provide memoranda for future reference, as seen in Jeake's careful record of his exact words on such important occasions as his proposal of marriage (14.6.80) or his taking oath as freeman of Rye (2.7.90). Concerning medication, too, he sometimes noted exact dosages for later use (16.4.86). Diaries dominated by such utilitarian notes were kept by people from many backgrounds in seventeenth-century England—a case in point might be the journal of the Revd Giles Moore of Horsted Keynes[2]—while Jeake's diary could at times be seen almost as an extension of his business records, as when it epitomizes his financial balance at the end of the year. Indeed the diary's neatness and precision parallels the comparably painstaking quality of Jeake's accounts, especially his surviving ledger for 1680–8.[3]

A third commonplace impulse to diary-writing of which Jeake partook to an extent was the desire to record historical events as they occurred. Indeed this 'urge to be a chronicler of the times' has been seen by William Matthews as 'probably the commonest reason for writing diaries'.[4] In Jeake's case it applies only sporadically, but a sense of witnessing history clearly underlies his extended account of the persecution of the Rye nonconformists in the 1680s or his relation of the French invasion threat in July 1690, where it is as if the excitement of the moment impelled Jeake to a narrative that took on a momentum of its own.

Apart from these general motives, however, there are two more specific ones, both of them alluded to in Jeake's title. As he there explains, his intention was partly to record the providences displayed in his life, and partly to investigate its astrological circumstances.

It is proper to take the non-astrological motive first, since Jeake tells us that he began to keep diary memoranda on 18 July 1666, in other words before he began to learn astrology on 25 June 1667, and the context of his initial essay in diary-writing is clearly provided by his Puritan background. The profuse evangelical exhortation to which he was exposed as a boy is revealed by a letter that his father wrote to him when he was in London in 1668, urging him to 'Looke into the freeness of grace in the Gospell tendered to unworthy soules, chiefe sinners, &c'.[5] This Puritan strain is also illus-

---

[2] Ruth Bird (ed.), *The Journal of Giles Moore* (Sussex Record Society, 68, 1971).

[3] RYE 145/11.

[4] Latham and Matthews, *Pepys* (see sect. 2 n. 1), i. cvii. Cf. Paul Delany, *British Autobiography in the Seventeenth Century* (London, 1969), ch. 2.

[5] FRE 4823. On Jeake's reading, see below, sect. 6.

trated at various points in the diary, for instance in Jeake's scruples about sightseeing on the sabbath at Rouen (19.4.74), while his early reading included a succession of godly books.

Among these were a number of Puritan biographies and autobiographies, works in which individuals' spiritual progress was chronicled and assessed and which, as William Haller and others have noted, overlapped in function with diaries.[6] The books Jeake read included Samuel Clarke's *Martyrologie* (7),[7] an anthology of the lives of godly Protestants of the sixteenth century, Henry Jessey's *The Exceeding Riches of Grace Advanced by the Spirit of Grace in ... Sarah Wight* (69), a classic narrative of despair and conversion, and, most telling of all, John Bunyan's *Grace Abounding to the Chief of Sinners* (71), which Jeake read within a year of its publication in 1666. In the first instance it may be deduced that Jeake intended to keep the kind of spiritual journal devoted to self-examination and the recording of God's mercies that was so common among the godly in seventeenth-century England, being disproportionately associated with nonconformists, and especially nonconformist ministers, after 1660.

The influence of Jeake's Puritan and nonconformist reading matter is also evident in another of his works of the mid-1660s. This is a carefully written volume containing 'Some Letters concerning the Return of the ten Tribes of Israel &c'—giving an account of the activities in the Near East in 1665–6 of the supposed messiah, Sabbatai Sevi—and 'Some Prodigies, Remarkable and signall Judgements on divers Persons &c beginning An° Christi 1664'. The latter comprised apparitions, strange natural effects, and the like, mostly taken from printed news-sheets and hearsay, but a few of which Jeake had observed himself. It clearly took its inspiration from published collections of omens indicating God's displeasure with the Restoration regime, another characteristic nonconformist genre of which the first and most influential specimen was also read by Jeake, Henry Jessey's *The Lords Loud Call to England* (40). Jeake's notes of abnormal celestial phenomena that he had witnessed provide examples of memoranda of the period when the diary was begun: for instance, under July 1665, 'A little before night two

---

[6] William Haller, *The Rise of Puritanism* (1938; new edn., New York, 1957), 38, 96 ff. See also Owen C. Watkins, *The Puritan Experience* (London, 1972), Dean Ebner, *Autobiography in Seventeenth-century England* (The Hague, 1971), and G. A. Starr, *Defoe and Spiritual Autobiography* (Princeton, 1965), ch. 1. For a penetrating study of another product of this tradition, see P. S. Seaver, *Wallington's World: A Puritan Artisan in Seventeenth-century London* (London, 1985).

[7] Here and in sects. 6 and 10 below, bracketed numbers in the text refer to numbered entries of books in the diary.

Rainbows were seen at Rye by me seeming about an ell distance the one from the other, one of them being exceeding bright'.[8]

Although—unlike this collection—the diary no longer survives in its original state, even in its present form it displays features typical of non-conformist journals of its day. The spiritual experiences recorded in the entries of 12 December 1664, 19 January 1671, and 23 May 1673 smack of the conversion narrative in their reference to 'assurance' and 'the Faith of Recumbency', and the diary may initially have overlapped with the 'Catalogue of sins' which Jeake notes that he discontinued in 1667. Equally characteristic is the theme announced by the diary's title, for the notion of recording God's providences as a guard against forgetfulness and ingratitude was a major impulse to autobiographical writing in Jeake's time. Others avowed this motive in their introductory remarks—like Henry Newcome or William Kiffin, for instance—while Ralph Josselin entitled his journal 'A thankfull observacion of divine providence and goodnes towards mee and a summary view of my life'.[9]

Jeake's diary is full of invocations of providence, concerning almost every aspect of his activities—from journeys safely negotiated to illnesses survived and commercial transactions successfully carried through, and not least the latter. Indeed, Jeake well exemplifies that shift towards the legitimization of 'mundane materialism' that R. H. Tawney traced in Restoration non-conformity in his classic study, *Religion and the Rise of Capitalism*.[10]

Apart from such passing references. Jeake also records fifteen near disasters from which he was saved by God's providential intervention—falls, riding accidents, and the like. Such episodes were often recorded by autobiographers, 'sometimes with more enthusiasm than judgement', as a modern scholar has aptly put it,[11] and Jeake is a clear case in point, since the 'disaster' that he feared almost invariably failed to materialize. His description of his near accident on 30 September 1693, for instance, reveals a

---

[8] Selmes MS 22 (unfoliated). Cf. the entry dated 11.11.65; those dated 30.9.65, 24.1, and 4.12.66 also mention events in Rye. See also the 'Prodigy' recorded below, 1663 (which does not appear in Selmes MS 22). The source of a good deal of the material in this MS, and perhaps of Jeake's interest in it, was his father's friend, the former Vicar of Rye, John Allin. See especially W. D. Cooper, 'Notices of the Last Great Plague, 1665–6; from the Letters of John Allin to Philip Fryth and Samuel Jeake', *Archaeologia*, 37 (1857), 1–22. For the background see Michael McKeon, *Politics and Poetry in Restoration England* (Cambridge, Mass., 1975), chs. 6–7.

[9] Richard Parkinson (ed.), *The Autobiography of Henry Newcome* (2 vols., Chetham Society, 26–7, 1852), i. 1–2; Orme, *Kiffin* (see sect. 1 n. 3), 1; Alan Macfarlane (ed.), *The Diary of Ralph Josselin, 1616–1683* (London, 1976), 1.

[10] Tawney, *Religion and the Rise of Capitalism* (see sect. 1, n. 11), ch. 4.

[11] Sara H. Mendelson, 'Stuart Women's Diaries and Occasional Memoirs', in Mary Prior (ed.), *Women in English Society, 1500–1800* (London, 1985), 188.

dwindling scale of seriousness which is almost comic: if not drowned, he might have been trodden underfoot by his horse, and at the very least he might have got all wet. Here as elsewhere, however, he was provided with an opportunity to affirm God's special mercy towards him, as is seen particularly strikingly on the occasion when a sudden flash of lightning alerted him to an obstacle in his path in the absence of street lighting (16.8.93).

If Jeake's diary initially had its roots in this Puritan tradition, however, it is less interesting for what it has in common with such writings than for the ways in which it differs from them, bearing witness to a significant trend in late seventeenth-century nonconformist thought. For one thing, apart from this almost formulaic invocation of providence, religion is not a prominent theme of the diary. Jeake occasionally refers to his preaching and other activities in the Rye nonconformist community, and (more rarely still) to his Bible reading (2.3.84), while godly books continued to dominate his reading throughout his life. But, considering that it came from a genre which classically subordinated mundane events to an overriding spiritual purpose, the diary has an overwhelmingly worldly air, especially after its earliest years. In Jeake we have none of the tortured spirituality of John Bunyan or the obsessive religious bookkeeping of Ralph Josselin.[12]

This is not to say that Jeake did not continue to be actively pious. Indeed, the danger of caricaturing beliefs that are by definition inscrutable on the basis of a limited range of sources is illustrated by a surviving letter to his daughter written not long before his death in 1699. In contrast to the more worldly tone of Jeake's business correspondence with his wife in his later years, this is reminiscent of the 1668 letter from his father than has already been cited in its exhortation to her to 'endeavor to make a sanctified use of all afflictions, & let all the dispensations of providence draw you neerer to God, & more off from the world in which you are but a stranger . . . It is a comfort to me that I have observed in you some good thing towards the Lord God of Israel & I trust he will perfect that good work he has begun in your Conversion to him to serve the Living God'.[13]

Sermon notes survive that Jeake kept in the 1680s, as in the 1660s, and it is conceivable that the diary's mundane tone results from the fact that he kept separate spiritual memoranda, like such other diarists of his day as Oliver Heywood.[14] But the fact that Jeake's record includes evangelical

[12] For Bunyan see *Grace Abounding to the Chief of Sinners*, ed. Roger Sharrock (Oxford, 1962).
[13] FRE 5359. For his letters to his wife see FRE 5301–33. For later religious references in Jeake's diary see 28.4, 23.5.73, 6.9.76, 21.9.79, 3.10.90, 21.5.99, and below, sect. 4.
[14] Turner, *Heywood* (see sect. 2 n. 1), iii. 9–15 and *passim*. For Jeake's sermon notes see Selmes MSS 48 (1684) and 16, 18, 27 (all dating from the 1660s).

experiences in its early years but not thereafter suggests on the contrary that the diary reveals a different process at work. In it, we arguably see a change towards a religious style on Jeake's part which, though perfectly sincere, was more comfortable and conformist than that which had characterized the Puritans of the earlier seventeenth century. Indeed, the diary is probably a more reliable source in this respect than the letter to his daughter just quoted, the self-consciousness of which is evident from Jeake's rider that 'these directions that I give you will be of use to you in after times as well as now even through the whole course of your Life'.

To a certain extent, Jeake may himself have been aware how his views were evolving. Commenting on the time when he first addressed the Rye meeting, he notes—apart from his preference for natural theology—how he found himself 'not so fit for points of Doctrine & Application', presumably in contrast to evangelists like his father (21.9.79). More significant, however, is evidence which the diary provides for a change even within the providentialism which remains so prominent in it. If closely examined, Jeake's providentialism is strangely limited in comparison with the writings of a Bunyan or a Josselin. Authors like these display a strong sense of sin; for them, God's providence was an ambivalent force, as likely to chastise the godly for their shortcomings as to reward them, so that suffering or bereavement were to be seen as trials sent by God to stimulate self-examination and repentance. 'The Lord helpe to heare the noise of it, and to prevent what is more threatened herein if wee mend not', Henry Newcome exclaimed when his servant was hurt by a cow, and Adam Martindale, for instance, experienced 'afflictive providences' as often as beneficial ones. Hence in a diarist like Oliver Heywood, the invocation of God's providence is constantly balanced by anxious self-examination and abasement.[15]

In Jeake, however, the ambivalence has virtually disappeared. Providence was almost invariably benevolent,[16] and the diary reveals little sense of sin. Indeed, in his business life, Jeake seems to have seen God as blessing selfish and uncharitable acts which might have sent Puritans of the earlier seventeenth century into paroxysms of conscience, as when no-one would stand bail for a man whom he had had arrested for failing to maintain his side of a bargain (12.11.92). Though he occasionally experienced scruples in a com-

[15] Thomas Heywood (ed.), *The Diary of Rev. Henry Newcome from September 30 1661 to September 29 1663* (Chetham Society, 18, 1849), 18; Richard Parkinson (ed.), *The Life of Adam Martindale* (Chetham Society, 4, 1845), 21 and *passim*; Turner, *Heywood* (see sect. 2 n. 1). For a discussion of this issue in the context of Josselin's diary, see Alan Macfarlane, *The Family Life of Ralph Josselin* (Cambridge, 1970), ch. 11.

[16] For the single instance of an unfavourable providence recorded by Jeake see 28.4.87.

mercial context, Jeake was apparently blithely unaware of any conflict between his self-interest and God's purpose for him, except in so far as God might actually know better where his true interest lay (13.7.79, 15.11.94). Jeake appears to display a shift towards that complacency and worldliness which has often been seen as characteristic of contemporary Anglicanism, and, though this may not have been the norm among nonconformists of his day, parallels may be found among other products of a Puritan background, such as Joseph Lister of Bradford. As Lister put it at one point in his *Auto-biography*, 'My soul-trouble began to wear off, as I was taken up with other things'. Moreover Lister has a complacent attitude to providence like Jeake's, which is also in evidence in Samuel Pepys' diary—perhaps especially in the diarist's annual assessment of his affairs—and, later, in the secularized and vestigial providentialism of the eighteenth century.[17]

Jeake was at a formative stage in this development, but what is particularly interesting about his providentialism is how his usage in the diary illustrates this concept degenerating into a virtual cliché, from an expression of God's special solicitousness for his elect to a description of something more non-committal. On one occasion he wrote how 'meer Providence' put an idea into his head on the spur of the moment (18.2.90), while in two other cases where one might have expected 'providence' to be invoked, it is instead replaced by the more neutral 'circumstance'—once in connection with his abortive courtship of Mary Weeks in the 1670s, the other concerning a financial transaction of 1690 about which Jeake was embarrassed, where he noted that the other party died before he could enquire about it (21.1.80, 11.10.92). Jeake's diary valuably documents the process by which a preoccupation with mundane affairs ousted the ascetic other-worldliness of earlier Puritanism.

In Jeake's case, a symptom of this change was arguably his curiosity about astrology, the second theme juxtaposed with the religious one in the diary's title. Jeake chronicles the growth of his astrological interests from the late 1660s onwards, and astrological motives clearly impelled him both to write up the diary in its current form in 1694 and, earlier, to record much of the precise data that appears in it. Indeed, it is not fanciful to see the spiritual component of the diary declining as the astrological one came to prominence.

---

[17] Thomas Wright (ed.), *The Autobiography of Joseph Lister* (London, 1842), 28 and *passim*. Cf. Delany, *British Autobiography* (see sect. 2 n. 4), 79–80. Latham and Matthews, *Pepys* (see sect. 2 n. 1), ii. 1, 241–2, and *passim*. For a recent assessment of how providentialism changed after 1660 see Blair Worden, 'Providence and Politics in Cromwellian England', *Past and Present*, 109 (1985), 59–60, n. 12.

The significance of astrology in this context is that it claimed to provide a key to understanding the circumstances of all actions and occurrences. Moreover, in its concern with the secondary causes of events it drew attention away from God's direct will to the manner in which He worked, in a way which—as moralists of the day often pointed out—could lead to a dangerous complacency about primary causation.[18]

Here again Jeake's diary provides valuable evidence, in connection with the near accidents that have already been referred to: for the passages dealing with these often juxtapose the invocation of providence with an exposition of the astrological circumstances at the time and the casting of a horoscope. Usually, Jeake presents this information in a manner which implies that the astrological configuration indicated impending catastrophe which would inexorably have followed had God not providentially intervened. The way in which providence remained a separate, higher force is similarly displayed by the dream that Jeake recorded with an illustration on 1 November 1678, itself one of the more remarkable components of the diary: he interpreted this in mainly astrological terms, but found within it evidence of God's 'Divine protection & special Providence' towards him.

Whereas normally astrological circumstances and providential intervention were polarized, however, Jeake sometimes saw the two as overlapping. Thus in his entry on 21 April 1694 both the impending catastrophe and his escape from it were explained astrologically, providence operating through the system of secondary causation that astrology offered. Indeed here we evidently see the role of a special providence transcending the course of nature being eroded by a stress on secondary causes as the way in which God worked out his design—a phenomenon long familiar in fashionable and scientific circles at the time but which is perhaps surprising in a nonconformist like Jeake.[19] What is equally interesting, however, is that Jeake was evidently aware of this shift and uncomfortable about it, appending to his comments on this occasion a slightly defensive expostulation on 'the admirably miraculous Textures' of God's dispositions (21.4.94).

If this suggests a simple polarization between a supernaturalist religion and a naturalistic astrology, however, elsewhere a more complicated situation is in evidence. For astrology was not purely naturalistic, and this too

---

[18] Keith Thomas, *Religion and the Decline of Magic* (London, 1971), esp. 358–9; Barbara Donagan, 'Providence, Chance and Explanation: Some Paradoxical Aspects of Puritan Views of Causation', *Journal of Religious History*, 11 (1980–1), 397–8 and n. 47. For comments on this subject in Jeake's *Diapason* of 1671–2, see Selmes MS 34, pp. [72–3].

[19] Donagan, art. cit., pp. 402–3; Thomas, op. cit., 80, 109, 639–40; R. S. Westfall, *Science and Religion in Seventeenth-century England* (New Haven, 1958), ch. 4.

caused Jeake problems, as is illustrated by what he says concerning 'elections', in other words the use of astrology to choose an auspicious time for an action. This practice was questionable in the eyes of authors who attacked astrology on religious grounds, in that practitioners indulging in such acts could be accused of gaining an insight into the future through contact with supernatural powers of doubtful legitimacy: though Jeake does not actually cite such views, it is interesting that he showed a similar moralism in his qualms in 1694 about the use of lotteries, which had been the subject of a fierce debate in godly circles earlier in the seventeenth century.[20]

Significantly, on the only occasion when Jeake admitted to making an election, he disguised the information in shorthand (3.8.71), while in three places in the diary he explicitly denies electing a time. There may have been an element of self-deception in this: on 9 April 1694 Jeake's disclaimer rings rather hollow in juxtaposition with his note of the advantages to be expected from a journey begun at that moment, while the time he selected to lay the foundation-stone for his new storehouse in 1689 was also so clearly astrologically propitious that it is unlikely that it was not deliberately chosen—especially as he had the horoscope let into the wall of the building like a kind of talisman.[21] To confuse matters further, in his *Diapason. The Harmony of the Signes of Heaven*, an exposition of astrological principles which he wrote in 1671–2, Jeake had actually defended elections against the accusation that their use constituted 'illicite Magick'.[22]

Despite Jeake's equivocation, however, it seems likely that it was precisely because of the overtones of 'Magick' that he was wary of this practice, and this is typical of his approach to astrology, evidently due not least to his religious principles. Indeed, if Jeake's diary reveals much about religious change in his time, it is equally telling concerning developments within contemporary astrology.

From a twentieth-century perspective it is easy to place all of astrology, along with alchemy and similar pursuits, in an undifferentiated 'occult' category, contrasting with more scientific modes of thought. In fact, however, both astrology and alchemy have experienced a conflict between more magical and more rationalistic strands throughout their history, in the case of astrology between a more divinatory and a more naturalistic tradition. The

---

[20] 13.4.94; on the background, see Thomas, op. cit., 118–24; Margo Todd, 'Providence, Chance and the New Science in Early Stuart Cambridge', *Historical Journal*, 29 (1986), 697–711.
[21] 13.6.89 and n., though in this case matters are complicated by the issue of whether astral causes applied to artefacts, which was denied by Jeake's mentor, J. B. Morin: *Astrologia Gallica* (The Hague, 1661), 490 ff. For the third case see 20.4.94.
[22] Selmes MS 34, p. 56.

former was seen quintessentially in the 'horary', the interrogation of the heavens at a specific time in what was effectively a magical act, significance being attached to the astrological circumstances of that moment in its own right and no need being felt for a rationale in terms of the astrological character of the person carrying out the act as defined in his natal horoscope. The alternative view was associated initially with the Hellenistic writer Ptolemy, and later with astrologers who accepted his basic precepts even if they refined his techniques. This saw astrology as comparable to other forms of natural causation: special stress was laid on the horoscope of the time of birth, on the grounds that it was then that heavenly influence was imbued in a human being, and more magical facets of astrological practice which could not be accommodated within this framework were rejected.[23]

In late seventeenth-century England there was considerable enthusiasm for a rationalistic form of astrology, and Jeake clearly exemplifies the aspiration to an exact, non-magical astrological science. Though he partook of the more divinatory streak to an extent, for instance in interpreting his dream on 1 November 1678, he made no use whatever of 'horarys', and his anxiety even about elections—which many rationalistic astrologers had no difficulty in justifying—is symptomatic of an unease with any magical aspect of the art. Indeed, some of his judgements in the diary show a matter-of-factness and lack of preparedness to read the magical significance of what could be discerned in a horoscope that some astrologers would find unimaginative. Instead, his enthusiasm was for what could be tested and rationalized.

This quest for precision and elaboration is in evidence even in Jeake's earliest writings on astrology, including the lengthy Latin analysis of his 'Nativity' that he compiled in 1668, which is notable for its degree of elaboration in giving numerical quantities to the good and bad testimonies of the various planets concerning different facets of his prospects.[24] Equally revealing is his concern with 'directions', in other words arithmetical calculations of the likely time of future good or bad events from the conjunction of 'significator' and 'promittor' in the natal horoscope (for these and other technical terms see Appendix 2 (i)). Directions figure frequently in the diary, and they were of particular interest to Jeake because they appeared to promise a more rigorous and objective form of astrology than the other com-

---

[23] See Geoffrey Cornelius, 'The Moment of Astrology', *Astrology*, 57 (1983), 97–112, 140–50; (1984), 14–24, 85–95; 59 (1985), 42–9, 207–21. For helpful remarks on the situation in alchemy in Jeake's time see B. J. T. Dobbs, *The Foundations of Newton's Alchemy* (Cambridge, 1975), 27–9, 40–1.

[24] Selmes MS 29. See also Selmes MS 35, a further analysis of 1672.

ponents of traditional horoscopy. Indeed, it was not least because his book devoted particular attention to such matters that Jeake was so impressed by perhaps the greatest astrological reformer of the seventeenth century, the French doctor and academic J. B. Morin, whose massive *Astrologia Gallica* (1661) Jeake read between 3 April 1684 and 22 January 1685. In the verse 'Encomium' to Morin that he was inspired to compose, Jeake singled out for praise the Frenchman's 'New Instructive Methods' for this facet of the art.[25]

Not only was Jeake preoccupied by the more rationalistic aspects of astrology; equally symptomatic was his aspiration to refine the techniques and test the principles of astrology by careful empiricism, an interest which he shared with a number of authors of his day, including Morin in France and John Gadbury in England. In this, Jeake may be aligned with the scientific movement of the seventeenth century, and it is therefore not surprising to find that he read a number of books associated with the new philosophy. His astrological writings show a constant sense of being on the side of the 'moderns', while he repeatedly appeals in them to 'Experience against which can be no dispute'.[26] Indeed, it was typical that the word he used to describe what he was doing when he was not making an election was 'Experiment', a term redolent of the new science which was also used by other astrological authors like Gadbury.[27]

Jeake's earliest attempts to reappraise astrological principles date from the 1670s. His *Astrologicall Excercitations* of 1675 comprised a series of technical proposals for refining horoscopic analysis. Another of his projects concerned the weather, which many astrological enthusiasts hoped might be better understood by collating its changes with their astrological circumstances. To this end Jeake kept a weather diary from 1670 onwards, in which full details of each day's sun and clouds were recorded in vivid style. This work has one feature in common with the present diary, in that for a time it was interspersed with horoscopes, from which Jeake attempted to deduce from the state of the heavens at the new and full moon what the weather would be like

---

[25] Selmes MS 49. On Morin see esp. Lynn Thorndike, *A History of Magic and Experimental Science*, 7 (New York, 1958), ch. 16. For evidence of Jeake's earlier interest in directions, see esp. Selmes MSS 35–6, which list and analyse directions for the 1670s.

[26] Selmes MS 34, p. 68 and *passim*. On Jeake's reading see below, sect. 6.

[27] 13.6.89, 9.4.94. See also 11.8.93. For the usage of 'experiment' see Bernard Capp, *Astrology and the Popular Press* (London, 1979), 183–5; B. S. Ingram (ed.), *Three Sea Journals of Stuart Times* (London, 1936), 75. On English astrological reformers see Capp, op. cit., 180 ff.; M. E. Bowden, 'The Scientific Revolution in Astrology: The English Reformers, 1558–1686', Yale Ph.D. thesis, 1974; and Michael Hunter, *John Aubrey and the Realm of Learning* (London, 1975), 119–21, 144–5.

in the period that followed, sometimes adding 'Error' if his expectations failed to be realized.[28]

In 1677, however, Jeake abandoned this enterprise, and there was then a gap in his astrological writings until the 1680s, when he set about a much more unusual programme of astrological enquiry, of which the diary forms part. Most writers who tried to test and re-evaluate astrological rules as applied to human affairs did so by deploying fairly superficial data about a wide range of people, as, for instance, in Gadbury's *Collectio Geniturarum* (1662). Indeed, Jeake had evidently engaged in such an enterprise himself in the 1670s, drawing up natal horoscopes for some 152 people, mostly from Rye, and collecting information on illnesses and other events that befell them with a view to collating their lives with the astrological circumstances of their birth.[29] Now, however, he abandoned this broader exercise and narrowed his focus to his own life. This may seem rather self-obsessed, but its result was to give his investigations a prominent autobiographical streak which adds greatly to their retrospective interest.

Perhaps the most significant of Jeake's writings of this kind was his *Astrological Experiments Exemplified*, the stages of whose composition are recorded in the diary (5.7.87, 16.10.88). In this work, Jeake attempted to correlate data about his affairs during a single year with their astrological circumstances, and specifically with the directions that could be observed in a horoscope drawn up for the moment of that year's solar revolution. He therefore compiled an elaborate list of these directions, juxtaposed them with a complete account of his activities from 4 July 1687 to 3 July 1688, and then wrote a series of painstaking 'Theoremes' in which he explored the nature of astrological causation and drew conclusions about the significance of differing positions and relationships of the planets and zodiac signs. The whole was neatly transcribed and prefaced by a manifesto for the refinement and improvement of astrology by careful empiricism, and in 1694 Jeake took it to London and showed it to the well-known astrologer Henry Coley, perhaps with a view to having it published, though nothing came of this.[30]

The diary continued Jeake's programme of astrological investigation based on his own life, and it appears to have had two functions. One, as the title states, was 'to investigate the Measure of Time in Astronomical Directions'. The Measure of Time was the formula by which allowance was made

---

[28] Selmes MSS 38, 33.

[29] See July/Aug. 70 and n. The data from which the horoscopes in Selmes MS 32 were compiled is to be found in Jeake MS 2, a collection of notes begun by the elder Jeake and continued and greatly elaborated by the younger; the events recorded go up to 1682.

[30] For the hope of publication see *AEE*, p. 21. The work's rather portentous style may also reflect this ambition: ibid., *passim*.

for a person's age in interpreting the directions in his natal horoscope: alternative methods of calculating it had been suggested by astrologers from Ptolemy onwards, including authors of the sixteenth and earlier seventeenth centuries like Johann Kepler, G. A. Magini, and Valentine Naibode as well as Jeake's English contemporaries John Eyres and John Kendal. Jeake notes that he wrote to Kendal on this subject in 1692, and it was perhaps at this point that he came up with the idea of collating a series of significant events or 'accidents' in his life with the directions which were deemed to have caused them, as a means of assessing which Measure was most reliable.[31]

He undertook this, not in the diary, but in a further work which he began in 1695 and to which the compilation of the diary is to be seen as a preparatory stage. This was an elaborate analysis of Jeake's natal horoscope or 'Nativity', which he left incomplete at his death. In it, Jeake not only tried to calculate as precisely as possible the position of the heavenly bodies at the exact moment of his birth so as to give a commentary on his character and prospects; he also sought to draw broader conclusions about astrological principles, and particularly about the most reliable Measure of Time and the most accurate method of calculating directions, vindicating Naibode in the former connection and Morin in the latter.[32]

For both purposes he required a list of accidents, which he derived from the full account of significant events in his life with their exact dates and times provided by the diary. From this he extracted almost verbatim a catalogue of 202 accidents, an abnormally large number, but typical of the almost obsessive pursuit of exactitude which is in evidence in the elaborate calculations and disquisitions which make up the work, and which is epitomized by the surpassingly detailed version of Jeake's natal horoscope with which it was provided.[33] Moreover, the relationship between the diary and *The Nativity of Samuel Jeake* probably explains why Jeake 'finished' the diary on 29 November 1694, four and a half months after beginning it, for he presumably felt that he had now collected enough data to move onto the next

---

[31] 4.7.92. Jeake also wrote to Coley, who had written a foreword to Kendal's Χρονομετρία (1684) and had divulged Eyres's system in his *Clavis Astrologiae Elimata* (London, 1669), pt. 2, pp. 181 ff. (see a manuscript n. on p. 644 of the British Library copy of the 2nd edn. of Coley's book, London, 1676, 8610.bbb.1). Ch. 7, sect. 5 of Coley's work provides a survey of views on the Measure of Time.

[32] Selmes MS 56/1, fols. 35v, 37, and *passim*.

[33] Ibid., 4v–9v. The only events in the list of accidents that did not derive from the diary date from the period after its completion: on these see below, sect. 3, n. 5. The remainder are almost all paraphrased or quoted verbatim, with nothing substantive added, though very occasionally Jeake's epitome provides a small amount of extra information or makes causal connections clearer than in his original account: see below, sect. 5 n. 19, sect. 8 n. 16. For the horoscope, see ibid., fol. 13.

stage of his programme, though it may also be significant that the penultimate entry concludes the narrative of his dealings with the East India Company.

This was not the only astrological purpose of the diary, however, for in it Jeake also attempted to analyse 'Astrall Causes', as promised in his title. At intervals in his text he paused to note the astrological circumstances of events and to comment on their significance, in passages which clearly reveal his astrological skill and his delight in and fascination by the precision with which sublunary affairs could be correlated with the positions of the planets according to the connotations assigned to them in astrological doctrine. Every so often he cross-referenced comparable events and influences or tried to draw new conclusions concerning astral causation—as concerning the 'Infortunes', Saturn and Mars (31.7.78, 8.1.86)—while in some cases he included a horoscope assessing the state of the heavens at the time of an important occurrence.

In its juxtaposition of events with their astrological circumstances, the diary can be seen as an extension of *Astrological Experiments Exemplified* (though, since it dealt with revolutional directions, there had been no need for that to be illustrated with a series of charts). Whereas the earlier work had dealt predominantly with day-to-day events during the year it covered, however, the astrological comments in the diary mainly concerned extraordinary occurrences, evidently in an attempt to establish a kind of typology for these. In part this was due to a typical astrological preoccupation with accidents, which were supposed to be critical events in an individual's life. But in Jeake's case a further reason may be sought in the concern with providential deliverances which helped to inspire the diary's initial composition, and on which the astrological component is, as it were, superimposed.

Indeed, this link to the providentialist tradition helps to explain certain features of the astrological commentary in the diary. One is that, just as the study of specific providences could by definition take place only after they occurred, so Jeake's astrological commentary frequently appears to be retrospective. 'Wherein these Remarkables are to be observed', Jeake often notes of the horoscopes that he included (16.6.70), proceeding to itemize their significance in an almost scholarly tone.

More puzzling is the haphazardness of Jeake's astrological notes. Whereas sometimes he elucidates matters fully as if for the astrologically uninitiated, elsewhere he takes a great deal for granted, sometimes breaking off his commentary with '&c' as if compiling an *aide-mémoire* for himself, or including a chart but failing to comment on it. Of course, the diary was in part a working paper, an arsenal of data intended for further analysis at a later date, as is shown clearly by Jeake's remarks under 2 May 1671: Jeake could hardly have known that he was going to die in his mid-forties. But the almost formulaic quality of some of Jeake's astrological comments suggest a rationale complementary to his analytical intent, implying that he was aware of a continuous astrological pattern to his life which it was only occasionally necessary to probe in detail. Indeed—both in this respect and in the extent to which its analysis was based on hindsight—the diary provides a valuable insight into the role that astrology played for devotees like Jeake. For it appears to have been most important in giving a sense of order and predictability to the world, offering a psychological prop rather similar to that which many had earlier derived from the doctrine of providence. It would not even be going too far to see Jeake's astrology as a kind of secularized providentialism.

But this kind of retrospective use of astrology was clearly not exclusive of its deployment in day-to-day decision-making, and on this, too, the diary provides some clues, though Jeake is not especially forthcoming on the subject, due in part to the embarrassment about elections which has already been referred to. On at least one occasion his remarks make it plain that the astrological circumstances affected a decision that he took (18.7.94), while his choice of a time to propose to his wife-to-be seems also to have been astrologically chosen (14.6.80). Moreover, Jeake's astrological expertise makes it almost inconceivable that the same was not more generally the case, and it would be naïve to have expected him to spell connections out except where he felt the need to prove them either to himself or to potential readers. Among his manuscripts are various lists of forthcoming directions, the significance of which would have been apparent to him without explicit commentary, while other brief notes in the diary of beneficial or malign planetary conjunctions, apart from those just noted, almost certainly date from the time when these occurred.[34]

What is not in doubt, however, is the value of Jeake's text in illustrating how astrological interests could inspire autobiographical writing. Indeed, Jeake's is perhaps the most remarkable specimen of a genre which has never received the attention it deserves, although it gives our understanding of autobiographical writing at the time an extra dimension, adding a further potential motive for such works to the religious and miscellaneous ones already outlined.

---

[34] This is particularly true of the shorthand diary for 1699: see below, sect. 9. For lists of directions see Selmes MS 29, pp. 57 ff.; Selmes MS 35, pp. 14–16; Selmes MS 36, fols. 1–4; *AEE*, pp. 15 ff.; and Selmes MS 56/1, fols. 24 ff.

At their most rudimentary, autobiographical notes compiled for astrological purposes might simply comprise lists of accidents prepared for analysis either by their author or by a professional astrologer. Such documents bear some relationship to Jeake's list in his *Nativity*, though they are invariably on a smaller scale, and they often provide crucial information about otherwise little-known figures.[35] Some, however, kept astrological notes about themselves on a more continuous basis, and, while these might comprise collections of one-off horoscopes cast for specific moments, they might become as continuous as Jeake's. Examples include the autobiographical notes that Elias Ashmole made for astrological purposes, or the 'diary' of the early eighteenth-century London clothier Norris Purslow, a series of revolutional horoscopes annotated with events in his life which he considered astrologically significant.[36] Most similar of all to Jeake's is the sea journal of Jeremy Roch, written between the 1660s and the 1690s and published in 1936, which is not only furnished with a retrospective commentary drawing conclusions from the data included, but is also illustrated by a series of specially drawn horoscopes.[37]

Though hardly any of these texts is as full or explicit as Jeake's, they have certain common features, which may be noted here as a background to the diary, illustrating how its astrological rationale may have affected its content. All these authors were intent on investigating the astrological circumstances of their own, rather than others', lives, which helps to account for the rather self-centred quality of such works, though the spiritual bookkeeping of Puritan diarists could have a similar effect. More important, astrology made it imperative to provide accurate data for analytical purposes, encouraging attention to minute detail in all these authors, and Jeake was far from unique in making painstaking records of the exact time to the minute at which he began a task, set out on a journey, or fell ill.

In some cases one also finds astrology tending to oust religion in the diarist's preoccupations. Norris Purslow, for instance, was a Quaker in his early life, but from the time when he discovered astrology in 1698 religion

---

[35] See e.g. such unpublished lists as Bodleian Library, Oxford, MS Ashmole 243, fol. 170, a letter of 5 June 1646 from the Shropshire schoolmaster William Roe to William Lilly. For published lists see e.g. John Aubrey, *Brief Lives*, ed. Andrew Clark (2 vols., Oxford, 1898), i. 45–8.

[36] C. H. Josten (ed.), *Elias Ashmole, 1617–92* (5 vols., Oxford, 1966), i. 4–7, and *passim*; Wellcome Institute, London, MS 4021. For a collection of horoscopes with brief commentaries see e.g. the notes by the lawyer John Stansby in Bodleian MS Ashmole 436, fols. 84 ff. See also ibid., fols. 61 ff., and MS Ashmole 174, item 1.

[37] Ingram, *Three Sea Journals* (see sect. 2 n. 27), 25–139. We are indebted to Keith Thomas for drawing our attention to this work.

virtually disappears from his memoranda except in occasional asides.[38] Equally important, these other works show a combination like Jeake's of the predictive and retrospective use of astrological data. Sometimes autobiographical material was used to expound broader theories, as in the case of Roch, who was trying to propound a refined doctrine of elections. But in other cases, authors had no special motive to elaborate on astrological circumstances whose significance was perfectly evident to them: they nevertheless valued such information either to help them make decisions or as cumulative evidence 'of the admirable force and Verity of Celestial influences' in their lives.[39]

Jeake's diary is therefore an outstanding example of a genre which ought to be better known. It offers a valuable insight into the uses to which astrology might be put by its devotees, as well as illuminating the nature of astrology and its relationship to religious changes in Jeake's day.

3. THE DIARY'S COMPOSITION

Diaries are often less straightforward documents than they appear at first sight, and Jeake's is no exception. Though he records beginning to keep a diary on 18 July 1666, the work as we have it is clearly based only in part on a continuous journal kept over many years, and the exact nature of Jeake's earliest 'Memorandums of my Life' is unknown. Rather, the present diary was compiled from more disparate sources at a specific time, between 12 July and 29 November 1694, and Jeake occasionally records his progress in writing it up: the entry for 1 November 1678 dates from 20 August 1694, for instance, and that for 16 March 1684 from 1 September 1694. What were the materials that he employed and how did he shape them?

Two sources for parts of the diary survive independently. Firstly, some shorthand notes by Jeake on the back of a letter from Thomas Miller of 27 June 1685 evidently comprise the journal of his movements that he kept while on the run during Monmouth's rebellion (25.6.85). By comparison with the diary, these are quite rudimentary, recording where Jeake stayed each night and little more. They lack the remarks about the weather during the perambulation which conclude this passage in the diary, as also the information about Jeake's wife coming to Bodiam and telling him about the

---

[38] Purslow did, however, feel the need to collect 'Scripture Proofs For Astrology': Wellcome MS 4021 (unfoliated), *passim*. Astrology seems similarly to have displaced religion for Ashmole, on whose religious views see Josten, *Elias Ashmole* (see sect. 2 n. 36), i. 47–8.

[39] Ingram, *Three Sea Journals* (see sect. 2 n. 27), 80 and 75–87, *passim*.

house being searched, and about the movements of Thomas Markwick.[1] It is unclear whether this information was interpolated in 1694 or whether there was an intermediate stage between the two extant versions which is now lost.

A second source is Jeake's detailed account of his activities in 1678–8 in *Astrological Experiments Exemplified*, of which both the fair copy and a draft survive: the latter is partly in shorthand and partly in longhand, and the oscillation between the two, together with slight changes of ink, indicate that it was written up a few entries at a time, presumably soon after the events recorded had elapsed.[2]

Jeake explains how, in writing the diary, he extracted from the earlier work what he deemed to be 'pertinent to my present design' (5.7.87). Often, the diary describes a transaction in a single general account rather than piecemeal as events occurred, sometimes filling in the background and adding comments from hindsight. In addition, many events which Jeake evidently regarded as trivial and details that he saw as incidental are omitted. For instance, 'accidents' which he did not consider worthy of inclusion in the diary range from being stung by a bumble bee to experiencing concern about a fire in the street where his wool was stored, while topics scattered through the earlier work which figure less often in the diary include national politics and Jeake's family affairs and social activities.[3]

Above all, *Astrological Experiments Exemplified* gives a much fuller view of the humdrum business of a merchant than does the diary. Jeake's memoranda faithfully record such 'petty businesses' as buying and packing wool and hops, negotiating with carriers, casting up prices, writing accounts, arranging loans, even giving a Christmas dinner for his customers and friends. 'An exceeding busy day', he often notes, and, quite apart from its interest as a document in the history of astrology, *Astrological Experiments Exemplified* is well worthy of publication for the very detailed picture of a year of Jeake's life that it gives, complementing the wider ranging but less comprehensive account printed here.[4]

A comparable but later item is a mainly shorthand journal which Jeake

---

[1] FRE 5209. Other additions comprise the references to the visit to Winchelsea *en route* to Westfield, and to staying with the Weeks there and with the Wightmans at Maidstone. There is one item in these memoranda which does not appear in the diary: 'Saw Tho. Fisenden's wife and Tho. ... the carrier' at Lamberhurst on 4 July. The letter's date suggests that it was brought to Jeake while at Bodiam, and that the notes were written up from then onwards; they terminate on 14 July.

[2] Selmes MS 54.

[3] *AEE*, 15.8, 18.10.87, and *passim*.

[4] Ibid., 19.11, 9, 28.12.87, and *passim*.

kept in the last year of his life, from 28 March to 19 October 1699, just over a month before his death: Appendix 1 provides a transliteration of the whole text. This, too, was clearly compiled soon after the events it records, as is suggested by repeated changes of ink and pen, and by such references as that on 17 April 1699 to 'tomorrow night'. It commences on the day when Jeake went to London for his last trip there, but that he had kept a diary for at least part of the time since 1694 is clear: for, whereas the last book entered in the main diary was numbered 283, the first in 1699 was no. 314, with a note that the last book had been no. 313. Though the intervening journal is lost, it is possible that a handful of memoranda concerning these years in Jeake's *Nativity* derive from it.[5] The 1699 fragment covers a range of topics not dissimilar to the main diary, including notes on astrological conjunctions— though it contains no horoscopes—and it might be supposed to represent a specimen of a draft diary kept continuously throughout Jeake's life, of which the 1694 diary is a fair copy.

Certainly, the unreflective style of the later text may illustrate the kind of raw material which Jeake embroidered when he wrote up his notes. But the frequency and length of the 1699 entries is almost certainly a misleading guide to Jeake's earlier practice, since the compilation of the diary in 1694 probably stimulated him to keep later memoranda on a scale matching the work's latest and fullest sections, which constituted an almost contemporaneous record. Earlier, there is reason to believe that Jeake's diary-keeping was more cursory and haphazard, and that he called on his memory and other sources to expand his notes when he wrote them up.

That Jeake did not normally keep a day-to-day record of his activities is suggested by his specific mention of the two surviving earlier records of this kind already referred to. He certainly kept memoranda, as is clear from the

---

[5] These comprise six 'accidents'. Two appear in the *Nativity*'s main list as nos. 217 and 218 (Selmes MS 56/1, fol. 9v):

217. Journey to London to print my fathers book of Arithmetick, with which & other expences [*shorthand*: demand [?] arrearage] was put to some straits at present in this Journey. 16 bags hops sold at £4 per hundred, little profit[.] Melancholy & a difficulty of breathing. Mar. 5 1694/5.

218. A daughter born. May 2 1695.

In addition, Jeake compiled two subsidiary lists for analytical purposes slightly later in the 1690s, each of which has two additional 'accidents':

Loss by fall of Bank stock from 110 to 85 per cent by the National Land Bank. Feb. 13 1696.

Ingraffment on the Bank by which it fell to 51 per cent & Extreme scarcity of money. Feb. 11 1697. [fol. 35]

Hops in partnership, lost £14. Sept. 18 1697.

Bought a farm of £1000 got £100 in 7 months. March 3 1698. [fol. 36v]

numerous passages in which he gives exact times for events or uses the present tense, referring on 7 January 1685, for instance, to the completion of a task begun 'yesterday', or on 13 April 1694 to 'Last night'. But the incompleteness of such notes is suggested by Jeake's reliance on his memory, not only in the diary's early years but thereafter, and from his use of sources like his incoming and outgoing correspondence to fill out his narrative.

It is also clear from the diary as we have it that Jeake kept particularly detailed records at specific times—perhaps particularly his 'Critical Register of the several Paroxysms' during his illness in 1670–1 (2.5.71)—with the result that the amount he wrote about his activities in different years varies considerably. The numbered and dated sequence of books that he read may have been kept as part of a journal or as a separate record, which was married with the main narrative when it was written up, as is suggested by the two occasions when whole batches of books were inserted at once (4.7.67, 14.10.82).

On the other hand, some of the diary's longer narrative passages were either written or adapted when Jeake composed the version we have, and alteration or addition is also in evidence where Jeake includes evaluations that are obviously retrospective: in one case—concerning his melancholy in 1667—he notes that it was 'not quite gone in 10 years time' (20.9.67).

Indeed, one should not underestimate the extent to which the diary is a conscious artefact, with more of the character of an autobiography than a diary, in the sense of an account of a person's life written up retrospectively at a specific time—often, as in Jeake's case, in middle age—as against a journal written piecemeal over a longer period. Jeake reveals that in many respects it is more helpful to think of diaries and autobiographies as a continuum than as two distinct types. Though differing from autobiographies of the period with a distinctive structure—for instance, the conversion narrative—Jeake's diary shows some similarity to purely narrative works of this kind.[6] Comparison may be made with Henry Newcome's *Autobiography*, based on a diary which is also partly extant, to which Newcome added a more formal element, presenting a briefer and more rounded selection of events and highlighting significant episodes; he also included introductory reflections and an account of his family which are not paralleled in Jeake's more functional document.[7]

The purpose of such reworking was usually to present the work to a wider

---

[6] On autobiographies with a distinctive structure see the works referred to above, sect. 2 nn. 4, 6.

[7] Parkinson, *Newcome* (see sect. 2 n. 9), i. 1–3 and *passim*. Cf. Heywood, *Newcome* (see sect. 2 n. 15).

audience, and Jeake, too, was clearly aware that other eyes than his might light upon his diary, illustrating an innate self-consciousness in autobiographical writing which E. P. Thompson has rightly observed in connection with Ralph Josselin. As Thompson points out, in such works 'we have evidence not of a spontaneous unmediated attitude but of this transcribed into an approved self-image (perhaps with approved doctrinal afterthoughts), like someone arranging his face in a looking-glass'—a metaphor which is particularly apt for Jeake, since one senses that he was doing precisely that in his self-portrait at nineteen.[8] Just who he thought this audience might be is not clear, in contrast to diarists and autobiographers, like Newcome, who addressed their descendants.[9] Nevertheless, this had both positive and negative effects on Jeake's composition and presentation of his work.

Perhaps most striking is his use of shorthand, evidently intending, like Pepys and other diarists, to commit to paper in this way information which he did not wish to be easily accessible.[10] Jeake's case is particularly interesting in that he used shorthand only for selected passages, thereby illustrating exactly what topics he deemed inappropriate for general consumption. He had earlier used shorthand for sermon notes, drafts of letters, and occasional memoranda, including the draft of *Astrological Experiments Exemplified*.[11] The idea of using it to disguise passages about which he was embarrassed seems to have occurred to him in *Astrological Experiments Exemplified*, where he actually erased a number of sentences in longhand in his fair copy, replacing them with shorthand: all of these concerned quarrels with his wife.

In the diary, he consistently used shorthand for entries on three topics, his abortive marital negotiations in the 1670s, sexual intercourse with his wife, and the progress of her pregnancies, thus showing a revealing bashfulness about procreational matters. He also used it for one-off entries, as concerning the single astrological election that he admitted to making and the sole domestic squabble referred to (3.8.71, 10.4.88). Otherwise, however, he employed shorthand for notes on various matters on which other entries were in longhand, and his use of the two does not seem to follow a clear pattern. For instance, though some intimate notes about his early religious

---

[8] 4.7.71; E. P. Thompson, 'Anthropology and the Discipline of Historical Context', *Midland History*, 1 (1972), 42.

[9] e.g. Parkinson, *Newcome* (see sect. 2 n. 9), i. 2; E. S. de Beer (ed.), *The Diary of John Evelyn* (6 vols., Oxford, 1955), i. 85.

[10] For analogues see Haller, *Rise of Puritanism* (see sect. 2 n. 6), 97–8; Mendelson, 'Stuart women's diaries' (see sect. 2 n. 11), 183–4; Matthews, *Diaries* (see sect. 1 n. 3), 14, 33, 36, 63.

[11] Selmes MS 54 and see e.g. FRE 4863, 4886, 5059, 5250 (p, q) and ESRO D 984/1 (drafts); Selmes MSS 27, 48 (sermon notes); Jeake MS 2/9, fol. 2 (memoranda: see also Selmes MS 40/1, Jeake's 1674 expense account).

experiences are in shorthand, others that seem hardly less frank are not; other topics which fall into this category include accidents, gifts, and notes on the deaths of friends.[12]

Jeake's apprehension of an audience also inspired him to omissions, perhaps most notably of the description of his mind in his self-portrait at nineteen, which he considered 'inconvenient for me to relate, and liable to certaine exposure' (4.7.71). That the diary suppresses all or part of episodes which reflected badly on Jeake is occasionally suggested by other sources. For instance, though Jeake's sale of the land near Pembury that he had inherited through his mother is recorded without comment in the diary, a surviving letter shows that his premature felling of much of the timber on the land reduced its value when he came to dispose of it.[13] But though in other cases we know of transactions which Jeake failed to note in the diary at all—as with the commercial venture in the West Country in 1678–9 evidenced in his correspondence and papers[14]—this does not seem to be due to deliberate selection. The miscellaneous information that went into the diary, if not that concerning the peaks of his career, appears to have been a little haphazard.

More significant is the positive effect on Jeake of his awareness of writing for an audience. 'You must know', he interjects at one point (29.8.81), and various retrospective comments seem aimed at a putative reader. There are also points where the diary takes on a veritably literary quality, often with reported speech carefully reconstructed, a technique which Jeake shares with other autobiographers of his day.[15]

The first episode of this kind concerns Jeake's marital negotiations with Elizabeth Hartshorne and her mother in 1680, but they increase in number in the diary's later stages. Jeake's long account of his dealings with Robert Grove in 1689–90 is followed in 1690 by his description of his father's last days and death, which is perhaps the most self-conscious passage of all, with its stress on the older man's resignation to providence. Here Jeake felt that he was writing a 'Relation', deliberately deferring details of his father's illnesses at the point where they would naturally have appeared so as to in-

---

[12] Some of these may have been placed in shorthand as being linked to Jeake's marital negotiations: see below, 2.8.75, 6.12.79, 8.7.80, and perhaps 16.7.74. But see also 25.9.73, 23.12.78, and, for religion, 23.5.73. For an instance where Jeake wrote the first word of a sentence in longhand before transferring to shorthand, see 11.11.70. Other shorthand entries will be referred to piecemeal according to subject throughout this Introduction.

[13] See George Castel to Jeake, 26 June 1676, and Jeake's draft reply (altered by his father), 29 June 1676, FRE 4851–2. Cf. Jeake's stock account, Selmes MS 39/3, where a 'loss' on the land of £19. 10s. is recorded. See 15.9, 10.11.75, 28.2, 25.5, 1, 28.6, 6.7, 2.8.76.

[14] See below, sect. 8, n. 25.

[15] Cf. e.g. Wright, *Lister* (see sect. 2 n. 17), 45 ff.

clude them in a connected narrative (30.6.90). Evidently he was aware of an extant literary tradition, not only in published lives but also in the reports of the deaths of local Puritans to be found in their correspondence, exemplified not least by his father's account of his grandmother Anne Jeake's death in 1640.[16] Indeed in such episodes we seem to move away from the diarist to the memoir-writer, a tendency also found in diarists like John Evelyn when they wrote up their notes from hindsight.[17]

But it would be wrong to differentiate too strictly between spontaneous memoranda and their retrospective elaboration, since Jeake's diary—like other similar documents—owes its character to a combination of the two. Whether or not conscious, the diary reveals a degree of literary skill in the way in which otherwise humdrum passages are repeatedly enlivened by the emergence of episodes recounted in a lively narrative. Even its main narrative shows a certain artistry, as when Jeake's account of his financial transactions in the diary's latter stages manages to communicate his own enthusiasm through what might otherwise have been a dull epitome of his correspondence.

William Matthews has pointed out with respect to Samuel Pepys how spontaneity does not automatically result from the immediate recording of events. Pepys also consciously embroidered his memoranda, though usually quite soon after the events involved, and there is an element of literary artifice in creating the sense of immediacy which is characteristic of the best diaries.[18] Jeake undoubtedly partakes of this compelling quality, if to a lesser degree than Pepys. Apart from its content and the significance that may be discerned in its mixed astrological and religious motivation, the diary is also worth reading for the talent as a writer that Jeake discovered as he converted his notes into the book as we have it.

4. RYE NONCONFORMITY AND ITS PERSECUTION

Jeake gives occasional glimpses of life in Rye throughout the diary. He reports meeting fellow businessmen at the tavern or the fish market, for instance (19.11.87, 25.6.94), or quarrelling with the mayor over the purchase of some pictures (3.1.93). A reminder of Rye's exposed position in the naval

[16] Cf. e.g. Turner, *Heywood* (see sect. 2 n. 1), i. 29 ff., and see Andrew Wear, 'Puritan Perceptions of Illness in Seventeenth-century England', in Roy Porter (ed.), *Patients and Practitioners: Lay Perceptions of Medicine in Pre-industrial Society* (Cambridge, 1985), 64. For the local context see Fletcher, *Sussex* (see sect. 1 n. 5), 68; Smart, pp. 58–9.

[17] de Beer, *Evelyn* (see sect. 3 n. 9), esp. i. 78–9, 83–5.

[18] Latham and Matthews, *Pepys* (see sect. 2 n. 1), i. cv–vi and i. xcvii ff., *passim.*

warfare of the period is provided by Jeake's mention of seeing the English and Dutch fleets during the Anglo–Dutch War of 1665–7 (though he refers to this only in connection with his eyesight, 28.7.66). It is also interesting that news of William of Orange's invasion reached Rye by 'a stragling vessell of that fleet that was put into our harbour' (7.11.88), while most striking of all is Jeake's graphic account of the panic which gripped the town in July 1690 when it was feared that the French might sack Rye after the defeat of the Anglo–Dutch fleet off Beachy Head.

Otherwise, the diary is a slightly disappointing source on the history of Rye except for one theme, and this is the political history of the town and the persecution of the nonconformists during and after the Exclusion Crisis. Persecution is a typical theme of autobiographical writings by nonconformists at this time, and Jeake may have felt expected to provide such a record.[1] In contrast to parts of the diary which seem to derive directly from notes made at the time, therefore, a disproportionate number of these passages have a retrospective air, being embellished with comments or evaluations which show that they were substantially embroidered after the events concerned.

Rye was typical of many towns in late Stuart England in being a centre of nonconformity. In 1669 it was reported that the Rye conventicle was attended by 100 people, and in Bishop Compton's census of 1676 the adult population of the town was said to be evenly divided between conformists and dissenters, a situation which might seem potentially troublesome in itself.[2] It was made worse by the broader context of Restoration England, in which politics and religion were inextricably linked. Politically, the nonconformists were the natural opponents of the extremes of Anglican loyalism which found support in many quarters in the aftermath of the Interregnum, seeing their interest as in a government with a tolerant attitude towards the free exercise of their religion.

Moreover, towns like Rye were not only hotbeds of dissent but also independent legislatures and constituencies for a large proportion of Members of Parliament. 'Every Corporation, is a petty free state, Against monarchy', the Duke of Newcastle complained at this time, specifically alluding to the

---

[1] Cf. e.g. A. W. Brink (ed.), *The Life of the Revd. Mr George Trosse* (Montreal and Toronto, 1974), 124 ff.; Henry Fishwick (ed.), *The Note Book of the Rev. Thomas Jolly, 1671–93* (Chetham Society, 33, 1895). For general accounts of the persecution see M. R. Watts, *The Dissenters: From the Reformation to the French Revolution* (Oxford, 1978), ch. 3; G. R. Cragg, *Puritanism in the Period of the Great Persecution, 1660–88* (Cambridge, 1957).

[2] G. L. Turner (ed.), *Original Records of Nonconformity under Persecution and Indulgence* (3 vols., London, 1911), i. 33; Anne Whiteman, ed., *The Compton Census of 1676: A Critical Edition* (London, 1986), 151.

religious connection by blaming 'Lecturers' for the problem.[3] This period therefore saw an attempt to eradicate dissenting influence in the municipalities by purging the electorate, turning out office-holders, and even altering the terms of municipal charters. At Rye, where the electorate comprised the freemen of the town, this process began in the aftermath of the contested election of 1661: the elder Jeake and others were deprived of their rights as freemen in October 1662 and quo warranto proceedings were begun against the corporation in the following year.[4]

The means by which dissenting worship could be curtailed were provided by the Conventicle Act of 1664 and the Five Mile Act of 1665 (which proscribed nonconformist preaching in built-up areas), but their enforcement was haphazard in the early years of the Restoration. Only in the 1670s and particularly the 1680s did nonconformists come under increasing threat, in connection with the political struggles of those years. Moreover as the leader of the local congregation and its principal preacher, the elder Jeake was a natural focus of attention: 'really a dangerous man', in the words of a government informer.[5]

The opening shot was fired by the Vicar of Rye in an abrasive letter to Jeake in the aftermath of the passing of the second Conventicle Act in 1670. But, though the town clerk, Thomas Tournay, an ally of Jeake's, was forced to take an oath rejecting the Solemn League and Covenant in 1673, inertia then again ensued until 1676.[6] A royal declaration of February 1675 had urged the enforcement of the laws against nonconformists, and in 1676 Jeake was cited to appear at the archdeacon's court at Lewes, and, failing to do so, was excommunicated. This would have had the effect of depriving him of his electoral rights had he not already lost them, while enforcement by the relevant secular authorities would have entailed his arrest: it was to avoid this that Jeake made a trip to Dover, the jurisdictional headquarters of the Cinque Ports of which Rye formed part.[7]

[3] T. P. Slaughter (ed.), *Ideology and Politics on the Eve of Restoration* (Memoirs of the American Philosophical Society, 159, 1984), 41 (we have modernized the Duke's spelling of monarchy). On the background see D. R. Lacey, *Dissent and Parliamentary Politics in England, 1661–1689* (New Brunswick, NJ, 1969), and John Miller, 'The Crown and the Borough Charters in the Reign of Charles II', *English Historical Review*, 100 (1985), 53–84.

[4] Ibid., p. 65, and Henning, i. 499–500. For the deprivation of Jeake and others of their rights see RYE 1/17, pp. 143–4.

[5] PRO SP 29/413, fol. 322.

[6] FRE 4521, printed in Smart, pp. 62–3; Vidler, p. 81. On the background see Anthony Fletcher, 'The Enforcement of the Conventicle Acts, 1664–1679', *Studies in Church History*, 21 (1984), 235–46.

[7] 24.5, 14.6.76; WSRO Ep. II/7/1, fol. 17; Lacey, *Dissent* (see sect. 4 n. 3), 71–2, and, on excommunication and voting, ibid., pp. 111, 153, 311 n. 58.

Matters became more tense in the national political crisis which followed the Popish Plot, and in Rye as elsewhere dissenters were increasingly aggressive in electioneering.[8] The younger Jeake notes in the diary that it was he who took a note from some of the freemen to Edward Polhill of Burwash, a lawyer and JP with low church sympathies, inviting him to stand as MP, though he refused (31.1.79). Trouble escalated from this point onwards, and in reconstructing the complicated sequence of events Jeake's diary can be supplemented by two principal sources, the Rye assembly books and a series of letters received by the government and preserved among the state papers. Indeed, Rye was seen as something of a *cause célèbre*, the secretary of state, Sir Leoline Jenkins, remarking in 1682 that 'the height of disaffection and contumacy that appears to be in the generality of Rye is the greatest scandal that I know of in the whole government'.[9]

Politically, Rye was split between court and country parties, with the balance held by floating voters.[10] The leader of the court party was Thomas Crouch, while others involved included Lewis Gillart, Joseph Radford, Moses and Aaron Peadle, and George Weeden, the last two both being local inn-keepers.[11] For the country, Jeake senior was said to be the ringleader, but since he and others were excluded from voting by the suspension of their rights as freemen the most active figure was the town clerk, Thomas Tournay. Others involved included Thomas Burditt, Michael Cadman, Thomas Miller, and Thomas Tutty.

In 1679 Benjamin Martin, a member of the country party, was elected mayor. Encouraged by Tournay and perhaps by Jeake, he proceeded to accept the votes of the freemen who, like the elder Jeake, had been disqualified in the 1660s, thereby assuring an electoral majority for the country party in the parliamentary election that October. It was evidently on this occasion that the elder Jeake ostentatiously declared that 'he was for noe Courtiour nor pentioner but a Countrie Gent', the exclusionist Sir John Darell.[12] Though the court party complained about Martin's action in 1680, nothing had been done by March 1681 when the problem arose again in connection

[8] Ibid., pp. 112 ff.

[9] *CSP Dom.*, 1682, p. 354.

[10] See particularly the analysis of the political state of the town by the government informer Robert Hall, in PRO SP 29/413, fol. 322. See also ibid., fol. 318, and *CSP Dom.*, July–Sept. 1683, pp. 151–2.

[11] For the link between Toryism and the drink trade see Colin Brent, 'The Neutering of the Fellowship and the Emergence of a Tory Party in Lewes (1663–88)', *SAC* 121 (1983), 101. This may help to explain Jeake's remarks on 9.12.84.

[12] *CSP Dom.*, 1679–80, pp. 526–8; PRO SP 29/413, fol. 322. For the hypothesis that Jeake was involved see Henning, i. 500. For parallel events elsewhere see Lacey, *Dissent* (see sect. 4 n. 3), 118.

with the election for the Oxford Parliament. Jeake notes the 'great heats & animosities' that accompanied this episode (10.3.81), and it was perhaps partly due to these circumstances that he had felt it best to be married incognito earlier in the month (1.3.81). In fact, however, the intervention of neutrals meant that the extremist Whig candidate, John Tudman or Tedman, was defeated by the sitting MP Thomas Frewen, a moderate from a local landed family (the other seat again went to Sir John Darell).[13]

At the mayoral election on 29 August 1681 matters came to a fresh climax with the 'usurpation' of the mayoralty 'in an insolent and Violent manner' by the loyalist Thomas Crouch at the expense of Tournay. Tournay claimed that he had been duly elected and went with Thomas Burditt and others to London to complain. His rivals, however, petitioned the King and Privy Council, who summoned both parties to Whitehall on 7 September, when adjudication was given in favour of Crouch and an order issued outlawing the elder Jeake's conventicle.[14] This was the occasion of the celebrated interview recounted by the diarist (29.8.81), and, though the details differ, the same defiant tone comes across from an account of the exchange between the elder Jeake and the King among the state papers.[15] Jeake challenged the King to appeal to the law, evidently aware of the questionable legality of the steps that the government was by now taking.

However heroic, his intransigence if anything made matters worse for the Rye nonconformists, since the court party took advantage of the royal order to proscribe their meetings. On 14 December 1681 Jeake, Miller, Thomas Markwick, Nicholas Skinner, and others were presented for not attending the parish church, while a telescoped and retrospective account of the persecution that now ensued appears in the diary.[16] The loyalist party also took the offensive politically, petitioning the government for a royal order to Tournay to give up the mayoral insignia he had defiantly retained, and attempting to deprive him of his post as town clerk and replace him by a loyalist, Samuel Stretton. In addition, they arranged for a whole series of their supporters to be elected freemen of the town as a means of altering the balance of parties in their favour.[17]

All this while an appeal by Tournay had been pending in the Court of King's Bench, at considerable expense, to which the younger Jeake

[13] *CSP Dom.*, 1680–1, pp. 173–5, 209–10.

[14] RYE 1/17, pp. 143–4, 58–61; *CSP Dom.*, 1680–1, pp. 422, 444.

[15] Ibid., p. 444.

[16] 29.8.81; Selmes MS 80 (notes on Rye dissenters' grievances, 1681–3). Cf. WSRO Ep. II/15/5, fol. 15, Ep. II/9/29, fols. 72v, 74–7.

[17] RYE 1/17, pp. 62, 63–5, 66, 67, 69; *CSP Dom.*, 1680–1, pp. 439, 583; Miller, 'Crown and Borough Charters' (see sect. 4 n. 3), 73.

contributed. As the matter dragged inconclusively on, Tournay seems to have despaired of the legal remedy which finally materialized in July 1682 (4.7.82). In May he and his supporters took advantage of Crouch's temporary absence from Rye to break into the town hall, change the locks, and take possession of the records and insignia.[18] They also emulated their opponents' tactics in trying to acquire an electoral majority by making their supporters freemen and ignoring the recent appointees of the rival faction, two prominent members of which, Lewis Gillart and Samuel Stretton, were gaoled. Meanwhile Crouch and his party counter-attacked, accusing Thomas Burditt of speaking treasonable words and trying to get him suspended.[19]

So matters stood when the new mayoral election occurred on 28 August. Thomas Crouch had died earlier that month, as Jeake notes with a certain satisfaction (8.8.82), and, when an attempt was made to find a compromise candidate, the court party obliged by putting up Joseph Radford rather than their first choice, Lewis Gillart. Tournay, however, was intransigent, and the upshot was that both he and Radford claimed to be duly elected. The events of the previous year were now repeated, with a royal order being issued against the defiant Tournay, while the loyalists proceeded to nominate even more of their supporters as freemen, subsequently declaring the elections under Tournay invalid.[20] At this point Tournay seems to have given up, moving to Hythe, where he was said to be favoured because of his experiences at Rye.[21] At Rye, however, the court party were left in undisputed control.

For the nonconformists this meant a new bout of the persecution that, here as elsewhere, was used by the Crown and its supporters to grind down their adversaries. There had been a moment of alarm in May 1682 when an attempt was made to arrest the elder Jeake in connection with the excommunication of 1676 and to serve him with a summons under the Five Mile Act, though he avoided this by leaving the town. In October proceedings were entered at the Crown Office against seven people in Rye for not attending church for eleven months. They were threatened with fines of £20 a month,

[18] RYE 1/17, p. 144; *CSP Dom.*, 1682, pp. 225–6, 234, 366–8. For Jeake's contributions see 14.11.81, 22.6.82, 21.4, 30.8.86 (all in shorthand) and 28.4.87 (in longhand). See also 4.7.82.

[19] RYE 1/17, pp. 71–4, 144; *CSP Dom.*, 1682, pp. 350, 367.

[20] *CSP Dom.*, 1682, pp. 367–8, 410, Jan.–June 1683, p. 147; RYE 1/17, p. 144. See also ibid., pp. 76–8, 79, 81, 83, 97–8. A subsidiary dispute that arose at this time concerned the records of Rye grammar school, which the Jeakes had in their possession and to which the rival faction required access in order to appoint a new master: ibid., pp. 92–3. Cf. *CSP Dom.*, 1679–80, p. 529.

[21] *CSP Dom.*, July–Sept. 1683, p. 152.

which seem rather arbitrary and excessive in terms of the penalties then in force under the 1670 Conventicle Act, which prescribed a £20 fine for the first offence of holding a conventicle. But this punitive multiplication of penalties was evidently intended to bankrupt the small traders and others involved.[22] A meeting was convened on 23 November and Thomas Miller was sent to London to get legal help, with the result that the case was contested and fought for the rest of the reign. More significant, on the same day the elder Jeake—no doubt selected as ringleader—was threatened with prosecution and forced to flee Rye to avoid arrest: he went with Miller to London and remained there for the next five years (23.11.82).

The letters that he exchanged with his son in the ensuing months echo the diary in illustrating the tribulations with which the dissenters left in Rye had to cope.[23] Meetings were broken up and Jeake's friends Miller and Markwick distrained for their nonconformist activities, while later complaints that the Tory jurats had failed to deal properly with money realized from goods that were seized for the fine testify to the kind of ugly, petty animosities that surfaced.[24] A fresh assault occurred in June 1683 in connection with the Rye House Plot, when Jeake's house was searched on the suspicion that he might be holding arms.[25] Jeake clearly believed this to be far-fetched in his case, as his indignant comment in the diary illustrates, but it was doubtless this succession of irritations which persuaded him to remove himself to London in the footsteps of his father on 4 October, returning only on 28 May 1684.

Even then, Jeake was not safe. Within a month of his return there were fresh moves against the Rye nonconformists, and the diary testifies to the constant vigilance that Jeake had to exert to avoid arrest by absenting himself from the town at strategic moments.[26] With the accession of James II the following year, the persecution mounted to a climax and then ceased. During the Duke of Monmouth's invasion, Jeake felt it prudent to stay away from Rye for days on end, while in October he was presented by the Rye grand jury for non-attendance at church (25.6, 5.10.85). But then came James' change in attitude towards the nonconformists, as he sought support

---

[22] Selmes MS 80 and see 23.11.82. Cf. WSRO Ep. II/15/5, fol. 35. On fines see Watts, *Dissenters* (see sect. 4 n. 1), 226–7.

[23] For extracts from these letters see Smart, pp. 63–6.

[24] Also rather questionable were the circumstances of the door of Miller's house being broken open after midnight on 14 June by the Tory faction. Selmes MS 80, and see 21.9.79, 18.3, 4.10.83.

[25] 29.6, 6.7.83. On the Rye House Plot, see below, sect. 5.

[26] 2.7, 20.9, 1, 9.12.84. See also FRE 5175, 5187, and Jeake's accounts for 1684 (RYE 145/11. fol. 55), which reveal the expenditure of £10 'towards the fines Levied on a meeting at Rye', of which £5 was subsequently returned.

in this quarter as a counter to the resistance that his pro-Catholic policy aroused in the Anglican church. Now the persecution subsided, as Jeake noted with relief. By the summer of 1686 it seemed safe for the elder Jeake to return to Rye (16.7.86), though in fact he did so only in 1687, when public meetings began to be held again (29.5.87). In 1688–9 Jeake recorded the abdication of James II, the accession of William and Mary, and the passing of the Act of Toleration, 'So that now through the mercifull Providence of God, we were freed from the fears of Popery & Persecution' (13.2, 22.5.89).

These years also saw dissenters return to a central position in Rye affairs. As part of James II's campaign of interference with municipal office-holding, Jeake's name was inserted in an abortive list of magistrates; he noted with relief, however, that he escaped preferment under a regime of which he, like many nonconformists, was highly suspicious.[27] In the new reign, the timidity of the freemen prevented them from electing prominent dissenters like his father and himself as clerk and deputy, and the clerkship instead went to Nathaniel Hartshorne, Jeake's brother-in-law (30.7.90). Jeake helped him in opposition to Thomas Tournay, who was now again active in Rye affairs but to whom Jeake had evidently developed an antipathy, perhaps due to Tournay's failure to repay the money that he had borrowed for his legal expenses in 1681–2.[28]

Though spared this responsibility, Jeake did acquire some offices in Rye in these years. In 1690 he was made a freeman of the town (2.7.90), at a time when the country party was in the ascendant after the court dominance of the 1680s. He also acquired two parish offices, of overseer of the poor in 1686 and surveyor of highways in 1693 (5.4.86, 9.1.93). Jeake does not seem to have relished such duties, however, noting the trouble that the latter post involved in his diary and rarely attending the town's assembly after his election as freeman.[29] Moreover, on 12 February 1694 he approached the assembly with the proposal that he would pay the town £60 at Michaelmas 1695 if within two years it paid off a mortgage it had incurred, one condition of this being that he be excused future office.[30]

Indeed, Jeake seems never to have been very politically active. Though embroiled with the dissenting party in Rye by dint of parentage, he appears

[27] 14.11.87, 14.4.88; see also *AEE*, 14.11.87. On the background, see Watts, *Dissenters* (see sect. 4 n. 1), 257 ff.; Lacey, *Dissent* (see sect. 4 n. 3), ch. 9.

[28] See above, sect. 4 n. 18.

[29] Jeake's only attendances are recorded in RYE 1/17, pp. 186, 198. For his election see ibid., p. 153, and see also ibid., pp. 179–80 for his being appointed to a committee of three to raise a tax to pay for repairs to the town's fortifications, 9 May 1692, a fact not noted in the diary.

[30] Ibid., pp. 198, 201 (a copy of Jeake's letter), and 215.

not to have been among its leaders, meetings tending to take place at his friends' houses rather than his own. A telling contrast may also be observed between his own and his father's reaction to the persecution. The latter took solace in characteristic evangelical exhortation and self-examination: 'Be not ashamed of, nor a shame to the Gospel of Christ', he wrote, 'Love the world less & Christ more'.[31] On the other hand, asides in the diary reveal the younger man's response to be more one of exasperation and derision—a sign of the times, perhaps, but significant nonetheless.[32]

The younger Jeake remained, however, a pillar of the local nonconformist community, and his role in it reached a climax with a plan which he was putting into effect at the time of his death. The 1699 diary shows that he had decided to erect a meeting house, a typical step in nonconformist circles in the aftermath of the Toleration Act of 1689, when permanent premises were frequently found by congregations who had formerly used private houses or rented rooms.[33] Jeake started raising money by various means, and he purchased the house next to his in Middle Street (now Mermaid Street) for conversion for this purpose.[34] His death delayed the project, but his widow brought her husband's wishes to fruition by completing and opening a meeting house on the site four years later, the licence for it being granted on 30 June 1703.[35]

5. JEAKE'S FAMILY AND SOCIAL LIFE

Jeake's diary is perhaps at its weakest on the kind of topics which certain other contemporary diarists record most fully, namely relations with family, kin, and neighbours. Jeake mentions few figures in Rye outside his immediate circle, while even friends and colleagues like Thomas Miller and Thomas Markwick remain shadowy as personalities, despite frequent references to them. Indeed a disproportionate amount of what we hear about Markwick is posthumous, arising from the trouble Jeake had in administering his will. Like other executorships, this merely forms part of a variety of

[31] FRE 5182 (letter of 19 Oct. 1684): cf. FRE 5187 and Smart, pp. 63–6.
[32] 29.8.81, 29.6.83, 9.12.84, 27.2, 5.10.85. See, however, 21.9.79 for Jeake's note of the juxtaposition of the onset of persecution with his exposition of a passage in the Apocalypse, and see below, sect. 6, on his reading at this time.
[33] Watts, *Dissenters* (see sect. 4 n. 1), 303 ff.
[34] 28.3, 11.4, 12.6, 2.8.99.
[35] RYE 1/17, p. 271. The account given in Holloway, p. 540 is erroneous in that the licence was granted in June, not May; that it was not for Mrs Jeake to preach there; and that it was not for a Presbyterian meeting.

minor legal business with which Jeake was involved in the course of his life and which the diary records.[1]

It is also clear that Jeake did not generally deem family matters appropriate for inclusion in the diary. This is perhaps significant in itself, and in this regard Jeake stands in contrast to other diarists of his day. His record would not lend itself to a study like Alan Macfarlane's *The Family Life of Ralph Josselin* (Cambridge, 1970).

On the other hand, this side of Jeake's life is not wholly absent. He provides interesting glimpses of his childhood, informing us of the ages at which he was weaned, at which he cut his first teeth, and at which he began to walk and speak. In his early manhood he records his attempts to find a wife, his unsuccessful efforts being disguised by shorthand. Mary Weeks, his first sweetheart, belonged to a local landed family for whom his father carried out legal work; her brother, John, was a friend of the diarist, with whom he stayed in 1671.[2] Mary proved elusive, since her kinsfolk evidently found Jeake unsuitable, despite the fact that he was prepared to wait till after her mother's death for the match to take place (20.3.76). In 1677, while the Weeks affair was going badly, Jeake briefly pursued a different quarry, Anne File, who lived surprisingly far off at Wye in Kent, but whom he may have met through his nonconformist connections.[3] Nothing came of this either, however, and in 1678 Jeake returned to Mary Weeks, at this point enrolling help in the negotiations from an unnamed cousin (16.3, 27.5.78). His optimism is suggested by the fact that in June 1678 and January 1679 he drew up plans suggesting alternative layouts for the marital home he would have liked to build. But, despite Jeake's persistence, the Weeks family remained adamant in rejecting him.

Success finally came with Elizabeth Hartshorne in June 1680, when the diary not only breaks into longhand but describes in detail the progress of Jeake's courtship and the hard bargaining over the dowry. That his thirteen-year-old bride was hardly more than a child is apparent from the crudeness of what is evidently her earliest letter to him, and it is hard to avoid the suspicion that the size of the dowry was one of the major attractions of the match. Jeake claimed, however, that he had borne her 'an Affection from her Infancy', while his expense accounts for 1675 record the outlay of a shilling 'To Betty Hartshorne'.[4]

---

[1] For executorships and administrations see 29.8.89 *et seq.* (Grove), 22.9.92 (Barham), and 11.8.93 *et seq.* (Markwick). On the narrowness of the circle covered by the diary cf. Burchall.

[2] FRE 4377, 4385, 4551–3; 19.6.71.

[3] For a Wye nonconformist called Thomas Markwick, perhaps related to Jeake's friend of the same name, see *CSP Dom.*, 1671–2, pp. 458, 502, 535.

[4] FRE 5108; 14.6.80; Selmes MS 40/2.

For a girl to be married in her early teens was unusual but not unknown in early modern England, particularly in mercantile circles.[5] What is extraordinary, however, is the fact that the match was immediately consummated: Jeake added a shorthand note concerning the 'devirgination' that followed two days after the marriage (3.3.81). The consensus of contemporary opinion was that parturition by girls below the age of about sixteen was dangerous, and it is unclear why Jeake was so out of step with normal practice.[6] The marriage survived, however, and correspondence suggests that an intimacy developed between the couple. 'My Dear', Elizabeth wrote to her husband when he was in London in 1683, 'I am much concerned for yo[ur] abscence. my Dear pray return as soon as possibly you can', while he refers to her in his letters as 'My dear & entirely beloved wife'.[7]

To his in-laws, Jeake no doubt seemed a respectable enough suitor. His father had earlier been friendly with Elizabeth's father, Richard Hartshorne, master of Rye grammar school,[8] while the younger man's commercial career was by this time well under way. What Jeake does not tell us in the diary may help to explain the anxiety of his prospective mother-in-law, Barbara Hartshorne, to secure a match at the time when Jeake approached her, for her husband had fallen ill and died in April 1680.[9] Though a son by her first marriage was living, Richard Holman, he was a seaman and merchant who was not resident in Rye, and she perhaps felt the need for a man about the house. In addition, the problems of her other son, Nathaniel, may already have been brewing.

These troubles, and Jeake's part in them, make up one of the diary's subplots in the 1680s. Nathaniel initially left Rye over some 'Infamy' which is never precisely identified but which was merely the prelude to a succession of tribulations (10.3.81). Indeed, though unfortunate, Nathaniel was clearly a highly unstable and difficult character. At London he was apprenticed to a lawyer, Richard Goodenough, but within weeks he was complaining of the treatment he had received from his master, who reciprocated by describing Nathaniel as 'so lewd & so unruly that 'twill be impossible for me to keep him in any due Decorum'.[10] In 1682 Nathaniel got into more serious trouble when he was indicted for theft and imprisoned. 'I feare he keeps very

---

[5] Ralph Houlbrooke, *The English Family, 1450–1750* (London, 1984), 66 and 89 n. 10.
[6] Lawrence Stone, *The Crisis of the Aristocracy, 1558–1641* (Oxford, 1965), 656–7. We are grateful to Ralph Houlbrooke for this reference.
[7] FRE 5107, 5242.
[8] See above, sect. 1 n. 8.
[9] Jeake MS 2/10.
[10] FRE 5025. Cf. FRE 5020, 5290, and 15.8.81.

bad company', one of Jeake's correspondents wrote in response to an enquiry about his brother-in-law, and now as later Jeake was involved, using his London contacts John Jaye, James Wightman, John Mackley, and Thomas Miller, to try to sort out Nathaniel's tangled affairs.[11]

Worse was to follow, for in 1683 Nathaniel became implicated in the Rye House Plot, a conspiracy said to have been devised by frustrated Whigs to assassinate Charles II and the Duke of York and to place the Duke of Monmouth on the throne. Nathaniel's master, Goodenough, was deeply implicated in this—it was a bad augury that Nathaniel had initially been apprenticed to him on the recommendation of John Tudman, the incendiary Whig candidate in the 1681 Rye election—and Nathaniel was sucked into a web of sedition.[12] In June 1683 he turned informer, like others in the fringes of the plot, and was employed with a former MP, Samuel Starkey, to search the houses of prominent Whig politicians who were suspected of involvement. Hartshorne and Starkey did this with the authorization of the Earl of Sunderland, secretary of state, but Sunderland and his colleagues subsequently decided that neither was reliable and did nothing to help them when the grandees whose houses had been searched, Lord Paget and Sir Roger Hill, challenged the legality of the warrant and accused the two of housebreaking. As a result they were arrested, imprisoned, tried, and convicted, first at the Old Bailey and then at the Buckinghamshire Assizes.[13]

As before, Jeake and his London contacts were involved, and extant letters to him and his mother-in-law supplement the laconic diary entries, illustrating the severe distress which Nathaniel's family suffered.[14] Nathaniel narrowly avoided hanging or transportation to the colonies, while his various adventures included escaping naked from custody and being pursued and shot at. Though the affair reflects badly on the more powerful figures involved, Jeake's brother-in-law comes across as none too savoury a figure. Finally, however, he achieved an unconditional pardon and, perhaps surprisingly, not only returned to Rye but became town clerk before his early death in 1693.[15]

---

[11] FRE 5072. See also FRE 5045–6, 5065, 5071–4, 5081, 5293–4, and perhaps 5296; *CSP Dom.*, July–Sept. 1683, p. 102; and 22.5, 16.11.82.

[12] On Goodenough see *DNB*; H. F. MacGeagh and H. A. C. Sturgess (eds.), *Register of Admissions to the … Middle Temple* (3 vols., London, 1949), i. 199. See also 10.3.81 and *CSP Dom.*, July–Sept. 1683, p. 11.

[13] Ibid., *passim*, and 1683–4, pp. 81, 282–3. On Starkey see Henning, iii. 478–9.

[14] These are as follows (in approximately chronological order): FRE 5291–2, 5297–8, 5300 (1683); 5172, 5178, 5180 (1684); 5208, 5218, 5223, 5225, and perhaps 5295 (1685); 5239, 5242, and perhaps 5299 (1686). See also 27.8, 3.9, 11.11.83.

[15] *CSP Dom.*, 1684–5, p. 209, 1686–7, p. 232; and see 16.4.88, 18.3.93. Cf. also FRE 5336.

Beyond that, the record of Jeake's family life is mainly limited to his wife's childbearing. Their first child was injured during delivery, perhaps not surprisingly with so young a mother (9.12.82). Thereafter four successful pregnancies and a miscarriage are recorded, though one of the former was complicated by a feared abortion which 'passed over'.[16] In addition, there are occasional notes of the illnesses and injuries of Jeake's children, and a unique report of a family quarrel due to 'letting the child go into rude company' (10.4.88). But the diary's incompleteness on such topics is clear from *Astrological Experiments Exemplified* and letters, and it is telling that there are as many references to Jeake's children's health in the detailed journal for 1699 as in the whole of the main diary.[17]

There are also glimpses of Jeake's relations with his numerous cousins, both on his father's and mother's side. Perhaps the most interesting of these was his refusal to be a party to the declaration of William Hartridge *non compos mentis* (12.5.93). Again the diary is clearly highly selective, but some of Jeake's references bear out the flexible, 'qualitative' significance of kinship relations in seventeenth-century England to which attention has recently been drawn.[18]

Lastly, while courting, and later in company with his wife, Jeake often made journeys 'for diversion'. These sometimes involved visits to friends in neighbouring parts of Kent and Sussex, on one occasion including indulgence in a syllabub (as Jeake noted in shorthand, 2.7.73). In the 1680s and 1690s he and his wife went more than once to London, and what might be entailed on such occasions is suggested by the fact that the visit of 22 May 1682 is elucidated in the list of accidents in his *Nativity* as 'to buy Cloths &c', although described in the diary merely as 'for diversion'.[19]

In addition, however, Jeake seems to have been quite a tourist, seeing the sights of London in November 1667, of Canterbury and of the dockyards of Chatham and Rochester in October 1672, and of Rouen—where he admired the view from the cathedral tower—in 1674. Here we evidently see a facet of that curiosity about the world around him which is also in evidence in his intellectual pursuits and which was perhaps imbued in him by the liberal education that he received from his father.

---

[16] 16.3.84, 3.1, 18.2, 13.3, 13.8.88, 8.11.92, 1.9.94, 21.7.99. See also 17.11.87, 27.7.94.
[17] 14.9.85, 6–7.7.90, 16.6, 3.8, 6.9.99. Cf. 25.2.90, 22.6.94. For letters see FRE 5206, 5315–6, 5324–6, 5328–9.
[18] David Cressy, 'Kinship and Kin Interaction in Early Modern England', *Past and Present*, 113 (1986), 38–69, and see p. 66 for the background to Jeake's use of the term 'cousin'.
[19] Selmes MS 56/1, accident no. 89 (22.5.82) (fol. 6). Cf. no. 181 (11.5.91) (fol. 8).

6. JEAKE'S READING AND INTELLECTUAL DEVELOPMENT

One of the most significant aspects of the diary is the information that it gives on Jeake's attitudes and beliefs and his view of the world. A major component of this is Jeake's complete—or almost complete—list of the books that he read, which illustrates unusually fully the intellectual influences to which he was subject. The diary also provides an interesting account of the education which Jeake received at the hands of his father, which may be supplemented by a remarkable series of school-books which still survive at Rye Museum.

The education of youth was evidently one of the elder Jeake's subsidiary sources of livelihood—letters survive requesting him to act as a tutor, not least in mathematics[1]—and he was therefore well equipped to teach his son. The schooling he provided included the staples of education at the time—grammar, both Latin and Greek, logic, and rhetoric—the latter intended to encourage clarity of thought and expression. On each topic the diarist notes his compilation of epitomes, which was evidently his father's preferred method of teaching, and most of the items referred to are extant.[2] Indeed these painstaking school-books suggest that it was to his father's influence that the younger man owed the methodical attitude to his affairs which is so much in evidence in the diary.

In addition, the older man gave his son a broader training in more modern subjects. One was mathematics, the subject of a book by the elder Jeake published posthumously by his son but mainly compiled forty years earlier.[3] There was also a substantial component of general knowledge—geographical, scientific, philological, and miscellaneous—as is illustrated by various surviving notebooks which the adolescent kept, including a substantial volume entitled *Miscelanea* and dated 1666.[4] Lastly, the younger Jeake was given a training in shorthand and scrivening: it was the latter that he was referring to in stating that he 'learned to write' in 1661–2. Numerous specimens survive of calligraphic exercises that he carried out, so that by his mid-

---

[1] FRE 4337a, 4568.

[2] See May 1666, 22.12.66, 1.6.69. The 'Epitome Rhetoricae' of 22.12.66 no longer survives, but a book on rhetoric in the hand of the elder Jeake, which may have been an adjunct to his teaching, is now Jeake MS 5.

[3] Samuel Jeake, senior, *Λογιστικηλογία* (1696), sig. B2 and *passim*. Selmes MS 28, *Of the Appendices to the Golden Rule or Discontinuall Geometricall proportion. &c.*, gives arithmetical problems and solutions in the hand of the younger Jeake.

[4] Selmes MS 25. For an earlier compendium of 1664 see Selmes MS 17. See also Selmes MSS 20 and 21.

teens he was capable of beautiful italic and other hands.[5] His artistic exercises, however, he notes were 'learn'd of my self' (26.4.64).

The elder Jeake must also have been responsible for the choice of the books read by his son during his adolescence, which form the start of the numbered list of books which Jeake thereafter kept throughout his life. The list begins with 124 books that the diarist had read by the time he was fifteen years old in 1667, a precocious but not abnormal rate of development in a seventeenth-century context. It continues on a piecemeal basis thereafter, being picked up again by the fragmentary diary for 1699.[6]

The amount that Jeake read at different times in his life fluctuated. During the latter stages of his adolescence from 1668 to 1671 he entered sixty-three books, whereas from 1673 to 1678 four and a half years elapsed when he was so preoccupied with commerce that no titles were listed at all. When commerce was slacker and persecution enforced leisure in the early and mid 1680s, Jeake's reading intensified, dwindling as trade burgeoned from 1687 to 1689 but rising again as it slackened at the start of the Nine Years War.

Of course, an aggregate of titles is potentially misleading, since some books that he read were much bulkier than others. Moreover, though the list indisputably proves that Jeake read the works included, it does not seem to be quite complete. Even in the diary Jeake refers to books that he read which are not included in the numbered list, perhaps due to oversight, including the writings of the divines William Ames and Thomas Gataker on the morality of lotteries (13.4.94). This is also true of the sources he employed for such compilations as his 1666 *Miscelanea*.[7] In at least some of these cases, this was possibly because Jeake merely skimmed a work, or read only part of it.

The main source of the books that Jeake read was the extensive library that his father had built up and to which both the elder and younger man added throughout the Restoration period. Though the collection itself is now almost entirely lost, its impressive size and range is illustrated by the painstaking 'Register' of it which survives, on which the two Jeakes collaborated:

---

[5] See Selmes MSS 10–15 (dated 1662–6), 26 (1668), and Jeake MSS 7–13 (1663–6). See also 24.2.70.

[6] Books were entered at the date when they were completed, rather than when they were begun (cf. 3.4.84, 22.1.85 concerning Morin's *Astrologia Gallica*). A number of titles which Jeake reread appear twice.

[7] These include H. C. Agrippa's *De Occulta Philosophia*, John Jonston's *Historia Naturalis de Avibus*, Philip Barrough's *Methode of Phisicke*, Nicholas Ling's *Politeuphuia*, and John Parkinson's *Theatrum Botanicum*, apart from various dictionaries etc.

this gives full details of all the volumes, even itemizing their prices.[8] Perhaps not surprisingly, the library's shelves were dominated by theology, and particularly Puritan theology, though room was found for works emanating from other traditions, including even *An Introduction to a Devout Life* by St Francis de Sales. More remarkable was the prominent showing of radical literature of the Interregnum, with tracts by authors like Richard Overton, Gerrard Winstanley, and the early Quakers. In addition, there were more general works like William Dugdale's *Antiquities of Warwickshire*, John Guillim's *Display of Heraldrie*, and Henry Peacham's *The Compleat Gentleman*. The library was also strong on books on science, medicine, and the occult, and on law and other professional interests of the elder Jeake, including school-books.

Not all the books that Jeake mentions reading were, however, to be found in the library, and others were presumably lent by friends in and around Rye. One source of loans in the 1660s was undoubtedly the lawyer and medical practitioner Philip Frith, who was to bequeath a large number of books to the younger Jeake at his death, particularly on medicine and natural science (16.10.70). Though the books that the diarist borrowed from friends rather than his father mainly comprise a fairly random selection of those he read, a disproportionate number seem to have been literary and popular historical works.[9]

Jeake could read Latin, but by far the bulk of his reading matter was in English, including English translations of classical writings and of books in contemporary foreign languages. Also notable is the number of highly topical works that Jeake saw in addition to older titles; these evidently reached Rye by carrier within a short time of their publication.

In view of his Puritan upbringing, it is perhaps not surprising that more of the books he read were on theology than on any other subject. The very first item to appear was a volume of John Foxe's *Acts & Monuments*, better known as the Book of Martyrs.[10] After this, the list of authors whom he read is like a roll-call of the classic godly divines of the period before the Civil War, including William Perkins, Thomas Brightman, William Fenner, Arthur Dent, Richard Rogers, Samuel Smith, and Thomas Cartwright (129). Many of the topics he studied were equally redolent of earlier seventeenth-century Puritanism—sabbatarian works, anti-Catholic writ-

---

[8] Jeake MS 4/1. An edition of this manuscript is currently being prepared by Michael Hunter, Giles Mandelbrote, and Nigel Smith.

[9] e.g. 16, 17, 30, 33, 46, 88, 151. Note also that two contemporary political works, 198–9, fall into this category.

[10] Bracketed numbers in the text refer to numbered entries of books in the diary. Works that appear in the initial list of 124 books under 4 July 1667 are not here separately numbered.

ings, the Puritan *Survey of the Booke of Common Prayer* (1606), John Rainolds' attack on stage plays, and Thomas Beard's collection illustrative of God's providential dispensations against evil-doers, *The Theatre of God's Judgements* (in the extended 1648 edition by Thomas Taylor). A further characteristic item was the *Relation* of the sixteenth-century Italian apostate Francis Spira, which was widely popular in Puritan and nonconformist circles in seventeenth-century England.[11]

From the years during and since the Civil War Jeake not only knew the biographical and autobiographical writings of Bunyan and Jessey which have already been noted as a possible inspiration for the diary, but also the works of such dissenting divines as Vavasour Powell, Thomas Brooks, John Flavell, Ralph Venning, William Dyer (128), John Owen (152), and his relation Christopher Blackwood. If such books suggest a fairly mainstream nonconformist position, more radical items include the mystical *Theologia Germanica*, works by Hugh Peter and Sir Henry Vane (169), the Republican pamphlet *Mene Tekel* (usually ascribed to Roger Jones), and the speeches and prayers of Major General Harrison and others of Charles I's judges executed at the Restoration.

But Jeake's reading was not wholly limited to Puritan works. He was also acquainted with such classics of Anglicanism as Archbishop Whitgift's response to the Elizabethan Puritan Thomas Cartwright, the works of Joseph Hall, Thomas Fuller, and James I, George Herbert's *The Temple*, and the life of the moderate Archbishop Usher. In addition, Jeake read such royalist items as the Εἴκων βασιλική attributed to Charles I and Thomas Bayly's *Worcesters Apothegme* (162), a collection of the witticisms of a leading royalist Catholic.

This broadmindedness perhaps provides the background to the diary entry for 21 September 1679 in which Jeake professed his admiration for the Huguenot Philip Duplessis Mornay, who defended Christianity by appealing to universal natural truths, in preference to the Dutch thinker Hugo Grotius, 'who (notwithstanding the Noise his learning makes in the world) fixes Religion on the Basis of Tradition'. Here we evidently see a parallel to the shift towards natural theology which has often been discerned in contemporary Anglicanism, but which is notable in a nonconformist like Jeake and contrasts with the preoccupations of his father.[12] If so, however, it is

---

[11] Cf. Brink, *Trosse* (see sect. 4 n. 1), 17–19.

[12] See e.g. G. R. Cragg, *From Puritanism to the Age of Reason* (Cambridge, 1950); R. E. Sullivan, *John Toland and the Deist Controversy* (Harvard, 1982), chs. 2, 8 (and, for a background to Jeake's view on Grotius, pp. 217–18). For a nonconformist parallel see M. B. Endy, *William Penn and Early Quakerism* (Princeton, 1973), ch. 5. On the elder Jeake's theological interests see esp. FRE 4223.

indicative of the limitations of the booklist that neither Duplessis Mornay nor Grotius actually appears in it, while one would have been hard put to draw quite this conclusion from Jeake's recorded reading, except for one work by the sixteenth-century French reformer, Sébastien Châteillon. It is unfortunate that the book on 'the trueness of the Christian Religion' that Jeake refers to writing in February 1672 has not survived.

Jeake's religious reading in the 1680s and 1690s ranged as widely as it had earlier. In this part of the list are such eirenic works as Sir Thomas Browne's *Religio Medici* (196) and a number of books by Anglican churchmen, including bishops like Robert Sanderson (201), Edward Stillingfleet (209–10), Gilbert Ironside (228), and John Wilkins (234). He also read that exemplar of Anglican casuistry, Jeremy Taylor (226), and a number of the writings of the Cambridge Platonist Henry More, including his *Enthusiasmus Triumphatus* (257).

In general, however, Jeake's reading continued to concentrate on low church authors, and especially Puritan ones of the early seventeenth century, together with a few items by Anabaptists and other radicals (208, 222, 241). Contemporary dissenting divines whose works he imbibed included John Owen (250), John Howe (275), Walter Marshall (277), and Vincent Alsop (315); his perusal of Bishop Burnet's life of the tolerant jurist Sir Matthew Hale with the *Additional Notes* of Richard Baxter may also be noted (212). But it is striking how many of the authors whom he read at this stage were of the earlier seventeenth century, evidently because much of the best devotional literature available to nonconformists dated from that period. Such writers included John Preston (243, 248), John Arrowsmith (270), Daniel Dyke (272), Henry Ainsworth (274), and Robert Bolton (283).

The persecution of the nonconformists in the 1680s evidently had the effect of giving Jeake a strong interest in apocalyptic speculation, which had been little apparent in his earlier reading. In the main, he studied books of the 1640s and 1650s by authors like Richard Mercer (238, 240) and John Tillinghast (235–6, 247), though he also read more recent millenarian works, including Pierre Jurieu's *Accomplishment of the Scripture Prophecies* (253). It was now that he read Milton's *Paradise Lost* (239), while significance may also be attached to his perusal of the Koran (242), which was widely seen at the time as a paradigm of the misuse of religion for political ends. Jeake read another recent millenarian work at the time of the French invasion scare of 1690 (263), while the last book in the list was Francis Potter's *Interpretation of the Number 666* (316).

Religious books were always Jeake's chief staple, but throughout his life he also read more widely. During his adolescence, the book list helps to

44

explain the grandiloquent list of subjects that he claimed to have 'somewhat acquainted my self with' by the age of nineteen (4.7.71). Predictably the classics were well represented in his early reading, including Josephus, Plutarch, Homer, Aesop, Virgil, Ovid, and Sallust. Also in evidence is the geographical interest which his father imbued in him, with such topographical works as Daniel King's history of the County Palatine, travel books like Giles Fletcher's *Of the Russe Common Wealth* and Samuel Purchas' *Pilgrimage*, and accounts of voyages by Thomas James and Sir Henry Blount. History figured prominently, with Grafton's abridgement of the English chronicles, Samuel Daniel's account of the Wars of the Roses, and William Camden's of the reign of Elizabeth (171); a related work was a treatise on heraldry by Sylvanus Morgan.

Jeake also read literary works, to a perhaps surprising extent in a Puritan context. He read Cervantes, Ariosto (151), and such works of English literature as Sidney's *Arcadia*, William Warner's *Albion's England*, James Howell's *Dodona's Grove*, Francis Quarles' *Emblemes*, and—more surprisingly—the royalist Sir John Suckling's *Fragmenta Aurea*. Also notable is Jeake's perusal of books by two authors suspected at the time of dangerously secular attitudes, Machiavelli's *Florentine History* and Francis Osborne's *Advice to a Son* (though these were balanced by the future archbishop, William Sancroft's, critique of Machiavellianism in *Modern Policies*).

The numerous books on the natural world which appear show a combination of the new science and of the occult traditions which enjoyed such vitality at the time. In the latter category were writings by Paracelsus and his follower Michael Sendivogius (160, 183), the Rosicrucian manifestos (174), and the alchemical classic, *Secrets Reveal'd* (149). Jeake read the latter in the year it was published and it is interesting that a month later he records in shorthand being told 'the first matter of the elixir as was supposed' —the great mystery of alchemy.[13] Earlier, he had read a selection of Hermetic and Neoplatonic works, including Iamblichus, Proclus, and the *Pimander* and *Asclepius* of Hermes Trismegistus; he also saw Jacques Gaffarel's *Unheard of Curiosities* (138), a discussion of the magical pursuits of the ancients. It is hardly surprising that there are a number of titles on his favourite study, astrology, including books by William Ramesey (131) and the Elizabethan Sir Christopher Heydon (135, 143), though Jeake's other writings make it clear that he read more on this topic than is indicated by the list.[14]

On the other hand, Jeake also read classics of the new philosophy,

---

[13] 15.4.69. See also Smart, p. 75, for a comparable reference by his father in 1685.
[14] For instance, he made extensive use of William Lilly's *Christian Astrology* (1647) and of computational works by authors like Vincent Wing.

including three books by Sir Kenelm Digby (130, 175, 187), Joseph Glanvill's famous methodological treatise, *Scepsis Scientifica* (148), and the works of Descartes (186). It is probably not coincidental that it was shortly after studying Descartes that Jeake refers in the diary to his 'Hypothesis about the Ebbing & Flowing of the Sea', since the explanation of the movement of the tides had been one of the classic problems of the new philosophy since the time of Galileo.[15] Though this item is unfortunately lost, the effect of such authors is certainly in evidence in another work that Jeake began that summer and which does survive, his *Diapason. The Harmony of the Signes of Heaven*. For in this exposition of astrological principles it is intriguing to find that Jeake, like certain other early modern astrologers, attempted to find a quantitative rationale for the influence of the heavenly bodies on sublunary events, arguing that the influence of the planets operated by 'subtil emanations or particles', and justifying this by allusion to 'the atomical hypothesis' of Digby and Descartes.[16]

In 1671 Jeake also immersed himself in medical books, to a greater extent than is apparent from his numbered list, since he refers to reading Nicholas Culpeper's translation of Lazarus Riverius' *Practice of Physick* (1655) without giving it a number (14.4.71). But the works in the list are themselves of interest, including various treatises which challenged the Galenic orthodoxy of the day by authors like Marchamont Nedham, Edward Bolnest, and George Thomson (179–81). Earlier, Jeake had read a variety of more or less up-to-date books on natural history, including writings by Edward Topsell, Thomas Moffett, Robert Lovell, and John Jonston (157), though it is noteworthy that only one work by Francis Bacon appears, his *Wisedome of the Ancients* (156).

Jeake's reading after the gap in the 1670s continued to cover many of the same topics as before. History books included Thomas May's *History of the Long Parliament* (202), John Speed's *History of Great Britaine* (203), and Sir Walter Ralegh's *History of the World* (195), the evident inspiration of his extraordinary dream on 1 November 1678. Geography recurred in Peter Heylyn's *Cosmographie* (205), whilst slightly *risqué* authors continued to be represented through the second part of Osborne's *Advice to a Son* (206). Another theme which appears at this point is contemporary politics, comprising Henry Neville's Republican tract, *Plato Redivivus* (199) and a work

[15] 25.8.71, and see E. J. Aiton, 'Galileo's Theory of the Tides', *Annals of Science*, 10 (1954), 44–57.
[16] Selmes MS 34, pp. 1, [72]. He also cited Sir Christopher Heydon in this connection. On the aspiration of Heydon and others to a quantitative astrology see Bowden, 'Scientific Revolution' (see sect. 2 n. 27), ch. 3 and *passim*.

by Slingsby Bethel (198): this had been barely in evidence earlier, although in 1672 Jeake had begun a book on politics which is now lost (18.12.72).

In 1682–3 Jeake engaged on a second bout of medical reading (213–18, 220–1), coinciding with his interest in apocalyptic works and perhaps to be seen as a further response to the persecution. In contrast to his earlier studies on this topic, however, his emphasis at this point was primarily on anatomy, including studies by such pioneering contemporaries as William Harvey, Jean Pecquet, and Thomas Bartholin. In addition, Jeake read another classic of the new science, Thomas Sprat's *History of the Royal Society* (258), though he was a little late in seeing this, as it had been published in 1667; more topical was his perusal of *The Sacred Theory of the Earth* by Thomas Burnet (265–6), a controversial work which attempted to provide a mechanistic rationale of the creation of the world. He also read William Charleton's translation of the *Ternary of Paradoxes* by the influential natural philosopher Joan Baptiste Van Helmont (259), while a more occultist flavour is seen in the alchemical *Ripley Reviv'd* (211). In astrology, the two works he studied at this time were both associated with the empirical tradition of the day, J. B. Morin's massive *Astrologia Gallica* (233) and John Goad's astrological analysis of the weather, *Astro-Meteorologica* (282).

Jeake's eclectic mixture of scientific and astrological reading is matched by the contacts that he made in these years. Perhaps most striking is his visit to the Royal Society in 1693, when he submitted the manuscript of his father's *magnum opus* on arithmetic to the society for its approval and received it back with the blessing of the president, Sir Robert Southwell (15, 21.6.93). The book was vetted for the society by the astronomer Edmond Halley, and it is possible that Jeake met Halley on this occasion and kept in touch with him thereafter.[17] For in attempting to establish the meridian of his place of birth as exactly as possible in his *Nativity*, Jeake was to collate his observations near Rye of a lunar eclipse on 6 May 1696 with those made by Halley at London, which do not appear to have been published.[18]

A further acquaintance was John Harris, a Fellow of the Royal Society and scientific author who was also Vicar of nearby Winchelsea and whose sermons in the lecture series founded by the scientist Robert Boyle was one of the last books Jeake read (314). Jeake cast Harris's horoscope, and through him he established contact in 1698 with the Astronomer Royal, John Flamsteed, asking him advice on some of the technical problems he

[17] Royal Society Archive, Copy Journal Book, viii. 180 (21.6.93).
[18] Selmes MS 56/1, fol. 4. Alternatively it is possible that Jeake came across Halley through George Parker's accurate almanac, which he used from 1690 onwards and to which Halley contributed.

encountered in attempting to calculate the positions of the heavenly bodies at the time of his birth with absolute precision in his *Nativity*.[19]

But Jeake was also in touch with fellow astrologers, noting his correspondence in 1692 with John Kendal and Henry Coley in a passage which itself manifests the intellectual vitality of astrology in his day (4.7.92). For Kendal sent Jeake an essay which no longer survives, in which he put forward a novel theory about astrological causation, while one of the topics on which Jeake consulted both Kendal and Coley were the ideas of the Italian astrological writer Tito Placido, which were championed in England at this time by George Bishop and John Partridge.[20]

Like many others in late seventeenth-century England, Jeake combined a commitment to the new philosophy with a strong interest in occult phenomena, which tinged his view of others more scientific.[21] The diary displays curiosity about natural phenomena like comets, eclipses, and an earthquake, while in the case of comets, Jeake even drew up an elaborate pair of diagrams in 1685 to suggest how their apparent paths might be explained.[22] But it was typical of Jeake to attach a personal, astrological significance to such astronomical phenomena (19.4.77, 2.7.84). Nor is it surprising to find him mapping the lines on his hands and taking an interest in physiognomy (8.9.70, 4.7.71)—a topic on which he read books in 1668 and 1670 (147, 172)—or displaying an apparent belief in the magical power of number in noting how he fell ill when he was exactly fourteen years, fourteen days, and fourteen hours old (18.7.66). Equally telling is the 'Hieroglyphick in picture' that he finished on 16 July 1670, which evidently owes something to the *Monas Hieroglyphica* of the sixteenth-century magus John Dee, in which Dee sought a single, complex symbol which would sum up all occult wisdom and about which Jeake waxed enthusiastic in his *Diapason* of 1671–2.[23]

The diary also records Jeake's interest in poltergeists (23.9.66, 19.6.71) and monstrosities (July 1667, June 1668), one of which he interpreted in

[19] Selmes MS 55/1 (which has a more precise birthdate—6 March 1665—than that given in *DNB*); Royal Greenwich Observatory Archive, MS 1/33, fols. 201–2 (Flamsteed to Harris, 8 March 1698).

[20] On these see Capp, *Astrology and the Popular Press* (see sect. 2 n. 27), 183. See also above, sect. 2.

[21] For parallels, see Hunter, *John Aubrey* (see sect. 2 n. 27), ch. 2; K. T. Hoppen, 'The Nature of the Early Royal Society', *British Journal for the History of Science*, 9 (1976), 1–24, 243–73.

[22] Selmes MS 50, and see 23.12.64, 1.6.76, 19.4.77, 17.2, 3.3.78, 11.12.80, 2.7.84, 8.9.92. Cf. also Jeake's reference to writing 'the Construction of an Instrument per Altitudinem Solis', 4.9.71.

[23] Selmes MS 34, p. 20. Cf. C. H. Josten, 'A Translation of John Dee's *Monas Hieroglyphica*', *Ambix*, 12 (1964), 84–221.

terms of the mysterious power of the imagination; a background to this is perhaps provided by Jeake's reading in the 1660s of such books as the account of the seemingly miraculous cures by 'stroking' of Valentine Great-rakes.[24] Such references date predominantly from Jeake's earlier years, but he saw no reason to suppress them when writing the diary up thirty years later, while continuity is also displayed by his note of an extraordinary cure in 1694, the truth of which he was able to establish for himself from the woman who had experienced it (20.4.94).

On the other hand, though both Jeake and the author of a contemporary pamphlet on the subject acclaimed the 1694 case as a 'Miracle', the latter did so in explicit response to those who sought a naturalistic explanation of the affair.[25] A challenge to Jeake's view of the world is also in evidence in another, rather surprising episode that the diary records, Jeake's contact in 1693 with the *Athenian Mercury* (12.4.93). The *Athenian Mercury* was a popularizing journal which looks forward to the literary periodicals of the eighteenth century; it published queries from readers with answers by the so-called 'Athenian Society', a group of intellectuals brought together by the bookseller John Dunton. Since the queries were printed anonymously, the identity of its correspondents is normally elusive, and it is only because Jeake explains in the diary what he wrote to the journal about that he can be identified as the author of a question in its pages. Indeed, this is one of the very few cases where the identity of a querist is known, and it further exemplifies the diary's unusual value as a source.[26]

More important, however, is what the query was about, and how it was answered by the *Athenian Mercury*'s compilers. For it concerned the Earth's motion, and Jeake—who had been sceptical of the Copernican hypothesis since the 1670s—clearly hoped to elicit the response that the doctrine was nonsense. 'If the Earth mov'd round,' he wrote, 'it would be very reasonable to conclude, that a Man running towards the East should rid more ground than if he ran towards the West; as also that a Gun would shoot much farther one way than another?' The Athenian Society, however, disagreed entirely,

---

[24] 142. See also above, sect. 2, on Jeake's reading of Jessey's *The Lords Loud Call to England* and his collection of 'Some Prodigies' etc. On the power of the imagination, see Hunter, *John Aubrey* (sect. 2 n. 27), 125

[25] *A Narrative of the Late Extraordinary Cure Wrought in an Instant upon Mrs. Eliz. Savage, (Lame from her Birth) Without the using of any Natural Means. With the Affidavits* (London, 1694).

[26] For the only other known querists, Sir William Temple and Elizabeth Singer, see John Dunton, *Life and Errors* (London, 1705), 261 and G. D. McEwen, *The Oracle of the Coffee House* (San Marino, 1972), 100, 105–6. On the *Athenian Mercury* see McEwen, op. cit.; Stephen Parks, *John Dunton and the English Book Trade* (New York, 1976), ch. 3.

putting Jeake down with a commonsensical refutation.[27] Jeake received a similar rebuff from John Flamsteed, who replied to John Harris' letter not only to point out an error that 'your Ingenious sober and candid freind Mr Jeake' had made in his calculations, but also to 'take Occasion from his Mistake to shew him how he may Imploy his time much better then in the study of Astrology'.[28] Jeake has left no record of his reaction to these assaults on his beliefs: but they are indicative of tensions in the transitional period in which he lived of which he can hardly have been entirely unaware.

7. JEAKE'S ILLNESSES AND MEDICATION

In the course of the diary, Jeake gives an account of his health which is extremely full and in some respects unique, particularly his almost obsessive chronicle of exactly timed ague attacks. Otherwise, however, his record is not atypical of autobiographies and diaries of his day. Such accounts are clearly of value to the historian, both for what they reveal about contemporary illness and treatment, and for the information that may be gleaned from their authors' comments as to how they perceived disease and health.[1] The preoccupation of authors like Pepys or Ralph Josselin with ailments and discomforts may breed the suspicion that many diarists were hypochondriacs rather than chroniclers of commonplace experiences of their day. But in Jeake's case such a characterization would arguably be unfair: his detail was purposeful rather than purely indulgent.

The amount of space devoted to illness in different parts of the diary certainly fluctuates, with its peak in the 1670s. This, however, is because that was the decade in which Jeake suffered his worst attacks of ague. It might be suspected that, as with his reading, there would be an inverse correlation between Jeake's attention to his health and the extent to which he was preoccupied by other matters like commerce. But in fact there is no shortage of

---

[27] *Athenian Mercury*, vol. 10, no. 11 (2 May 1693). The reason given is taken straight from Varenius: see Richard Blome (trans.), *Cosmography and Geography in Two Parts* (London, 1683), 24. For Jeake's view of Copernicanism see esp. Selmes MS 38, pp. 12–13; in addition, Selmes MS 50 postulates a static earth.

[28] Royal Greenwich Observatory Archive, MS 1/33, fol. 202. In fact, Flamsteed's draft is incomplete and does not contain an explicit critique of astrology. On this episode and its background see Michael Hunter, 'Science and Astrology in Seventeenth-century England: An Unpublished Polemic by John Flamsteed', in Patrick Curry (ed.), *Astrology, Science, and Society* (Woodbridge, 1987), 260–300.

[1] For parallel accounts see particularly Lucinda M. Beier, 'In Sickness and in Health: A Seventeenth-century Family's Experience', in Porter, *Patients and Practitioners* (see sect. 3 n. 16), 101–28, and other contributions to the same volume. See also Roy Porter, 'The Patient's View: Doing Medical History from Below', *Theory and Society*, 14 (1985), 175–98.

medical notes at times when we know that he was inordinately busy, as in the later 1680s. Indeed, collation of the diary with *Astrological Experiments Exemplified* suggests that the diary's record of Jeake's illnesses is relatively complete, in contrast to its selectiveness on themes like his commercial activity.[2]

That Jeake had been constitutionally weak from his earliest years is possibly suggested by his father's letters to him during his stay in London in 1668, which seem to show more than normal parental concern about the adolescent's health.[3] It is worth noting that none of Jeake's siblings survived infancy, and it may be significant that 'one of the first things that I remember' was an illness (31.5.56). On the other hand, the childhood ailments that Jeake briefly records were fairly typical, notably measles and worms (though he seems to have been interested only in when he 'voided' these, a fact which he saw it as appropriate to consign to shorthand).[4] Then, in 1666, he had an attack of smallpox, which 'came out but kindly, & I was not disfigured by them' (21.7.66).

Thereafter, the rest of Jeake's life settles down to a predictable pattern, and especially to an endless succession of more or less serious colds and 'agues', the latter evidently attacks of the malaria which was endemic in the low-lying coastal lands surrounding Rye. The colds started in his childhood—indeed his smallpox developed from a cold (18.7.66)—while the agues began in 1667 and recurred frequently, with particularly severe attacks in 1670–1 and 1678. Colds were characterized by headaches, hoarseness, blocked nose (5.5.72), and 'abundance of thin Rheum' (2.11.73), with side-effects such as soreness (29.4.88). In addition, they overlapped with ague, and Jeake sometimes conflated the two, both with one another and with the 'fevers' from which he also suffered. The agues were preceded by symptoms such as 'a great pain in my head' (7.10.81); they then took the form of successive more or less severe attacks, involving sweating, vomiting, giddiness, drowsiness, and shaking. There were often also accompanying pains and other corollaries.

Jeake describes his agues according to the standard terminology of the time, which classified them principally according to the cycles in which attacks returned. The commonest types were tertian and quartan. The former involved attacks of some twelve hours' duration, recurring on alternate

---

[2] For illnesses and medication not mentioned in the diary see *AEE*, 28.8.87 (melancholy), 4.9.87 (toothache), 8.9.87 ('purging diet drink'), 2, 6.12.87 ('ocular internal medicine'). On accidents see above, sect. 3. As will be seen, all are fairly minor.

[3] FRE 4823, 4824, 4827, 4832, 4833, 4838.

[4] 3.12.52, 6.4.53, 31.5.56, 13.3.71. Cf. Beier, 'In Sickness' (see sect. 7 n. 1), 107 ff.

days ('simple'), daily ('double'), or with three fits every two days ('triple'). A quartan, on the other hand, involved a visitation every fourth day if simple, on two succeeding days with a third day free if double, or daily if triple: the triple always emerged from the single or double. The rarer quotidian ague involved daily bouts, while Jeake also uses the concept of 'irregular' for agues which failed to fit into any of these categories. Apart from the pattern of attacks, the various agues were distinguished by different symptoms: quartan, for instance, was characterized by melancholy, while the onset of a tertian was marked by great shaking fits, as against a light shivering and coldness in a quotidian.[5]

In addition, Jeake complains of a miscellany of other ailments, such as swellings and twitches in different parts of his body, stomach pains, diarrhoea, dizziness, toothache—of which he had a particularly severe bout in 1671—and 'noise in the Ears' which began in the 1660s (4.3.68) and continued throughout his life. He was also concerned about his eyesight, which was affected by his smallpox in 1666, and he notes a succession of attempts to ameliorate it over the following years, including a special trip to London in search of medication (28.5.72); none, however, proved successful. A further lifelong complaint was 'melancholy', in other words depression, which Jeake seems to have suffered to an extreme extent, complaining of its duration for ten years from 1667, reaching a 'most intolerable' climax in the winter of that year but continuing 'with Violence' till the summer of 1670 (20.9.67). Later, perhaps the worst attack 'I ever were afflicted with' came in 1680, causing him prolonged sleeplessness (29.9.80).

Another of Jeake's recurrent troubles was apparently an anal fistula, which was evidently 'confirmed' on 21 May 1672. This caused him much pain in his adolescence and early manhood, and in 1677 an unsuccessful attempt seems to have been made to deal with it by surgery (7.9.77). On this topic, as on his eyesight, a high proportion of Jeake's memoranda are in shorthand, something which is not otherwise the norm in the diary's medical entries.[6]

On the whole, none of the illnesses from which Jeake suffered was serious, causing inconvenience more than any real risk of debilitation: some of the things of which he complains are as trivial as a painful crick in the neck (5.2.93). It is only fair to acknowledge, however, that agues and other ail-

---

[5] Cf. Lazarus Riverius, trans. Nicholas Culpeper, *The Practice of Physick* (London, 1655), 580 ff.

[6] 28.7.66, 11.11.70, 17.1, 21, 28.5, 21.9, 26.10.72, 28.1, 11.4.73, 7.9.77, and perhaps 20.9.67, 31.1.78. One topic which Jeake noted once in the diary (in shorthand) was having his hair cut: 13.6.57. Thereafter he did not vouchsafe such notes to his diary, though a record of his haircuts in the 1670s survives in his expense accounts (Selmes MS 40/1–6; see also Selmes MS 56/2).

ments could develop more serious complications, and Jeake was therefore justified in monitoring even the first signs of illness and decay. Although the cause of his death at the age of forty-seven is not entirely clear, it was not preceded by notes on any illness in the shorthand diary which survives for his last months, and it seems likely that he suffered a stroke: the author of an anonymous broadsheet lamenting Jeake's death was evidently being more than metaphorical when he referred to Jeake as

> crop't off in blooming Years
> By fatal Stroke.[7]

Jeake shows a knowledge of medical terminology, almost self-consciously using technical terms like 'Gutta Serena' or 'Sonitus Aurium' in describing his ailments (2.8.67, 4.3.68). He also had a clear sense of the signs of illness and recovery, as seen, for instance, when he noted his urine 'turning pale as in health' (21, 23.10.78). Perhaps because of this know-how, he sometimes expresses puzzlement when a disease failed to follow a predictable pattern, while on other occasions his interest in symptoms seems to diminish once he had identified the disease. A case in point is the fever from which he suffered in the summer and autumn of 1678, about which he seems to have been perplexed until he deduced that it was part of an illness which had spread all over Europe (23.10.78).

Jeake's expertise is already in evidence in his comments on his smallpox in 1666, when he remarked on the lack of any 'surfeiting disorder' as a preliminary symptom (18.7.66), and this was an attainment that he clearly owed to his father and his friends. Medical knowledge seems to have been more widely disseminated among non-professionals in early modern England than might have been expected, and there is evidence of a considerable amount of skill in the circles in which Jeake moved. This is documented not only by the medical advice in his father's letters to him but also by a surviving commonplace book of the Jeakes' friend, the surgeon-apothecary Philip Frith, which comprises a miscellany of medical lore, recipes, and prescriptions for different diseases, to which the elder Jeake made additions.[8] One item in this is a

---

[7] *In Obitum Vere Deploratum Samuelis Jeake, Gent.* (*qui Obiit 22 Novembris, 1699*) *Carmen Lugubre* (London, 1700).

[8] FRE 606 (an earlier recipe book with substantial additions by Frith); ibid., fol. 107 for Jeake senior's additions. For his letters see FRE 4823, 4832. On the commonness of medical knowledge among non-professionals see Paul Slack, 'Mirrors of Health and Treasures of Poor Men: The Uses of the Vernacular Medical Literature of Tudor England', in Charles Webster (ed.), *Health, Medicine, and Mortality in the Sixteenth Century* (Cambridge, 1979), 237–73; Porter, *Patients and Practitioners* (see sect. 3 n. 16), *passim*; and Roy Porter, 'Lay Medical Knowledge in the Eighteenth Century: The Evidence of the *Gentleman's Magazine*', *Medical History*, 29 (1985), 138–68.

short tract, evidently by Frith, entitled *Some Kindling Sparks In Matter of Physicke*, of which the younger Jeake made a transcript.[9] But although this recommends a fairly extreme form of anti-Galenic therapy—suggesting that all diseases be treated with fiery substances, since fire was the source of life—there is no evidence that the younger Jeake was much influenced by such ideas.

In any case, Frith provided the wherewithal for the younger Jeake to educate himself medically by the extensive series of books on this subject that he bequeathed him in his will, the titles of which can be identified from the Jeakes' surviving library catalogue.[10] Jeake's medical reading has already been referred to, and it is interesting that he particularly singles out Culpeper's translation of Riverius, since some of his terminology, and some of the concepts he uses to describe his illnesses, can be paralleled in this work and the glossary issued with it.[11]

Like many contemporaries, Jeake approached illness with a pathology which might be described as an eclectic Galenism. His commentary on his 1670–1 ague attack shows that he associated the progress of illness with 'morbifique matter' in the body and that he believed that there was a link between health and the seasons (2.5.71). His subscription to a generalized humoral view of disease is illustrated by his reference elsewhere to the need to 'draw away the noxious humours that offended' parts of his body (3.8.71), while he also uses the humoral terminology of phlegm, yellow choler, and so on.

As for the causation of illness, Jeake, like others, tended to presume that colds and related ailments were caught by going out on cold days (30.11.78, 14.4.88) and made worse by drinking cold beverages (3.7.67), travelling (18.7.76, 2.6.88), or even overwork (6.11.86).[12] Once contracted, he appears to have seen diseases as having a kind of natural cycle, though medication might affect this, while he also seems to have seen specific organs, such as his eyes, as 'naturally infirme' and hence 'the apter to receive injurious impressions' (28.7.66).

In Jeake's case, there was also the influence of the stars. On at least one

---

[9] FRE 606, fols. 135–40. The transcript is Selmes MS 23.

[10] It is clear from the Library 'Register' (Jeake MS 4/1) that the Frith bequest comprises the main clump of books entered under each letter of the alphabet in the younger Jeake's hand, which are disproportionately on medicine and natural philosophy.

[11] See, for instance, Riverius, *Practice of Physick* (see sect. 7 n. 5), 50 (melancholy: cf. 31.8.80), 580 (ague: cf. 30.1.77). The concepts of 'morbifique matter' and 'Peccant Humour' are both to be found in Culpeper's appended *Physical Dictionary*.

[12] For parallels, see Porter, 'The Patient's View' (see sect. 7 n. 1), 178–9; Wear, 'Puritan Perceptions' (see sect. 3 n. 16), 82–3.

occasion Jeake appears to have seen astrological causes as distinct from natural ones, implying that he invoked astrology in the absence of more mundane explanations (18.7.66), but elsewhere astrology formed part of his view of natural causation. The casting of horoscopes and the noting of astrological circumstances at the moment he fell ill is to be seen in this light, for at one point he paused to try to generalize as to which positions of the planets tended to bring illnesses out, suggesting that while astrology explained the time at which he was taken ill, nature was responsible for the buildup of 'peccant humours' which then became apparent (31.7.78).

Indeed it is in this context that one should see perhaps the most extraordinary feature of Jeake's record of his health, his curiosity about the time to the minute at which his illnesses, and especially his attacks of ague, occurred. This concern about exact moments in sickness is not normal among diarists of his day, and to us it may seem rather trivial. But to an astrologer like Jeake it was crucial, and it is revealing that he began to record such information in the early 1670s, in his first period of intensive astrological study, not including it in the diary in connection with previous ailments.[13]

Evidently Jeake hoped that an explanatory pattern might become apparent by collating the movements of the heavens with the timing of attacks in conjunction with their intensity, symptoms, and side-effects, which he also carefully noted. That his motive was astrological is suggested by the astrological metaphors that he employed in his disquisition on the 'Critical Register' he kept of the ague attacks that he suffered in 1670–1, though he never carried out a full analysis of this (2.5.71). Jeake's special interest in ague is not surprising, for agues were arguably precisely the kind of illness likely to appeal to him, their regularity of timing and the qualitative difference that could be observed between the various attacks being highly susceptible to the type of exact astrological analysis in which he specialized. Hence astrology made the recording of detail even more mandatory than would otherwise have been the case.

Moving from diagnosis to treatment, the evidence suggests that Jeake deployed astrology less than might have been expected. Though he cast horoscopes at the moment when he was taken ill (the so-called practice of 'decumbiture'), Jeake does not seem to have used these as a guide to therapy, as some astrologers of his day did. Only on one occasion—which he

---

[13] On the effects of astrological interests on medical observation cf. Michael MacDonald, *Mystical Bedlam: Madness, Anxiety, and Healing in Seventeenth-century England* (Cambridge, 1981), 28–30.

significantly disguised in shorthand—does he note that he elected a time for a medication, which produced 'little benefit' in any case, despite the fact that the medical use of elections was a topic that he wrote about at some length in one of his astrological works in the 1670s.[14] Instead, the diary suggests that he used a fairly predictable armoury of non-astrological therapies, in this as in his diagnosis displaying a degree of expertise as to what treatment would be appropriate in different circumstances which evidently derived from his background and reading.

In treating himself, Jeake employed a number of herbal and chemical recipes, either externally as ointments or internally as palliatives or as purges and vomits intended to remove noxious substances in the body by defecation or vomiting. He administered substances either direct—as with the leaves of deadly nightshade that he placed on his forehead to induce sleep (11.8.78)— or in simple compounds, as with the mixture of salt, oil, and vinegar with which he treated shingles (22.5.87). Tobacco might either be applied externally, as with the concoction of tobacco, frankincense, and beaten currants that he applied to his wrists (11.10.70), or taken internally (16.1.70).[15] Other internal remedies included herbal ones like rosemary beer (10.10.81), pills made from aloe (9.10.69), and various 'theriacs', including the celebrated Venice Treacle, a compound prophylactic based on classical prototypes which Jeake used from 1678 onwards.[16] In addition, there were vomits like Crocus Metallorum, an antimony preparation (8.10.70, 14.9.78), while Jeake also made use of oil of sulphuric acid as a general palliative.[17]

Jeake clearly purchased at least some such compounds ready made, but it is likely that he also made chemical preparations himself: an interest in distillation and other processes was something that he had inherited from his father and from Philip Frith, whose widow bequeathed the diarist various

---

[14] 3.8.71; *Diapason. The Harmony of the Signes of Heaven*, Selmes MS 34, pp. 57–8. On Jeake's attitude to elections see above, sect. 2.

[15] On the use of tobacco see F. N. L. Poynter and W. J. Bishop (eds.), *A Seventeenth-century Doctor and his Patients: John Symcotts, 1592?–1662* (Bedfordshire Historical Record Society, 31 (1950)), p. xxxiii. For Jeake's purchase of tobacco see his expense accounts, Selmes MS 40/4–5.

[16] On Venice Treacle see Poynter and Bishop, *Symcotts* (see n. 15 above), 116; Richard Palmer, 'Pharmacy in the Republic of Venice in the Sixteenth Century', in A. Wear, R. K. French, and I. M. Lonie (eds.), *The Medical Renaissance of the Sixteenth Century* (Cambridge, 1985), 108–10; and 16.10.78, 10, 14.10.81, and 20.10.86. See also 18.2.78. On Jeake's purchase of 'Aq[ua] Theriac[alis]' on 19 and 21.9.78, see Selmes MS 40/5.

[17] 9, 23.7, 16.8.72. Cf. FRE 4635, illustrating the elder Jeake obtaining 'Spirit of Sulphur Viva per Campanum' from Dr Relfe of Cranbrook in 1672. Jeake's expense accounts (Selmes MS 40/2, 4, 5) refer to the purchase of Sulphur Viva on 7.10.75, 15.3.77, and 2, 27.7.78 (the latter from Dr Relfe).

stills at her death.[18] In addition, an element of eclecticism is in evidence, as when Jeake abandoned one—evidently expensive—nostrum, 'Volatile Salt of Vipers', in favour of a cheaper and more everyday substitute in the form of brandy, at a time when he evidently had a large supply of such liquor from his trading activity.[19]

Medication of this kind was clearly self-administered, though Jeake sometimes makes it plain that it was based on advice or on a consensus of opinion.[20] The same is true of Jeake's references to putting himself into 'a Physical sweat' (2.10.78), for instance, or treating his eyes both externally and internally (25.5.71). Other treatments, however, and particularly surgery, must have involved the services of a medical practitioner. Thus he refers in the passive tense to having a cataplasm or poultice applied to his neck (27.6.72), to a 'Fontinell' being used to remove undesirable humours (3.8.71), or to the operation he had in 1677 (7.9.77). Frustratingly, however, Jeake never names the practitioner or practitioners involved, though in the 1670s it might have been the barber-surgeon Edward Gee and his one-time apprentice Thomas Crouch, both of whom are recorded in Jeake's accounts as cutting his hair and providing him with medicaments.[21]

Sometimes Jeake records that medication worked, as when tobacco 'conquer'd' a pain in his head (16.1.70), or when other potions abated his pain or caused him to sleep soundly; of vomits, too, he sometimes noted that they 'wrought well', as on 14 September 1678. Moreover, on one occasion he specifically notes that it was because a medication 'agreed very well with my body' that he recorded the dose (16.4.86). On the other hand, he sometimes observes that, though a medication had a direct effect, it failed to help his illness, as when a dose of Crocus Metallorum gave ten vomits and three stools 'but no benefit as to my Ague'.[22] On yet other occasions he frankly noted that 'all means I used proved ineffectuall' (1.10.88), while medication might have harmful side effects. The worst instance of this is described in a short-

---

[18] 11.10.71. For an endorsement to a letter of 1674 in the younger Jeake's hand, which gives references to various books on chemistry concerning the distillation of spirit of sulphur, see FRE 5632. One of the plans for a house that Jeake drew up in 1678–9 (that dated 9.1.79) includes a laboratory (Selmes MS 47/4). On the chemical interests of his father's circle see especially T. W. W. Smart, 'A Notice of the Rev. John Allin, Vicar of Rye, AD 1653–1662; An Ejected Minister', *SAC* 31 (1881), 151–2.

[19] 21.8.79. For the purchase of half an ounce of Volatile Salt of Vipers and its transport to Rye in September 1679 see Selmes MS 40/6 and 42/4.

[20] See e.g. 21.5.72 ('confirmed'), 26.4.84 ('advised').

[21] Selmes MS 40/2–6. Cf. Burchall, p. 105. FRE 4859 is a letter from Dr Relfe of 15.8.77 giving medical advice about the elder Jeake in which Gee is mentioned (cf. Selmes MS 40/6 for payment for a 'Letter from Dr Stacy', 15.3.79).

[22] 8.10.70. Cf. Beier, 'In Sickness' (see sect. 7 n. 1), 119–20.

hand entry on 7 and 13 September 1677, in which Jeake notes how the surgery on his fistula was done 'unskilfully' and he was 'like to bleed to death'.

Jeake also mentions quite often that an ailment 'went away of it self' (4.3.68), without—or in spite of—medication. His comments on the ague of 1670–1 show his conviction that, if strong enough, 'Nature' could overcome illness (2.5.71), while, either in addition to or instead of other explanations, he was sometimes inclined to invoke God's direct intervention, as in the last entry of the main diary, where 'it pleased God somewhat to asswage the pain in 3 or 4 days' (26.11.94). This is a facet of Jeake's invocation of providence which has already been discussed, and it is symptomatic that God might be directly responsible for a cure, but never for the onset of disease: Jeake stands in contrast to those earlier seventeenth-century Puritans who saw illness as a divine chastisement.[23]

What effect did illness have on Jeake? Some of his pains were 'not very violent' (18.7.79) and clearly caused him only inconvenience. Melancholy, in particular, was something that he just had to live with, though aware that it made him bad-tempered, as at the time of his marriage negotiations in 1680 (29.9.80). In connection with his cold in 1667 he notes retiring to bed as if this was unusual.[24] Even the agues seem to have caused only intermittent trouble, so that in 1670–1, for instance, he was able to continue reading, learning geometry, and the like during gaps between the recurrent attacks. Perhaps the only really serious illness was his smallpox in 1666, which completely incapacitated him for several days, and it is interesting that here, like other diarists, he records almost ritualistically the stages of his return to normality from the abnormal condition of the sickbed.[25] Otherwise, Jeake's chronicle is mainly of intermittent pain and inconvenience: as such, it may well be that his experience was typical of his age, and that he was abnormal only in his obsession with writing it down.

8. THE MERCHANT OF RYE

The theme that occupies more space than any other in Jeake's diary is his activity as merchant, money-lender, and investor. Diaries and memoirs kept by tradesmen and businessmen in the seventeenth and early eighteenth cen-

[23] Cf. Wear, 'Puritan Perceptions' (see sect. 3 n. 16), esp. 70–2. On providence see above, sect. 2.

[24] 4.7.67. Cf. *AEE*, 19.3.88, when he records an ague attack 'but forced to bear up, being busied about the Cloth all the afternoon'.

[25] 27–30.7.66. Cf. Beier, 'In Sickness' (see sect. 7 n. 1), 124.

turies are rare. Among the most notable are those of the Lancashire shop-keeper Roger Lowe and the Lancaster merchant William Stout, both of which have been deployed to help remedy 'the collective ignorance of economic historians regarding the structure and organization of commerce at local and regional levels'.[1] Jeake's represents a worthwhile addition to this literature.

In Jeake's case, though the diary is the most accessible source concerning his commercial activity, a profusion of other material survives. Indeed this is sometimes paraphrased in the diary, as when Jeake gives his net profit for a year as represented by the amount transferred to stock to balance his books. Jeake's accounts survive from the 1670s and 1680s, the former on loose sheets, the latter in the form of an elaborate ledger with separate entries for each client with whom he dealt or commodity in which he traded, all neatly cross-referenced to stock and cash accounts, and with his expenses and profits separately totalled.[2] His business correspondence survives up to 1686, providing detailed information on such matters as his credit transactions, while for the year 1687–8 *Astrological Experiments Exemplified* gives a day-to-day account of the more humdrum details of a merchant's life.[3]

What the diary offers is a sense of priorities and preoccupations, and of the risks involved in commerce at the time. Small businessmen in the late seventeenth century lived under a constant threat of bankruptcy. 'The Lord keape me from miscaryinge, for the Lord's sake!', prayed Jeake's tradesman contemporary, Roger Lowe,[4] and the diary notes various people who 'broke', including Jeake's cousin, John Mackley (16.8.89). Though himself spared this fate, the risk undoubtedly contributed to the caution which is so much in evidence in Jeake's text, which sometimes seems inordinate. The diary reveals Jeake's doubt and indecision in commercial matters, recording regrets over lost opportunities to buy and sell at advantageous prices. He also hesitated to try new ventures, though sometimes surprising himself by doing better in these than on more established commodities. Other problems included the risk of shipwreck in cross-channel or coasting trade and the impact of war, felt particularly in 1678 and 1689, which was only marginally compensated for by the proceeds available from prizes.

Also in evidence is the sense of timing required to make the best of market

[1] Marshall, *William Stout* (see sect. 1 n. 3), 14. See also W. L. Sachse (ed.), *The Diary of Roger Lowe of Ashton-in-Makerfield, Lancashire, 1663–1674* (London, 1938) and T. S. Willan, *The Inland Trade* (Manchester, 1976), ch. 3.
[2] Selmes MSS 39–45; RYE 145/11. For references to the accounts in the diary see 26.2, 31.5.80, 8.2, 31.12.81, 30.1.82, 19–21.5.83, 1.1.85, 1.1, 31.12.87.
[3] FRE 4845 *et seq.*; *AEE, passim.*
[4] Sachse, *Roger Lowe* (see sect. 8 n. 1), 60.

forces, as commodity prices fluctuated according to demand and to harvests and the weather. Even the travel which commerce necessitated had its difficulties, as seen in Jeake's almost obsessive concern with weather conditions, reminding one of a vulnerability to the elements to which modern travellers are immune.

Bankruptcy was a matter of particular concern to businessmen from backgrounds like Jeake's because of the overtones of moral unworthiness associated with it,[5] and the diary illustrates Jeake's scrupulous, even moralistic, approach to his dealings with others. This is seen in his concern about smuggling (13.7.79) or his keenness to repay the kindness of his friend Thomas Miller in the 1690s (30.6.94). More remarkable is a breathless shorthand passage in which Jeake expressed the pangs of conscience that he experienced about what he saw as a slightly questionable transaction on his part, for which he attempted to compensate by repaying the illicit profit that he believed he had taken (though even then suppressing the reason 'for my reputation') (11.10.92).

The exact date of Jeake's earliest trading venture is unclear. He computed 'the first of my Profits' from April 1673 (11.12.73), but these probably derived at first not from merchandising, but from another activity which hardly figures in the diary although it is clear from Jeake's accounts and other sources that it provided a significant source of income for him in the 1670s and a minor one thereafter. This was scrivening, for which, encouraged by his father, he had been prepared by an extensive calligraphic training during his adolescence. Jeake evidently earned money by writing out indentures, bonds, certificates, wills, and the like, some specimens of his work surviving among his correspondence reused as palimpsests.[6]

At some stage probably in 1674, however, Jeake seems to have consciously decided on trade as a career. In a reply of 18 April 1674 to a lost letter of Jeake's, his cousin Christopher Blackwood of Dublin noted Jeake's 'Intentions: as to Asume [*sic*] Merchandize for your Imployment', and it is doubtless significant that 1674 is the first year for which Jeake kept detailed accounts.[7] In an entry under December 1673 in which he declared his intention to devote a tithe of his profits to charity from 19 January following,

[5] Cf. Marshall, *William Stout* (see sect. 1 n. 3), 8–9.

[6] FRE 4868v, 4870v. For the supply of bonds and other documents see FRE 4879, 4882, and e.g. 5011. Jeake's accounts, *passim*, have references to the purchase of blank bonds as well as to profits from this source, while there are many allusions to this activity in *AEE*. For the single reference in the text below see 25.6.94.

[7] FRE 4845; on the Blackwood family see T. W. W. Smart, 'Original Letters, Hitherto Unpublished, of the Rev. Christopher Blackwood', *Baptist Magazine*, 59 (1867), 369–76, 435–40, 519–24, 579–85.

Jeake makes it clear that he expected these to come 'by Trade'. Hence, although Jeake gives 27 August 1674 as the date of his 'first entrance into Trade', he must mean by this his first large-scale enterprise, by contrast with smaller transactions in goods like honey, roses, and lace which both diary and accounts illustrate that he had carried out earlier that year.

In opting for commerce in this way, Jeake followed a common career pattern among Restoration dissenters. Christopher Blackwood was a minister's son who had effected this transition—it was perhaps for this reason that Jeake had written to him for advice—while Jeake's major trading contacts locally were also with nonconformists. These included Thomas Markwick and Nicholas Skinner or Shinner, both of whom left Jeake legacies in their wills, and above all Thomas Miller, 'a great Nonconformist', in the disapproving words of a government informer.[8] This did not, however, preclude occasional links on Jeake's part with merchants with other affiliations, including Lewis Gillart, one of the leaders of the court party in Rye politics in the 1680s.[9]

Jeake's venture into trade is abnormal in that he does not seem to have served an apprenticeship, a most unusual circumstance, and contrasting, for instance, with the career of Christopher Blackwood.[10] Possibly this was due to the financial independence that Jeake had as a result of family money, which was what made his business activities possible in the first place. But it is more likely that Jeake's early steps in trade were overseen by Thomas Miller, the fellow merchant with whom his earliest major ventures were carried out, who was already established in commerce. Such an informal arrangement may have been facilitated by the commercial links of Jeake's family, his uncle, William Key, having been a mariner whose estate the elder Jeake administered.[11]

Jeake, Miller, and their friends were typical of the small factors or middlemen of which late seventeenth-century England was full. Based on ports or market towns, such men engaged in a variety of trading activities, importing goods and distributing them to a local catchment area and collecting and exporting the staple products of the region in exchange. Though

---

[8] *CSP Dom.*, July–Sept. 1683, p. 151. For bequests see 7.12.89, 11.8.93, and 29.12.91, the latter that of Richard Naldread, on whom see 15.2.85, FRE 5126, and RYE 145/11. For parallels see Watts, *Dissenters* (see sect. 4 n. 1), 363–4; Marshall, *William Stout* (see sect. 1 n. 3), 13, 53.

[9] FRE 4856, 5250(f); RYE 145/11; and see below, p. 65.

[10] Smart, 'Original Letters' (see sect. 8 n. 7), 580–1. Cf. e.g. Willan, *Inland Trade* (see sect. 8 n. 1), 95–6.

[11] See 20.12.66 and n. See also above, sect. 1, on the commercial activity of the man who was probably Jeake's great-grandfather.

they frequently remain rather shadowy, dealers like these were crucial in the period's economic development.[12]

Rye, the centre of Jeake's operations, was a port of intermediate size which had seen better days in the late Middle Ages and the sixteenth century: at that time it had been one of the chief outlets for the products of the Wealden iron industry, a role which now survived only in an attenuated form. In addition, the port had earlier had a flourishing fishing fleet, whereas by this time the local fishing industry was increasingly attracted to nearby Hastings. Rye remained, however, a significant outlet for various staple products of its hinterland, particularly wool from Romney Marsh and hops from the Weald. Other exports included cereals from the Battle area and herrings from coastal fishing. In return, imports of general merchandise were required, especially from London, while in the 1670s Rye had some significance as a centre for the import of wine, cloth, and canvas from France, though its role was secondary to that of Dover. It also acted as a port of refuge for ships in the Channel, and this sometimes provided commercial opportunities to its merchants, especially with ships carrying deals from Scandinavia.[13]

In the course of his career, Jeake was to become involved in many of these commodities, though there were some he never dealt in, such as iron, oats, or barley. The port books kept by local customs officials suggest that Jeake was typical of the Rye merchant community in the nature and scale of his operations, though some who used the port worked on a much larger scale, such as the London merchant Thomas Western.[14] In addition, Jeake never owned ships of his own, always having to subcontract the actual carriage of goods to shipowners, either in Rye or (equally often) in Hastings, where by now more boats were moored. On the other hand, though based on Rye, Jeake was never limited to a purely local sphere, engaging in transactions which bypassed Rye, such as the direct shipment of cloth from France to Falmouth.

---

[12] R. B. Westerfield, *Middlemen in English Business, Particularly Between 1660 and 1700* (1915, repr. Newton Abbot, 1968); J. A. Chartres, *Internal Trade in England, 1500–1700* (London, 1977), 50–2 and *passim*. See also Richard Grassby, 'England Merchant Capitalism in the late Seventeenth Century: The Composition of Business Fortunes', *Past and Present*, 46 (1970), 96–7.

[13] See esp. J. H. Andrews, 'Geographical Aspects of the Maritime Trade of Kent and Sussex, 1650–1750', London Ph.D. thesis, 1954, which corrects in various respects the older work of T. S. Willan, *The English Coasting Trade, 1600–1750* (1938; repr. Manchester, 1967). See also C. E. Brent, 'Urban Employment and Population in Sussex between 1550 and 1660', *SAC* 113 (1976), 35–50.

[14] e.g., for 1674–5, PRO E190, 772/13, 773/9, 12. On Western see Woodhead. A useful guide to the Rye port books is provided in Andrews, 'Maritime Trade' (see sect. 8 n. 13), 374–5.

In the first instance, Jeake became involved through Miller in imports from France. While they were in Dieppe together in April 1674, the two bought a parcel of bone-lace in partnership. Then, in July, Jeake bought a barrel of meal at Dieppe through James Le Griell, a contact of Miller's, while in August Miller and Jeake collaborated in importing French linen from St Malo.[15]

Their scale of operations enlarged early in the following year, assisted by gifts amounting to £110.11.6 in capital from Jeake's father and subsequent loans from the same source. On 13 March 1675 (as Jeake succinctly explained in his *Nativity*, being slightly more explicit than in the corresponding passage in the diary) he 'First began to Trade to Morlaix & money given by my Father to Trade Jan. 6 & Mar. 29 which Encreas'd much in 1675 & 1676'. The *Nativity* also makes it clear that it was to raise further capital 'to trade with' that in July 1676 he sold for £85. 10s 0d. the land at Pembury that had come to him by descent from his mother, having already disposed of the timber on it for £58. 5s. 0d.[16]

The staple of Jeake's and Miller's trade at this point was the purchase of cloth—particularly 'lockrams', a type of coarse linen—at St Malo and (above all) Morlaix in the *arrondissement* of Finistère in Brittany. These were bought either directly or through London contacts, and the goods were then shipped either straight to Rye or via London. The latter was commoner, since Jeake and Miller were working on too small a scale to import complete cargoes on their own, and they had to share with others. Moreover, even if a joint cargo came to Rye first it was not always possible to locate the requisite parcels of goods.[17] The cloth was then resold in the surrounding countryside at a profit, and Jeake's diary reveals how his customers were widely scattered: he mentions seeking custom or collecting debts for lockrams in Eastbourne and other places (10.4, 26.6.77), and it is clear that many other journeys elsewhere in East Sussex and Kent that he refers to were similarly inspired.

In 1676 this basic trade was supplemented by other ventures. In one, Jeake and Miller collaborated to send herrings from Rye and Hastings to France and London, the former in exchange for cloth, though some loss was made.[18] A more ambitious project involved shipping a cargo of cloth directly from Morlaix to Falmouth in Cornwall, 'the greatest Venture that ever I had by Sea before this time', as Jeake notes (6.1.77). The identity of his

[15] 15.4, 27.8.74. For the barrel of meal see FRE 4847.
[16] Selmes MS 56/1, accidents nos. 50, 54 (fols. 5, 5v); see 6.1, 29.3, 22.7.75, 19.1.76, and Selmes MS 39/1-3. On the land at Pembury, see above, sect. 3, and below, 27.8.73 and n.
[17] See e.g. 6.3.76, 2, 15.5.77, 2.3.88. For payment see 5.8.75 or e.g. Selmes MS 42/1.
[18] See Selmes MS 45/6; FRE 4856; 27.10.76 *et seq.*

contact there is unfortunately unknown, but there was a well-established link between Rye and the West Country at this time.[19] In addition, Jeake continued to deal on a smaller scale in commodities like beeswax, honey, and paper.[20]

Despite disappointments like the herrings, Jeake's accounts show that his transactions with Miller in French cloth proved highly lucrative, and in the mid 1670s his profits from commerce swiftly grew to outstrip the proceeds of his scrivening. The substantial quantities in which linens were imported is indicated by the figures given both in the diary and his accounts—often amounting to hundreds of pounds—and his clear profits rose from £24. 12s. 0¼d. in 1675 to a peak of £70. 2s. 6½d. in 1678.[21]

In that year, however, this phase of Jeake's commercial activities was abruptly brought to an end when Parliament prohibited trade with France. This trade embargo was a major blow not only to Jeake but to local prosperity more generally. Dr J. H. Andrews has argued that the impact of war was as significant in Rye's commercial decline as the silting up of the harbour, although the latter attracted more attention in Jeake's day and has often been blamed since for the port's decline: in fact, most of the ships involved in trade at the time were small enough to negotiate the reduced channel. Not only did this—and subsequent—French wars cut off trade: they also endangered harbours like Rye and their shipping through the threat of enemy action, while the pressing of sailors was a further wartime hazard.[22]

As with other embargoes of which Jeake was to be a victim, this one was not watertight, and a series of letters to French businessmen survives in which Jeake explored fresh lines of communication across the Channel, resulting in the import in 1678 and 1679 of paper, wine, brandy, gloves, and fans from Dieppe and Rouen. But the illegality of the operation appears to have caused him concern, while in 1679 he was left with a substantial quantity of merchandise on his hands, so that he put the transaction down in his diary as representing a loss and thereafter abandoned the trade.[23]

Instead, he investigated other possibilities. In 1678 he enquired of his cousin Christopher Blackwood about obtaining tallow from Dublin 'for a Triall'. His partners in this were Thomas Miller, Richard Freebody—a Rye

---

[19] See PRO E190, 773/12, 25, 775/4.

[20] Selmes MS 41/3–4.

[21] Here and hereafter all figures given in the text are derived from Jeake's accounts, referred to in sect. 8 n. 2, unless otherwise stated.

[22] Andrews, 'Maritime Trade' (see sect. 8 n. 13), chs. 3, 7; and below, 20.2, 7, 22.3.78.

[23] FRE 4886–92, 4895, 4897, 4899, 4902–4 and 5250(c, o, r); Selmes MSS 39/5, 41/6, 42/4, 44/3–4; RYE 145/11, fol. 1; and below, 9.3.78, 29.4, 26.5, 13.7.79.

'cousin'—and Jeake's London cousin, the tallow-chandler John Mackley, with whom Jeake now seems first to have established contact. But though another merchant, Daniel Hayes, dispatched some tallow from Dublin in July, it sold at a slight loss and no further imports were made.[24] A further venture of 1678–9—not noted in the diary—involved sending hops from the Rye area to the West Country and in return shipping wheat from Devon and Cornwall to Rye.[25]

The impression of an almost desperate search for new sources of income is given by the miscellaneous smaller ventures noted at this time. In 1679 Jeake went into partnership with another of his nonconformist friends, Thomas Markwick, to sell timber, again making some loss (27.5.79), while with Lewis Gillart he purchased French boats captured in the Channel and sold as prizes, laying out some £200 and having to borrow money to be able to do so (3–7.7.79). He also sought 'some Factory, & Correspondencyes at several places' in London, though without success (3, 11.3.79); he dealt in salt on commission; and he seems to have tried to interest Rye customers in Madeira obtained in London.[26]

A more significant activity which Jeake had begun in 1678 was the lending out of money at interest, either on simple bond or by mortgage on people's property: this was another typical activity of small capitalists in the early modern English countryside, the commonness and significance of which in the economic life of the time has been underlined by recent research.[27] Jeake's earliest recorded loans date from 1678, but in 1679 and 1680 they proliferated, while the sums involved became larger, often amounting to £100 or more, and this established a pattern which was to continue throughout the period covered by the diary.

These loans could occasionally cause tense moments, for instance when those in debt to Jeake died and problems ensued concerning payment, while he sometimes notes with relief when he was repaid a loan shortly before the other party went bankrupt, as with his cousin Richard Freebody in 1685

---

[24] FRE 4863–4, 4866–71, 4874–7, and 5250(i); and below, 9.7, 14, 23.9.78. The letters do not mention Daniel Hayes, who was probably related to Jeake's London business contact Claude Hayes (who is mentioned in connection with the venture in FRE 4874).

[25] FRE 4880–5, 4894, 4898, 5250(p), 5251. This involved Thomas Morris, a London nonconformist with whom Samuel Jeake senior had had contact in the 1660s: Smart, pp. 67–71. See also FRE 5250(q) and 4917.

[26] Selmes MS 44/6 (salt); FRE 4886 (Madeira). On the timber see also FRE 5250(j).

[27] B. A. Holderness, 'Credit in English Rural Society before the Nineteenth Century, with Special Reference to the Period 1650–1720', *Agricultural History Review*, 24 (1976), 97–109. For the figures see Jeake's accounts, *passim*. For an isolated earlier loan of 1676 see Selmes MS 42/2.

(5.6.85). But it was nevertheless a potentially profitable business and worth the risks involved, interest being paid at a standard rate of 6 per cent.

Apart from simple loans and mortgages, in 1679 Jeake began to lend money on bottomry, 'which used frequently afterwards' (22.5.79). Bottomry was a type of mortgage whereby a shipowner borrowed money at an agreed rate of interest for the period of a voyage, pledging his ship as security, the lender taking the risk that if the ship was wrecked, his money would be lost with it.[28] Having begun modestly in 1679–80, Jeake's profits from this source rose to £12. 13s. 0d. in 1681 and a peak of £17. 1s. 0d. in 1682.

Then, on 3 July 1679, Jeake began to negotiate bills of exchange, and again this proved a lucrative activity, as shown by the rise of the proceeds from £5. 11s. 10¼d. in 1679 to £25. 8s. 2d. in 1680 and £20. 16s. 10d. in 1681. It depended on the contacts in London and France that Jeake had accumulated during the 1670s, using business transactions to convey credit around the country and across the Channel; at the London end he increasingly relied on his cousin John Mackley. The system of credit involved was not dissimilar to that which has been documented for the eighteenth century, with an extensive system of promissory notes to named payees obviating the need for cash to be transferred; the rate of commission on bills varied, but seems most often to have been 1 to 1½ per cent or 4 pence in the pound.[29] Risks occasionally surfaced, as when bills were 'protested' (e.g. 8.4, 22.8.86), but again it was a rewarding and satisfying business, and there is a clear note of pride in Jeake's record of his ability to be able to draw £350 'all in one bill 3 days sight' in 1686 (30.10.86).

Another new venture was wool, in which Jeake traded for the first time in 1680, as he notes under 19 June that year. Here he acted as a wholesaler, buying wool from producers in East Sussex and Kent like Richard Hill of Woodchurch, for instance, and exporting it to London or further afield.[30] Jeake's profit from this source was £24. 13s. 2d. in 1681 and £12. 6s. 1¼d. in 1682, though this, too, was not without problems, due to the Restoration government's concern about the illegal export of wool and its more or less effectual attempts to curb it, which focused on Romney Marsh.[31] Even perfectly honest dealers could suffer from these measures, as Jeake found when

---

[28] For background see Ralph Davis, *The Rise of the English Shipping Industry* (London, 1962), 84–5.

[29] T. S. Ashton, *An Eighteenth-century Industrialist* (1939; repr. Manchester, 1961), ch. 8; T. S. Willan, *An Eighteenth-century Shopkeeper* (Manchester, 1970), ch. 7. For the rate see Jeake's accounts, *passim*. Cf. also 16.1.80.

[30] For Hill see 19.6.80 and FRE 5254.

[31] Andrews, 'Maritime Trade', (see sect. 8 n. 13), 171 ff.; P. J. Bowden, *The Wool Trade in Tudor and Stuart England* (London, 1962), 194 ff.

some wool which he had sold to a chapman partly on credit was seized by officers on the Marsh on 10 September 1681 and he was worried that he might not be paid.

The result of such diversification was to give Jeake's affairs a sounder basis than previously, meaning that he was never again as dependent on a single commodity as he had been in 1678. Instead, it was now possible for him to juggle between his different commercial activities, so that as the proceeds from one dwindled, their place could be taken by profits from another. In this Jeake seems to have been typical of country merchants and shopkeepers, such as Abraham Dent of Kirkby Stephen a century later.[32] Moreover, as Jeake shifted from his role as factor to that of moneylender and back, he was often dealing with the same people. Peter Waters, for instance, appears in Jeake's 1681 accounts both as a supplier of wool and as a borrower.[33] It is clear that Jeake was able to respond to local needs as well as market fluctuations to make the best use of his capital.

This is illustrated by changes in the way his earnings were made up over the next few years. In 1680, his clear profits rose to £175. 8s. 4¾d., due not least to the fact that the difficulties over French goods had now evaporated again, enabling his profits from cloth imports to reach a new peak of £104. 6s. 3d. In this year he derived only £20. 7s. 5d. from interest, but in the following year interest accounted for £54. 4s. 5d., by far the largest single component of his total profit, rising to £81. 12s. 0d. in 1682 and remaining at a similar level for the next few years, although his total income fell at this point to under £100 per annum. In the mid 1680s Jeake's trading and exchanging activities virtually ceased due to the persecution of the nonconformists and the need to be repeatedly absent from Rye, and, had he still been dependent on such business, he could not have survived these years.

Even allowing for interest from loans, the time of persecution brought Jeake closer to ruin than at any other stage in his career. While in London in 1683 he sought employment either with the East India Company or as an accountant, which would perhaps have utilized his calligraphic skills (24.11.83). But nothing came of either idea, and the diary notes how in the following year he had to transfer £54. 13s. 1d. from stock to his current account to balance the books due to lacking employment, 'not daring to put my self into any business by reason of the persecution' (1.1.85). Indeed it was fortunate for Jeake that his estate had been substantially enhanced through his marriage settlement in 1681, which provided him with a greater degree of security than hitherto.

[32] Cf. Willan, *Eighteenth-century Shopkeeper* (see sect. 8 n. 29), e.g. 127.
[33] RYE 145/11, fols. 17, 22. Cf. 9.11.81.

In 1686 Jeake began to trade again, and his fortunes took a general upturn, his profits in that year reaching a new peak of £165. 15s. 11¾d. £73. 8s. 2d. of this came from interest, but he also made a healthy £47. 8s. 2¾d. from buying and selling wool. In addition, he began to deal on a substantial scale in hops, selling them partly to London and partly to the West Country, where he was able to make fresh trading arrangements with Edward Cross of Exeter, a former contact of Thomas Miller's (21.9.86). He also returned to negotiating bills, and again the sums involved quickly rose, from a mere £2. 0s. 1d. in 1685 to £18. 19s. 5d. in 1686, £25. 1s. 4d. in 1687, and £20. 16s. 1½d. in 1688, while the diary notes a climax in such business between 10 January and 8 February 1689 (10.1.89). His chief London contact for this and other purposes was now Thomas Miller, formerly his trading partner in Rye: Miller had been installed in London since 1683 and he increasingly took over the role served in the 1670s by Jeake's cousin John Mackley, who was to go bankrupt in 1689, and of whom Jeake was perhaps already suspicious at this stage.

In 1687 and 1688 Jeake's profits came to £160. 4s. 7d. and £143. 12s. 4¼d. respectively. By now he had responded to the state of the market so that relatively little of his revenue was coming from interest. Instead, almost all his profits derived from exchanging bills and from the sale of wool, hops, and— once again—lockrams and other fabrics. The diary notes Jeake's return to the Morlaix trade in the spring of 1687 (28.12.86, 12.2, 11, 30.4.87) and he began to invest large sums in importing French textiles, so that by 1688 his profits from this source came to £50. 18s. 1¼d. As earlier, he was also prepared to invest cautiously in new ventures. In 1688 he imported some French lace and purchased deals and malt from some ships that put in to Rye: on the latter he made a profit of £41. 14s. 1d., despite his initial reluctance to undertake it, 'having no Experience in it, & fearing it would not sell'.[34]

After the difficulties of the mid-1680s, Jeake's affairs were thus by now back on an even keel. It is appropriate that at this point the diary gives a hint of the relatively luxurious life-style in which Jeake could by now indulge in its mention of his purchase of pieces of Japanned furniture, though these modish items were damaged in transit to Rye (1, 15.6.88).

Jeake's correspondence does not survive after 1686—except for his letters to his wife during his trips to London—and neither do his accounts after 1688: the absence particularly of the latter make it difficult to compare the level of his business with that of previous years. It is clear from entries in the

---

[34] 19.1.88. See also *AEE*, 25.2.88. For further new ventures see below, 1.6.88, 6.10.92.

diary, however, that he continued to lend money and to trade around Rye and on the London and Exeter axes in wool and hops. Moreover, optimism is suggested by his erection of a storehouse at considerable expense in 1689–90, of which the foundation-stone was laid on 13 June 1689 to the accompaniment of a horoscope.

But, as ever, Jeake remained vulnerable to circumstances beyond his control, and the outbreak of the Nine Years War had its effects on commerce. Most immediately, it brought his trade in French cloth to a halt: Jeake just failed to get a shipment of canvas out before war broke out (28.1.89), and whatever the 'Proposal for managing the Trade of French Linens at Rye' was that he was writing while rumours about impending hostilities were rife, it did not prevent the complete collapse of this side of his activity (18.2.89). Worse still, the war did long-term damage to his money-lending activities as well as his merchandising: he had already given up his trade in bottomry due to the hostilities (12.2.88) while he complains in the diary how after a few years of war he was only making 5 per cent interest on mortgages and bonds, 'upon which I could but barely maintain my family' (16.4.94). Various events in 1693 proved the final straw, including the loss of the Smyrna convoy in June and the defeat at Neerwinden in July, 'which put a great Stop to Trade' (17.7, 2.8.93). Once again, international events seemed to be conspiring to threaten Jeake's hard-won success.

The solution was suggested by his experiences during a visit to London in April 1694 in connection with the executorship of his friend Thomas Markwick, as a result of which he began to consider 'Several Projects' as a means of increasing his income (16.4.94). It is symptomatic that in describing his new ideas Jeake used the vogue word 'project', as also that he specifically notes that his London visit made him consider things which he would not have bothered with in Rye (13.4.94). For what had inspired him was his first encounter with the financial experimentation which burgeoned in London in the 1690s, and he now resolved to invest more in the financial institutions of the City.[35]

The reason he gives for this in the diary is the low level of commercial activity in Rye. There may, however, have been a further reason which he did not vouchsafe to the diary, but which is revealed by the letter which he wrote to the corporation at this time offering to help pay off the town's debt

[35] For background see esp. P. G. M. Dickson, *The Financial Revolution in England* (London, 1967), and W. R. Scott, *The Constitution and Finance of the English, Scottish, and Irish Joint-stock Companies to 1720* (3 vols., Cambridge, 1910–12). For 'the general Projecting Humour' of the period, see Daniel Defoe, *An Essay upon Projects* (London, 1697), p. ii and *passim*.

in return for being absolved from civic duties. For he was clearly concerned that his offer would 'subject me to the injurious Consequence of an imagined great Estate', his expressed wish 'to obviate the malice of all sordid reflections either upon my Profession or Person' also suggesting local resentment of his money-making activities, perhaps exacerbated by the pressure of war-time conditions.[36] Be that as it may, though he continued to trade in hops and the like, at this point the focus of the diary moves from Rye to London, giving a unique insight into the Financial Revolution then in progress, in which he and other middling investors participated.

The exigencies of the Nine Years War stimulated many ingenious schemes for raising funds for government expenditure in these years. Jeake's first encounter was with the Million Lottery, the bill for which had been passed in March 1694. This was a project to raise one million pounds from subscriptions in multiples of £10 in return for guaranteed basic annuities and the chance of winning supplementary ones, the fund for paying the dividends being provided by a duty on salt, beer, vinegar, cider, and brandy. Investors could either buy prize tickets or blanks, which gave a 10 per cent dividend for 16 years after which interest ceased without repayment of capital.[37]

While in London, Jeake also learnt about a parliamentary bill then pending for the most famous and lasting of the fund-raising schemes mooted at this time, the Bank of England. Assent was given later in April to the bill, which offered two further investment opportunities that Jeake noted in his diary (16.4.94). In the first place, loans were invited for a total of £1,200,000 at 8 per cent interest, a marked improvement on the rate to which Jeake was accustomed; those who offered such loans by 1 August were to be incorporated as 'The Governor and Company of the Bank of England'. The remaining £300,000 required was to be raised by life annuities, an elaboration of a scheme that had begun the previous year though Jeake had evidently not known of it, by which investors could collect 14 per cent interest on one life, 12 per cent on two, or 10 per cent on three, the names of those whose lives were thus covered being submitted by a set date.[38]

Thirdly, Jeake resolved to buy stock in the East India Company, a rather longer-established concern with which, as we have seen, he had abortively attempted to establish contact in the 1680s. Jeake noted that the company's shares 'were now fallen to 82 per cent & probably supposed to fall lower'

---

[36] RYE 1/17, p. 201. Jeake also invoked his bequest from Thomas Markwick as a reason for his generosity.

[37] C. L'E. Ewen, *Lotteries and Sweepstakes* (London, 1932), 127 ff.; Scott, *Joint Stock Companies* (see sect. 8 n. 35), iii, 275, 290.

[38] Dickson, *Financial Revolution* (see sect. 8 n. 35), 48–9, 53–5. See 13.10.94.

(16.4.94), and his diagnosis was absolutely correct. East India stock had reached a peak in 1690 from which it then declined, and from 1694 to 1699 its price was actually below par, due largely to the threat during these years that the company's monopoly might be challenged by a rival enterprise, the New East India Company. In the short term, too, stock was subject to quite violent fluctuations: thus in 1693 it had oscillated between 66 per cent in May and 97 in November, and potential existed for significant killings as the value of stock rose or fell with the arrival of news of the fortunes of East India Company ships or of successes or reverses in the war.[39] It was said that Sir Josiah Child, one of the company's directors, had private intelligence of such matters,[40] and Jeake's diary well illustrates the excitements and opportunities that existed.

Jeake began his speculations while in London, buying ten tickets in the Million Adventure on 20 April, while on his way home he set to work calling in loans so that he could invest the proceeds. Indeed the diary shows a complete turn around at this point, from the lending of money to a feverish search for funds that he could borrow from others; he also realized 'unnecessary' bullion (30.4.94). The result was that at least once over the next few weeks he found himself perilously short of cash (8.9.94), though by 17 October, when a substantial mortgage came in, he seems to have been back on an even keel. He also showed the zeal of a convert in persuading his mother-in-law to invest, and in organizing a partnership to do so in Rye.[41]

Subsequently, Jeake moved on to annuities and the other types of investment he had outlined, including the Bank, though the latter may have seemed less immediately attractive to him than the other opportunities available: he apparently had to ask Thomas Miller for his advice about it, and was evidently taken by surprise at the speed with which the Bank's subscription was filled (14, 18, 25.6.94). He did, however, become one of the Bank's first subscribers, increasing his stake from an initial £200 to £500, the minimum required to qualify to vote at the Bank's General Court, a privilege of which he was to avail himself over the next few years.[42] Jeake's subsequent notes show his satisfaction with the profit that he derived from his investment during the Bank's first few months: at this stage the actual rate of interest was over 13 per cent, since, whereas only 60 per cent of the subscription had to

[39] Scott, *Joint Stock Companies*, i. 318 ff., ii. 150 ff.
[40] Wilson, *England's Apprenticeship* (see sect. 1 n. 11), 221.
[41] 30.4, 7, 8, 11, 15, 29.5.94.
[42] Bank of England Archive, original Subscription Book, 1694, pp. 25, 28 (nos. 812, 924, 25–6 June 1694). For Jeake's attendance at the court see the General Court Minutes, Bank of England Archive MS G7/1, pp. 61 (misspelt 'Peake'), 63, 71, 72, 163, 167, 169. Since it is noted on other occasions that 'divers others' were present, however, he may have attended more often. On the rate of interest see Scott, *Joint Stock Companies* (see sect. 8 n. 35), iii. 206–7.

be paid at first with the remainder following later, the interest of 8 per cent was calculated on the whole sum promised.

Lastly, there was the £400-worth of East India stock which Jeake bought, and the diary gives a cliff-hanging narrative of his 'long & fluctuating Consultation in my own thoughts' about first its purchase and then its sale, the latter complicated by the possibility of accepting a 'refusal'—a commission paid by a putative buyer for the option of acquiring the stock at a set price within a fixed period.[43] Jeake was apparently premature in his wish to sell, but Miller's strategy and the exigencies of communication between Rye and London prevented him from doing too badly (or too well): though he failed to capitalize on the highest point in the market, he had made a profit of 12 per cent by the time Miller took the initiative and disposed of the stock for him on 24 November.

Though the main diary ends in November 1694, a kind of coda is provided by Jeake's shorthand diary for 1699. This shows him well established in the London financial world, spending £500 on Bank of England stock in April that year, and having a further £700-worth transferred to him by Thomas Miller on 17 May. The Bank's ledger shows that Jeake had become quite adept at trading in stock in the interim since 1694, having purchased a further £200-worth in September 1695 and £600-worth between June and December 1697, then selling £200-worth in June and £500-worth in November 1698.[44] In 1699 Jeake also bought and kept for a few weeks some shares in the 'Lustring Company', a typical projecting venture of the time devoted to the manufacture of glossy black silk.[45] The profit that resulted was worth while, particularly through a dividend that was declared before he disposed of his holding, though the shares themselves seem to have hung on the market by comparison. At this point, Jeake still retained at least some of the exchequer annuities that he had purchased in 1694, but on 4 April he sold his 14 per cent annuity—presumably that on the life of his wife (13.10.94)—evidently in order to invest the proceeds in the Bank: though annuities could provide a steady income, stock had the advantage of being more easily transferable.[46] In any case, Jeake was satisfied with the 'good bargain' he made on the sale.

---

[43] On this see John Houghton, *A Collection for Improvement of Husbandry and Trade* (London, 1694), no. 99 (22.6.94). See also 28.7, 12.9.94.

[44] Bank of England Archive, Bank Stock Ledger, 1, fol. 145; 2, fol. 637. Cf. FRE 5253, a letter of attorney of 8 June 1697 concerning one of these transactions (and a letter of attorney to Miller to sell bank stock, 7 Oct. 1699, though in fact none was sold at this point).

[45] See Scott, *Joint Stock Companies* (see sect. 8 n. 35), iii. 73 ff., esp. 85 concerning the dividend, which Jeake's evidence proves was declared, something of which Scott was uncertain.

[46] Wilson, *England's Apprenticeship* (see sect. 1 n. 11), 223.

The 1699 fragment reveals the affluent Jeake as a well-connected figure in London circles through such hints as his dinner engagement with Robert Bristow, one of the directors of the Bank of England (18.5.99). It is also clear that Jeake still retained local commitments, arranging for hops and flax-seed to be conveyed from Rye to London and experiencing concern about price fluctuations, as earlier in his career (3.8.99). In addition, there were residual problems with debts, particularly those of Mr Benge of Wadhurst.

Some of the story of the intervening years can be pieced together from biographical notes in Jeake's *Nativity* and from his letters to his wife while on visits to London, when she acted as agent in his Rye business transactions and he advised her in detail on what to do. These show that flax-seed was a commodity with which Jeake had become involved in the mid 1690s, though the market for hops was also often anxiously assessed. Other topics covered include the acceptability of guineas in the aftermath of the recoinage of 1696, and the grievance that Jeake shared with others who held annuities under the 1694 Act over the payment of the dividends to which they were entitled.[47]

Above all, Jeake showed ceaseless vigilance over the rise and fall of bank stock: 'you know how much it concerns us', he explained to his wife, apologizing for an extended stay in London to monitor its fluctuations in 1697. He kept her informed of political and other events which might affect the price of stock, though modestly telling her—presumably in response to an enquiry as to the secret of the technique—'As for telling when 'tis a good time to purchase that's past my skill or any body's else'.[48] In addition, his biographical notes illustrate the alarm that he—with other investors—experienced between 1695 and 1697, when the Bank of England seemed in genuine danger of collapse due to the crippling cost of the war, exacerbated by the challenge posed by the rival Land Bank that was set up in 1696, and the repercussions of the recoinage of the same year.[49]

9. CONCLUSION: ASTROLOGY AND THE NEW AGE

As these events must have revealed to Jeake—and as was apparent even in the easier periods of 1694 and 1699 for which we have fuller memoranda—the stock market in the 1690s was a tense and hazardous place. It is this

---

[47] FRE 5246 (misplaced) and 5301–23. On the history of the grievance concerning the annuities, see Ewen, *Lotteries* (see sect. 8 n. 37), 130.
[48] FRE 5318, 5329.
[49] See above, sect. 3 n. 5. On the fortunes of the bank in these years see Scott, *Joint Stock Companies* (see sect. 8 n. 35), i. 347 ff.; iii. 208 ff.; Dennis Rubini, 'Politics and the Battle for the Banks, 1688–97', *English Historical Review*, 85 (1970), 693–714.

constant element of risk which explains a juxtaposition which might otherwise seem to us surprising, namely of astrology and financial speculation. One of the striking components of the latter part of the main diary are the horoscopes which Jeake cast for the moments at which he invested in the Million Lottery and the Bank of England: his intention was doubtless to assess the auspiciousness of the heavens for such transactions, though on at least one of these occasions he self-righteously denied choosing the time of purchase according to such criteria. Perhaps most striking is the sequence of horoscopes he cast on 20 April 1694, for the time at which he entered the shop where tickets for the Million Adventure were sold, at which he handed over the money, and at which he received his tickets.

The 1699 diary fragment, which was clearly written up piecemeal at the time of the events it records, is even more revealing from the point of view of seeing how Jeake used astrology in his business (though, interestingly, this was not something that he divulged to his wife in his letters to her at this time).[1] For it shows him noting favourable aspects of the planets on several days running, with occasional climaxes arising as short-term beneficial transits and other correlations occurred. Evidently astrology affected his judgement at two levels, partly in assessing the broad circumstances in which he came to important decisions and partly in choosing exact moments at which to execute his plans.

In the earlier diary there are also occasional hints of the way in which Jeake's decision-making was affected by his knowledge of the astrological circumstances at the time—perhaps particularly the entry on 18 July 1694, though in this case astrological factors were outweighed by other ones. Moreover, commerce is one of the topics in connection with which astrology was most frequently invoked, not only in the diary but also in Jeake's other astrological writings. The subject-matter of his *Astrological Experiments Exemplified* is predominantly commercial: indeed, the exercise was carried out in a year when Jeake was more than ordinarily busy with mercantile activities. Similarly, the accidents that Jeake extracted from the diary for analysis in his *Nativity* were disproportionately commercial, many of the transactions included being surprisingly minor.[2]

Arguably there was a special rapport between astrology and commerce for Jeake, and that he was not unique in this is suggested by clues surviving elsewhere: for instance, the diary of Norris Purslow, referred to in section 2 of this Introduction, shows a comparable preoccupation with business trans-

---

[1] FRE 5324–33.
[2] *AEE, passim*; Selmes MS 56/1, fols. 4v–9v.

actions, often of a rather trivial nature.[3] Neither is it difficult to understand the appeal of astrology to such entrepreneurs, with its impressive mathematical complexity and its ability to give a sense of rationality and control in a difficult business environment. It would be hard to argue that astrology was irrelevant to the needs of the age of the Financial Revolution.

Extrapolating more broadly, it may be argued that, for all the complexities and tensions in his ideas, Jeake was a distinctly modern figure in his anxious self-preoccupation, his love of precision, his increasing worldliness, even his curiosity about the natural world. Moreover much the same is true of the other astrological autobiographers referred to in the second section of this Introduction, all of whose life-styles were forward-looking in different ways. Apart from the thrusting bureaucrat and virtuoso Elias Ashmole, we have the lawyer John Stansby, the shopkeeper Norris Purslow, and the sea-captain Jeremy Roch, the latter a brisk, self-reliant individual likened by his twentieth-century editor to a figure from Fielding or Smollett.[4] It was precisely because astrology was so compatible with their preoccupations and ambitions that such men devoted so much time to it.

It is therefore difficult to accept that the problems that astrology and other magical beliefs encountered in this period had anything to do with a failure to 'keep pace with changing social circumstances'.[5] Jeake's case suggests that astrology's predicament resulted not from an inability to fulfil the needs of those who believed in it, but from a failure to retain credit as a belief-system among the leaders of opinion of the day. To these, a man like Jeake was arguably more peripheral, and here something can be learnt from the conflicts of ideas manifested in the episodes in the 1690s referred to in section 6 of this Introduction, and especially his brush with the *Athenian Mercury*. For that arbiter of fashionable opinion not only put down Jeake's belief in a static Earth but also issued broadsides against astrology which look forward to the satirical attack of Swift which emanated from a comparable milieu a decade and a half later.[6] This not the place to sketch the complex

---

[3] Wellcome Institute MS 4021, *passim*. A further astrological notebook associated with a late seventeenth-century tradesman, William Bellgrave of Chesham, Bucks., was sold at Sothebys on 24 July 1978; its present whereabouts is unknown.

[4] See above, sect. 2, nn. 35–7. See also Michael Hunter, *Elias Ashmole, 1617–92* (Oxford, 1983), 2–3 and *passim*; Ingram, *Three Sea Journals* (see sect. 2 n. 27), p. xxv.

[5] Keith Thomas, *Religion and the Decline of Magic* (see sect. 2 n. 18), 656. But see also ibid., chs. 10–11 and 22, *passim*, for alternative ideas which are more compatible with what is suggested here.

[6] *Athenian Mercury* (see sect. 6 n. 27), vol. 1 no. 6 (11 Apr. 1691), vol. 9 no. 8 (7 Jan, 1693). See also ibid., vol. 1 no. 14 (9 May 1691), vol. 2 no. 9 (23 Jan, 1691), and vol. 10 no. 23 (13 June 1693).

reasons for this rejection:[7] but the way in which Jeake's account of his life juxtaposes astrology with the new aspirations of late Stuart England should illustrate the dangers of uncritically presuming that all the progressive forces of his day were equally antithetic to astrology.

10. JEAKE'S MANUSCRIPT AND THE PRESENT EDITION

The manuscript of Jeake's diary from 1652 to 1694 is William Andrews Clark Memorial Library MS J43M3/D540. It is a quarto volume measuring 8 inches by 6 inches, bound in parchment wrappers.

On the front cover are some endorsements which throw a small amount of light on the history of the manuscript between its use by nineteenth-century scholars like William Holloway and its purchase by the Clark Library in 1959. At the centre the name 'M. Frewen' had been written in ink in a nineteenth-century hand: 'M' could be for Moreton J. E. Frewen (1794–1871), to whom the Jeake manuscripts passed on the death of his aunt Philadelphia Frewen in 1841, probably together with the Jeake family portraits which are known to have been in her hands in 1837 and which survive today at Brickwall, Northiam, Sussex. The handwriting does not appear to be Moreton Frewen's, but it might be that of his wife, née Sarah Jenkins.[1] It was Mrs Frewen who lent and subsequently gave to Dr Wake Smart the Jeake manuscripts which are now in Rye Museum, though Smart does not seem to have had the two manuscripts which are now in the Clark, since these do not appear in a list that survives of the items that he borrowed in May 1858.[2]

In addition, the price '21/-' has been marked in pencil near the left-hand top corner of the cover; this has subsequently been erased, while above and to the left of this is a further pencilled endorsement which is not easily legible.[3] The price may be that at which the volume was sold to C. H. Sp.

---

[7] For a consideration of some of the issues involved see Hunter, 'Science and Astrology' (above, sect. 6 n. 28).

[1] For Moreton Frewen's hand see FRE 4021; for his wife's, FRE 4156. The handwriting is not that of Smart or of Thomas Frewen IV. On Philadelphia and Moreton Frewen and the Jeake manuscripts see H. M. Warne, *A Catalogue of the Frewen Archives* (Lewes, 1972), 25 and pedigree; and a MS note by Thomas Frewen IV on the flyleaf of a copy of the elder Jeake's *Λογιστικηλογία* in the Bodleian Library, Oxford, classmark Vet A 3 c 66. For Holloway's use of the diary see above, sect. 1.

[2] Selmes MS 64/1–2. The fact that in his 1861 paper Smart cited the *Nativity* and Holloway concerning episodes that are more fully related in the diary suggests that he did not have access to it at that stage: Smart, pp. 63, 66. By 1880 he had evidently seen the diary, however, since he quotes from it in 'A Notice of the Rev. John Allin' (see sect 7 n. 18), 153 n. 67.

[3] It appears to be '11/ Surrey'. The same endorsement appears on the front cover of *AEE*. The handwriting could conceivably be that of Perceval, who was evidently the author of jottings on the front fly-leaves of both manuscripts.

meddled with them. In this course (tho' with
sometimes of Intermission) I proceeded so far
till I came in order to the 9th Chapter of the
Revelation: & was prepared on Mar. 11. ☉. 168$\frac{2}{3}$.
to have interpreted the effects of y.e fifth Trumpet
consisting in the opening of the bottomless pit,
the smoke thence arising, the Locusts thence
issuing &c. When, before I began, The Tribe
of Persecutors, Enemies of all Righteousness
disturbed us, & we were afterwards forced to
meet in several parcells in o.r own families.
with 3 or 4 besides, Praying together, and
repeating a Sermon.

Nov: 19. ♂ Aguish all day, & ill with a little Cold: so till
    22. ♄. then pretty well again. 23. ☉. ill again
    with y.e Cold, & so most part of the Week.

Dec. 6. ♄. 1/6.h p.m. ♒ o.l w m.s ɔ.ni.º j.s r.º h.r 8 ∠ ♃ ♄
    5, ♑ o 1. gr ♒ o. ♃ ☿ — 1. √ l sw.s l. ∠ hu.ρ
    ∠ ɲ.s h. gr ♃ ♃. ⸗ ♓ g gr ♃ ⊼.ᵛ

11. ♃. N.º 195. Six W. Raleigh's History of y.e World. Fol:

23. ☉⸗. About 10.h a.m. r.z l. ɔ v t w l. s.ᵉ ⁊ l √ ∠
    h.z 3 s.l. l) + gr lov. ɔ.º l/ gr ♂ ☌.z ☌.ᶜ ♀.ˢ⁻ˡ

Jan. 1. ♃. I began to keep my Accompts in a Liedger
    after the method set down in Chamberlain's
    Accomptant's Guide; which course I al-
    waies continued henceforward.

13. ☉⸗. N.º 196. Tho: Browne, Religio Medici. 8.º

16. ♀. Negotiated some Bills of Exchange & more
    afterwards as they were brought to me,
    till I went to London in 1683. and a-
    gain after my Return till the War broke
    out between England & France.

21. ♀. About 8.h 30.l or 9.h a.m. r.z l. ɔ v t w l.r
    ↑ ʋ.ᵛ ⁊ l) ꝝ 7.z — ⸗ a ⸗ ♂ g ♃.ᵛ ɲ 7.ᵘ.z
    o — ♂ s.l ʋ/ 1.h.30.l p.m. — ☌.º o.z √ 2.h.30.l p.m.
    — ♀.z l. r. √ o.ni.l p.m. — r.z j.ᵛ l √ l ☌.ᵛ r.º l.z
    — g.ᵛ s.z s.ᵉ ⸗ /ʌ l √ g º ☿ o.º ♃ʋ r.º ⸝.
                                Feb. 26. ♃

Perceval in the early 1890s: it was because he had recently acquired this and *Astrological Experiments Exemplified* that he wrote to *Notes and Queries* about them in 1893. Alternatively, it could date from some point between Perceval's ownership of the manuscript and its acquisition by the booksellers R. D. Steedman of Newcastle-upon-Tyne, who sold it to the Clark.[4]

Internally, the manuscript is a fair copy, neatly written in Jeake's characteristically clear and methodical hand. The overall tidiness and lack of alterations and insertions in the existing text suggests that it may have been copied from a draft:[5] though there is no direct evidence of this, a parallel may be sought in Jeake's analysis of the 'Nativity' of his wife, Elizabeth, compiled in 1685 and recopied the following year, of which both a draft and a fair copy survive among the Selmes manuscripts at Rye Museum.[6]

Since the manuscript of the diary is a fair copy, editorial problems have been few, and this edition attempts to reproduce Jeake's text as literally as possible. However, it has been necessary to introduce consistency in a number of matters, and to alter Jeake's usage in a handful of cases where it could distract or mislead the reader.

Jeake's spelling and capitalization have been consistently followed. His punctuation has also generally been retained, but obvious inconsistencies have been corrected, while insertions have sometimes been made to clarify the sense: in such cases, the insertions have been enclosed in square brackets. In addition, whereas Jeake frequently places a full-stop after (and sometimes also before) a numeral, these have been omitted throughout.

Jeake makes considerable use of abbreviations, but he seems to have seen these as purely functional, enabling words to be fitted into a limited space, and is himself inconsistent in their use: for instance, in his title he gives 'partly' once abbreviated and once in full. Here, therefore, all such purely mechanical abbreviations have been expanded. In order to retain at least some of the original flavour of the text, however, the following abbreviations have been retained. All shortened versions of proper names have been left, including 'Exon' for Exeter and 'E.I.C.' for the East India Company; where Jeake gives initials only and these have been expanded for the reader's convenience, this has been indicated by the use of square brackets. Jeake's ampersands have also been reproduced, as has his use of '8°', '4°', etc. (i.e.

---

[4] *Notes and Queries*, 8th ser. 4 (1893), 147. Messrs R. D. Steedman have no information concerning the provenance of the manuscript (letter of 24 December 1984).

[5] The following entries were inserted into the text after it had been written out: 3.1.62, 26.11.64, 21.1.65, the last sentence under 28.7.66, 29.10.69, 25.8.71, and 4.9.71. In addition, other entries very occasionally incorporate minor insertions.

[6] Selmes MSS 52 and 53/1.

octavo, quarto, etc.) when describing the format of books. His usage of 'h' for hours and ′ for minutes in his notes on the times of day has also been retained. Dipthongs have been spelt out as two separate letters throughout.

In transliterating Jeake's symbols, we have adopted a compromise position which we hope will minimize potential confusion. Jeake throughout uses standard symbols for the planets and planetary aspects in his astrological notes (see Appendix 2 (ii)). In addition, he uses the same seven symbols for the days of the week as for the planets, and, at the start of each diary entry (and occasionally within his text), he juxtaposes the date with the day of the week thus expressed in an almost formulaic way. To have retained all his symbols would have been potentially misleading, and we have therefore transliterated all the symbols for the planets and aspects and for the days of the week where Jeake refers to these without date, so as not to interrupt the flow of his prose. On the other hand, we have left the symbols for the days of the week where these are mechanically juxtaposed with the date, since this seemed the best way of retaining this information without devoting as much space to it as would have been required to transliterate it in full. We hope that readers will not mind having to familiarize themselves with these seven symbols, to which a key is given on p. xii above.

Jeake is inconsistent in his use of a margin in his manuscript. Entries are generally indented with only the date going forward to the margin. But in longer entries, or entries lacking dates, he often dispenses with this indentation and writes across the whole page (cf. Fig. 1). In view of this inconsistency, a margin has here been adopted throughout.

A further editorial alteration which has been made to avoid confusing the reader concerns the date of the new year. Whereas Jeake follows the old style, beginning the new year on 25 March, here the new style has been adopted and each year begun on 1 January.

Passages transliterated from Jeake's shorthand are printed in italic throughout. The only exception to this is the text of the shorthand diary for 1699, Rye Museum Selmes MS 57, printed as Appendix 1: since this is mostly in shorthand, the shorthand text has been printed in roman type, while the passages that appear in longhand in the original have been printed in italic. Punctuation has throughout been silently added to shorthand passages.

The system of shorthand that Jeake used is outlined in Appendix 5. Though it has been possible to identify virtually all Jeake's symbols, a few puzzles and ambiguities remain, particularly where Jeake merely gives a capital letter to denote a word. If satisfied that we have accurately transcribed what Jeake wrote we have interfered with it as little as possible, even if it reads slightly awkwardly. This is particularly the case with the 1699 text, which was written up piecemeal: see, for instance, the entry for 11 April 1699.

Editorial interpolations into the text are enclosed in square brackets. The bulk of these relate to Jeake's references in the diary to books that he read, since cumbersome footnotes have been avoided by elucidating the titles of these works within the diary text. For each book we have inserted in brackets the data of first publication—or later edition, if it is clear from the title or format given that Jeake is referring to an edition which differs significantly from the first—and any other data necessary to identify the work involved (e.g. the authors of works published anonymously). Where Jeake para-phrases a title rather than quoting it exactly, his paraphrase has been retained: his descriptions of the author and title are generally accurate, if often succinct. Footnoting has only been used where Jeake's description bears too little resemblance to a book's actual title for piecemeal elucidation in the text to be feasible, or where it has proved impossible to identify the work that Jeake refers to.

The booklist has been elucidated partly through standard bibliographical aids and partly by collation with the extant 'Register' of Jeake's and his father's library. Identification has been made easier by Jeake's notes of the format of the books he read, which evidently stemmed from his father's practice in the 'Register'. In three cases, Jeake includes as a single item in his list a collection of separate works which happened to be bound together in the Jeakes' copy (19, 170, 191). In addition, whereas Jeakes often uses '&c.' to denote a longer title which he abbreviates, in a few instances it evidently indicates a similar collection of tracts (34, 40, and perhaps 56). Sometimes comparison with the library catalogue clarifies exactly which edition of a work Jeake consulted, and dates have been inserted accordingly.[7] In a hand-ful of cases the Jeakes owned an earlier edition than any that has survived.[8]

Footnotes to the text have deliberately been kept to a minimum so as to provide the least possible distraction to the reader. Jeake's comments in the text are often elucidated in the relevant section of the Introduction, and we have refrained from constant cross-reference to this. Writings by Jeake that he mentions may be presumed lost if not footnoted. The notes are supple-mented by the following: (1) Appendix 2 gives an introduction to the techni-

---

[7] See 1, 59, 67, 122, 161, 171, 186, 191, 194, 273. See also 29. Where the Jeakes owned what was effectively merely a reprint it has seemed more helpful to give the original date of publica-tion. For the Library 'Register', see Jeakes MS 4/1.

[8] See 65, 83, 118, 176. 278 may be a lost work, as may the two wholly unidentified items, 153 and 245.

calities of Jeake's astrology. (2) Appendix 3 offers a biographical guide to all those whose names appear frequently in the diary, in alphabetical order. Those who appear only briefly are identified in footnotes at the point in the text where they are mentioned. (3) Appendix 4 gives a glossary of technical terms—astrological, medical, commercial, and legal—together with some notes on quantities and measures.

A
DIARY

of the Actions & Accidents
of my Life: tending part-
ly to observe & memorize
the Providences therein
manifested; & partly
to investigate the Measure
of Time in Astronomi-
cal Directions, and to
determine the Astrall
Causes, &tc

Rye
Begun July 12 1694.

A Diary of Actions & Accidents in the Life of Samuel Jeake Eldest Son of Samuel Jeake & Frances his Wife; as followeth.
Viz.

I was born at Rye in Sussex July 4 1652 on the Lord's Day. ¼ of an hour past 6 a Clock in the morning, according to the aestimate time taken by my Father from an Horizontal Dial, the Sun then shining.

1652

Nov. 27 ♄ *I fell out of the bed but had no hurt.*

Dec. 3 ♀ *Voided a great worm downwards.*

1653

Feb. 12 ♃ Weaned from the breast.

Apr. 3 ☉ Ill all day.

　　 6 ☿ *Voided a great worm downwards.*

　　 9 ♄ My under teeth first seen. *just broke the flesh.*

　　21 ♃ I had 2 upper teeth.

May　　 from 14 ♄ to 21 ♄ Ill & untoward.

June 29 ☿ My Brother Thomas born.

　　 I began to go at a year old; & to speak at a year & a quarter.

1654

Sept. 20 ☿ & 21 ♃ ill. 22 ♀ very ill with a cold & feaver. 23 ♄ somewhat better.

Nov. 30 ♃ My Mother taken sick of the smal pocks.

Dec. 3 ☉ My Sister Frances born & died the same day.

　　 9 ♄ My Mother died.[1]

1654 　[1] These early memoranda may derive in part from notes kept by the elder Jeake for astrological purposes, some of which survive as Jeake MS 2/1.

1655

July   4   ☿   Being 3 years old, my stature was 2 Feet 10⅜ Inches.

1656

Apr.   21   ☽   I went first to School to *Moses Peadle's wife* about 10 a Clock in
the forenoon;[1] under this face of heaven.

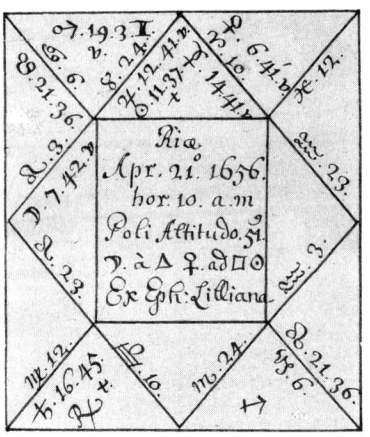

May 31 ♄ Ill. June 1 ☉ Also ill. At night the Measells came out upon me
(not being elsewhere in the Towne). 2 ☽ & 3 ♂ ill. Afterwards
began to mend (This is one of the first things that I remember).

July   6 ☉ My Brother Thomas died: after which I never went to School,
but was taught by my Father.

1657

Feb.   I entred reading in the Bible.

June 13 ♄ *Had my hair cut.*

Aug.   8 ♄ Had a Cough. 10 ☽ very ill all day. 11 ♂ mended.

1656 [1] Margaret or Mary Peadle was the wife of Moses, glazier. The Peadles were a long-established family of Rye craftsmen. For references to two other members of the family see 8.8.82, 4.6.88. Burchall, p. 106; LAWR 40, p. 99.

1660

About this year (but I remember not exactly) as I was catching of Crabs at full Sea; I fell from a Rock into the Tide up to the midle.

1661, or 1662

I learned to write, & in 1663 could write well, severall hands.

1662

Jan.　3 ♀ Received for Mrs. Miller's Legacy of 40s—36s 3d.[1]

1663

I entred into the Greek Grammar; having before learned the Latine Authors.

About this year I began to learn Rhetorick (but I remember not justly when).

This year (as I mind) on a Lord's day in the evening; a Prodigy (whether true or false I know not) related at my Father's house *by John A.*[1] was the first occasion of my Conversion, & serious thoughts about my future condition. The Prodigy (as my memory serves me) was thus. A Throne appeared in the heavens, & one like a King sitting thereon, over whose head were the 2 letters C.R. After which another Throne, & another person in royal apparel seated on it, over whose head were the two Letters I.R. which my childish apprehensions interpreted, That after the then present King C[harles] 2 Jesus Christ should come to reign: and reflecting on my unfitness to receive him (as who may abide the day of his coming, that is in a natural state) I was greatly afraid. And the next day, it pleased God to work more effectually upon me in convincing me of Sin. But after, these impressions were worn off again, & I grew more negligent.

1662 [1] Possibly Sara Miller, of Aldersgate, London. PCC PROB 11/309 1662: 156.
1663 [1] Not identified.

1664

Apr. 26   By this time I could draw pictures indifferent well, learn'd of my self.

Nov. 26 ♄ Given by my Father in pieces of Gold £24: 8: 9d Silver 16: 7d.

Dec. 12 ☽ It pleased God to work in me a more effectual sorrow for sin, yet I received not at this time the assurance of his Love; but after this degenerated.

    19 ☽ I began the imitation of 30 Pictures of the Primitive Fathers printed from Copper plates, & finished them Jan. 21 ♄ next following. Many other Pictures made this year & next.

    23 ♀ I beheld the Comet which then appeared in the Evening; & another in March following, in the morning.

Dec. Jan.
&c.   Troubled with a kind of Haemorrhoids, excessively painful every evening but without either swelling or bleeding, Continuing for 2 or 3 months if not longer: & supposed by me to be the Effect of the direction of Sol ad Corpus Saturni.

1665

Jan. 21 ♄ Given by my Father in several sorts of Gold. 6: 11: 4, silver 0: 12: 7¾.

Sept. 9 ♄ By this time I had learned to write Shorthand.

      In this moneth I began to learn Hebrew.

    21 ♃ My Aunt Anne Key (my Fathers Sister) died.[1]

1666

In the moneth of May, I went a Journey for diversion to Lydd, Dengeness & New Romeney returning in 4 days. viz. from Monday to Thursday.

In May I finished a Manuscript for my own use called Epitome Grammaticae Latinae.[1]

1665 [1] Anne Key died in childbirth. She was the wife of Willam Key of Rye, mariner (see 20.12.66); her first husband had been William Dallet of Rye. Smart, p. 78.

1666 [1] This compilation from the textbooks of William Lily and Charles Hoole and comparable sources is now Selmes MS 24.

July   4 ☿ Being 14 years old my stature was 4 Feet 10⅝ Inches.

      18 ☿ I began first to set down Memorandums of my Life in a Diary.

ditto   About 8h p.m. (being 14 years 14 days 14 hours old) I was taken sick of the small pocks (as it proved afterwards, though now only cold) under the ensuing positure of heaven. And as it seemed from an Astrall Cause; that distemper not being in the Town of Rye before nor after for a considerable time, nor I having been any where to catch it, nor conscious of any surfeiting disorder. I conceive it therefore occasioned by the directions of the Ascendant ad Cor Leonis & Mars ad conjunctionem Solis both then operating: & the rather because I well remember my self to be then infected with an unusuall Ambition & haughtiness of spirit, more than before or after, which I suppose did proceed properly from the nature of Cor Leonis.

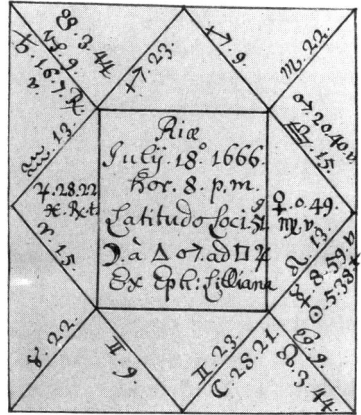

19 ♃ In the morning cut my right forefinger, & vomited up my breakfast.

20 ♀ The smal pocks came out, but favourably; so that I went not to bed, but kept in my Study.

21 ♄ About 11 a clock in the morning I arose, but was like to faint in the Chamber. I lay upon the bed all day in my Cloths & more of the small pocks came out but kindly, & I was not disfigured by them. In the night I slept but little, & talked idly.

July 22 ☉ Something better; but kept my bed till 27 ♀ then I rose.

28 ♄ I went into my Study. 29 ☉ down stairs. 30 ☽ into the garden.

The small Pocks prejudiced my Eyesight; which being naturally infirme, was the apter to receive injurious impressions; a movable cloudiness sometimes appearing & then again vanishing, disturbed it for several moneths; & this succeeded by a kind of Suffusion, whose symptoms were perpetual and without intermission. *Yet I found no sensible decay* Sept. 1 & 2 *following, when the English fleet went by on Sunday; for then it being a cloudy close day I could* [?] *plainly and distinctly perceive each ship. But my sight was so much decayed in* 1667 *about* July 9 ♂ *that the Dutch fleet going by in a clear day I could not see one of them, unless it were the sail of one ship a little before night, on which the sun shining caused it to give a brighter gloy* [sic] (*though perhaps they went by at somewhat greater distance than the English before mentioned*). *After which again by little and little my sight grew worse and worse, so that in* November 1667 *I could not perceive what it was a clock by the church dial, though I stood in the yard as nigh to it as I could on the ground. At which decay it stood ever afterwards, only the suffusion gradually increased, but through mercy at a very slow rate; for at the age of* 42 *at which I write this my sight enables me to read and write as well as almost any other ordinary man.*

This year I made a Miscellaneous Collection, of 54 sheets 4°.[2]

Sept. 23 ☉ Just as I went into my bed, I thought I heard a great Sigh at the further end of my Chamber.

Dec. 17 ☽ & all that week had a great Tumor on my Eye called Aegylops, with which I had very frequently been troubled for 2 or 3 years before; but rarely afterwards.

20 ♃ My Unkle Key died*; which brought a great deal of trouble to my Father as his Executor in Looking after his estate & 5 children.[3]

* Legacy £5. [*written in margin*]

[2] Now Selmes MS 25. It contains notes on such subjects as proverbs and the nomenclature of places, minerals, animals, plants, and diseases. On its sources, see Introduction, sect. 6.

[3] William Key of Rye, mariner, whose wife had died the previous year (see 21.9.65), left £20 to 'my loving brother-in-law' Samuel Jeake senior, asking him to act as executor and bring up his five youngest daughters, Jane, Anne, Elizabeth, Mary, and Sarah. Jeake's volume of notes and accounts relating to the Key estate, 1666–79, survives as Selmes MS 6. PCC PROB 11/325 1667: 155.

22 ♄ Finished a Latine MSS for my own use entituled Epitome Rhetoricae.

1667

Jan.   10 ♃ I made a Map of the Towne of Rye.[1]

In March I began to learn Arithmetick, and learned as far as Proportions.

Apr.   1 ☽ I went to Hasting, & 2 ♂ to Westfield.

3 ☿ About 8h a.m. Taken with a Tertian Ague or rather feaver; the first fit held me till night.

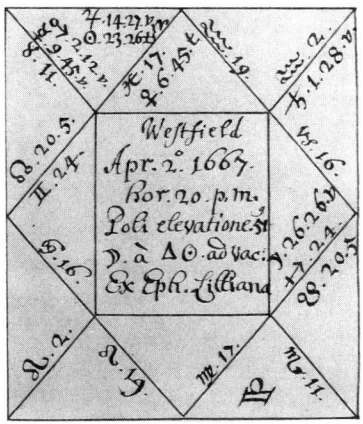

4 ♃ I came home. My Ague remained a Tertian till Apr. 14 ☉ then turn'd to a Quotidian.

May   1 ☿ Took a vomit, having before taken a Purge without effect.

8 ☿ My Ague began to decrease 9 ♃ & 10 ♀ it could hardly be perceived.

11 ♄ Quite gone; but my head aked till June 25.

30 ♃ By this time, indifferently skilled in the Theory or Rules of Poetry, both English & Latine; but my fancy never ran much to practise[.]

1667 [1] The original of this map is now lost, but a copy of it made by William Wybourn in 1728 is now RYE 132/15. The central portion of this is reproduced as pl. 13 in R. F. Dell, *Records of Rye Corporation* (Lewes, 1962), and the whole in *SAC* 122 (1984), 112.

June 22 ♄ Ill in my stomach in the forenoon.

  25 ♂ About noon I began to learn Astrology.

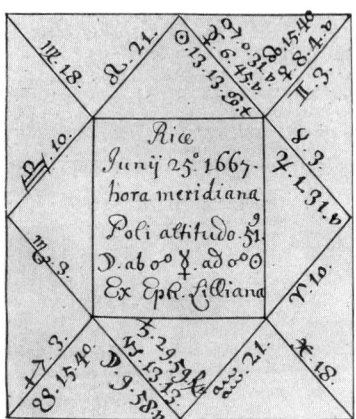

July 2 ♂ In the evening troubled with an hoarsness.

  3 ☿ In the afternoon went to Iden; where by drinking Cold beer & eating cold milk, my hoarsness increased.

  4 ♃ It increased more & I was greatly troubled with the headach, so that afternoon I lay down upon the bed. After supper, ill in my stomach, but continued not long. In the evening a Vesicatory was applied to my neck, yet it took not away the pain of my head, though it after decreased & in process of time went away.

Being now, 15 years old my stature was 5 feet ⅛ inch.

Before this time I had read over
the following Books.

Folios

No.

  1. John Fox, Acts & Monuments [7th edn., 1632]. Vol: 1.
  2. Flavius Josephus his Works [trans. Thomas Lodge, 1602].
  3. Eusebius, Socrates, Evagrius &c. translated by [Meredith] Hanmer [1577].

4. Tho: Fuller, Pisgah sight of Palestine [1650].
5. Jo: Richardson, Observations &c. on the old Testament [1655].
6. Tho: Beard & Tho. Taylor, Theater of Gods Judgments [4th edn., 1648].
7. Sam: Clark, English Martyrologie &c. [1652].
8. Plutarch's Lives of the noble Graecians & Romans [trans. Sir Thomas North, 1579].
9. Homer's Batrachomyomachia, Hymns & Epigrams [trans. George Chapman, 1624?].
10. Nic: Machiavel, History of Florence [trans. Thomas Bed-ingfield, 1595].
11. Samuel Purchas his Pilgrimage [1613].
12. [Edward] Topsel's history of Beasts & Serpents; [Thomas] Mouffet's of Insects [1658].
13. John Reynolds, God's Revenge against Murther [1635].
14. Daniel King, Vale Royal of England &c. [1656].
15. Sylvanus Morgan, Sphere of Gentry [1661].
16. Philip Sidney, Countess of Pembrook's Arcadia [1590–3].
17. Miguel de Cervantez, Exemplary Novells [trans. James Mabbe, 1640].

Quartos.

18. John Weemse, Christian Synagogue [1623].
19. Wm. Warner, Albions England. English Tragedies.[2]
20. Jo: Wigan, Antichrist's strongest hold overturned [1665].
21. A.V. History of the Siege of Ostend [trans. Edward Grimeston, 1604].
22. Cyprian Valera, Of the Pope, & the Masse &c. [trans. John Golburne, 1600].
23. John Saltmarsh, Some drops of the Vial &c. [1646].
24. Edwin Sandys, Europae Speculum [new edn., 1629].
25. John Rainolds, Conference with John Hart [1584].
26. John Rainolds, Overthrow of Stageplays [1599].
27. Tho: Parker, Visions & Prophecies of Daniel expounded [1646].

---

[2] This entry refers to a volume in the Jeakes' library comprising William Warner's *Albions England* (1589) and 'English Tragidies [*sic*]. by Baldwin &c'. The latter was perhaps an edition of *A Mirror for Magistrates* (1559), of which William Baldwin was editor and to which he contributed.

28. Vavasor Powell, Sufferers Catechisme.[3]
29. Wm. Perkins, Order of Causes, Exposition of the Creed & several Treatises.[4]
30. Tho: Maleor [i.e. Malory], History of King Arthur [new edn., 1634].
31. Jo: Whitgift, Answer to the Admonition [1573].
32. Sam: Daniel. Civil Wars of England [1595].
33. Tho: Danett, History of Lewis 12. Francis 1 & Henri 2 [1600].
34. Speeches & prayers of King Charles I's Judges. &c.[5]
35. [Donald Lupton] Glory of their times, or Lives of the primitive Fathers [1640].
36. John Bulwer, Man Transform'd [1650].
37. Tho: Brightman, his Works [1644].
38. Chr. Blackwood, Exposition of the 10 first Chapters of Matthew [1659].
39. Robt. Barker, Discourse of the Powder Treason &c.[6]
40. Hen: Jesse[y], Lords Loud Call to England. Prodigies &c. [1660].[7]
41. R.J. Short History of the World.[8]
42. Tho: James, Voiage for discovery of the NW passage [1633].
43. Menasseh ben Israel, Hope of Israel [1650].
44. Hen: Blount, Voyage into the Levant [1636].
45. Jo: Cartheny, Voyage of the Wandring Knight [trans. William Goodyear, 1607].

[3] Possibly Powell's *The Scriptures Concord: or a Catechisme, compiled out of the Words of Scripture* (1646). Alternatively, Wing gives a work entitled *The Sufferers-Catechism* (1664), not attributed to Powell. Both, however, are octavos.

[4] 'The Order of the Causes of Salvation and Damnation' is the subtitle of Perkins' famous work *Armilla Aurea*, or *A Golden Chaine* (1590). What Jeake read was evidently a 1597 collection of Perkins' writings, of which there was a copy in the Jeakes' library.

[5] Evidently a volume in the Jeakes' library comprising *The Speeches and Prayers of Some of the late King's Judges* (1660), dealing with Thomas Harrison, Hugh Peter, and others, and comparable works of 1662 concerning John Barkstead and John James.

[6] i.e. *His Maiesties Speach in this last Session of Parliament ... Together with a discourse of the maner of the discovery of this late intended Treason* (1605), a compilation put together by the printer Robert Barker.

[7] 'Prodigies &c.' probably refers to the works that were bound with the Jeakes' copy of Jessey's book, a set of the three *Mirabilis Annus* tracts (1661–2) and a work entitled *Strange News from the West* (1661).

[8] Probably Robert Johnson's translation of Giovanni Botero, *Relations, of the Most Famous Kingdoms and Common-Weales thorough the World* (1608), of which the Jeakes had a copy in their library.

46. Ro: Codrington, Life of Robert Earl of Essex [1646].
47. Evan Price, Eyesalve for England [1667].
48. Reginald Scot, Discovery of Witchcraft [1584].
49. Jo: Spittlehouse, Unchangeable Morality of the 7th day Sabbath.[9]
50. Will: Aspinwall, Abrogation of the Jewish Sabbath [1657].

Octavos 12°s 16°s &c.

51. Jo: Frith, Answer to More concerning the Sacrament [1533].
52. William Fenner, Riches of Grace [1641].
53. Tho: Farnaby, Index Rhetoricus [1625].
54. Arthur Dent, Ruine of Rome [1603].
55. William Dyer, Cabinet of Jewells [1663].
56. Tho: Goodwin, Return of Prayers &c. [1636].
57. Ric: Grafton, Abridgment of the Chronicle of England [1562].
58. T.G. History of Fortunatus [trans. from Dutch, 1640].
59. Aesopi Fabulae &c. [London edn., 1647].
60. Fra: Osborn, Advice to a Son [1656].
61. Jos: Hall, Epistles, Vol: 2 [1608].
62. Jos: Hall, Contemplations, Vol: 2 [1614].
63. Joseph ben Gorion, Wars of the Jews [trans. Peter Morwyng, 1558].
64. Geo: Herbert, Temple, Sacred poems [1633].
65. Chr: Blackwood, Soule searching Catechism [c.1650].[10]
66. Nic: Bernard, Life & Death of Bishop Usher [1656].
67. Iamblichus de Mysterijs. Porphyry, Proclus, Psellus, Hermes [trans. Marsilius Ficino, Lyons edn., 1570].
68. K. James, βασιλικον Δωρον [1599].
69. Hen: Jesse[y], Relation of Sarah Wight [1647].
70. John Bunyan, Holy City, or New Jerusalem [1665].
71. Jo: Bunyan, Grace abounding to the chief of Sinners [1666].
72. Tho: Brooks, Heavenly Cordial [1666].
73. John Vernon, Life of Caleb Vernon [1666].

[9] Presumably William Saller and John Spittlehouse, *An Appeal to the Consciences of the Chief Magistrates of this Commonwealth touching the Sabbath-day* (1657).
[10] The earliest edition recorded by Wing is the second, of 1653, a quarto. The copy owned by the Jeakes is given in the library 'Register' as 'N.D.', and was perhaps the first.

74. Tho: Cooper, Sermon preached at Lincolne [1575].
75. Seb: Castalion, Dialogus sacrorum Libri 4 [1552].
76. Sam: Clark, Looking-glass for saints & sinners [1646].
77. Sam: Clark, Englands Remembrancer [1657].
78. James Howell, Dodona's Grove [1640].
79. Survey of the book of Common Prayer &c. [1606].
80. Robt. Lovell, History of Animals & Minerals [1661].
81. Sufferings of Ka: Evans & Sar: Cheevers in Malta [1662].
82. Nic: Chewney, Hell & the torments thereof asserted [1660].
83. John Flavell, Navigation Spiritualiz'd &c. [1665].
84. Ralph Venning. 2d part of Canaan's flowings &c. [1654].[11]
85. Virgils' Eclogs Englished by W[illiam] L[isle, 1628].
86. Wm. Mason, Little Star or Catechism [1653].
87. K. Charles 1. 'Εικών βασιλικὴ [1649].
88. T.B. Tragedy of Massenello [1649].
89. Tho: Hall, Treatise against the Millenaries [1658].
90. Ovids Heroical Epistles, englished by [Wye] Saltonstal [1636].
91. Ovids Metamorphosis, englished by G[eorge] Sandys [1626].
92. Jo: Playford, Englands black Tribunal [1660].
93. Marcellus Palingenius, Zodiack of Life [trans. Barnaby Googe, 1565].
94. Joh: Piscator, Expositio Capituum Catecheseos [1603].
95. Scipio du Plessis, Resolver of Curiosities of Nature [Eng. trans., 1635].
96. Hugh Peters, Last Legacy to his daughter [1660].
97. Fra: Quarls, Emblems & Hieroglyphicks [1635–8].
98. Jo: Quarls, God's Love, Man's unworthiness &c. [1651].
99. Jo: Reynolds, the flower of fidelity [1650].
100. Ri: Rogers &c., Garden of spiritual flowers [1609].
101. Wm Robertson, Hebrew Text of Psalms & Lamentations [1656].
102. [Nathaniel Bacon] Relation of Francis Spira [1638].
103. John Suckling, Fragmenta Aurea, or Collection &c. [1646].
104. Jos: Salmon, Antichrist in Man [1647].

[11] In fact, Venning's *Canaans Flowings* of 1654 formed the second part of his *Milk and Honey*.

105. Sam: Smith, David's blessed Man [1614].
106. C. Salustius, his Works [trans. William Crosse, 1629].
107. [Vital d'Audiguier] Tragicomical History of these times [trans. William Duncomb?, 1627].
108. Virgils' Works, englished by Jo: Ogilby [1649].
109. John Veron, Hunting of Purgatory [1561].
110. P. Vincent, Miserable estate of Germany [1638].
111. Geo: Withers, Motto & Poem, mistress of Philarete [1621–2].
112. Tho: Williamson, Sword of the Spirit against Antichrist [1613].
113. Wm. Winstanley, Englands Worthyes [1660].
114. Geo: Withers, Memorandum to London [1665].[12]
115. Jo: Eaton, Discovery of dangerous dead Faith [1642].
116. Weak Christian resolved.[13]
117. Val: Wigelus [Weigel], Life of Christ [1648].
118. Ralph Venning, New Command renewed [1648].
119. Robt Chamberlain, Nocturnae [*sic*] Lucubrationes [1638].
120. Theologia Germanica [Eng. trans., 1646].
121. [William Sancroft] Modern Policy [1652].
122. Justini historiarum ex Pompeio Trogo Libri 44 [Lyons edn., 1555].
123. Ralph Venning, Orthodox Paradoxes [1647].
124. G. Fletcher, History of Russia [1591].

Monstrosities seen by me before this time

1. *William Greenes child at Rye which had no eyes, a piece of flesh much like a nipple hanging between the places of the eyes instead of a nose; a turkeys claw growing outwards from each little finger and little toe (the mother had a mind to a turkey).*[14]

2. *Pet. Harmers girl at Winchelsey that had no passage for its vectites but one leg; a skin growing between the fore and middle fingers, and between the ring and little fingers, like that of a goose; but the middle fingers were not joined to the ring fingers.*[15]

[12] A transcript of this work by Jeake, dated 25 Aug. 1665, survives as Selmes MS 19.

[13] Perhaps *The Weak Beleever Resolved. In a Dialogue between a worthy Minister and a weak Beleever* (1644).

[14] William Greene was a Rye Carpenter. Burchall, p. 107.

[15] The birth of a son of Peter Harmer at Winchelsea on 27 Nov. 1667 is recorded in Jeake MS 2/1, fol. 6v. 'Vectites' seems to derive from the word 'vectitation', denoting the action of being conveyed.

I kept formerly a Catalogue of sins committed by me, in order to a deeper humiliation. But now considering, that God hath blotted out as a thick Cloud my Transgressions, & as a Cloud my Sins: why should I give occasion to Man to revive the memory of that which God will remember no more.

Aug.   2 ♀ A little after dinner, troubled with a dark cloud before my sight of the nature of Gutta Serena, so that I could hardly see, & with the headach; but quickly gone: A Diarrhoea which continued till the 6 ♂. Another Book read over this day. viz. No. 125 [?Roger Jones] Mene Tekel. 4° [1663].

5 ☽ No. 126. Liber perlectus. Anthony Monday, History of Palmerin d'Oliva. 4° [1597].

16 ♀ A little Aegylops on my Eye—21 ☿ .

25 ☉ No. 127. Liber perlectus Jo: Vicars, God in the Mount. 4° [1642].

28 ☿ About 4h p.m. Headach & cold; next day well.

Sept. 2 ☽ About 10 a Clock in the forenoon, I had such a Cloud before my sight as August 2 last. After that ill with a pain of the head and stomach. After dinner, vomited & recovered.

17 ♂ Finished this day my Calligraphy, which had taken me up at spare times a great part of this Summer; being 41 Copyes fairly written in Folio of about 28 several sorts of hands.[16]

20 ♀ *The F*[irst] *and P*[   ].[17] About this time I was seized with an excessive Melancholy, which continued with Violence till July 1670. In the winter 1667 most intolerable. In December 1669 somewhat diminished. But its' continuance was full 7 years; Nay not quite gone in 10 years time.

27 ♀ I began to learn Logick; but ineffectually.

In Oct: & the Winter, troubled with such a kind of Haemorrhoids as in the Winter 1664. but not so long nor so violently.

Nov. 7 ♃ No. 128. Liber perlectus. Will: Dyer, Christs famous titles, & a Believers golden Chain. 8° [1666].

11 ☽ I went first to London with my Father; & several other in Company. This evening we lodged at Tunbridge, & 12 ♂ rode from Tunbridge to London.

[16] This no longer survives, but it was seen by William Holloway in the early nineteenth century after being found in a house in Rye. Holloway, p. 571.

[17] Jeake's shorthand reference has not been understood.

13 ☿ Saw the Ruines made by the great fire at London in the year 1666. very few houses being yet rebuilt.

14 ♃ I went to see the Tombs in Westminster Abby & Henry the 7ths Chappell &c.

15 ♀ I went to Deptford & Greenwich.

16 ♄ Went to the Tower, & saw the Crown & other Regalia, the armoury, & other things there to be seen.

21 ♃ Returned back to Tunbridge. & 22 ♀ to Rye.

1668

Feb. 21 ♀ No. 129. Liber perlectus Tho: Cartwright, Reply to Whitgift. 4° [1573?].

22 ♄ No. 130. Liber perlectus K. Digby, Discourse of the Sympathetic powder. 8° [1658].

27 ♃ No. 131. Liber perlectus Wm Ramesey, Lux Veritatis. 8° [1651].

Mar. 4 ☿ Or thereabouts, I began to be troubled with the Sonitus Aurium or noise in the Ears, which increased much in few days, & continued all my Life, yet without any deafness. About this time the Suffusion began also to be sensible, the Objects being represented when far distant with holes in them, this continued & increased (but slowly). That which most afflicted my sight about this time was a wavering mist before it; which went away of it self after the year 1668.

20 ♀ No. 132. Liber perlectus Ger: Malynes, Lex Mercatoria. Fol: [1622].

29 ☉ No. 133. Liber perlectus Felo de se, or the Bishops condemned &c. 4° [1668].

Apr. 9 ♃ No. 134. Liber perlectus [George Walker] Manifold Wisdom of God. 12° [1640].

23 ♃ About 10 a Clock in the forenoon I was taken ill of a Tertian feaver, of which had two fits.

30 ♃ In the morning taken in bed with a Quotidian ague, which held me till May 5 ♂.

May 4 ☽ No. 135. Chr: Heydon, Astrological discourse of influence. 8° [1650].

May 10 ☉ No. 136. [John] Jackson, Sober word to a Serious People. 4°
[1651].

17 ☉ Had another fit of an Ague. 18 ☽ took a vomit.

28 ♃ No. 137. N.R. Proverbs, English, French, Italian, Spanish,
Dutch. 12° [1659].

June 13 ♄ No. 138. James Gaffarel, Unheard of Curiosities. 8° [trans.
Edmund Chilmead, 1650].

About this time saw the 2 monstrously great Irish children,
Laurence & Katherine Duff; she but 5 year old.[1]

15 ☽ No. 139. Tho: Goodwin, Tryal of a Christian's growth. 8°
[1641].

July 4 ♄ Being 16 year old, my Stature was 5 feet 2⅞ Inches. *About this*
time my beard began to appear.

About this moneth, troubled with a violent Cholerick humour,
breaking out in pimples upon my Nose, & Face, from which
never totally free after: but sometimes more rarely & sometimes
more frequently troubled with it.

In July & August handled my Nativity Astrologically, after the Method
proposed in Lilly's Introduction; which took up (with the Cal-
culation of the directions) most part of a Quire of paper.[2]

Aug. 7 ♀ No. 140. John Angelus of Astrology. 8°.[3]

Sept. 25 ♀ No. 141. Tho: Hall, Loathsomnesse of Long Haire. 8° [1654].

27 ☉ No. 142. Brief Account of Val: Greatraks. 4° [1666].

30 ☿ No. 143. Chr: Heydon, Defence of Judicial Astrology. 4°
[1603].

Oct. 13 ♂ I rode towards London to tarry there some time for diversion,
15 ♃ came thither.

Nov. 13 ♀ No. 144. Geo: Thomson, Pest Anatomiz'd. 12° [1666].

18 ☿ No. 145. Joh: Bulwer, Pathomyotomia. 12° [1649].

Dec. 15 ♂ No. 146. Thomas Erastus, Nullity of Church Censures. 8°
[Eng. trans., 1659].

23 ☿ No. 147. Joh: Bulwer, Chirologia et Chironomia. 8° [1644].

1668 [1] No other reference to these children has been found.
[2] Now Selmes MS 29. By 'Lilly's Introduction' Jeake means William Lilly's *Christian*
Astrology (1647).
[3] i.e. Johann Engel, trans. Robert Turner, Ἔσοπτρον Ἀστρολογικόν: *Astrologicall Optics*
(1655).

Jan.   9 ♄ About 5h p.m. As I went over London bridge to go to the post-
house then in Bishopsgate street; there being a great stop on the
bridge, & I having gone as far as the uncovered place a little
before the drawbridge; was thrust to the Eastside close to the
stonewall; where a Cart passed so nigh to the wall, that I had
scarce room left to stand between; & if I had not providentially
lift up my Foot, & stept into a puddle of mud I believe the Cart
had run over it & broke it.

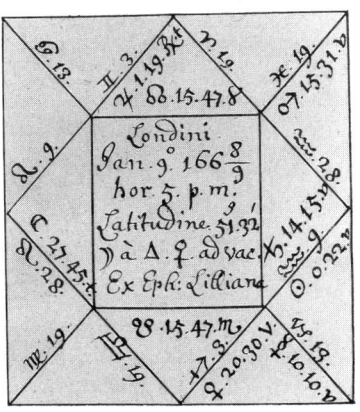

   19 ♂ No. 148. Jos: Glanvil, Scepsis Scientifica, &c. 4° [1665].
Feb. 26 ♀ About 10h a.m. I began to learn Geometry.

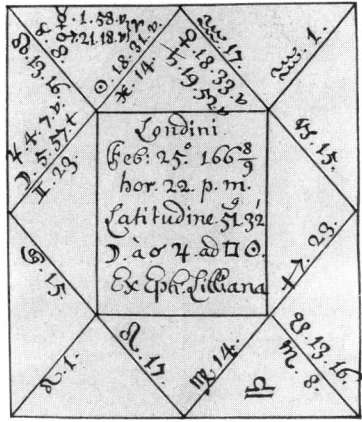

Mar. 17 ☿ No. 149. ['Eirenaeus Philalethes'] Secrets Reveal'd. 8° [1669].

25 ♃ I came from London to Gravesend by water: & thence to Maidstone that night.

26 ♀ From Maidstone to Hedcorne. 27 ♄ thence home to Rye. Had no very good weather this journey; sometimes Snow.

Apr. 11 ☉ No. 150. Hugh Broughton. Concent of Scriptures. 4° [1590].

13 ♂ No. 151. Lodowick Ariosto, Orlando furioso. Fol. [trans. Sir John Harington, 1591].

15 ♃ *My C[ousin]* told me the f[irst] *matter of the elixir as was supposed.*

21 ☿ No. 152. Jo: Owen, Doctrine of the Trinity vindicated. 12° [1669].

May 2 ☉ No. 153. Advice to the Parliament Temp. Hen: 8. 8°.[1]

11 ♂ About 1h p.m. I began effectually to learn Arithmetick under this positure of heaven.

27 ♃ No. 154. J. F. Sober Inquiry or Christs reign &c. 8° [1660].

June 1 ♂ About 10h a.m. I began effectually to learn Logick under the ensuing face of heaven. Then also began my synopsis thereof for my own use, being chiefly a contraction & translation into

---

1669 [1] Not identified.

English of Burgersdicius his Logical Institutions. This took me up till August 20 ♀ next following, when finished it about 10h p.m. consisting of 74 pages, in 4°.[2]

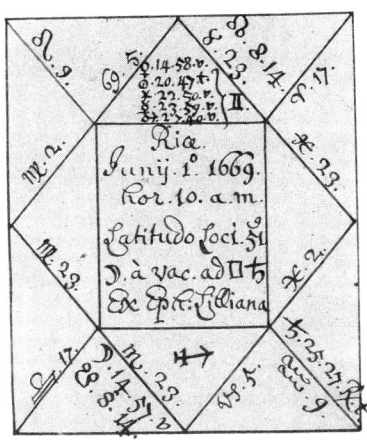

10 ♃ No. 155. Nath: Homes, Resurrection Revealed. Fol: [1653].

July   4 ☉ Being 17 year old, my stature was 5 feet 3½ inches.

     7 ☿ No. 156. Fra: Bacon, Wisdom of the ancients. 12° [trans. Sir Arthur Gorges, 1619].

   24 ♄ No. 157. John Johnston, Constancy of nature. 8° [trans. John Rowland, 1657].

   31 ♄ No. 158. Franco Burgersdicius, Institutionum Logicarum Libri 2 & Synopsis. 8° [1634].

Aug.   1 ☉ No. 159. Testamentum Graecum, cum Epistola H: Stephani &c 12°.[3]

Sept. 15 ☿ No. 160. Mich: Sendivogius, New light of Alchymy. & Paracelsus of the nature of things. 9 books. 4° [trans. John French, 1650].

Oct.   4 ☽ No. 161. John Fox, Acts & Monuments. Volume 2d. Folio [7th edn., 1632].

---

[2] This volume, entitled *A Synopsis of Logick*, is now Selmes MS 30. The work by Franco Burgersdijck on which it was based was one of the standard school-books of the day.

[3] This seems likeliest to have been the 1587 London edn., except that that was in 16mo. The Jeakes also owned a 16mo edn. of 1617 with this epistle.

Oct 8 ♀ All day ill with the headach cold & hardness of my Throat: in the night troubled with great heat.

9 ♄ A little better: took 3 Pills Aloephanginae

29 ♀ Mr. Marshal buried. Nov. 25 following I received his watch which he had given me by will.[4]

Nov. 12 ♀ No. 162. Tho: Bayley, Worcester's Apophthegms. 8° [1650].

13 ♄ Francis Sack the most intimate of all my Friends died this day of the smal pocks.[5]

Dec. 17 ♀ No. 163. [Josiah Ricraft, collected by] Joh: Leycester Civil wars of England. 8° [1649].

20 ☽ No. 164. Tho: Pye. An Houreglass. 4° [1597].

Jan. 9 ☉ I was troubled with a great pain in my head all the afternoon till night.

11 ♂ No. 165. Tho: Fuller. Holy State &c. and Holy War. Fol: [1639–42].

16 ☉ I began first to take Tobacco, about 2h 24 p.m. had conquer'd it by Feb: 8 following.

22 ♄ As I remember this day I began my MSS entituled English Stenography, or Short writing &c. methodized Logically; & finished it May 27 ♀ 1670 about 11 a clock in the forenoon.

Feb. 24 ♃ Made an end of writing fairly in Print hand the Decalogue, Lords Prayer & Creed, in Hebrew, Greek, Latine & English.[1]

Apr. 4 ☽ No. 166. Nic: Bernard, Judgment of the late Archbishop of Armagh, &c. 8° [1657].

23 ♄ No. 167. [John Owen] Truth & Innocence vindicated. 8° [1669].

May 1 ☉ No. 168. Jer: Burroughs, Moses his Choice. 4° [1641].

---

[4] In his will, in which he was referred to as a gentleman, Thomas Marshall of Rye left 'my silver watch with my arms engraved' to Samuel Jeake junior, and 20 shillings for rings to each of his overseers, his 'kinsman' Thomas Miller (see Appendix 3), and his 'loving friend' Samuel Jeake senior. PCC PROB 11/332 1670: 38.

[5] The burial of 'Francis Sacke a young man of the Pox' on 14 Nov. 1669 is recorded in Rye Parish Register. ESRO PAR 467/1/1/3, p. 182.

1670 [1] This exquisite piece of calligraphy is now Selmes MS 31.

19 ♃ I rode to Cranbrook faire; taken ill there about noon with a pain in my head & illness in my stomach; came home that night.

June 16 ♃ About 11h p.m. Going into a Room by dark part of which some few days before was fallen into a Cellar that was underneath; I not minding it; fell down into the Cellar almost up to the middle in Water. But through the good Providence of God, did neither fall into the Well, nor dash my head against the Cellar Walls, though neer both: so that I had not the least hurt. Behold the position of heaven at that instant.

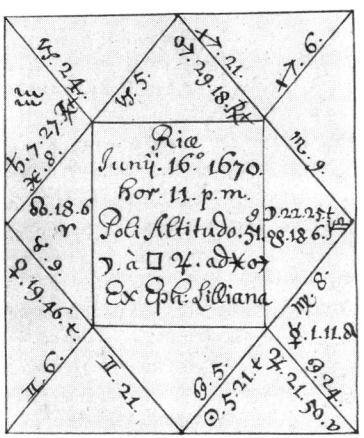

Wherein these Remarkables are to be observed. First that Saturn is just arising in Pisces a watry sign, & neer the degree of the Cusp of the house of death in the Radix (as when my Leg was in danger of being broke Jan: 9 1668/9 Saturn was just descending or setting in Aquarius, (which is supposed to signify the Legs) & opposite to the Radical Ascendant) 2dly Mars is almost culminating. 3dly Jupiter Lord of the 8th in the Radix on the Radical place of the Sun there Lord of the Ascendant in square of the Moon. 4thly The Sun neer the Radical place of Mars &c.

July 4 ☽ Being 18 year old my stature was 5 feet 4⅝ Inches. After which I never grew in heighth.

July 16 ♄ I finished my Hieroglyphick in picture: after the manner following. But vide exactly in the Prototype, too long & superfluous
here to interpret.[2]

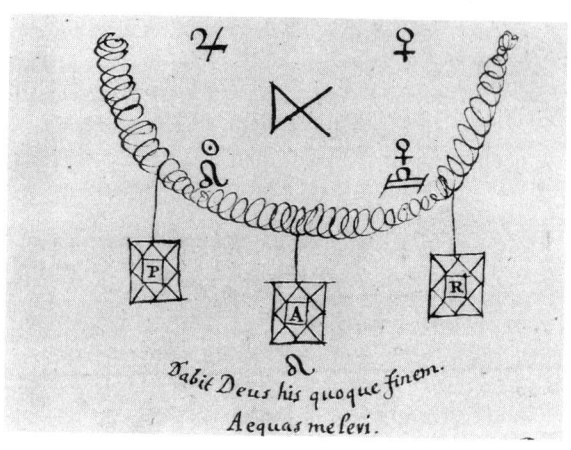

20 ☿ No. 169. Hen: Vane, Epistle General & Face of the Times &c.
4° [1662].

30 ♄ No. 170. Al: Ross, Chymaera Pythagorica, [Robert] Gells' 2
sermons &c. 4°.[3]

July & Aug: Drew out the Nativityes I had by me, in Schemes.[4]

[2] A more elaborate version of this scheme appears as the frontispiece to Jeake's *Diapason.
The Harmony of the Signes of Heaven* (Selmes MS 34). Briefly, it appears that the symbols at the
top, of Jupiter and Venus, were intended to denote the leading features respectively of Jeake's
father's and mother's natal horoscopes. These are linked by an ampersand to the Sun and
Venus, which Jeake evidently saw as the leading features of his own natal chart—in which the
Sun was ruler of the ascendant—together with the zodiac signs, Leo and Libra, in which they
there appeared. The three pendant horoscopes (which are filled in in detail in the version in
Selmes MS 34) are (from right to left) for his 'Radix', and for the 'Aestimatum tempus' and the
'Perfectum tempus' of his conception. Then Leo, the zodiac sign in the ascendant in Jeake's
horoscope, is repeated, followed by a motto which may be roughly translated: 'God puts an end
to these also'. 'Aequas me levi' is an anagram for 'Samuel Jeake' which may be rendered:
'[Matters] fitting to my littleness'. Dr J. C. Eade has kindly helped to interpret this drawing.
[3] This entry refers to a volume of tracts in the Jeakes' library comprising Alexander Ross'
Commentum de Terrae Motu Circulari (1634) (of which the title given on pp. 1 and 36 is
'Chymaerae Pythagoricae'), Hardick Warren's *Magick & Astrology Vindicated* (1651), [*The
Late*] *Storie of Mr William Lilly* (1648), and two sermons by Gell, *Stella Nova* (1649) and
Ἀγγελοκρατία Θεοῦ (1650).
[4] This evidently refers to Selmes MS 32, a folio volume each page of which has been drawn
up to form six horoscopic charts, of which 152 have been completed. See Introduction, sect. 2.

Aug. 11 ♃ No. 171. Will: Camden, Annals of Queen Elizabeth. Fol: [trans. Robert Norton, 1630].

29 ☽ I began to observe a diary of the weather at Rye. beginning yesterday; which I continued for 7 years containing 23 sheets in 8°.[5]

31 ☿ About 7h p.m. I were taken with a Quartan Ague.

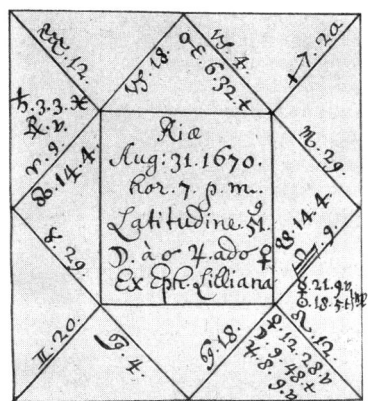

the Heavens being disposed, as before in the precedent Page specified.[6] At first I was taken cold as usual; but when I were in bed, hot; accompanied with aches of the bones, & giddiness of the head. This Ague lasted 8 months.

Sept. 1 ♃ Ill all day with the headach, pain in the bones, & oppression of the Stomach.

3 ♄ About 7h p.m. the 2d fit of the Quartan began: Worse than the first; most violent of all.

6 ♂ About 6h 30′ p.m. the 3d fit, very bad.

8 ♃ Delineated the Lines of my Hands on Paper; to observe the Variations thereof afterwards.

9 ♀ About 6h 30′ p.m. the 4th fit; so little that it could hardly be perceived.

---

[5] In fact each sheet was divided into two, and 41 out of these 46 sections survive as Selmes MS 33.

[6] This entry appears at the top of p. 22 of Jeake's manuscript; the chart for 31.8.70 had appeared at the bottom of p. 21.

Sept. 12 ☽ About 3h 25′ p.m. the 5th fit: cold, accompanied with pain of the head & drowsiness; continued till about 8h 30′ p.m.

15 ♃ About 3h 1′ p.m. the 6th fit, like to the 5th but somewhat worse.

18 ☉ About 4h 10′ p.m. the 7th fit, more benevolent than the former in the beginning without the headach; but a greater shaking.

21 ☿ About 3h 44′ p.m. the 8th fit like to the 7th but more sleepy.

24 ♄ About 3h 37′ p.m. the 9th fit like the 7th but gentler, continued till about 9h p.m.

27 ♂ About 4h 7′ p.m. the 10th fit, with shaking, giddiness, drowziness, headach & inclination to vomit; continued till about 9h p.m.

29 ♃ No. 172. Ri: Sanders. Physiognomy & Chiromancy, Treatise of Moles, Artificial memory &c. Fol: [1653].

30 ♀ About 3h 25′ p.m. the 11th fit, like the 10th but milder, not off till about 9h p.m.

In September or October I set my self again to learn Geometry, spending most of the ensuing winter (when my Ague was off) about it, & with good effect.

Oct. 2 ☉ No. 173. London Assembly, Jus divinum Ministerii Evangelici, & Anglicani; with an Appendix. 4° [2nd edn., 1647].

3 ☽ About 2h 46′ p.m. the 12th fit, like the 11th & besides a great palpitation of the heart; staid till 9h p.m.

6 ♃ About 3h 1′ p.m. the 13th fit, with shaking, giddiness, drowsiness & headach; continued till about 9h p.m.

8 ♄ I took a vomit of the Infusion of Crocus Metallorum, with which had 10 vomits, & 3 stools, but no benefit as to my Ague.

9 ☉ About 4h 14′ p.m. the 14th fit, like the 13th went off about 9h p.m.

11 ♂ Tobacco, Frankincense & Corants beaten were applied to my wrists for the Ague; but without effect.

12 ☿ About 4h 59′ p.m. the 15th fit, like the 14th continued till about 9h p.m.

15 ♄ About 4h 1′ p.m. the 16th fit, like the 15th continued till about 9h p.m.

16 ☉ About 7h p.m. Taken with another fit; first cold, then shaking, then giddiness, lastly headach: but not so bad as the former;

continued till about 9h p.m. This was the 17th fit, my Ague now degenerating into a double Quartan.

About this time I received Mr. Philip Frith's Books of his Executrix, being mostly Physick Books, given me by his Will, & worth about £25. He died August 17th last 7h 50′ p.m.[7]

18 ♂ About 6h 59′ p.m. the 18th fit, milder than the former; like the 16th except drowsiness; continued till about 9h 30′ p.m.

19 ☿ About 5h 15′ p.m. the 19th fit, like the 17th except giddiness, yet worse; continued till about 8h 30′ p.m.

21 ♀ About 4h 45′ p.m. the 20th fit like the 18th abode till about 9h p.m.

22 ♄ About 5h 37′ p.m. the 21th fit, like the 19th went off about 9h p.m.

24 ☽ About 5h 37′ p.m. the 22th fit, without any great shaking; yet remained till about midnight.

25 ♂ About 7h 26′ p.m. the 23th fit; with a great shaking, like the former, continu'd till about 11h p.m.

27 ♃ About 7h 8′ p.m. the 24th fit, with a little shaking drowsiness & headach: continuing till about midnight.

28 ♀ About 7h 31′ p.m. the 25th fit: like the 24th except drowsiness; continued till about midnight.

30 ☉ About 6h 51′ p.m. the 26th fit; like the 25th continuing till about midnight.

31 ☽ About 7h 44′ p.m. the 27th fit: like the 26th continuing likewise till about midnight.

Nov. 2 ☿ About 5h 40′ p.m. the 28th fit, like the 27th continued till about 10h p.m.

3 ♃ About 6h 29′ p.m. the 29th fit like the 28th but milder; continued till about 10h p.m.

5 ♄ About 4h 59′ p.m. the 30th fit: fierce, with a great shaking, continuing till about 9h p.m.

6 ☉ About 6h 57′ p.m. the 31th fit; very gentle but like the 29th continuing till about 11h p.m.

[7] Philip Frith of Rye, a lawyer and surgeon-apothecary, was referred to as 'gentleman' in his will. His executrix was his widow, Elizabeth, who was instructed to give Jeake those of his books which she did not want. PCC PROB 11/334 1670: 134 (copy in ESRO SAS/B/41).

Nov. 8 ♂ About 4h 59′ p.m. the 32th fit, like the 30th but somewhat more favorable; lasted till about 10h p.m.

9 ☿ About 6h 7′ p.m. the 33th fit: like the 31th but sharper, yet without any great shaking; continued till about 10h 30′ p.m.

11 ♀ About 5h 18′ p.m. the 34th fit; without the great shaking; but else like the 32th continued till about 9h 30′ p.m.

About *this month began to be troubled with the* F[   ] M[   ]⁸ *whilst I had my ague.*

12 ♄ About 6h 26′ p.m. the 35th fit, like the 33th but milder; continued till about 10h p.m.

13 ☉ Sweat in the night; as I did also whilst I had a simple Quartan for 4 fits or thereabouts in the nights next following those in which the Quartan came. And when my Quartan came to be double (the first fit whereof was Oct. 16 ☉) on that night & every 3d night after I did sweat much. But scarce at all on my other ague nights.

14 ☽ About 5h 4′ p.m. the 36th fit like the 34th & drowsiness & sweat beside; lasted till 10h p.m.

15 ♂ About 6h 58′ p.m. the 37th fit like the 35th continued till about midnight.

17 ♃ About 6h p.m. the 38th fit like the 34th & sweat in the night besides, continued till about 11h p.m.

18 ♀ About 7h 4′ p.m. the 39th fit like the 38th continuing till about 11h 30′ p.m.

19 ♄ About 8h p.m. Taken with another fit; gentle, with a little sweat. This was the 40th fit: now turned to a Triple Quartan.

20 ☉ About 6h 15′ p.m. the 41th fit, like the 38th continued till about midnight.

21 ☽ About 7h 30′ p.m. the 42th fit, like the 41th continuing till about midnight.

22 ♂ About 8h 59′ p.m. the 43th fit; with a little shaking, headach & sweating, continuing till about 10h 30′ p.m.

23 ☿ About 7h 44′ p.m. the 44th fit; with a great shaking; else like the 42th continuing till about 11h p.m.

---

⁸ This may refer to Jeake's fistula: see Introduction, sect. 7. Cf. 21.5, 26.10.72.

24 ♃ About 7h 59′ p.m. the 45th fit, like the 44th continued till about midnight.

25 ♀ About 9h 14′ p.m. the 46th fit, like the 43th continued till about midnight.

26 ♄ About 7h 32′ p.m. the 47th fit, like the 45th yet with a great shaking, continued till about midnight.

27 ☉ About 7h 44′ p.m. the 48th like the 45th in all respects.

28 ☽ About 9h 15′ p.m. the 49th fit, like the 46th went off about 11h p.m.

29 ♂ About 7h 51′ p.m. the 50th fit, like the 48th remained till about 11h p.m.

30 ☿ About 7h 28′ p.m. the 51th fit, like the 50th continuing till about 11h p.m.

Dec. 1 ♃ About 8h 52′ p.m. the 52th fit like the 49th but worse, continued till about 10h 30′ p.m.

2 ♀ About 8h 7′ p.m. the 53th fit, like the 51th continued till about 12h 30′ p.m.

3 ♄ About 8h 14′ p.m. the 54th fit like the 53th continued till about midnight.

4 ☉ About 8h 30′ p.m. the 55th fit. like the 52th continued till about 11h p.m.

5 ☽ About 8h p.m. the 56th fit, like the 54th and drowsiness besides, continuing till about midnight.

6 ♂ About 7h 56′ p.m. the 57th fit, like the 54th but my sweating was almost gone; continuing till about 11h p.m.

7 ☿ About 7h 48′ p.m. the 58th fit, like the 55th but worse & some sweat: continuing till about 10h p.m.

8 ♃ About 8h 28′ p.m. the 59th fit, like the 56th with sweat: continued till about 10h p.m.

9 ♀ About 8h 12′ p.m. the 60th fit, like the 57th continued till about 10h 30′ p.m.

10 ♄ About 8h 57′ p.m. the 61th fit, like the 58th but more gentle: continuing till about 10h p.m.

11 ☉ About 8h 43′ p.m. the 62th fit, like the 59th but without great shaking, continued till sleep came, in which I used to sweat.

Dec. 12 ☽ About 8h 54′ p.m. the 63th fit, like the 62th but gentle & short.

13 ♂ About 9h 28′ p.m. the 64th fit, scarce sensible.

14 ☿ About 8h 20′ p.m. the 65th fit; gentle: remained till about 10h p.m.

15 ♃ About 9h 1′ p.m. the 66th fit, as the 65th continuing till about 10h 30′ p.m.

16 ♀ This day I had no fit.

17 ♄ About 7h 31′ p.m. the 67th fit; as the 66th continuing till about 9h p.m.

18 ☉ About 8h 44′ p.m. the 68th fit; very gentle continued till about 9h 15′ p.m.

19 ☽ About 8h 31′ p.m. the 69th fit; mild & short.

20 ♂ About 6h 17′ p.m. the 70th fit, worse, continued till about 10h p.m.

21 ☿ About 8h 1′ p.m. the 71th fit gentle & short. This day altered the Sundial 30′ backwards supposing it went to fast.

23 ♀ About 4h 44′ p.m. the 72th fit; sharper; continued till about 10h p.m. My Ague now altered again, & became irregular.

26 ☽ About 5h 3′ p.m. the 73th fit. as the 72th continued till about 10h p.m.

28 ☿ About 7h 53′ p.m. the 74th fit; little: continued till about 9h p.m. My Ague became now again a double Quartan.

29 ♃ About 4h 32′ p.m. the 75th fit, like the 73th continued till about 10h p.m.

31 ♄ About 7h 37′ p.m. the 76th fit, like the 74th continued till about 9h p.m.

1671

Jan. 1 ☉ About 5h 30′ p.m. the 77th fit; worse, with sweat; continued till about 10h p.m.

3 ♂ About 6h 28′ p.m. the 78th fit, like the 76th continued till about 10h p.m.

4 ☿ About 5h 44′ p.m. the 79th fit, sharper, lasted till about 10h p.m.

6 ♀ About 6h 7′ p.m. the 80th fit, like the 78th continued till about 12h p.m.

7 ♄ About 5h 59′ p.m. the 81th fit, like the 79th continued till about 9h p.m.

9 ☽ About 6h 3′ p.m. the 82th fit, sharp; continuing till about 10h p.m.

10 ♂ About 5h 2′ p.m. the 83th fit: fierce; lasted till about 9h p.m.

12 ♃ About 6h 12′ p.m. the 84th fit, like the 82th continued till about 10h p.m.

13 ♀ About 5h 25′ p.m. the 85th fit, worse than the former, continued till about 10h p.m.

14 ♄ No. 174. Fame & Confession of the Rosie Cross. 8° [Eng. trans., 1652].

15 ☉ About 5h 18′ p.m. the 86th fit, better then the former; lasted till about 10h p.m.

16 ☽ About 4h 46′ p.m. the 87th fit, like the 85th continued till about 10h p.m.

18 ☿ About 4h 55′ p.m. the 88th fit, sharp, lasted till about 9h 30′ p.m.

19 ♃ About 5h 19′ p.m. the 89th fit, mild; continued till about 10h p.m.

This day my Faith was strengthned to believe on the Lord Jesus Christ for the remission of my sins; & that with a Faith of Assurance. The Faith of Recumbency having been through mercy formerly bestowed on me: & since my illness, especially in this moneth of January, my thoughts having been occupied with most assiduous Reflections & Meditations upon the encouragement given in the Gospel to believe on the Lord Jesus. chiefly in these Scriptures, Acts 10. 43. To him give all the Prophets witness, that through his name, whosoever believeth in him, shall receive remission of Sins. Chap. 13. 39. And by him all that believe are justified from all things, from which ye could not be justified by the law of Moses. 1. John. 3. 23. And this is his Commandment that we should believe on the name of his Son Jesus Christ &c. Chap. 5. 10. He that believeth on the Son of God hath the witness in himself: he that believeth not God hath made him a liar, because he believeth not the record that God gave of his Son.

Jan. 21 ♄ About 4h 32′ p.m. the 90th fit like the 88th continuing (as also those that follow) till about 10h p.m.

22 ☉ About 5h 26′ p.m. the 91th fit; gentle.

24 ♂ About 4h 18′ p.m. the 92th fit; sharp.

25 ☿ About 5h 44′ p.m. the 93th fit, gentle.

27 ♀ About 4h 1′ p.m. the 94th fit, sharp.

28 ♄ About 4h 58′ p.m. the 95th fit, gentle.

30 ☽ About 3h 57′ p.m. the 96th fit, sharp.

31 ♂ About 5h 37′ p.m. the 97th fit, very gentle.

Feb. 2 ♃ About 4h 28′ p.m. the 98th fit, sharp.

3 ♀ About 4h 44′ p.m. the 99th fit, very gentle.

No. 175. Ken: Digby, Discourse of the Vegetation of Plants. 16° [1661].

5 ☉ About 2h 30′ p.m. the 100th fit; fierce.

6 ☽ About 4h 45′ p.m. the 101th fit, gentle.

8 ☿ About 2h 30′ p.m. the 102th fit, sharp.

9 ♃ About 5h p.m. the 103d fit; very short & gentle.

11 ♄ About 2h 44′ p.m. the 104th fit, sharp.

12 ☉ About 4h 55′ p.m. the 105th fit very short & gentle.

14 ♂ About 2h 14′ p.m. the 106th fit, sharp.

15 ☿ About 4h 52′ p.m. the 107th fit, mild & short.

17 ♀ About 2h 59′ p.m. the 108th fit. sharp.

18 ♄ About 5h 7′ p.m. the 109th fit, mild & short.

20 ☽ About 2h 37′ p.m. the 110th fit, sharp.

21 ♂ About 5h 29′ p.m. the 111th fit, most gentle.

23 ♃ About 2h 31′ p.m. the 112th fit, sharp.

24 ♀ About 4h 55′ p.m. the 113th fit, scarse sensible.

25 ♄ By this time I had learned Dialling: and Geometry, indifferently.

26 ☉ About 2h p.m. the 114th fit; fierce & cruel. Now turned again to a Simple Quartan.

Mar. 1 ☿ About 2h 15′ p.m. the 115th fit; fierce.

4 ♄ About 1h 34′ p.m. the 116th fit, more favorable than the 115th.

7 ♂ About 1h 52′ p.m. the 117th fit, worse than the 116th.

10 ♀ About 1h 37′ p.m. the 118th fit, sharpe.

13 ☽ About 2h 14′ p.m. the 119th fit, sharp. *This day voided a worm.*

15 ☿ About 5h 45′ p.m. the 120th fit, gentle. My Ague now again turning into a Double Quartan.

16 ♃ About 2h 20′ p.m. the 121th fit, sharp.

18 ♄ About 5h 30′ p.m. the 122th fit, gentle.

19 ☉ About 2h 14′ p.m. the 123th fit. with sweat milder than the 121th.

21 ♂ About 5h 30′ p.m. the 124th fit, worse than the 122th.

22 ☿ About 4h 44′ p.m. the 125th fit, sharp.

24 ♀ About 4h 59′ p.m. the 126th fit, worse than the 124th.

25 ♄ About 4h 59′ p.m. the 127th fit, like the 125th.

27 ☽ About 4h 30′ p.m. the 128th fit; gentle.

28 ♂ About 4h 29′ p.m. the 129th fit, better than the 127th. By this time I had learned the Mathematical part of Navigation.

30 ♃ About 4h 46′ p.m. the 130th fit, moderate.

31 ♀ About 5h 33′ p.m. the 131th fit, gentle.

Apr. 2 ☉ About 4h 59′ p.m. the 132th fit, gentle.

3 ☽ About 5h 56′ p.m. the 133th fit, gentle; but accompanied with a little toothach.

5 ☿ About 4h 58′ p.m. the 134th fit, very short & favorable. Now changed again into a Simple Quartan.

8 ♃ About 5h 2′ p.m. the 135th fit, worse.

11 ♂ About 3h 59′ p.m. the 136th fit, as the 135th.

14 ♀ About 2h 28′ p.m. the 137th fit; worse than the 136th. This day first perceived my sight to be vitiated with a Suffusion: upon which I began to read Physick, viz., Riverius's Practice of Physick &c,[1] and continued reading mostly on that Subject till September 14 ♄ 1672 & sometimes afterwards.

17 ☽ About 1h 37′ p.m. the 138th fit, worse than the 137th.

20 ♃ About 2h 44′ p.m. the 139th fit. worse than the 138th.

23 ☉ About 2h 29′ p.m. the 140th fit, like the 139th.

1671 [1] i.e. Lazarus Riverius, trans. Nicholas Culpeper, *The Practice of Physick* (1655).

Apr. 26 ☿ This day I missed my fit.

29 ♄ About 3h 1′ p.m. the 141th fit, accompanied only with the headach.

May 2 ♂ About 2h 30′ p.m. the 142d and last fit; very mild & short.

This Critical Register of the several Paroxysms, I undertook the
rather, to investigate the cause of their Regular Returns. I shall
only observe in this place, That, as the morbifique matter
encreased, or the constitution or habit of body was vitiated by
the continuance of the Quartan; so it became in less than two
moneths a Double Quartan, viz. on the 16th of October last.
And encreasing more it became a Triple Quartan on the 19th of
November which continued till December 21. When it became
irregular & uncertain (or as a Planet having run out his direct
course, becomes Stationary to Retrocession) failing of the fits
that were expected, 22th 24th 25th & 27 December (besides the
Chasme of December 16) Then as if it took it's course Retrograde, it was again reduced to a Double Quartan, on the 28th of
December continuing regularly so for 2 moneths viz. till February 26 when it was further reduced to the narrower Compass of
a simple Quartan; but more violent, as if the strength of both fits
were now united in one. Thus it continued till March 15 when
as if nature were not strong enough to overcome it; it relapsed
once more into a Double Quartan: & so remained till April 5
when Spring coming on apace, & Nature growing stronger, it
was lastly reduced again to a Simple Quartan; which continued
till it made a halt on April 26 & finally expired on May 2 after
full 8 moneths duration.

25 ♃ No. 176 James Janeway, Token for Children. 16° [1671].

In May, began to make use of several Medicines both Topicals
& Internals for the preservation & recovery of my Sight; which I
continued most part of the summer, & at times all next year; &
now & then afterwards, though more rarely. But my Sight continued much alike only with some very small gradual diminu-
tion as I grew in years: neither suffering the decay that I feared;
nor receiving the melioration that I expected.

June 1 ♃ No. 177. John Wynel, Lues Venerea. 8° [1660].

9 ♀ No. 178. Tho: White, Controversy-Logick. 8° [1659].

12 ☽ No. 179. Mar: Nedham, Medela Medicinae. 8° [1665].

13 ♂ No. 180. Edw: Bolnest, Medicina Instaurata. 8° [1665].

14 ☿ No. 181. Geo: Thomson, Galenopale. 8° [1665].

15 ♃ No. 182. Ever: Maynwaring, Medicus Absolutus. 8° [1668].

16 ♀ No. 183. And: Tentzelius, Sympathetical Mummy. 8° [trans. Ferdinando Parkhurst, 1653].

18 ☉ About 6h 30′ p.m. I was seized with a violent fit of the Tooth-ach, which lasted 3 hours.

19 ☽ About 6h 30′ a.m. I went with Mr. John Weekes to his Father's house at Westfield, to tarry there 5 or 6 days: where lodging with him; we saw on the 23th ♀ in the morning, when we awaked; that a bedstaff which in the evening before was stuck up at his side of the bed, was now found placed on my side between 2 others which were set there the night before. And that Two other Bedstaffs that were missing the same evening; & as we well remembred; sought for in a Chair that stood on my side of the bed, were this morning when I arose found lying in the same Chair. This seemed somewhat strange; & being pretty well satisfied; that none of the family were concerned in it, I cannot yet resolve it into any other Cause, than the ridiculous & trifling actions of some of the meanest rank among the Infernal Spirits. Especially for that, upon discourse of this, I had the Relation of some other such like trifles acted in the very same Chamber.

24 ♄ About 1h p.m. Returned home to Rye.

26 ☽ No. 184. [Christopher Irvine] Medicina Magnetica. 8° [1656].

30 ♀ No. 185. John [i.e. Joseph] Hall, Balm of Gilead. 8° [1646].

July   4 ♂ Being now 19 Years of Age, I had by this time somewhat acquainted my self with the Latine, Greek & Hebrew, Rhetor-ick, Logick, Poetry, Natural Philosophy, Arithmetick, Geometry, Cosmography, Astronomy, Astrology, Geography, Theology, Physick, Dialling, Navigation, Calligraphy, Steno-graphy, Drawing, Heraldry, and History.

My stature was short, viz.; the same that was noted July 4 1670. My Complexion Melancholy, My Face pale & lean, Forehead high; Eyes grey, Nose large, Teeth bad & distorted, No. 28. Hair of a sad brown, & curling: about this age & till after 20 had a great quantity of it; but from thence it decayed & grew thin. My voice grew hoarse after I had the small pocks. My Body was always lean, my hands & feet small, I was partly left handed & partly Ambodexter. In my right hand was found the perfect Triangle composed of the Vital, Cephalick, & Hepatick Lines, all entire; but the Cephalica broken in my left hand.[2] The Moles or Naevi, five: Viz. 1. one under the right arm almost as high as the armhole. 2. one in the left hand upon the Mount of Jupiter. 3. one upon the right side, under the short Ribs. 4. one (the largest) on the Abdomen. 5. one, at the left side of the right heel.

The Description of my Mind must be totally omitted as inconvenient for me to relate, and liable to certaine exposure: it being not possible for me in this particular to saile between Scylla & Charybdis.

July   5 ☿ Troubled with the pain of the Teeth, which continued, but moderate.

     6 ♃ No. 186. Ren: des Cartes, Opera Philosophica. 4° [3rd edn., 1656].

     8 ♄ In the night I had a most violent fit of the Toothach; & another 9 ☉ in the afternoon & night.

   28 ♀ No. 187. Kenelme Digby, Treatise of Bodies, and Treatise of Man's Soule. 4° [1644].
No. 188. Rich: Edlyn, Observationes Astrologicae, with Shakerly's Discourse of the Systeme of the World. 8° [1659].

Aug.   3 ♃ About 1h 15′ p.m. I had a Fontinell made in my Neck to draw away the noxious humours that offended my Face Eyes & Teeth &c. *on an elected time which the former med[ic]ations were not*. But finding little benefit by it I had it dryed up the next year.

This day my Teeth aked again. which continued till 6 ☉.

     5 ♄ In the afternoon ill with a pain in my left Eye & Cheek; Teeth & Head: worse at night.

   10 ♃ About noon taken ill with a great pain in my left side: continuing till 13 ☉.

   18 ♀ No. 189. James Primrose, Popular Errors. 8° [trans. Robert Wittie, 1651].

   25 ♀ My Hypothesis about the Ebbing & Flowing of the Sea.

---

[2] These are all technical physiognomical terms denoting lines etc. on the hand. A broken cephalic line was a sign of weakness. For an exposition see Richard Sanders, *Physiognomie and Chiromancie* (1653), which also includes 'A Treatise of Moles'.

28 ☽ No. 190. Cuthb: Sydenham, Christian Exercitation. 8° [1653].

Sept. 4 ☽ Wrote the Construction of an Instrument per Altitudinem Solis.

Oct. 11 ☿ Given me by Mrs. Eliz. Frith's will (who died this day 8h p.m.) a Copperstill & some glass stills.³

16 ☽ No. 191. Hebrew Bible of Menasseh ben Israel's edition with points [1639], & Greek Testament of Richard Whitaker's impression. 8° [1633].⁴

Dec. 26 ♂ Troubled with a Cold, which encreased, 27 ☿ so that I was very hoarse; after, decreasing.

1672

Jan. 3 ☿ This day I finished my Book entituled Diapason, or The Harmony of the Signes of Heaven: being a juvenile Essay or Enquiry into the Rationality of Astrological Maximes; consisting of 9 sheets in 4to. & begun last Summer.¹

6 ♄ About 1h 15′ p.m. I began to learn the Art of Memory, but followed it not long.

17 ☿ F[irst] *impulse to pray for the recovery of my eyesight.*

In this moneth or February following I made some Genethliacal Observations.² In February wrote a rough draught of a short Exercitation about the trueness of the Christian Religion. In the beginning of March wrote the Astrological judgment of the 20th year of my Age.³

Mar. 11 ☽ & from thence to the 17 ☉ Exclusive I was occupied about Mnemonick Images.

24 ☉ About 2h p.m. ill in my stomach. but of no long continuance.

28 ♃ Busied about making the Alphabet in great florid Letters: & about this time imploy'd much in learning to flourish Letters & Knots.

---

³ Elizabeth Frith was the widow of Philip Frith (see 16.10.70). No copy of her will appears to have survived.

⁴ The Jeakes' copies of these two works were bound together; the editions have been given from the library 'Register' (Jeake MS 4/1).

1672 ¹ Now Selmes MS 34.

² Now Selmes MS 35.

³ Now Selmes MS 36.

Apr. 1 ☽ About 4h p.m. A kind of Ague fit. I had also been somewhat indisposed ever since the 24th past.

2 ♂ Made some new knots a la quevé.

4 ♃ About 5h p.m. Taken with a pain in the head, which continued
till about midnight; sweat much in the night.

8 ☽ About 8h 15′ a.m. went for diversion to Mr. Weekes's house at
Westfield; came thither about ¼ hour before noon. Tarried there
till 13 ♄ when returned at 10h a.m. & came to Rye about 1h
p.m.

16 ♂ Ill in the afternoon, cold & aguish; pain of the head in the evening; sweat in the night.

18 ♃ Aguish in the afternoon, sweat in the night.

19 ♀ About 2h p.m. Taken with another aguish fit, the worst of all,
continuing till 11h p.m. with headach & much sweat in the
night.

25 ♃ A Cold & hoarsness till 30 ♂. Then decreasing. About 15h 40′
p.m. a Diarrhoea with a Cough following.

29 ☽ About 4h 1′ p.m. Taken with a fit of an Ague; inclin'd to shivering, after headach and sweat in the night.

May 1 ☿ About 5h 18′ p.m. Taken with another fit of an Ague, but very
moderate.

5 ☉ A Cold in my head & stoppage of the nose continuing till 24 ♀ or
thereabouts.

6 ☽ About 9h 15′ a.m. Several pieces of Gold of divers sorts of Coins
given me by my Father. in all about £18 14s. And 9 ♃ about 3h
15′ p.m. Seven dollars £1 11s 6d. And 11 ♄ about 3h 48′ p.m.
more in different Coins 14s 10d. And 15 ☿ 21 ♂ 23 ♃ 24 ♀ &
July 9 ♂ Severall curious fishes shells stones & other rarities.

8 ☿ Rode with Cousin Hen: Wightman to Brenset Appledoor &
Tenterden, & back to Rye.

21 ♂ *About this time the F[   ] M[   ] confirmed and very troublesome.*[4]

28 ♂ About 10h a.m. I rode to London, where I arrived safe. 29 ☿
about 3h 30′ p.m. Excessive hot weather which discomposed
me. *The intention of my journey was to find a medicine for my eyes.*

[4] Cf. 11.11.70, 26.10.72.

June 5 ☿ About noon I was taken ill of a Quartan Ague, which continued all day, but moderate. Troubled also with a soreness in my Neck not far off from my Issue.

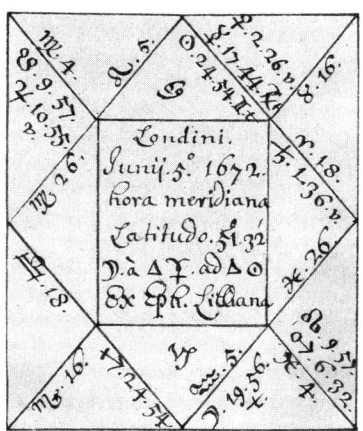

8 ♄ About 3h p.m. the second fit: little, accompanied with breaking out of the Lips.

9 ☉ Troubled all day with a twitching pain in my right Eyebrow till toward even; then some respite after a short sleep.

10 ☽ The pain returned & encreased till about 3h p.m. after, remitted. And till 18 ♂, afflicted thus every forenoon, with remission in the afternoons & nights.

11 ♂ About 3h 48′ p.m. the 3d fit: but little.

13 ♃ Came from London about ½ an houre before noon, & home to Rye, 14 ♀ about 5h 30′ p.m.

14 ♀ About 2h p.m. taken ill upon the road with the 4th fit of my Ague, but pretty moderate. About this day there began a swelling in my neck from a confluence of humours occasioned by neglecting to dress my Issue orderly in this Journey.

17 ☽ About 1h 15′ p.m. the 5th fit. somewhat violent yet without shaking; lasted till night.

20 ♃ About 0h 45′ p.m. the 6th fit, violent, held till night, no shaking, but after the cold fit was over pain in the head.

23 ☉ About 0h 37′ p.m. the 7th fit; not so bad.

June 24 ☽ Began to dry up my Issue. the swelling in my Neck encreased on the left side.

     26 ☿ About oh 54′ p.m. the 8th fit, like the 5th & 6th.

     27 ♃ About 9h 15′ p.m. A Cataplasm laid to my Neck to break the swelling.

     28 ♀ About 8h 8′ a.m. The swelling in my Neck was lanced, & part of the matter let out, opened again at night, & so twice on 29 ♄ & 30 ☉ & afterwards healed up.

     29 ♄ About 2h 12′ p.m. the 9th fit, not quite so violent as the 5th.

July   2 ♂ About 2h 12′ p.m. the 10th fit, lasted till 6h p.m. not so violent as the former.

     5 ♀ About 2h 12′ p.m. the 11th fit. of the same duration with the 10th but not quite so bad.

     8 ☽ About 2h 27′ p.m. the 12th fit, lasted till about 7h p.m. somewhat worse than the former: sweat in the night. By this time my Issue was dryed up & the swelling well.

     9 ♂ This day as I Remember, began to take Oyl of Sulphur per Campanam, 4 drops daily, for some years.

   11 ♃ About 2h 39′ p.m. the 13th fit: lasted till night; somewhat milder than the former.

   14 ☉ About 2h 40′ p.m. the 14th fit; of like duration with the former, but much more moderate.

   17 ☿ About 2h 40′ p.m. the 15th fit, lasted till night but very moderate: troubled most with a lassitude in my limbs. especially the feet.

   18 ♃ A Tumour began under my left Armhole; which encreased till 25 ♃ & was painful from 22 ☽ to 29 ☽ discussed by an Unguent, and almost quite gone by August 1 ♃.

   20 ♄ About 2h 20′ p.m. the 16th fit: like the 15th.

   23 ♂ About 2h p.m. the 17th fit: moderate. Took 5 or 6 drops of Oyl of Sulphur per Campanum a little before the fit; & repeated it till the ague was gone.

   26 ♀ About 2h 14′ p.m. the 18th fit. moderate.

   29 ☽ About 2h 15′ p.m. the 19th fit, milder then any of the former.

Aug.   1 ♃ About 2h p.m. the 20th fit; scarce perceptible.

4 ☉ About the former part of the afternoon, the 21th fit so little that the time of it's beginning was uncertain.

7 ☿ About 2h 30′ p.m. the 22th fit. like the 21th.

10 ♄ About 4h p.m. a little touch of the Ague but scarce sensible.

16 ♀ By this time the constant use of Oyl of Sulphur had brought me to an excellent good Appetite & digestion.

26 ☽ No. 192. G[eorge] S[winnock] Life & death of Tho: Wilson. 8° [1672].

Sept. 11 ☿ About 7h 19′ p.m. Going in the dark I was like to run my head against a ladder that stood aslope in the street, but Providentially discerning it just as I came to it; clapt up my hand & saved my self. The same evening about 7h 34′ p.m. going to a friends house, I broke my right shin against a Tub that stood unsuspected in the midst of the Kitchin. Note, that Mars was at this time in Pisces neer the Cusp of the 12th. Saturn in Pisces in the 12th in partil opposition of Sun & Jupiter in the 6th & platique opposition of Venus & the Moon, &c.

21 ♄ Troubled with a wearisome pain in my left leg beginning insensibly about 1h 30′ p.m. & after 6h p.m. very painful.

Troubled about this time with the prism [?] and again in October. mostly when asleep.

27 ♀ About 2h 30′ p.m. One shooting at a bird that stood between him & me (not seeing me as I was of the other side of the Pales in a Garden) some of the shot flew about me but praised be God I had no hurt. Mars Stationary exactly opposite to the Cusp of the 8th Saturn & the Moon in the 2d opposite also to the 8th The Sun, Jupiter, Venus & Mercury all in Libra in the 8th So that as in the Accident of Sept. 11th all the Planets were in the 12th & 6th here they are all in the 8th & 2nd.

Oct. 21 ☽ About 11h 36′ a.m. Went to Westfield & 22 ♂ about 6h 15′ a.m. Rode with J[ohn] W[eeks] junior for diversion to Maidstone. came thither 2h 15′ p.m. a calm clear day.

25 ♀ About 8h a.m. we rode to Canterbury & got thither about 2h 20′ p.m. where took a view of the City, Cathedral & Tombs.

26 ♄ About noon, went back towards Maidstone & came thither about 6h p.m. a little Rain in the evening. *The F[   ] M[   ] somewhat painful till 28 ☽.*

Oct. 29 ♂ About 9h 15′ a.m. Rode to Chatham and Rochester to see the ships docks & yards &c. came back to Maidstone that night about 6h 15′ p.m. a little rain in our return.

31 ♃ About 9h 15′ a.m. Returned from Maidstone & came to Westfield about 5h 40′ p.m. Cloudy, & a little misling in the forenoon.

Nov. 2 ♄ About 2h 7′ p.m. went to Rye, & came thither about 4h 54′ p.m.

Dec. 18 ☿ 19 ♃ & 20 ♀ Occupied my self about writing some Politicks for my own use: enlarged them gradually afterwards, to 104 Precepts with their Commentaryes taking up 7½ sheets in Quarto.

24 ♂ About 9h 45′ a.m. Went with J[ohn] W[eeks] junior & another in Company to Westfield. About 1h 50′ p.m. going over an hedge, I received a blow casually on my right Eyebrow by a Staff of one in the Company, which struck off the skin, & made the place swell & red, & afterward black for a fortnight. And it was a great Providence that the stroke did not light full in my Eye. The Sun neer the Cusp of the 8th opposite to the radical place of Mars & in square to Jupiter & Mars & in opposition of the Moon. all in Cardinal Signs. Came to Westfield about 2h 30′ p.m. had fair weather overhead.

28 ♄ About 11h 40′ p.m. Rode back to Rye & came to the ferry about 2h p.m. when it fell a raining hard, & the ferriman not being there I was fain to go back in the wind & rain to an house almost a mile off; & came not to Rye till 4h p.m.

1673

Jan. 19 ☉ Troubled in the night with a Griping in my Stomach, & by fits sometimes before.

28 ♂ 8h p.m. F[irst] *assurance about the recovery of my sight. Vowed £50 to the poor on the healing of my eyesight.*

Apr. 11 ♀ *In my evening prayer I believed that God would heal my eyesight with joys.*

May 13 ♂ About 9h a.m. Went over Guldeford ferry[1] with Cousin H[enry] W[ightman]. Thence rode with him to Brookland, after which it rained continually all the day, & we rode therein to several places, & mistaking the way from Appledoor, came back

---

1673 [1] i.e. the ferry across the Rye harbour channel to East Guldeford. Cf. 6.10.74, 23.5.88.

to Guldford; & there being no boat, could not get to Rye that night: Nor next day till noon, after having waited 3 hours on horsback in the wind & cold on the Gravelly Ground.

23 ♀ *In the act of evening prayer a most illustrious and sweet support of faith given in fullness of faith, patience, joy, submission. On this I resolved when G[od] gave me a son to call his name Manasseh, for G[od] hath made me forget all my toil; and all my C[are]s house [?] a mediocrity from this time till* June 7 ♄.[2] *From thence desolations till* June 16 ☽ *following. Yet with faith but sorrow. When in the afternoon about* 3h p.m., *exactly I remember not, a most solid instantaneous comfort; prayer immediately answered, being but the instant before in the depths of sorrow.*

July   2 ☿ About 9h a.m. Rode to Tenterden for diversion. *sillabub.* & returned next day.

Aug.   8 ♀ No. 193. [Jeronymo Lobo, trans. Sir Peter Wyche] Short Relation of the River Nile &c. 8° [1669].

13 ☿ About 6h 15′ a.m. Rode with Mr. Thomas Miller (with whom had contracted an intimate friendship about July 17 ♃ last, occasioned by a casual discourse) to Lewes; came thither about ·7h 15′ p.m.

16 ♄ About 9h 30′ a.m. Returned thence & came to Rye about 10h p.m. had good weather all this journey.

27 ☿ About 7h a.m. Rode with my Father to Pembury to see the land that came by my Mother, & finish the settlement thereof in severalty with the rest of the Coparceners.[3] Had some hindrance by rain in the way so that we came not thither till 4h 30′ p.m.

28 ♃ About 8h 30′ a.m. My Father released to me the right that he had by the Curtesy, in the Land & Annuity that was my Mother's. About 9h 15′ a.m. Returning I viewed the Land & about 6h p.m. came back to Rye. Rain in the afternoon for 6 or 7 miles riding.

[2] The sense of part of this passage is rather obscure, although the shorthand outlines are written clearly. For the story of Manasseh see 2 Chr. 33: 1–20.

[3] Through his deceased mother, Frances, Jeake inherited land near Pembury in Kent and an annuity of 40 shillings a year on land at Ashburnham, Sussex, which was owned by his uncle, John Wagon of Pembury. The agreement for the partition of these and other lands divided between him and his maternal kinsmen was drawn up in 1660; the partition itself was executed on 20 April 1675. The lawyer involved was Edward Polhill of Burwash. ESRO D 984/1.

Sept. 5 ♀ Began again to take medicines for my eyes, both purgers & alter-
atives, continued it almost daily till December 28 following. viz.
the altering medicines: the other but 1 month.

   25 ♃ *Widow Shoesmith taken sick* 5h p.m. *with a pain in the side. Died
   October 5th 13h 30' p.m.*[4]

Nov. 2 ☉ A Cold, which increased much & at it's height 4 ♂ in the night.
very hoarse with it, & abundance of thin Rheum, for which took
Carraway seeds & Treacle ♂ & Marmalade on 5 ☿ when, after
7h p.m. it sensibly decreased.

Dec. 11 ♃ Resolved to set apart the Tenth part of my Annual Income &
Profits arising by Trade, for the Relief of the Poor & other
Charitable uses; & to begin from January 19th following. But
afterwards on January 5th Resolved to begin the decimation
from April 11th last; that it might comprehend the first of my
Profits.

About this time Mercury being directed ad conjunctionem Solis
I was inclined to the study of Geometry as far as it refers to
Navigation, which humour continued till April.

1674

Feb. 1 ☉ At supper, after eating of a piece of Duck taken with a soreness
in my right Eye, & many glutinous humours flowing to it; which
troubled me for a fortnight: but chiefly in the nights. 8 ☉ the
humour came into the left Eye, & both, equally affected afterwards.

Apr. 14 ♂ About 5h 30' p.m. I went from Rye with Mr. Tho: Miller to
Dieppe in France in a Double Shallop belonging to Dieppe[.]
About 6h p.m. we set saile, with fair weather & a gentle fresh
gale, so that I was not sick above ¼ of an houre all the way.

   15 ☿ At 11h 30' a.m. we arrived safe at Dieppe. at 11h 45' a.m. went
   on shore. & the same day viewed the Towne. 16 ♃ & 17 ♀
   tarried at Dieppe. & on ♀ bought a smal parcel of bone lace in
   partnership.

   18 ♄ About 7h 15' a.m. we rode from Dieppe to Rouen. had some
   rain at first, but after pretty good weather. about 4h 30' p.m. we

---

[4] Perhaps Elizabeth, widow of John Shoesmith of Rye, bricklayer, who also died in 1673.
Both Jeakes witnessed his will. LAWR 33, p. 90.

came to Rouen; & that evening viewed the River & part of the City.

19 ☉ In the forenoon we went to the Protestant Church about 3 miles out of the City below the bridge; Returned in the afternoon & went over the Bridge of Boats, & after that up into the middle spire of Nostredame (so called) about 700 Steps from the ground besides the top-spire into which was no asscent; then to see the great Bell there reported to weight 40000 lb. the Clapper at the biggest being about 17 inches diameter. The middle of the whole building affoorded a fine prospect of the City, Bridge, River & Islands therein. But it has been to my Regret ever since; that instead of keeping holy the Sabbath day, I profaned it, by presenting to my eyes such Objects, as ought either to have been viewed on other days, or else to have been totally omitted.

20 ☽ In the morning after having seen the Exchange, returned about 8h 30′ a.m. for Dieppe[;] had good weather & came to Dieppe about 5h 30′ p.m. & at 6h 45′ p.m. went aboard a Barque of Hasting, & went presently to Sea, got out of the harbour just as the Sun was setting viz. 7h 14′ p.m. with very good weather & winds. I was a little more sick then when I went.

21 ♂ The wind coming Easterly at noon: we came on shore at Hasting about 2h 7′ p.m. And about 4h 45′ p.m. took horse for Rye. the weather rainy & wind now high. Left our horses at Winchelsea, & coming on foot to Rye it began to rain hard & the wind was stormy; so that when we came to the ferry, the Tide being up, we could neither get over, nor make the ferriman hear, but were fain to go back in the rain to Cadborough house almost a mile; came thither about 9h 30′ p.m. wet to the skin.

22 ☿ At 5h 15′ a.m. went towards Rye with good weather & got over the ferry after a long stay by 6h 30′ a.m.

May 5 ♂ About 9h 30′ a.m. Rode to Pembury to receive arrears of Rent & agree on a meeting to seal the writings of partition. came thither about Sun set.

6 ☿ About 9h a.m. came back, & at 8h p.m. to Rye, had good success & weather; only this day a gentle shower &c.

June 10 ☿ About 6h a.m. Rode with my Father to Burwash to meet with the Coperceners about partition of the Lands, came thither at

9h 45′ a.m. but we could not agree about the doing it. I went that night to Tunbridge & next day back to Rye.

July 16 ♃ About 10h a.m. Rode to Cranbrook with some of my kindred that had been at my Fathers' house; returned back to Rye that night about 10h 30′ p.m. *Riding back about 7h 30′ p.m. was pulled off my horse by Jane Key who rode behind me, but had no hurt.*[1]

Aug. 5 ☿ Finished the Projection of my Nativity on the Sphere in Plano.[2]

7 ♀ Ill with a pain in my head: aguish also and my Throat sore. 8 ♄ worse, troubling me to swallow, aguish at night & headach. 9 ☉ at night the soreness began to amend.

27 ♃ I sent with Mr. Tho: Miller in partnership for a small parcell of Linens to St Malo. not above £160 in all & this was my first entrance into Trade.

Oct. 6 ♂ About 11h a.m. Went over Guldeford ferry to Brookland & Snave about my Father's business, returning home at 6h p.m.

16 ♀ News that part of the Linens sent for August 27 last, viz. 40 pieces of Kentings value £16 were safely arrived at London.

Dec. 13 ☉ News that the residue valued about £88 were likewise safely arrived there.

1675

Jan. 6 ☿ About 4h 30′ p.m. My Father gave me £25 to imploy in Trade.

Feb. 1 ☽ Received the Linens safe at Rye.

Mar. 13 ♄ Returned £100 to London, between Mr. Tho: Miller & my self; to be remitted to Morlaix to buy Lockrams.

29 ☽ My Father gave me £40 to Trade with.

Apr. 12 ☽ About 7h 30′ a.m. I rode to Pembury to agree about the settlement of the lands & to receive my Rent, both which effected, though the first with much adoe. At Hawkhurst I met with some showers of hail, else had fair weather. I came to Pembury at

---

1674 [1] On Jeake's cousin Jane Key see 20.12.66.

[2] Jeake evidently refers to making a projection into two dimensions of the three-dimensional state of the visible heavens at the moment of his birth (in contrast to the standard horoscope, which was purely diagrammatic). This was a standard astological practice. Cf. Selmes MS 56/1, fol. 13v.

2h 15′ p.m. And having concluded concerning raising the fines & settling the land, I returned the next day about 2h p.m. & came to Rye about 8h p.m. having fair & sunshine weather, but the wind high.

May 14 ♀ News that the first parcell of Lockrams costing per Invoice 1107L 14s french, were arrived safe at London.

25 ♂ They came safe into Rye harbour.

26 ☿ I rode with my Father to Burwash to joyn in the acknowledging the fine about the partition of the Lands & sealing the Indentures leading to the uses: which after some opposition was effected. Returned home at night, & wet pretty much with rain the last 5 mile.

July 21 ☿ Linens to the value of 579L 9s french, between Mr. Tho: Miller & my self, arrived safe at London from St Malo.

22 ♃ About 1h 30′ p.m. My Father gave me £45 11s 6d all in Gold, to trade with. This I am much inclin'd to think the Effect of the Direction of the 2d house ad sextilem Solis. & that there is a Sympathy between the Planet Sol & that metall. For once before I observed a Significatrix in the 2d house Venus directed to the very same Promittor, to signify a Gift in Gold, May 6 1672.

29 ♃ Remitted 433⅓ crowns at 57⅜d per crown to Morlaix in partnership with Mr. Tho: Miller for Linens bought there.

Aug. 2 ☽ *Silver tobacco box engraven given me by my C[ousin]* 2h p.m.

5 ♃ Received the St Malo's Linens safe at Rye. The same day sent over to Dieppe 193 crowns to be remitted to St Malo.

8 ☉ News that the 2d parcell of Lockrams costing per Invoice 1789L 10s were arrived safe at London.

12 ♃ About 8h a.m. I Rode to Westfield with Mr. Th: Miller, where met accidentally with my Aunt Dighton, *who mentioned me both to* Mrs. *Weeks and her daughter without my approval.*[1] Returned the next day.

Sept. 15 ☿ About 1h p.m. Rode with Mr. A.G.[2] to Pembury to take

---

1675 [1] Elizabeth Dighton was sister of Samuel Jeake senior and wife of Christopher, a glazier of Wapping. She had been married three times, her first husband being Abraham Goph of Rye and her second Nathaniel Bonnick. Smart, p. 79; PAB 299.

[2] Perhaps Allan Grebell, a Rye acquaintance of the Jeakes, whose will was witnessed by the elder Jeake. Burchall, p. 105; PAB 298; Selmes MS 40/4–5.

accompt of the value of the Timber on my Land. Came home next day at 6h p.m. had good weather.

Sept. 16 ♃ Lockrams to the value of £160 sterling between Mr. Miller & my self; came safe to Rye.

This summer I made 13 Astrological Exercitations, comprehended in 45 pages in 4°.[3]

Nov. 10 ☿ I sold my Timber at Capell for £58 5s of which £30 5s to be paid this month & £28 Sept. 29 next.

Dec. 19 ☉ News that 29 pieces of Lockrams between Mr. Miller & my self, were arrived at London.

1676

Jan. 10 ☽ Resolved to seek *Mrs. Weeks in marriage.*

19 ☿ About 8h p.m. £20 given me by my Father which I borrowed of him August 23th last.

Feb. 12 ♃ The 29 pieces of Lockrams value about £130 arrived in the harbour of Rye.

28 ☽ About 10h a.m. Rode to Pembury to enquire a Chapman for my Land. came thither about 6h 30′ p.m.

29 ♂ Returned home by Brenchly & Goudherst. came to Rye 6h p.m. had very good weather.

Mar. 6 ☽ 34¼ pieces of Lockrams between Mr. Miller & my self came into Rye harbor from Morlaix: but stowed at bottom that could not be took out.

20 ☽ About 10h a.m. *I spoke to John Weeks about my intentions of seeking his sister in marriage if unmarried at his mother's death.*

24 ♀ News that the 34¼ pieces of Lockrams were safe at London, & that another Vessel wherein were 32 pieces ditto, was arrived in the Thames.

31 ♀ News that another ship wherein 30½ pieces of Lockrams were laden between T[homas] M[iller] & me at Morlaix was arrived at London.

Apr. 26 ☿ 96¾ pieces of Lockrams cost about £440 sterling between T[homas] M[iller] & my self came safe from London into the harbour of Rye.

[3] Now Selmes MS 38.

May 1 ☽ About 7h 30′ a.m. Rode to Burwash fair to receive some Rent, & home about 10h p.m. the weather fair, but very hot.

10 ☿ About 2h p.m. *having some conference with John Weeks and by him his sisters answer. I wrote her a letter* 2h 30′ p.m. *which sent by him.*

24 ☿ About 8h 45′ a.m. my Father went to Dovor to see to prevent the serving the writ de Excommunicato Capiendo, if the Court at Lewes[1] should excommunicate him & take out the writ, he having been cited Apr. 21 ♀ last.

25 ♃ About 5h p.m. News of a Chapman for my Land.[2]

June 1 ♃ Eclipse of the Sun in the forenoon. About 6h 15′ a.m. I rode to Pembury to treat with him, but he failed of coming, nor was he at home so returned next day, re infectâ,[3] & came home about noon. Windy weather all the journey, & misling rain for 15 miles outwards.

14 ☿ About 10h p.m. News per post in a Letter to my Father that he was excommunicated.

28 ☿ News from G[eorge] C[astel] the before mentioned Chapman offering £80 for the Land.

July 5 ☿ I rode to London to examine the Record of a Fine for Mr. Lewis Gillart senior to testify it at a Tryal he was to have at Sussex Assizes, lodged at Goudherst that night.

6 ♃ Rode to Somerhil to Geo: Castel & sold him my land about 11h a.m. for £85 10s[;] came to London about 5h 30′ p.m.

7 ♀ Examined the Record at the Chirographers office.

10 ☽ I came out of London about 6h a.m. got to Tunbridge about noon, staid there neer 2 hours, came to Rye, about 8h p.m.

15 ♄ About 11h a.m. Rode to the Assizes at East Grinsted, to witness the Record; like to be through wet with a Thunder shower about ½ a mile from Groombridge, but secured by a Lodge; else had good weather. Lodged at Groombridg.

17 ☽ Rode to Grinsted, & came thither about 8h a.m. & the business

---

1676 [1] i.e. the archdeacon's court.

[2] i.e. George Castel: cf. 28.6, 6.7.76. Probably the cook (and landowner) from Tonbridge, Kent, whose will was proved in 1696. KAO DRb/PWr/28: 44.

[3] Latin for 'without accomplishing the matter'.

being put to reference I returned next day about 10h a.m. & came home 8h p.m. the sky clear & weather very hot.

July 18 ♂ Almost as soon as I came home, perceived some pimples on my left side inclining toward the Spine, which proved the Shingles being I suppose bred with the heat of the weather & disorder of the Journey; next day very sore & 20 ♃ they itched extremely especially in the night. so 21 ♀ on which day I used Unguentum Nutritum, whereby the pain was abated that night, & by next Wednesday almost perfectly well.

Aug. 2 ♀ About 5h a.m. Rode to Pembury to receive the money for my land which having done & delivered possession, I came home that night about 9h 30′ p.m. had very good weather *and cheerful on the road. The last deep fit of melancholy being* July 18. *Lost in my return from Grinstead; from hence became more cheerful.*

29 ♂ About 10h p.m. A kind of aguish fit succeeded by the headach & an extreme lassitude all 30 ☿ & a sweat in the night after.

Sept. 6 ♀ Rode to the Meeting at Tenterden & home at night.[4]

14 ♃ About 10h a.m. Rode to Robertsbridge Fair *to get opportunity to speak to M[ary] W[eeks] but could not.* came home about 8h p.m.

Oct. 9 ☽ A small parcell of Noyals between T[homas] M[iller] & my self arrived safe at Rye from London.

19 ♃ About 6h p.m. An Aguish fit, but gentle.

27 ♀ Upon advice from Morlaix that Herrings might sell well there. Mr. Miller & I rode to Hasting about 7h 45′ a.m. & bought 83 barrels; & having left order for 40 more to be bought, we came home next day about 4h 30′ p.m. had very good weather.

Nov. 2 ♃ About 10h a.m. we rode again to Hasting & brought more herrings making up 136½ barrels, came back 3 ♀ at 4h p.m. & home at 6h p.m. had stormy & rainy weather in the last 4 miles as we went, else good.

6 ☽ I rode again to Hasting about 9h a.m. to repack the herrings to save freight[;] came thither about 11h 30′ a.m. & imployed men presently, staying to see it done till 8 ☿ when they were reduced to 105½ barrels; Then, having bought some more & left

---

[4] This was probably a nonconformist meeting held at Robert Harding's house between Smallhythe and Tenterden, which the elder Jeake had been invited to attend in 1665. FRE 4426.

them to be repackt &c. came back to Rye at 4h 30′ p.m. & home 6h 30′ p.m. had very good weather.

10 ♀ I rode again to Hasting about 9h a.m. to get boats to lade the Herrings aboard of R.M.'s sloop (which we had fraighted to Morlaix) but the Sloop came not that Tide into the Road; so returned that night.[5]

13 ☽ Mr. Miller rode thither about the same business, & the Sloop coming into Hasting road the herrings were all put aboard this day: & the next day returning into Rye harbour, was filled up by 15 ☿.

15 ☽ About 1h 15′ p.m. The Sloop set saile for Morlaix with $135\frac{1}{2}$ barrels of Herrings between Mr. Miller & me. The weather very fair & wind at North East.

29 ☿ News per post this evening from Procter & Sedgwick of Morlaix, that the Sloop was Thanks be to God arrived safely there on the 19th ☉.

Dec. 11 ☽ News per post of the arrival of $48\frac{1}{4}$ pieces of Lockrams worth about £180 between T[homas] M[iller] & me, safe at London.

25 ☽ News per post that R.M.'s Sloop with $143\frac{3}{4}$ pieces of Lockrams to the value of 6906L 8s french or about £530 sterling between Mr. Miller and my self, was thanks be to God safe at Falmouth the 17th Instant having put to Sea from Morlaix the 14th.

30 ♄ News per post, that he arrived at Cowes in the Isle of Wight the 23th Instant having put out from Falmouth the 21th.

1677

Jan. 6 ♄ About 1h p.m. After we had expected the coming in of the Sloop til $\frac{1}{2}$ or $\frac{3}{4}$ Ebb, & were gone home in some discomposure: because the wind was fair, though high, & very thick misty misling weather, She came into the harbour, assoon as we were at home: having put out of Cowes yesterday about 10h a.m. This was the greatest Venture that ever I had by Sea before this time, in the safe Return whereof I shall allwayes acknowledge the gracious Providence of God.

8 ☽ Unladed our goods, 5 or 6 ballots damaged by wet, but inconsiderable.

5 'R.M.' was probably the Hastings mariner Robert Moore. FRE 4856; Selmes MS 40/3.

Jan. 22 ☽ About 8h a.m. Mr. *Jenkins offered his advice to my* C[ousin] *to speak for my marriage with* Mrs. *Ann File which my* C[ousin] *told me of about* 9h a.m.[1]

28 ☉ About 11h a.m. Taken with a Tertian Ague, the cold fit continuing about 2 houres, afterwards a violent headach till 12h p.m.

30 ♂ About 10h 45′ a.m. the 2d fit. cold for 2 hours & more violent than the former, with vomiting, & breaking out of the Lips. The hot fit & headach much more gentle than last & pretty well off before I went to bed.

Feb. 1 ♃ About 8h a.m. the 3d fit much like the 2d lasted till 6h p.m.

3 ♄ About 7h 45′ a.m. the 4th fit, like the 3d but much gentler, & mostly off by 2h p.m.

5 ☽ About 7h a.m. the 5th & last fit, very gentle, without any vomiting or much shaking, & pretty well off before noon. Very weak with this ague so that my strength was not recovered in some time.

This morning the 48¼ pieces of Lockrams to the value of £200 that arrived some time since at London, came safe to Rye.

26 ☽ A violent pain in my Teeth all day.

Mar. 5 ☽ News per post of some loss by Herrings we sent to London. And by several posts from Morlaix before (the first about February 7 last) News that our herrings went off very slowly & at some loss.

7 ☿ News from thence of 40 barrels more sold at somewhat more loss than the former; so that we feared there would be £40 loss in the whole; but in conclusion we lost but £20.

8 ♃ About 7h p.m. Taken with a very violent pain of the Teeth, continuing all night & next day & till midnight after: then my Cheek swelled & the pain abated.

Apr. 6 ♀ A Cold: violent 7 ♄ & 8 ☉. then abated.

10 ♂ About 7h a.m. Rode to Bourne[2] & other places to get in debts & Customers for Lockrams, lodged at Haylsham that night.

1677 [1] George Jenkins was a gentleman from Hothfield, Kent. The Files were gentlefolk from Wye, Kent. Ann File later married Elhanan Tucker (see 30.10.86) by licence. Cowper, p. 583.
[2] i.e. Eastbourne. Cf. 26.6.77.

11 ☿ Came back to Battel, Seddlescombe & Westfield; & 12 ♃ home. had fair weather over head, but the wind extreme high.

13 ♀ About 9h p.m. News per post from Morlaix that all our herrings were sold; & the losse but £19 2s much less then at first we feared. News also that our last orders for Linens were almost completed & would speedily be shipt.

29 ☉ News per post that 5 ballots Lockrams value about 1200L french between Mr. Miller & my self were safe as far as the Downes.[3]

A Comet appeared April 19 in the morning in the NNE between the left foot of Andromeda & the Base of the Triangle, almost on the Line of my Medium Coeli: about the bigness of a Star of the first magnitude, with a Tail visibly about ½ a yard long, & seen for several days.

May 2 ☿ News per post of the arrival of the before-mentioned Lockrams at London; & of the arrival of 5 ballots more there, of the like value, in another Vessell.

14 ☽ About 8h p.m. Coming down out of a neighbour's Garret (where had been to prevent a fire &c) at the bottom step, it being only a Stave; my foot slipped & I broke my left Shin, & it was a great mercy that I did not break my leg. Saturn & the Sun in conjunction in the beginning of Gemini in opposition to the Cusp of the 1st.

15 ♂ The 10 ballots Lockrams value about £200 came safe from London into Rye harbour.

June 11 ☽ About 10h a.m. Rode to Appledoor fair to meet with Mr. Geo: Jenkins, & thence to his house with him *to see* Mrs. *Ann File.*

12 ♂ Rode with him & his wife to Wye to Mrs. File's. *here saw her daughter about* 1h p.m. lodged there that night. Next day to see Mr. Scot at Lymindge & back to Wye at night.

14 ♃ About 5h p.m. went from Wye to Hoathfield to Mr. Jenkins's house, & 15 ♀ about 9h 30′ a.m. from thence home about 2h 30′ p.m. had good weather.

26 ♂ About 4h 30′ a.m. Rode to Bourne to receive debts for Lockrams, came home at 9h 30′ p.m. very hot weather & little wind.

---

[3] Part of the sea within the Goodwin Sands, off the east coast of Kent.

July 7 ♄ *A letter from* Mr. *Jenkins that he had spoke to Mistress File and her daughter but refused.*

  25 ☿ About 10h a.m. Rode to Ewherst fair, came home at 10h p.m. good weather, only hot.

Aug. 4 ♄ About 10h p.m. my Father taken ill with an Ague, & ill all next day. 6 ☽ About noon a second fit very violent with vomiting & a lasque, very ill all night & next day & full of pain. 8 ☿ a most violent fit, with a terrible pain in the back for about 3 hours; very neer death; but it pleased God he recovered by degrees, in a moneth or two.

  21 ♂ About 13h 30′ p.m. An oppression in my stomach; much Rheum running out of my mouth, but could not vomit: soon over.

Sept. 7 ♀ About 8h a.m. *part of the pre*[   ] *cut to cross the F*[   ]*, but being done unskilfully was fain to be done again* September 13 ♃ *about* 7h 45′ *a.m. like to bleed to death by cutting one of the veins not well till* 28th ♀.[4] Mars on the Eastern finitor in conjunction with Venus.

Oct. 1 ☽ Taken with a Quotidian Ague, or rather a double Tertian about 2h p.m. Gentle a little shivering. Went off with a pain in the head & sweat.

  2 ♂ About 5h p.m. a 2d fit; scarce sensible.

  3 ☿ About 1h p.m. a 3d fit; as the 1st but worse.

  4 ♃ About 4h p.m. a 4th fit: gentle.

  5 ♀ About 4h p.m. a 5th fit: gentle, off by 8h p.m. but sweat as before in the night.

Nov. 30 ♀ About noon rode over to Stone being sent for to make Jno Hall's will, who put me in Executor, which I afterwards desired to be freed from & he put in another:[5] Return'd at night, weather Rainy.

1678

Jan. 4 ♀ Finished 4 accompts of Goods in partnership with Mr Tho: Miller & received £22 profit & £3 balance.

  31 ♃ *The pre*[   ] *began to run back and after* March 1 *never restored.*

---

[4] Evidently a reference to an operation to deal with Jeake's fistula. See Introduction, sect. 7.
[5] John Hall was a yeoman from Stone, Isle of Oxney, Kent. In his lengthy will, Hall referred to an inventory drawn up by himself and Jeake in 1677. AMS 5742/17; KAO PRC/17/76: 49.

Feb. 12 ♂ No. 194. Littletons Tenures in English. 8° [new edn., 1621].

 17 ☉ About 7h 30′ p.m. I saw at Rye the rare conjunction of Saturn & the Moon where the Moon eclipsed Saturn. She about this Instant beginning to cover him: the unilluminated part of the Moon first coming over him; for, just before; they stood thus.

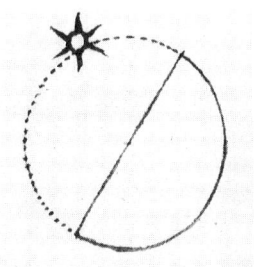

 ditto In the night taken with a Cold and hoarseness, which encreased much by morning.

 18 ☽ At night my Cold being much worse, took some Theriaca Andromachi, which through God's blessing sensibly abated it before morning.

 20 ☿ News of a Ship worth £30000 sterling coming from Morlaix for London, cast away neer to Calais, all the men, & most part of the goods lost. Supposed to be one of the Ships that Procter & Sedgwick, advised T[homas] M[iller] & me to have goods by; in December last, before the war. But we being apprehensive of no war, gave no order: & so providentially escaped the Losse.

Mar. 3 ☉ In the Evening, Venus cast a perfect and distinct shadow, as the Moon a little after the New.

 7 ♃ Intentions of sending for Canvas upon the news of the Prohibition of french goods that would commence the 20th Instant. But my mind altered the next day; & it was well it did, for those that sent overstockt themselves, so that they could not sell it, till some of it was seiz'd: the time of sale allowed by Parliament being elapsed, &c.

 9 ♄ Sent for a small parcell of Paper, Wine & Brandy to Dieppe. in partnership with Mr. Harris & Mr. Shinner; which came over

safe 14 ♃ about noon. being no more in all then 5 Punchions of Brandy. 1 of Wine & 2 bales Paper, Sold with profit.[1]

Mar. 16 ♄ *Finished my address to my C[ousin] about seeking M[ary] W[eeks] in marriage, which presented to him* 19 ♂ *a little after noon, and in the evening he gave me his consent. Whereon* 20 ☿ *resolved to go next Tuesday.*

22 ♀ News, that the Act for prohibiting the importation of French goods for 3 years was passed the 20th Instant whereby I lost my trade with France.

26 ♂ About 8h a.m. Rode to Battell. *and thence to Westfield whither came about* 4h 15′ p.m. *and about* 5h p.m. *spake to M[ary] W[eek]s' mother for her consent to seek her daughter in marriage; and* 27 ☿ *about* 9h a.m. *spake to her C[ousin] but had no encouragement from either; only liberty to speak to her, which did about* 11h a.m. *But she told me her mother had that day bid her deny me though she had [. . .] given me her consent. Had 3 hours talk with her and after this came away at* 3h 30′ p.m. *and home about* 6h p.m.

Apr. 4 ♃ About 8h 45′ a.m. Rode to Rolvenden & came home again at 9h p.m.

9 ♂ About 7h 30′ a.m. Rode to Battel market *to speak to* Mr. *Weeks and his son about the premises, but he desired me to forbear any further applications.* came home at 8h 30′ p.m.

22 ☽ About 8h 45′ a.m. Rode to Stone to make another will for Jno Hall, wherein as before I was made Executor with a Legacy &c. but altered afterwards at my desire, as before mentioned.[2] came home at 6h 15′ p.m.

May 27 ☽ About 8h a.m. Rode to Bodiham faire *to speak to* Mr. *Weeks about* 3h 30′ p.m. *who with much importunity and unwillingly granted me leave to mention it once more to his daughter.* came home about midnight. 29 ☿ *about* 9h a.m. *I rode to Westfield and came thither about* 11h a.m. *with a letter from my C[ousin] to Mrs. W[eeks] but not being accepted returned home* 30 ♃ *after dinner and came to Rye about* 3h p.m. *unconcerned.*

1678 [1] Edmund Harris, mariner, was one of the richer inhabitants of Rye in 1660. Burchall, p. 108. On Shinner or Skinner see Appendix 3.

[2] See 30.11.77.

June 18 ♂ About 10h a.m. A fit of the Toothach, continuing without intermission for 24 hours but not very violent: then swell'd & went away.

25 ♂ 26 ☿ & 28 ♀. Busied in drawing Groundplots of houses, & considering the laws of Architecture thereabouts.[3]

July 9 ♂ sent to Dan: Hays of Dublin, for 4 Tons of Tallow between my self & others for a Tryal.

23 ♂ About 7h 15′ a.m. Rode to Goudherst, Brenchley & Pembury, came thither about 9h p.m.

24 ☿ Came to Maidstone about noon.

26 ♀ About 4h p.m. went thence & came to Cranbrook about 9h 30′ p.m. next day went home by Rolvenden & Tenterden came to Rye about 7h p.m. had fine weather.

31 ☿ About 2h p.m. Taken ill of a Feaver, which proved a very bad & irregular one: accompanied with great restlessness. Not free from it & it's consequents in some months time. This first fit lay much in my head a little in my back & thighs, I was not very cold nor shaking, but toward night hot, yet did not sweat at all.

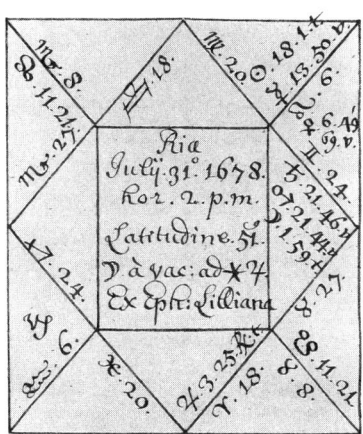

[3] These plans showing possible alternative layouts for the ground floor of a house survive as Selmes MS 47/1–4: the first three date from the period noted in the diary, the fourth from the following January.

Saturn & Mars are remarkably posited here in exact conjunction, on the Cusp of the 8th[.] And indeed I have often observed that when the body is full of peccant humours, they usually discover themselves, when the Planets especially the Infortunes are in some Critical places viz: the Cusps of the 8th 12th or 6th houses, or the Cusps of some of the Angles. And that violent falls or suddain & unthought of Accidents fall out when either Saturn or Mars are upon the Cusp of some Angle.

Aug. 2 ♀ The 2d fit of my Feaver. Very hot in the night.

3 ♄ I took a scruple of Extractum Rudii, which wrought well. I was free from the feaver all day, but stomachless. In the night had a 3d fit of the Feaver, somewhat bad; could not sleep a wink nor sweat at all.

5 ☽ An extreme bad night with the 4th fit. & so restless, that I put on my Cloths at 1 a clock in the morning, & lay upon the bed, where fell a sleep till 7 a clock & the feaver gone.

6 ♂ In the night had a 5th fit. Very little, but I hardly slept at all.

7 ☿ Weak, stomachless, & could not sleep, in the night had a 6th fit.

9 ♀ In the night a 7th fit; but not very much.

10 ♄ Could not sleep in the night.

11 ☉ In the night the 8th fit, but very little. Took some Diascordium to procure sleep, & laid some leaves of deadly nightshade to my forehead & temples & through mercy slept better than I had done at all since this illness.

13 ♂ I took another scruple of Extractum Rudii, which wrought much & I slept well at night. But the 3 next nights could not sleep till toward Saturday morning, then a fine sleep which much refresht me; but the night following slept very badly again.

18 ☉ Slept very well all night & sweat much. and had the like good nights till 23 ♀.

23 ♀ About 3h p.m. Rising from off the bed I felt my self ill & aguish, till even, then my feaver took me, viz. the 9th fit, & held me all night though moderately; but very little sleep.

25 ☉ A little feaver the 10th fit; in the night: not much sleep.

27 ♂ First went abroad; slept ill at night.

30 ♀ About 2h p.m. Taken a little aguish & then feaverish (the 11th fit) then a little sweating, but all went off in 2 hours, in the night slept indifferently & sweat very much.

Sept. 1 ☉ About noon vomited, & taken with the cold fit being the 2d of my ague (or 12th of the feaver) but moderate, lasted an houre, then vomited again, after came the hot fit, & lasted till 3h p.m. then went off in sweat.

3 ♂ About 11h a.m. taken with the 3d fit of my ague, vomited twice, the cold fit lasted 3 hours, & the hot fit as long. then went off in sweat.

5 ♃ About noon, taken with the 4th fit, & vomited yellow Choler several times, about 1h 15 p.m. the hot fit, but very gentle, held till 3h p.m. sweat afterwards, very weak.

7 ♄ About 11h 30′ a.m. the 5th fit. very moderate, but one vomit. about 1h p.m. the hot fit exceeding gentle lasted 1½ hour, then sweat.

9 ☽ About noon, the 6th fit, very gentle, slept till 2h p.m. then waked in the hot fit which very little & soon went off in sweat. slept better then usual in the night & sweat extraordinarily.

11 ☿ About 1h p.m. A little inclination to vomit no cold fit but about 2h p.m. grew feaverish (the 7th fit) till 3h 15′ p.m. then went off as 9 ☽.

13 ♀ About 11h a.m. The 8th fit of my Ague worse than before, vomited, after the hot fit came pretty strong lasted till 3h p.m. then went off as before.

14 ♄ In the morning news per post, that the 4 Tons of Tallow were safe arrived at London. This day I took a vomit being Infusion of Crocus Metallorum, which wrought well. slept very little in the night.

15 ☉ About 10h 30′ a.m. The 9th fit, worst of all (except vomiting) the cold fit held till about 1h p.m. the hot fit till 2h 45′ p.m. & at its' latter end very violent, then sweat till neer 6h p.m. Slept well in the night as I usually did in this Ague on the Ague nights, but very little on the other.

17 ♂ About 9h 30′ a.m. The 10th fit, the cold fit lasting till 1h 30′ p.m. moderate. the hot fit till 4h p.m. gentle, succeeded by a little sweat.

Sept. 19 ♃ About 9h a.m. The 11th fit, cold till 1h p.m. hot till 3h p.m. moderate. Troubled with the falling down of the Uvula, worse 20 ♀.

21 ♄ About noon, The 12th fit. no cold fit but all hot, lasted till 3h p.m. moderate. This day & next my throat worse, spit much thick flegm, Scorbutick pains in my Limbs &c.

23 ☽ News that the Tallow was sold to some small loss, not above 15s for my part.

24 ♂ About 10h a.m. Taken with a pain in my Back, shoulders & Legs, for 3 or 4 hours. About 10h a.m. A Brick fell from the Top of the Chimney as I sate by the fire; but hearing it fall I avoided the place, but it fell in the midst of the fire, & not where I sate.

26 ♃ About 10h a.m. Taken cold. About 11h a.m. A violent shaking fit of an Ague, lasted for an hour; made my Teeth chatter in my head, had 2 or 3 vomits & as many stools, in the shaking fit. After that was over; the hot fit was very gentle. Off by 3h p.m. but no sweat.

28 ♄ About noon the 2d fit, shook me very much, with 3 vomits &c, after 1h 15 p.m. the hot fit all the afternoon.

30 ☽ About 3h p.m. the 3d fit. cold but without shaking, & but 1 vomit &c. lasted till 6h p.m. the hot fit very little.

Oct. 2 ☿ I put my self into a Physical sweat yet had some small matter of my Ague about 5h p.m. Slept indifferent well all the time of this Ague, & sweat not much, on the intermitting days sometimes troubled with a pain in the back.

8 ♂ After dinner an Aguish fit, moderate but long cold viz till 4h p.m. feaverish till next morning, & neither sweat nor slept scarce at all.

9 ☿ About 1h p.m. A 2d fit. cold, but gentle, like to vomit at 3h p.m. the feaver held till 5h p.m. then sweat & went off.

10 ♃ About 2h p.m. A pain in my back, & after a little aguish & not well all night.

11 ♀ Took 1 scruple of Extractum Rudii. wrought well. about 3h p.m. a little aguish & pain in the back.

12 ♄ In the afternoon, the same pain & aguishness. but none afterward till Wednesday next.

16 ☿ About 4h 30′ p.m. A little fit of an Ague, shivering till 8h p.m. then the feaver. Took some Venice Treacle, & sweat.

18 ♀ About 5h p.m. A 2d fit. cold till 8h p.m. then the feaver till 10h p.m. both moderate.

20 ☉ About 6h p.m. A 3d fit, cold & shivering till 9h p.m. but moderate; after the feaver & sweat.

21 ☽ About 9h p.m. A little aguish, but slept well, with a little sweat. Afterwards began to recover, sleeping well, & my Urine turning pale as in health, the pain of the back gone, & my strength & appetite returning.

23 ☿ Mended more, & my Urine now free from the white Gravell that used to be in it; in my Agues. About 8h p.m. a little remembrance of an Ague for an houre. Very hungry & a good digestion (as alwaies after the last dose of Pills) Slept very well & my sweating much decreased.

Note. That whilst I had this Sickness it was an exceeding sickly time all over England with the like distemper, & also in the Netherlands France & Sweden: Very mortal at some places; but through mercy not so at Rye; yet I observed that all were a long time recovering, & commonly relapsed into an ague again before quite well.

24 ♃ At this time I may esteem my self by God's blessing recovered, only my strength not fully restored, which gradually encreasing by the middle of November I was very well.

Nov. 1 ♀ or about this Time; In the night I had a dream, which made some more than ordinary impression upon me: the Circumstances of which I well remember at the writing hereof viz: August 20 1694. & are as followeth. I dreamed that I saw the Sun appearing in the West as if he were about the Cusp of the 8th house of Heaven, of so great a magnitude that his Diameter was thrice as long as the visible diameter of the Sun, which made him shew 9 or 10 times bigger than the true Sun: but he lookt so pale & watrish, that I could stedfastly behold him without the least injury to my sight. But which was more strange, all his Superficies (excepting only the middle just about the visible bigness of the Sun in the firmament) was fill'd with horsemen & their horses, all in Confusion; trampling upon one another; some riding, some overthrown; as in the rout of an Army: &

much like to that depicted in the figures of the Battel of Cannae in Raleighs' history of the world, especially the first, in the confused posture of the first skirmishers of the Roman & Carthaginian horse.[4] And moreover about the Circumference of the Sun's body I saw in my dream the Characters of the 12 Signes, described in aequidistance; Libra being uppermost towards the Zenith; all perfect only that of Pisces defective, thus ♓. I thought I beheld this appearance a long time, & that it continued so, without the least Variation. Behold a rough Idea thereof.

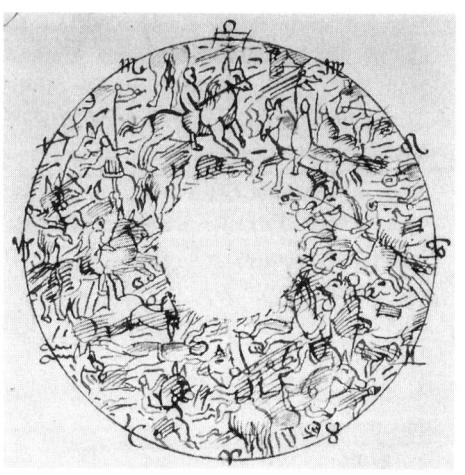

Whether my looking on those Figures in Raleigh, in whom I used to read at that time, did any way contribute to the constitution of those confused formes represented to my Fancy in the aforesaid Dream, I know not. Nor will I be positive in determining that it was Fatidical. I shall only set down what Conjectural Thoughts I then had of it's probable Signification; viz. Because the Apparition was of the Sun environed with the Characters of the 12 signs, I conjectured that it was to be interpreted consentaneously to Astrological Principles: & that therefore I was signifyed by the Sun because he was Lord of the

---

[4] The Battle of Cannae is dealt with in Bk. 5, ch. 3, sect. 8 of Ralegh's *The History of the World* (London, 1614, and subsequent edns.); the illustrations of it appear between pp. 452 and 453, and 454 and 455 in the 1614 edn.

Ascendent in my Nativity. And that his appearing of so great a Magnitude, denoted a proportionable encrease of my estate, & the figure that should attend it. But his looking so pale, that any one might behold him as long as they pleas'd without prejudice to the sight; portended that I should never be in any Place of Honor or Authority over others. The surrounding of his Center with the horsemen in their confused postures, presignifyed a multitude of Enemies, & their motion endeavouring to penetrate to the Center it self; noted their many Efforts to destroy me. But whereas the middle part of the Sun during the whole time of the appearance remained perfectly clear & free from being invaded by the horsemen, notwithstanding all their perpetual attempts to enter it; so that they seemed to be restrained by an invisible power: this I thought signifyed the Divine protection & special Providence of God still preserving me out of the hands of mine Enemies: & never suffering them to ruine me: & hath often brought to my mind that passage of Jacob in his blessing to Joseph, Genesis 49. 23, 24. The Archers have sorely grieved him, & shot at him, & hated him. But his Bow abode in strength, & the arms of his hands were made strong, by the hands of the mighty God of Jacob: from thence is the shepherd, the stone of Israel. And whereas I beheld this Phoenomenon a long time without any variation of Magnitude or other circumstances, & still as it were fixed on the Cusp of the 8th house, which is the house of Death: I supposed it to denote the continuance of my estate & condition for several years, even untill the time of my Death. Moreover as Libra seemed to occupy the Medium Coeli, which was quite opposite in my Radix: so it seem'd that the Heavens were revers'd to me: & I might (as in a glass) see them turn'd topsy-turvy, as to any hopes of preferment by Honors or Offices. And as the Character of Pisces was broken off & defective, so it signifyed that my Father, whose Ascendent that Sign was, should receive some prejudice & be partly separated from me; but not totally, nor for ever: because the greater part of the Character remained.

30 ♄ About 1h p.m. Going out in a very cold day, caught a great pain in my head, which after I came home turned to the fit of an Ague, & then hot & sweat, but not violent.

Dec. 23 ☽ About 9h 30′ a.m. 5 *limned pictures given me by Robert Brown.*

145

1679

Jan. 31 ♀ About 7h a.m. Rode to Burwash with a Letter from some of the Freemen to Mr. Polhill to stand for Burgess of Rye, but he refus'd it.[1] came home 7h p.m. good weather, but bad ways.

Mar. 3 ☽ About 8h a.m. I rode to London, to get some Factory, & Correspondencyes at several places, but it succeeded not. came to Riverhead about 6h p.m. wind pretty high & cold & at Sevenoke a little Snow. Next day snow'd all the forenoon, at noon went for London, snow'd when at Bromly & Lewsham, came to London 5h p.m.

5 ☿ And all the rest of this week, spent about getting Correspondents: but came to no effect.

10 ☽ About 8h 30′ a.m. Came from London, & to Lamberhurst that night: some rain by the way; frequent, but moderate.

11 ♂ About 7h 30′ a.m. Went from Lamberhurst & home to Rye about 30′ p.m. very foggy & some rain the first part of the way.

After I came home, at my Leisure, especially March 19 wrote to divers Correspondents, but the times favoured not my indeavours.

Apr. 29 ♂ Wrote to Rouen for the value of 200 Livres in Fans, Gloves &c. for a Tryall.

May 22 ♃ Lent £10 first on Bottomarie, which used frequently afterwards.

26 ☽ Advice that the Fans &c. were sent to Dieppe.

27 ♂ Bought a small parcell of Timber in partnership with Mr. Tho: Markwick, by which lost some small matter.

July 3 ♃ Bought a prize taken by an Ostender in partnership with L: Gillart for £100 to be redeemed at 2s per £ profit.[2] 4h p.m. This day first began to negotiate bills of Exchange, which used several years after.

4 ♀ About 7h 45′ a.m. Rode out to Brede & Westfield to borrow money for the present for the buying of Prizes; met with £168 which borrowed, returning home at 5h 30′ p.m.

7 ☽ In the forenoon we bought 2 fisherboats prizes, for £97 4s.

1679 [1] Edward Polhill of Burwash was a lawyer, JP, and compiler of religious tracts. *DNB*; ESRO D 984/1; AMS 5744/12–16. See also note to 27.8.73.
[2] By an Ostender, Jeake means a ship from Ostend.

13 ☉ The goods I sent for from Rouen were brought to Rye, & 19 ♄ 10h p.m. I received them. Sold after to some Loss; & I never sent for any more; finding this Trade too full of Snares & Temptations to be exercised with a good Conscience. And therefore I esteem my self happy, that the Providence of God always prevented me from being imployed & engaged in the smugling Factoryes: even when for want of due Consideration of the Temptations, I endeavoured to procure them.

18 ♀ Rode to Brede & paid £100 of that I borrowed to buy prizes the 4th Instant. came home about 5h p.m. At night a pain in my teeth continuing by fits till 20 ☉. then no intermission day nor night but not very violent.

21 ☽ About 1h 45′ p.m. A fit of an ague, but little.

23 ☿ About 8h p.m. My Teeth having been uneasy a good while, began to ake thoroughly continuing till 7 a Clock next morning. then ceased; but neer noon began again, lasting all the afternoon & night, then decreasing & by morning 25 ♀ swelled very much & the pain almost quite gone.

Aug. 12 ♂ In the Evening, the pain began again but not violent held all night, & continually till Thursday morning 6 a Clock. swell'd pretty much.

N.B. When I received the mony for one of the prizes July 12 ♄ there were 48 Gold pistols, & August 19 ♂ in the receiving of £35 17 Guineys, & September 1 ☽ in the receiving of £40 35 Guineys. Q[uestion] whether the receiving Gold (not usually so frequent in payments here) be any way referrable to the Direction of Luna ad trinum Solis in my Nativity.

21 ♃ The swelling in my Jaws which proceeded from the Toothach, continuing grew hard & strumous, & my head out of order, with a vertiginous swimming: for both which had a vesicatory laid to my Neck this Evening with good success. The Tumor afterwards returning & becoming more obstinate I had another blister September 5 ♀ which run well & the Tumor abated. September 29 ☽ I began to take Volatile Salt of Vipers to discuss it's remaining hardness. 10 grains per diem till ½ an Ounce was out viz. till October 22 ☿ . all this time the swelling kept abating & was not troublesome. But after it returned & I was not free from it a long time, at length I found washing the Mouth with

Brandy to be a far Cheaper & much more speedy & effectual Medicine, which took it quite away.

Sept. 21 ☉ I began first in our Evening Meeting or conference, to speak about the Demonstration of the Trueness of the Christian Religion in an Argumentative way & according to Du Plessis his Method;[3] which I esteemed far beyond Grotius (who (notwithstanding the Noise his learning makes in the world) fixes Religion on the Basis of Tradition).[4] This I continued usually every Lord's day; till finished. Then I made an Entrance on Interpreting of the Revelation, In a way of short Comments & observing the Scope of the Prophecy. & having compared the Expositions of several writers, among which I generally found cause to prefer the sentiments of the Profound Apocalyptical Commentator Joseph Mede.[5] I found my self then not so fit for points of Doctrine & Application, & therefore more rarely meddled with them. In this course (though with sometimes of Intermission) I proceeded so far till I came in order to the 9th Chapter of the Revelation: & was prepared on March 11 ☉ 1682/3 to have interpreted the Effects of the fifth Trumpet, consisting in the opening of the bottomless pit, the smoke thence arising, the Locusts thence issuing &c. When, before I began, The Tribe of Persecutors, Enemies of all Righteousness disturbed us; & we were afterwards forced to meet in several parcells in our own families with 3 or 4 besides, Praying together, and repeating a Sermon.

Nov. 19 ☿ Aguish all day, & ill with a little Cold: so till 22 ♄ then pretty well again. 23 ☉ ill again with the Cold, & so most part of the Week.

Dec. 6 ♄ *About* 6h p.m. *news that old* Mrs. *Weeks was dead, whereon being* conc[eived?] *some engagement to her daughter though she conc*[eived?] *none to me I resolved to be absolutely discharged from her if she continued in her refusal.*

11 ♃ No. 195. Sir W: Raleighs' History of the World. Fol: [1614].

---

[3] Cf. Philip Duplessis Mornay, *De La Verité de la Religion Chrestienne* (1581).

[4] i.e. Hugo Grotius or de Groot (1583–1608); Jeake probably refers to his *De Veritate Religionis Christianae.*

[5] Joseph Mede (1586–1638), the Cambridge scholar and author of *Clavis Apocalyptica* (1627). See Booklist 204.

23 ♂ About 10h a.m. *rode to Westfield to see if I might be admitted as S[uitor] to M[ary] W[eeks] after her mother's death, but her C[ousin] refused. Came home that night.*

1680

Jan.   1 ♃ I began to keep my Accompts in a Liedger after the method set down in Chamberlain's Accomptants' Guide; which course I alwaies continued henceforward.[1]

13 ♂ No. 196. Tho: Browne, Religio Medici. 8° [1642].

16 ♀ Negotiated some Bills of Exchange, & more afterwards as they were brought to me, till I went to London in 1683. and again, after my Return till the War broke out between England & France.

21 ☿ About 8h 30′ or 9h a.m. *rode to Westfield to take my leave of M[ary] W[eeks], which finding no inclination in her did finally do the next day about 1h 30′ p.m., and came thence at 2h 30′ p.m., and home to Rye about 6h p.m. Nor were I at all concerned about it, and have since seen it a most happy circumstance that prevented it.*

Feb. 26 ♃ I sent £12 on Bottomarie or Adventure & continued that Trade for several years afterwards.

Apr. 27 ♂ In the night my Father taken very sick of a Feaver & pain in the right breast, continued very ill the 2 following dayes, & for a whole week: then began to mend very slowly, And after this time never enjoyed his health so well as formerly.

May 31 ☽ Received £100 of Mr. Tho: Miller for Lockrams in partnership; & this year we finished most of all the Accounts between us; & I got £104 6s 3d by the last Account of Linens. And gained £25 8s 2d by Negotiating Bills this year.

June 7 ☽ Resolved to seek Mrs. Elizabeth Hartshorn of the Age of 12 years & 8 moneths in Marriage, with the Consent of her Mother Mrs. Barbara Hartshorn of Rye. And this day about 3h p.m. went to her house to mention it; but prevented by Company from a convenient Opportunity.

1680 [1] i.e. Robert Chamberlain, *The Accomptants Guide or Merchants Book-Keeper* (1679). Cf. Jeake's surviving ledger for 1680–8, RYE 145/11.

June 8 ♂ About 1h p.m. I went again, & finding Mrs. Barbara Hartshorn alone had a fit opportunity to propose it immediately, which was accepted, & the portion argued, I insisting upon £1200. she first offered £500 in money, & the house she lived in (one of the best in the Towne)[2] which she rated at £200 & at last said she would make her a Fortune to me of £1000 viz. £700 in money £100 in Houshold Goods & the House valued at £200 which was above the Moiety of her whole estate, except her Joynture of £40 per annum during life, & she having a Son to provide for besides.

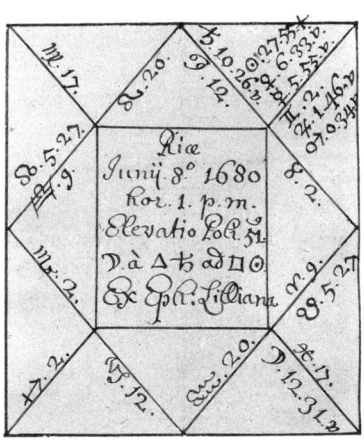

Note a Congeries of Jupiter, Mars, Venus & Mercury in conjunction in Gemini in trine to the Ascendant.

9 ☿ In the morning I acquainted my Father with what I had proposed &c. for his consent: for I had not acquainted him with it before. In the Evening I was at Mrs. Hartshorn's: & had some further discourse amongst which she told me that should she ask advice, none would advise her to give so much, & that she would not make the like offer to any other person in the World.

11 ♀ About 1h p.m. I went thither again, and staid about 4 hours; but we came to no conclusion. In the Evening I came to a Resolution in my own thoughts, & had my Father's consent to proceed as I pleased; & having a fit Opportunity of waiting on Mrs.

[2] i.e. Hartshorne House in Middle Street (now Mermaid Street).

Hartshorn to her own house, I told her about 9h p.m. that I had advised with my Father, and perceived him satisfied: And that I did comply with those termes she had proposed, & declare my self to be her most humble & most obedient son and servant for ever: which she respectfully accepted with expressions of satisfaction.

14 ☽ About 1h 30′ p.m. I went to Mrs. Barbara Hartshorn's; having her Consent to propose it to her Daughter Mrs. Eliz: Hartshorn; for whom I had an Affection from her Infancy. My first motion was as I remember to this Effect. My Dear Lady, the deep impression your person & vertues have made upon my mind oblige me to become your servant, and I beseech you Madam be pleased to believe the greatness of my Affection, to which be pleased to return me the favour of having a place in your heart. Sir (said she) it is so weighty a business that I am not capable of returning you an Answer without a long time of Consideration.

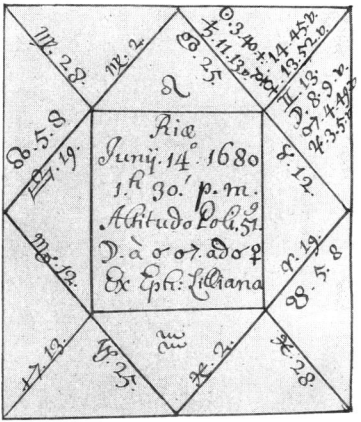

The rest of our discourse may be superfluous & impertinent to memorize, being continued till 4h p.m. After which I went to walking with her Mother & her & Cousin Mary Key,[3] & returning staid there till past 8h p.m. Note the Cluster of Planets in Gemini as before hinted & the Moon in the midst here carrying

---

[3] See 20.12.66.

the Influence of Jupiter & Mars to Venus & Mercury. Venus & Mars being Lords of the 1st & 7th. This seem'd to shew a successfull time for such addresses.

June 16 ☿ About 6h p.m. I went to Mrs. Barbara Hartshorn's, & having her approbation before, had now the declared consent of her Daughter.

19 ♄ I bought Rich: Hills's wooll;[4] this being the first year that I dealt in wooll, which I continued for several years afterwards. This year I bought about 29 packs.

22 ♂ Paid Mr. Jno Robins for his wooll, & weigh'd it; this being the first parcell that ever I weigh'd.

28 ☽ Having drawn up the termes of the Marriage & settlement & shewn it to my Father I went in the Evening to carry it to Mrs. Hartshorn; which when she had perused she told me she liked nothing in it, and insisted upon the repayment of £500 if her Daughter died without issue. which I not granting, she seemed so much averse that I thought she repented of what she had offered, & she was very pressive for me to take my leave of her Daughter that night, which I desired her not to importune, for I were resolved not to do. I returned home somewhat concerned. And she came after to me, with many pleasing & perswasive words to return part of the portion as aforesaid.

29 ♂ About 7h a.m. Being sent for by Mrs. Barbara Hartshorn, I went thither. She told me she perceived I was troubled, & that she would not have me concern'd: she then mentioned the repayment of £200 & I mentioned the repayment of £300 if I died without issue. But without coming to any Conclusion, I was sent for home, & she perceiving my Concern, told me she would resolve me by night. As soon as I was gone she sent for Mr. Mich: Cadman & shew'd him the Rough draught which I had left with her, acquainting him of the difference between us: he thought that what I had drawn up in writing was reasonable & that she ought not to insist on the Repayment of any part of the Portion. Whereupon she sent him to me to tell me, that if I had no other discouragement; then she did accept of the propositions I had made according to the Paper which I had drawn up, wherein was conteined a reservation of £40 per

---

4 No further information has been found on Richard Hill.

annum to her during life; in case her Daughter died without issue &c. This assurance he came & gave me about 10h a.m. I replied that I had no other discouragement, & that I did return her my thanks that she was pleased to consent: & went to her house with him to make my acknowledgements.[5]

July 6 ♂ Paid Rich: Hill £122 for his wooll.

    8 ♃ *News that* Mr. *Weeks senior died the 4th instant in the morning.*

  12 ☽ About 2h p.m. (the writings concerning the Marriage being sealed just before by Mrs. Barbara Hartshorn & my self) I was betrothed or contracted to her Daughter Mrs. Eliz: Hartshorn in the presence of my Father, & her Mother, Mr. Mich: Cadman & Mr. Tho: Miller, in form following viz. Taking her by the right hand I said I Samuel take thee Elizabeth to be my betrothed wife, & promise to make thee my wedded wife in time convenient: in token whereof is this our holding by the hand. Then loosing my hand, She took me by my right hand; repeating the same words mutatis mutandis.

Aug. 30 ☽ I lent Mr. Edw: Scot, £150 & Sept. 18 following £200 more for all which took a Mortgage at 6 per cent which was continued for several years, and the Interest allways exactly paid.

  31 ♂ I removed with my Father to the house which was Mrs. Hartshorn's, & which I was to have in part of the portion: & first began to keep house there. Surprized the same week with an excessive Melancholy; which lasted all September & October: & without any just Cause.

Sept. 25 ♄ Taken with a Tertian Ague in the morning about 8h a.m.

  27 ☉ Another fit about 4h a.m.

  29 ☿ or rather 28 ♂ 12h p.m. Another. But all three moderate.

By Reason of my Melancholy in this Month & the next, being perhaps the most violent I ever were afflicted with: & which made me pass some whole nights without sleep: there arose great displeasure & difference between me & my intended Mother in Law & Wife. But in the beginning of November it pleased God, out of his abundant mercy to chear & raise my

---

[5] Michael Cadman was a woollen draper and Rye jurat. His son, of the same name, was later apprenticed to Jeake's friend Thomas Miller (see Appendix 3). LAWR 49, p. 68; AMS 4621/22; PCC PROB 11/419 1694: 82.

spirit without any known occasion; but as the seed sown springeth up we know not how. Even so the mercifull God day after day made my spirit chearfull & lively. So that by degrees I recovered easily my repute again with them.

Dec. 11 ♄ I first saw the great Comet, whose prodigious Coma reached from the Horizon farther than the Zenith. The Comet being very neer the Sun could not or at least was not seen by me this Night in it's body; but only the Coma as before: Afterwards I observed it by the Eye every night that it was to be seen till January 30 ☉. The Coma being 70 degrees long a good part of that time. my observations thereof I omitt because they could not be so accurate as if performed by an Instrument. Yet they well agree with those set down in Lilly or rather Coley's Almanack for 1683.[6]

1681

Feb. 11 ♀ Perceiving myself sufficiently again in favour with my Mother in Law, I moved her about 3h p.m. for the Consummation of my Marriage with her Daughter: which without any reluctancy she granted, & it was appointed to be celebrated on March 1 next. And in the interim all things providentially concurred to favour it with happy Omens.

8 ♂ Began for this year to imploy money on Bottomary; imployed £117 all (except £15) between this day & April 4 gained by it this year £12 13s viz. before January 1 next.

Mar. 1 ♂ About 9h 35' a.m. I was married to Mrs. Elizabeth Hartshorn at Rye by Mr. Bruce,[1] in the presence of Mr. Tho: Miller, Mr. Nath: Hartshorn, & the Sexton we going though in the day time, yet so much incognito, that there was no concurse, or notice taken either of our going or coming. The day was cloudy, but calm. The Sun shone out just at tying the Nuptial Knot: & also just at his setting. *devirg*[ination] 3 *Thursday night.*

---

[6] Lilly had died in 1681; in 1682 and 1683 his *Merlini Anglici Ephemeris* was continued by Coley, though the title-page still retained the legend 'By William Lilly', and only in 1684 was this changed to 'According to the Method of'.

1681 [1] Not identified. For a certificate dated 22 Feb. 1681 giving permission for the marriage to take place at Playden see FRE 5255.

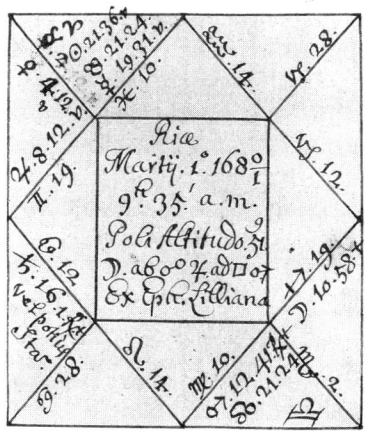

The Positure of Heaven seems not very fortunate for though the
Sun & Saturn Lords of the 1st & 7th in my Nativity are here in
trine, & Mercury and Jupiter Lords of the same in her's in Reception, & moreover the Sun & Mercury Lords of the
,Ascendant in both, here in conjunction. Yet Jupiter is cadent
detrified & opposed by the Moon, squared by Mars. Mercury
detrified in opposition to Mars & in square of the Moon. Seeming to presignify divers troubles & discontents, as Saturn in the
2d portends variance about parsimoniousness, or indigence of
money. Mars as likewise ill posited & moreover ill aspected in
the 5th[:] Violences, Death or mischief to Children. But the Sun
& Mercury in the 11th prenote good friends, & Venus & Jupiter
in the 12th take off all mischief by Enemies.

By my Marriage I came into actuall possession of about £800 of
my wife's portion, and the remainder was paid me gradually in
1681.

10 ♃ This day was an Election of Burgesses at Rye, to serve in the
Oxford Parliament; which had been managed with great heats &
animosities, wherein I was somewhat concerned. Sir Jno Darell
& Mr. Tho: Frewen were chosen: the former without contradic-
tion; the latter had Mr. Jno Tudman, a Candidate against him,
who having the minor number of votes, lost it; & went to

London, assoon as the Election was over:[2] & with him my Mother in law sent her son Brother Nath: Hartshorn; because of a report of Infamy that she heard of him a day or two before. After his coming to London being designed for an Attorney at Law, by Tudman's recommendation he was put Apprentice to Rich: Goodenough with £100 which was not only all lost; but he also ruin'd by Goodenoughs ill usage of him, & neglecting to look after him & keep him from the ill Courses he was inclined to.

July   4 ☽ Began to pay for the wooll I had lately bought this year: in this moneth, and September I bought about 18 packs.

Aug. 15 ☽ About 6h a.m. I rode to London at my· Mother's request to compose the differences that were already arisen between my Brother Nath: & his Master Goodenough. I came to London that night about 8h p.m. But it was Thursday before I could speak to Goodenough—he was either so full of business or pretences: then composed all things for the present and 19 ♀ about 2h 30′ p.m. Came from London & that night to Sevenoke; & next day home. Had good weather both going & coming not wet, nor very hot. But at Beckley going outwards on 15 ☽ my horse threw me on a Gallop & with the fall I broke the Combs in my pocket & squeesd a Copper tobacco box flat, yet through God's providence I had no hurt at all. My horse ran away towards Rye till some Company coming that way stopt him.

    29 ☽ This being the day of Election of Maior at Rye. Mr. Tho: Crouch usurped that office having the usuall oaths administred to him & a staff delivered him in Court by his own party: though Mr. Tho: Tournay was legally chosen by the Maiority of Votes at the same time. Who because he would not deliver his staff & surrender his place to Mr. Crouch was in 3 or 4 days served by him & his Partisans with an Order of Councill for the said Tournay, & other's of his party, amongst whom were my Father & other Dissenters that voted for Mr. Tournay, to appear before the King & Councill at Whitehall in the beginning of September. Who accordingly appearing, the King Charls 2d was

---

[2] Sir John Darell, who had been elected MP for Rye in October 1679 and was to serve again in 1689, had formerly been recorder at Canterbury. Thomas Frewen, of Brickwall, Northiam, was MP for Rye in 1679, 1681, and 1685: see also 21.1.94. On John Tudman or Tedman see Introduction, sect. 4. On Richard Goodenough see Introduction, sect. 5. Henning, i. 499–500, ii. 194, 368–9.

informed by Crouch that my Father who voted for Tournay was a Preacher to a seditious Conventicle (for you must know that the name of a Preacher was always a Name of reproach amongst such Fools as had never considered the Ecclesiastes of the wise Solomon)[3] And upon Crouch's information the King asked which was he. Whereupon my Father drew neer, & told the King that he was the person so charged, but that he did preach any sedition he denyed: the King asked him why he transgressed the Laws in preaching in a Conventicle; to which he replyed That if he did transgress the Laws, his Majesties Courts were open. Then the King told him if he were so much for Law, he should have it; & bid the Attorney General[4] to prosecute him upon the Oxford Act, & commanded Crouch to shut up the doors of our meeting place at his return. So that from this time we were forced to meet in great privacy & mostly by night; & were persecuted, cited, inform'd against in the Crown office &c. till most of us were driven out of Town for a Time.

Sept. 10 ♄ This day (my Father being not yet returned from London) I sold weigh'd & delivered my wooll being about 18 packs to Tho: Smith, & besides what I received of him I trusted him of £126. The same Night he lost all the said wooll it being seized by the Officers in Romny Marsh: which when I heard of I was much concern'd, fearing he would either never be able or willing to pay me. But making no stir about it; he came very honestly & paid me £26 the 21th Instant & gave me a Mortgage of his house & land that cost him £100 for the remaining £100 so I lost nothing.

Oct. 7 ♀ At night taken with a great pain in my head, lasting all that night & next day.

8 ♄ Aguish, & then a feaver; in the night cold & not sleepy.

9 ☉ About 2h p.m. Another Aguish fit, with a little vomiting, then a feaver: & restless all night.

10 ☽ About 2h p.m. Another fit with vomiting then hot & burning. At night took some Venice Treacle & Rosemary beer; & slept well.

---

[3] The Book of Ecclesiastes is devoted to 'the Words of the Preacher, the Son of David, King in Jerusalem'.

[4] i.e. Sir Robert Sawyer, Tory MP and Attorney General between 1681 and 1687. His wife Margaret was the daughter of Ralph Suckley (see 18.12.83). Henning, iii. 399–403.

Oct. 11 ♂ The feaver all night & no sleep.

    12 ☿ In the afternoon took 1 of Matthew's Pills[5] gr[ains] x. sweat from 11h p.m. 2 hours, slept little.

    13 ♃ Feaver all night, very restless; no sleep at all.

    14 ♀ Took some Venice Treacle, & some Aqua Theriacalis mixt with Syropus Caryophyllatus. After it I missed my feaver & slept well; & from this time began to recover. 17 ☽ came down.

Nov. 9 ☿ Bought Peter Waters's wooll & after that others at a dear rate, & lost some small matter by it afterwards.[6]

    14 ☽ *Let* Mr. *Tournay have £8 by contribution for the charge of recovering his right, which lost.*

    15 ♂ My Mother assigned me bonds for about £160 & 18 ♀ paid me the balance of the Portion.

Dec. 19 ☽ She took most of the bonds again, and paid me money instead, viz. £144 15s 1d.

    31 ♄ When I cast up my accounts for this year computed I had gained by Accounts of Exchange £20 16s 10d Wooll £24 13s 2d. And that since January 1 last my Estate was increased in this One year £1100 Clear: viz. my wife's portion £1000. Gifts from my Father in Plate & curious pieces of Gold & Silver this year £60 & Profit clear by Trade £40 all Charges of housekeeping &c. paid.

1682

In January I went to Canterbury with Mr. Tho. Markwick & to other places, went on Tuesday & return'd Saturday after. Bad ways, & wettish weather.

Jan. 30 ☽ From hence to February 25 delivered upon Bottomarie £100 & £62 afterward. Profit thereby computed December 31 1682 £17 1s.

In Easter Terme (falling this year in May) the Bodar of Dovor

---

[5] A popular opiate which was the subject of a dispute over proprietorship in the early 1660s. See Richard Mathew, *The Unlearned Alchymist his Antidote* (1660), and R. S. Wilkinson, 'George Starkey, Physician and Alchemist', *Ambix*, 11 (1963), 140–1.

[6] Peter Waters could have been either a gentleman from Beckley who owned lands in Northiam, Peasmarsh, and Old Romney, or his cousin of the same name who came from Udimore. LAWR 52, p. 243; AMS 3209/10.

Castle came to take my Father upon the writ de Excommunicato Capiendo: & Mr. Stretton (Mr. Crouches Clerk) came to my house to serve him with a Summons out of the Crown Office to appear upon the Oxford Act at the suite of Sir Robert Sawyer then Attorney General. But my Father having intelligence of their proceedings withdrew himselfe out of the Town for some days.

May 22 ☽ I rode with my wife & Mother in Law to London for diversion: came thither 23 ♂. had hot & dry weather. Were well entertained & treated by Kindred & Friends. Composed Nat's business once more & placed him again with his master at Mr. Firmin's motion.[1]

June 22 ♃ Mr. *Tournay had £6 more which lost.*

23 ♀ We returned from London in the Stage Coach to Tunbridge, &c. 24 ♄ came to Rye at night. Had pretty good weather & escaped being wet; though the weather then much inclin'd to rain.

July 4 ♂ News in the morning that Mr. Tournay was declared Maior by Course of Law; having yesterday carried it against Mr. Crouch by Verdict in a Tryal at the King's Bench bar at Westminster, before Sir Fr: Pemberton. L.C.J.[2]

10 ☽ Advise that Jno Mackley had bought some Tallow per my order; & more September 11 which cost in all £89 16 8d the price falling: he took it afterwards at the price it cost; & so I lost the Interest of my money.

12 ☿ My Father taken ill with an Ague, which after turned to a kind of running Gout & vehement racking pains in the back; very neer death by it. He continued very ill all July & most part of August; after began to recover & by the end of September indifferent well again.

Aug. 8 ♂ Our late usurping Maior & Persecutor Mr. Tho: Crouch having lately surrendred his Staff to Mr. Tournay according to the Verdict before mentioned; & since being cast in a Tryal at Sussex Assizes, came home thence ill, & after 2 or 3 days sickness, died this day, about 3h 15′ p.m. And October 2 ☽ about 1h p.m. died

---

1682 [1] i.e. Richard Goodenough: see Introduction, sect. 5. Thomas Firmin was a London business man and philanthropist. *DNB*; Woodhead.

[2] i.e. Lord Chief Justice. On Sir Francis Pemberton see *DNB*.

Aaron Peadle one of his greatest Abettors in Arbitrary Power & Persecution.[3]

Aug. 28 ☽ The same Interest that last year had set up Mr. Crouch; did this Election set up Mr. Jos: Radford for Maior against Mr. Tournay; & being still encouraged and countenanced; did at length with perpetual Contention weary out Mr. Tournay & his party; & grasp all the government & offices of the Towne into their own hands: & held it till the Coming of the Prince of Orange in 1688.

Oct. 14 ♄ Between January 13 1679/80 & this time I had read over the following Books, viz.

No. 197. P.D.C. The French Politicks. 8°.[4]

No. 198. Slingsby Bethel, Interests of the States of Europe. 8° [1680].

No. 199. [Henry Neville] Plato Redivivus. 8° [1681].

No. 200. [Robert Fleming] The fulfilling of the Scriptures. 8° [1669].

No. 201. Robt. Sanderson, Cases of Conscience. 8° [trans. Robert Codrington, 1660].

No. 202. Tho: May, History of the Parliament. Vol. 1 Fol: [1647].

No. 203. Jno Speed, Chronicles of the English Kings. Fol:[5]

No. 204. Jos: Mede's Works of Dr. Worthington's Edition. Fol: [1663–4].

No. 205. Peter Heylyn, Cosmography. Fol: [Enlarged edn., 1652].

No. 206. Fr: Osborn, Advice to a Son part 2d & other works. 8°.[6]

No. 207. John Selden, Theogonia. 8°.[7]

---

[3] Aaron Peadle was a Rye innholder, who may also have been a shoemaker like his father. It was he who claimed to have overheard the seditious words which Thomas Burditt was accused of uttering in 1682. Burchall, pp. 104–5; LAWR 36, p. 104; *CSP Dom.* 1682, p. 350.

[4] Perhaps P. D. C[ardonnel], Gent., *Complimentum Fortunatarum Insularum . . .*, Eng. trans., 1662, with verses by Edmund Waller and John Dryden included.

[5] i.e. Speed's *The History of Great Britaine* (1611).

[6] Probably Osborne's *Works*, of which the first edition so titled was the 'seventh' of 1673. Previously, however, volumes comprising the sixth edition of *Advice to a Son* together with the second edition of the *Advice, Second Part* and part or all of Osborne's three other works were widely available.

[7] Conceivably John Selden's Θεάνθρωπος: *Or, God made Man* (1661), an octavo.

No. 208. Sir Henry Vane, Retired Man's Meditations. 4°
[1655].

No. 209. Edw: Stillingfleet, Origines Sacrae. 4° [1662].

No. 210. Edw: Stillingfleet, Answer to the Jesuits Reply. 8°.[8]

No. 211. ['Eirenaeus Philalethes'] Ripley Reviv'd or Sir G.
Ripley commented on. 8° [1678].

No. 212. Gilb: Burnet, Life & Death of Sir Mat: Hale &c. 8°
with [Richard] Baxter's Additions. [1682].

20 ♀ No. 213. Jo: Veslingus, Anatomy of the Body. Fol: [trans.
Nicholas Culpeper, 1653].

Nov. 16 ♃ Advise per post from Cousin Jay of London that Brother Nath:
Hartshorn, had been under restraint for Debt; & to free himself
had perswaded Tho: Clerk to be bound with him for 43s which
he being unable to pay (being very poor) was in danger of being
imprisoned for; & came to him with a grievous Complaint about
it.[9] And 3 or 4 days after a Letter from Mr. Medley a Mercer in
Fenchurch street that Brother Nath: had taken up £14 or £15
worth of goods there.[10] But that proved afterwards his coming
with some idle women into the shop; & so Medley being cheated
of his goods by them: would having imposed the payment upon
my Mother in Law.

23 ♃ News that I was informed against in the Crown Office for not
coming to Church; & that an Attachment was granted out
against my Father upon the Oxford Act. And that 5 or 6 Dissenters more of us were informed against in the Crown Office
for 11 moneths not coming to Church at £20 per mensem.
Upon which they met this Evening at my house & concluded
that Mr. Tho: Miller being one of the number should go to
London next day, to imploy an Attorney to defend themselves &
to advise about it. And my Father seeing he could not be safe at
Rye because of the Capias & Attachment aforesaid resolved to
go with him. So next morning about 6h a.m. whilst it was yet
dark they both took horse for London: where my Father continued till the Summer 1687.

[8] This seems likeliest to be Stillingfleet's *A Reply to Mr J[ohn] S[ergeant] his 3d. Appendix,
Containing some Animadversions on the Book Entituled, A Rational Account of the Grounds of
Protestant Religion*, issued as an appendix to John Tillotson's *The Rule of Faith* (1666).

[9] Thomas Clerk was a pipemaker in Clerkenwell. FRE 5073.

[10] John Medley wrote to Barbara Hartshorne from 'the Angell Corner shop of Forechurch
Street' in London in November 1682. FRE 5293–4.

Dec. 2 ♄ or thereabouts, Advice of Brother Nath's being in custody at Westminster for £3 13s which Cousin Wightman paid & releas'd him; & he was sent down to Rye.

6 ☿ No. 214. Alex. Read, Anatomy of the Body. 8° [1638].

8 ♀ I weighed & delivered the Wooll I bought this year of Ste: Wilmshurst, being 22 packs ferè, to Tho: Knight & Tho: Videan, at £9 per pack, by which got 10s per pack. though much troubled before I could get all the money paid.[11]

9 ♄ My wife fell in travel in the Evening & had violent pains before the Midwife could be fetcht she living 6 mile off, and after a very hard travell was difficultly delivered of a Daughter next day at 11h 32' a.m. the Child being hurt in the Birth in the right Temple; died of that hurt & of the Thrush. 18 ☽ following about 15h p.m.

1683

Jan. 13 ♄ About 5h p.m. I was taken with a fit of an ague which with the feaver succeeding at midnight lasted till next morning; & I was not well till the night following.

22 ☽ Sold my Tallow for what it cost at first to Jno Mackley to have £40 present, and £49 16s 8d afterwards.

Feb. 21 ☿ No. 215. Realdus Columbus, de Re Anatomica. Libri 15. 8° [1559].

26 ☽ No. 216. Tho: Winston, Anatomy Lectures. 8° [1659].

27 ♂ No. 217. Wm Molins, Anatomical Administration of the Muscles. 8° [1676].

Mar. 8 ♃ No. 218. Wm Harvey, Anatomical Exercitations of the motion of the Heart & Blood; with J. de Backs Discourse of the Heart; & Two Exercitations of Dr. Harvey to Riolanus the Son. 8° [Eng. trans., 1653].

---

[11] Jeake had lent money to Stephen Wilmshurst, of Cadborough in the parish of Rye, in 1681. In the 1670s Wilmshurst had been threatened with prosecution by the commonalty of Rye for inning marshes. Thomas Knight wrote to Jeake from Lydd. This name was common in Sussex and Kent, but it has not been possible to make a positive identification. Videan probably lived in Romney. For a Dieppe promissory note which he and Knight endorsed, see FRE 5250c. 'Fere' is Latin for 'approximately'. FRE 4931, 5107, 5228; RYE 1/17, p. 5; 145/11.

11 ☉ No. 219. Nat. Homes, Resurrection Revealed Raised Fol: [1653].

As I remember it was* this Lord's day in the evening, that I being with other of our friends at our meeting at Mr. Tho: Miller's house; we were disturbed by Mr. Radford the usurping Maior, with the Jurats & others' their associates; and because we refused to open the doors, they beset the house** & brake them open in the night; & took our names but committed no body to prison, Afterwards they distreined Mr. Tho: Markwick for £20 for preaching, & Mr. Miller for £20 for having a Conventicle at his house. But me they distrained not; though they fined me & my wife at 5s a piece & distrained some others as auditors.

* It was Mar. 18 ☉ [*written in margin*]   ** 9h p.m. [*written in margin*]

14 ☿ No. 220. Jno Pecquet, Anatomical Experiments with [Thomas] Bartholinus, of the Lacteal Veins of the Thorax. 12° [Engl. trans., 1653].

Apr.　5 ♃ No. 221. William Harvey, Anatomical Exercitations concerning the Generation of living Creatures. 8° [1653].

May　19 ♄ & 21 ☽ I delivered £40 on Bottomarie, by which & by £30 out before I gained this year (viz. before January 1 next) £12 8s 6d.

June 18 ☽ No. 222. Wm Mason, Little Star or Catechism. 8° [1653].

29 ♀ About noon my house was searched for Armes by an ambulatory Messenger assisted by Mr Radford, Captain Hall & others.[1] This being the time wherein the Earl of Essex & my Lord Russell were seized: and so our good neighbours would fain have perswaded themselves that the Dissenters of Rye must needs be concern'd in a Plot.[2]

July　1 ☉ No. 223. Jno Saltmarsh, Dawnings of Light. Free Grace. Sparkles of Glory. 8° [1645-7].

6 ♀ This afternoon Mr. Radford Captain Hall Mr. Gillart & their followers, not satisfied with their former diligence, searched my house again for armes.

10 ♂ Rode with my wife in company of Mr. Tho: Miller to Mr. Edw: Hawksworth's at Warbleton for diversion; next day a Fellow

---

1683 ¹ Robert Hall was a customs officer at Rye and a jurat. He provided the government with information about the state of affairs in the town. *CSP Dom.* 1679–83, *passim*.

² i.e. the Rye House Plot, in which the Earl of Essex and William Lord Russell were said to be involved. See Introduction, sect. 5.

turn'd our horses out of the ground for stray horses, & we could not hear of them till Saturday, when riding home upon others, we found them at Brightling. Good weather this journey.[3]

July 18 ☿ About 8h a.m. I rode to London with Mr. Tho: Miller; he to dwell there, being wearied out with the troubles & persecutions he met with at Rye; & I to see my Father. We got to London, 19 ♃ about 8h p.m. I found my Father ill of the Gout, of which he had been very bad before; but 'ere I came away he was much better. In this Journey I resolved to remove to London, to prevent being informed against at Rye Sessions for £20 per mensem.

27 ♀ About 3h p.m. I came from London, & home to Rye next day about 4h 30' p.m. Had good weather going & coming.

Aug. 11 ♄ No. 224. Jno Saltmarsh, Some drops of the Vial. 4° [1646].

27 ☽ Upon news of Brother Nath: Hartshorn's being in Prison in the Gatehouse at Westminster for a Felony committed in searching the houses of the Lord Paget & Sir Roger Hill & that he was to be tryed next Wednesday, I rode with my Mother in Law to London;[4] set out about 2h p.m. came to Tunbridge that night, had pretty much rain about Plimwel[5] & a little afterwards. 28 ♂ we came to London about 3h 30' p.m. having good weather. Went forthwith to him who perswaded his Mother to give £200 to buy him a pardon; from which she was diswaded till she had inquired about the Circumstances of the Crime, finding that he was not to be tryed till Lent Assizes the fact alleaged being done in Buckinghamshire. I spent the time of my stay principally about that business.

Sept. 3 ☽ My Mother staying at London about that business, I returned this day about 1h 45' p.m. & came to Tunbridge about 7h 30' p.m. & next day to Rye about 2h 30' p.m. in good weather.

[3] Edward Hawksworth was a gentleman of Warbleton, son of Joseph, former Rector of Burwash, by Jane, daughter of Edward Polhill, who had acted for the Jeakes in the partition of the lands inherited from the Hartridge family: see note to 27.8.73. Information kindly provided by Liz Doff.

[4] The Gate House was a notorious gaol adjoining College Court (north of Dean's Yard) at Westminster, demolished in the late eighteenth century. William, 6th Baron Paget, and Sir Roger Hill of Denham, Bucks. (MP for Amersham and later Wendover) were both active Whigs. *DNB*; Henning, ii. 550.

[5] i.e. Flimwell.

23 ☉ No. 225. [John] Jackson, Sober Word to a serious people. 4°
[1651].

Oct. 4 ♃ Having resolved to leave Rye; because I was informed that I
should be prosecuted there by Mr. Lewis Gillart then Maior &
the rest of that party for Non-conformity at £20 per mensem, as
divers other of my Friends had already been. I this morning
departed privately with my wife (then with Child) from Rye to
live at London: leaving a Neighbour to look after my house &
goods. We took horse without any Company about 9h a.m. &
went first to Udimer to secure £100 due to me on Bond from
Mr. Jno Waters who besides had £200 of me on a Mortgage of
£300 sealed August 24 ♀ last, & was to have had the 3d £100 on
Saturday last for which I had given him my bond. But he was
taken sick the beginning of last week, & died on Friday the 28th
past, which I not hearing of (but only that he was ill) had put up
the money on Saturday & was just riding out to carry to him;
when at that Instant a letter was brought me from him which he
wrote in his sickness to tell me that he could not come to receive
it according to appointment; & withall the messenger told me
that he was dead. Which was very Providential for me that he
had not received & disposed of the last £100 before he died; for
he died poor in personal estate.[6] But now it being not actually
paid & gone his Widow, who was very just, consented when she
had taken Administration to give me in my Bond of £100 in
Exchange for his Bond of £100 that so I might secure my self
wholly upon the said Mortgage. Went thence to Westfield to
Mr. Jno Weekes's with whom I left Mr. Waters his bond, to
exchange for mine with the Widow. After, to Hasting whither
we came about 6h 30′ p.m. Fine weather: cloudy, but no wind
nor rain.

6 ♄ about 11h a.m. we rode from Hasting to Lydd a tedious way
round by Appledoor, to get in or secure £66 10s owing to me
from Knight & Videan of Lydd & Romney for the wooll that
they bought of me last year; & for which I had already made 3
journeys this Summer without more effect then promises. We

---

[6] Jeake had had various dealings with Waters of Udimer. Though Jeake states that when
Waters died he was 'poor in personal estate', his widow, Bridget, bequeathed some land when
she wrote her will in the same year. She asked her cousin, Edward Polhill (see 31.1.79), to act as
overseer. RYE 145/11; LAWR 41, p. 4.

came to Lydd safe through God's Providence about 6h 30′ p.m. to Cousin Ric: Freebody's house, where had the good news that Videan had lately paid £30 thereof into his hands & Knight £20 into the hands of Mr. Will: Finch of Romney, whom I had lately ordered to sue for it.[7] The weather this day just like that Thursday last.

Oct. 8 ☽ In the afternoon went to Romney to speak to Mr. Finch, & ordered him to arrest Knight for the residue £16 10s a little Rain in our Return.

9 ♂ We rode to Dengeness Light to see it & speak to Tho: Smith about 1 years interest due to me. Fine weather only cloudy.

10 ☿ About 9h a.m. I departed with my wife from Lydd for London; got to Woodsgate that night about 6h 15′ p.m. having a sunshine day, but the wind troublesome.

11 ♃ About 7h 45′ a.m. we departed from Woodsgate & came to London about 5h p.m. a very fine day, sunshine & calm. Being through the good hand of God safely arrived after this solitary & troublesome journey, we went immediately to Cousin Jay's at the Golden Lion in Fenchurch street, where my Father & Mother in Law boarded, whom we found in health. And there we boarded & dwelt all together till next Spring. At my coming heard that Brother Nath: was escaped out of the Gatehouse; but in few days he was taken again.

Nov. 24 ♄ About 11h 45′ a.m. spake to Mr. Tho. Morris about getting me a place in the East India Company, or as an Accomptant to keep a Merchant's Liedger: which he pretended but performed not: Nor could I fall into any Imployment whilst I staid at London.[8]

26 ☽ About 7h p.m. News per post from Mr. Weekes that he had received my Bond of £100 from Mrs Bridget Waters: & delivered in the other.

Dec. 6 ♃ Mr. Edw: Scot proposed to me to lend him £5 or £600 more upon a General Mortgage of his Whole Estate; which I took a days time to consider of, & on Saturday returned him Answer in the negative. But afterwards my mind Changing, I resolved to

---

[7] On Knight and Videan see 8.12.82.

[8] Thomas Morris of Southwark had corresponded with the elder Jeake on religious matters in the 1660s; the younger Jeake was in contact with him on commercial matters in 1678-9. Smart, pp. 67-71; see Introduction, sect. 8 n. 25.

take it, & acquainted him so, on 12 ☿ about 10h a.m. Q[ques-
tion] if this might not be the Effect of Venus directed ad sextilem Saturnis in Libra in my Nativity.

13 ♃ Advise that Mr. Finch had received for me £16 15s of Knight in
full of that debt.

18 ♂ About 2h p.m. Went with Mr. Scot to a Tavern in Nicolas
Lane, where he sealed the Mortgages for £600 & I paid him
£200 & gave him bond for £400. The Mortgages being made for
£600 to secure his Estate the better; if he should be convicted
upon an Information or Indictment rather then depending
against him for Non-conformity at £20 per mensem. But I
afterwards considering that it were better to try to prevent his
Conviction than for me being a Dissenter my self, to undertake
to screen him from the penaltys by force of the said Mortgages:
though for better security they were made in Mr. Weekes's
name in Trust for me: Resolved, Providence putting it into my
mind & my Father approving of it to endeavour to procure for
him a Noli Prosequi from Sir Robt Sawyer Attorney General by
means of Mr. Suckley his Father in Law who was indebted to
my Cousin Jaye: wherewith having acquainted Mr. Scot by
Letter; though he had little hopes of it's success, having himself
made a journey to London not long before for that purpose
without effect: yet by his Answer of January 19 he accepted of
my endeavours; & accordingly Cousin Jaye proposed it to Mr.
Suckley, promising him 13 or 14 Guineys if he could perform it;
who moving the Attorney General obtained a promise if he
could find a flaw in the Indictment to ground it upon; so procuring a Copy I happily found two or 3 errors; which being certi-
fied at Mr. Scot's request by Sir Wm Honywood & another
Justice of the Peace for the County of Kent as I remember the
Certificate was carried to the Attorney General & he granted a
Noli Prosequi; which Cosin Jaye & I carried to Mr. Luke Clerk
of the Assizes, by vertue whereof Mr. Scot only appearing at
next Assizes to plead it, was happily discharged; & removing his
habitation to London was never after prosecuted.[9]

---

[9] On this matter see also FRE 5132, 5138, 5143, 5153, and 5155 (which shows that the other
J.P. was Captain William Kingsley). A 'Noli' or 'nolle prosequi' was an entry in a court's record
when a prosecutor abandoned his suit. Sir William Honeywood of Elmsted and Canterbury was
a Canterbury alderman who was elected MP for the city in 1685. Henning, ii. 577–8.

1684

Mar. 2 ☉ I finished my reading of the Bible through out: which I had begun in the English last Translation,[1] since I came to London, intentionally & deliberately, on purpose to observe the revealed will of God therein, both as to matters of Doctrine & Discipline: endeavouring therein to mind diligently the scope of the words, & to free my self from prejudice.

16 ☉ About 37′ past 5 a Clock in the morning my Wife was through God's mercy, happily delivered of a Daughter at Cousin Jay's house in the parish of Gabriel Fenchurch London. The Child was named Elizabeth & is praised be God now living at the writing hereof viz September 1 1694.

18 ♂ No. 226. Jer: Taylor, Liberty of Prophesying. 4° [1647].

Apr. 3 ♃ No. 227. Apocrypha in English. 4°.[2]

About this time I began to read Morinus's Astrologia Gallica, & spent most of my Leisure time therein till January 22 next.

20 ☉ About 4h p.m. Taken with a little fit of an ague; first a pain in the head, after a smal chilness, ending in a feaverish heat, which lasted till 12h p.m.

21 ☽ News about 6h p.m. by Letter from Cousin Freebody; that I was warned to appear at the Exchequer the 23 instant, upon a Controversie concerning the title of Tho: Smith's Land which I had in Mortgage. At which somewhat alarm'd, but my Title being good I heard no more of it.

22 ♂ About 9h a.m. Taken with a 2d fit of an Ague; cold for 2 houres & vomited 3 or 4 times; after very hot & feaverish, till about 5h p.m. then a pain in the head & limbs, & inclin'd to sweat. lasting till 11h p.m.

24 ♃ About 4h a.m. Taken with a 3d fit, cold for some houres & vomited as before, after very hot & feaverish till about noon: then a pain in the head & inclin'd to sweat 2 hours or more.

26 ♄ About 5h a.m. A 4th fit, which was the last; cold but more moderate & without vomiting, after hot & then sweating; pretty

---

1684 [1] By this Jeake meant the Authorized Version, of which the Jeakes owned more than one edition.

[2] Probably an edition of the Apocrypha which formed part of a quarto volume in the Jeakes' library comprising the Bible, Prayer Book and Psalms, published in London in 1586.

well off by noon. Yesterday my mouth begain to be sore & my lips broke out. And this day my mouth was very sore, & in the night so extreme that I could not sleep quietly. 27 ☉ it was worse & pained me much. Then being advised to wash it with Brandy by night it was somewhat better, & thence forward the soreness rather decreased.

May 11 ☉ No. 228. Gilb: Ironside. 7 Questions of the Sabbath. 4° [1637].

28 ☿ About 9h 15′ a.m. I returned from London to Rye with my Mother in Law, Wife, Child & Servant in a Coach which I hired to carry us; & came to Tunbridge that evening about 6h 30′ p.m. And next day at 8h a.m. we departed from Tunbridge & came to Rye about 7h 30′ p.m. having fine sunshine weather & very good ways.

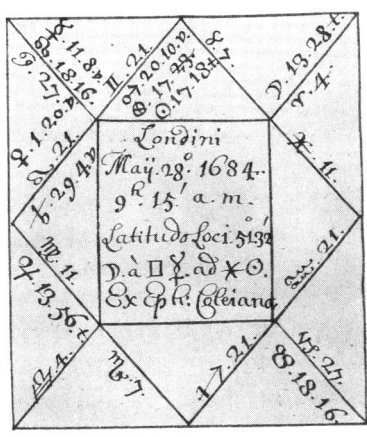

About the beginning of June. News of the death of my good friend Mr. Edw: Hawksworth.[3]

June 21 ♄ or thereabouts, News by Mr. Tho: Miller's letter of the 19 Instant that he with Mr. Markwick & other of our friends had been outlawed upon the former Information of £20 per mensem, and with some difficulty & charge had gotten it reversed till Lent assizes.

[3] See 10.7.83.

July   2 ☿ In the afternoon the Sun Eclipsed in the 21 degree of Cancer the very Cusp of the 12th house, & very neer his radical place in my Nativity: which seemed to portend many efforts of Enemies against me.

27 ☉ No. 229. Controversial Letters of my Father in Manuscript about Visible Churches. Fol:[4]

Sept. 15 ☽ No. 230. Jus Divinum Ministerii Evangelici & Anglicani, with an Appendix; by the Assembly of Divines. 4° [2nd edn., 1647].

20 ♄ Mr. Lewis Gillart threatned to send for me next Court day, & tender me the Oaths of Allegiance & Supremacy, & upon refusall committ me to prison, & 24 ☿ he repeated the same Threats before his Brother & Mr. Curteis:[5] & accordingly October 17 ♀ being a Session I was sent for about 10h 30′ a.m. by the Sergeant George Weeden to appear before the Maior & Jurats.[6] But I was providentially gone to Benenden that morning about an hour & half before being subpena'd for a witness by vertue of a Commission out of the Chancery to testify the sealing of a writing: which I accordingly did the next day at Cranbrook before the Commissioners & at night returned to Rye.

Dec.   1 ☽ Suspecting that I should be again sent for this day to the Session, I went to Hasting about 9h 30′ a.m. & came thither a little before Sunset. Towards Evening the Maior & Jurats sent the Sergeant again to my house for me to come before them; but I was out of their way. 3 ☿ I came back to Rye, & arrived there, about 5h 15′ p.m. had indifferent good weather.

9 ♂ News by one of the Grand Jury that Mr. Wm Williams the Vicar of Rye designed to have the Dissenters indicted on the Statute of 23 Elizabeth & that the Jury were then warned to the Court to be held on the morrow in order to receive such a Charge, Lewis Gillart being Deputy, because the Maior was out

---

[4] Evidently the elder Jeake's letter-book, now FRE 4223, many of the letters in which deal with this topic.

[5] Curteis was a common name in the area. Jeake may have been referring to the Rye grocer named John Curteis, Thomas Markwick's friend William Curteis (see 3.1.93), or possibly Jeremiah Curteis of Tenterden, who was related to several of Jeake's acquaintances. RYE 2/5; Berry, p. 65.

[6] George Weeden, the sergeant at mace, was a carpenter and alehouse keeper in Rye. RYE 2/4, 19/53.

of Towne:[7] whereupon I thought it best to absent my selfe next day, & did so: but Gillart being drunk (as was said) the night before Court, overslept himself I suppose, for there was no Court kept.

14 ☉ No. 231. Tob: Crisp, Christ alone exalted. 11 Sermons 8º [vol. 3, 1646].

No. 232. Peter du Moulin, Anatomy of the Mass. 8º [trans. James Mountaine, 1641].

27 ♄ Finished my Encomium on Jo: Bapt: Morinus & his Astrologia Gallica which I had begun about 10 days before, consisting of 382 lines of English Heroicks.[8]

1685

Jan.　1 ♃ When I cast up my Accompts for the year past I found that I had gone behind £54 13s 1d out of the stock or Principal of my Estate; Occasioned by my removal to London & being out of Imployment; not daring to put my self into any business by reason of the persecution.

7 ☿ Finished my Demonstration or Diagram of the Illustration of the Coince of Blazing Stars in Two Figures, entituled Comae Cometarum Adumbratae; & begun yesterday.[1]

12 ☽ About 6h p.m. Taken with a Quartan Ague. this 1st fit exceeding gentle.

15 ♃ About 6h p.m. A 2d fit, lay pretty much in my head but not very cold; sweat in the night.

16 ♀ Rode to Robertsbridge, being subpena'd as a witness, & return'd at night. good weather.

18 ☉ About 6h p.m. a 3d fit. moderate in cold. at 8h p.m. headach but less then in the 2d fit. sweat in the night.

[7] It is not entirely clear which Elizabethan statute is referred to. It might have been the anti-Catholic act of 1580 (23 Eliz., c. 1), the 'Act against Seditious Words' of the same year (23 Eliz., c. 2) or the act against sectaries of 1593 (35 Eliz., c. 1), which was still being invoked at this time (Watts, *Dissenters* (see Introduction, sect. 4 n. 1), 224, 255). William Williams was a jurat as well as Vicar of Rye. RYE 19/59.

[8] Now Selmes MS 49.

1685 [1] This pair of diagrams, in which Jeake tried to account for the apparent paths of comets and the way in which they 'coincided' in terms of their movement in elliptical orbs, is now Selmes MS 50.

Jan. 19 ☽ Wrote to Mr. Miller about joyning in partnership to Negotiate Bills, which he consented to; but by reason of the King's death soon after we proceeded not.

21 ☿ About 6h p.m. A 4th fit. like the 3d but less.

22 ♃ No. 233. Jo: Bapt: Morinus. Astrologia Gallica. Fol: [1661].

24 ♄ About 6h p.m. A fifth fit: like the 4th or less.

27 ♂ About 6h p.m. The 6th & last fit: exceeding gentle.

Feb. 4 ☿ About 6h 30′ a.m. Went to Lydd & Romney to speak for bills to be negotiated. Came to Lydd about noon. Went to Romney in the afternoon, & having spoken for that purpose returned to Lydd. Came home 5 ♃ about 8h p.m. the wind blew exceeding sharp & cold when I went to Romney: else very good weather.

9 ☽ In the morning, News that King Charles the 2d was dead.

12 ♃ About 9h a.m. News by letter from my Father that Cousin Mary Jaye was dead.[2]

15 ☉ About 10h a.m. News of my Friend Mr. Naldread's being under restraint at Hasting.

16 ☽ About 9h a.m. Went to Hasting, came thither about 1h p.m. & found him then at Liberty again. Next day returned home; had exceeding fair & sunshine weather.

27 ♀ About 8h 15′ p.m. Mr. Tho: Markwick being at my house, was sent for by the Maior & Jurats; occasioned by one Simon Smith as I remember who was Uncle to Mr. Markwick, & coming to Rye to see or speak to him; was by their Worships very learnedly taken for a Plotter. But when they saw they could make nothing of it they dismissed them both.

May 9 ♄ No. 234. Jo: Wilkins, Discourse of the Gift of Prayer; & of Preaching. 8° [1651].

18 ☽ About 7h or 7h 30′ a.m. Went with Mr. Rich: Naldread to see my Father at London; on Foot to Tenterden, whither we came about 1h p.m. & Mr. Naldread being taken ill of an ague there, we hired horses & next day went to Maidstone, and about 2h p.m. thence by water to Rochester, & thence at 6h p.m. Walked to Gravesend & came thither about 9h p.m. And 20 ☿

---

[2] Mary Jaye was the wife of John Jaye (see Appendix 3) and a daughter of William Key (see 20.12.66).

about 7h a.m. in the tilt boat to London, where we landed about 30′ p.m. Very good weather all the way, not very hot little wind, no rain. Found my Father in health. In this journey Cousin Jno Mackley sealed me a bond for £25 which I had lately lent him, which he never repaid.

June 1 ☽ About 8h 30′ a.m. came from London with Mr. Naldread & my Mother in law in the Stage Coach to Tunbridge, where we arrived about 6h p.m. & next day about 6h 30′ a.m. we went thence & having parted with Mr. Naldread at Plimwell[3] came safe to Rye at 4h 30′ p.m. having very good weather, little or no wind or rain, but this day a little heat.

5 ♀ Lent Cousin Rich: Freebody £10 & June 11 ♃ lent him £20 more; which he paid September 10 following to my order in London & soon after broke.

25 ♃ Upon the late Duke of Monmouth's landing at Lyme, a great many persons were imprisoned; & I apprehending I must run the same fate, if I tarried at Rye; thought best to withdraw my self out of the Towne till the business was over; & not expose my self to be sent a Prisoner to Dovor Castle for nothing; as some others were serv'd, who staid in Towne. And accordingly Mr. Markwick & I went this morning from Rye about 9h 30′ a.m. On foot, & travelled about incognito till the business was past & the Duke taken, & the Prisoners that had been seized on suspition, released: And because we might have been examined afterwards we kept a Journall of our motions as followeth, viz. This day we went to Winchelsea & thence to Mr. Jno Weekes's at Westfield, where we staid that night & 26 ♀ & till 27 ♄ in the afternoon: then we went to Mr. Sam: Hylands at Bodiham,[4] & lodged there till July 2 ♃ & having sent for my wife thither who acquainted me with the house being searched for me to have sent me to Dovor Castle &c. we rode this day to Lamberhurst, and lodged there that night. July 3 ♀ we went to the Wells, & lodged that night at Cousin Jno Wagon's.[5] July 4 ♄ Rode back to Lamberhurst & thence to Brenchley, where

---

[3] i.e. Flimwell.
[4] Samuel Hyland of Bodiam may have been the son-in-law of John Weeks, Jeake's close friend, whose grandchild was named Samuel Hyland (see Appendix 3).
[5] John Wagon or Waghorne of Pembury, bricklayer, was married to Jeake's aunt, Elizabeth Hartridge, and had to pay Jeake an annuity on land at Ashburnham. See 27.8.73.

lodged at Geo: Jansons, & tarried there all the Lords day. And July 6 ☽ we rode to Maidstone where Mr. Markwick left us about some business of his own, but I & my wife continued there at Cousin Anne Wightman's house[6] till July 10 ♀ when we returned from thence to Hawkherst & lodged at Mr. Collier's, July 11 ♄. We lodged at Mr. Tho: Woodgate's in Hawkherst where Mr. Markwick met us again;[7] & there we continued till July 20 ☽. When (my wife being return'd 3 or 4 days before) I ventur'd home again to Rye coming on foot from Hawkherst & arriving at Rye 11h p.m. My Persecutors having then no power to meddle with me. The weather in these journeys pretty much inclin'd to rain, especially toward the latter end, yet we scaped pretty well, & I had a very fine day for my return; but severall days before were wet, & the next day very rainy.

Aug. 2 ☉ No. 235. Jno Tillinghast, Generation Work. Parts 1 & 2. 8°
[1654].

  31 ☽ No. 236. Jno Tillinghast, Generation Work. Part 3. 8° [1654].

Sept. 5 ♄ Finished my Wife's Nativity Astrologically handled, exactly: according to the Method & Principles of Jo: Bapt. Morinus the Rough Draught of which I transcribed at leisure times & finished by August 30 1686 consisting of 8 sheets in 4°.[8]

  9 ☿ About noon exactly or very neer, I was taken with a Tertian ague; cold but not Shaking; after it lay in my head from 6h p.m. till next morning, & I sweat very much in the night. NB when I was first seized Saturn was just past the Cusp of Medium Coeli & Mars partilly opposing the Cusp of the 8th.

  11 ♀ About 11h a.m. A 2d fit, cold at first & vomiting, the vomit exceeding sowre, after an hot fit & sweat much in the night.

  13 ☉ About 10h a.m. A 3d fit, cold & vomiting but not so bad as the 2d fit: afterwards hot & sweat in the night. This was the last fit though I were indisposed on the well daies, & after I had lost the

[6] Ann Wightman was first cousin of Jeake and daughter of William Key (see 20.12.66), married to James Wightman, a London watchmaker. By the 1680s she was living in Maidstone. Smart, p. 78; PCC PROB 11/428 1695: 195; ESRO D 516/34.

[7] Thomas Woodgate may have been related to the yeoman of the same name from East Grinstead who wrote his will in 1677. No information has been found on George Janson or Mr Collier. LAWR 34, p. 333.

[8] The draft of this work is now Selmes MS 52 and the fair copy Selmes MS 53/1.

ague for neer a week troubled with the spleen, costiveness & a sore mouth.

14 ☽ About 2h 45′ p.m. I rode to Tenterden being subpena'd to witness the sealing of a deed at Maidstone assizes. I left my Child very ill of a feaver, & I was indisposed with my ague; came to Tenterden 5h 30′ p.m. And next day about 7h a.m. rode thence & came to Maidstone about noon, having very good weather. That evening news was brought me by one that came from Rye that my Child had a fit of Convulsion, a little after I was gone towards Tenterden, whereat I was much concerned. But 16 ☿ after I had given my Testimony at the Tryal in the forenoon, the rest of the day proved so rainy, that I was forced to stay till 17 ♃ when about 9h a.m. departed from Maidstone, & came to Rye about 5h p.m. without any rain or other trouble; & at my return found that there had been no more of the Convulsion fits, though the feaver continued still.

27 ☉ No. 237. Jo. Archer, Personal reign of Christ on Earth. 4° [1642].
No. 238. Ric: Mercer, Some discoveryes of the Mystery of the last times &c. 4° [1649].

Oct. 5 ☽ This day I was presented by the Grand Jury at Rye, for not coming to Church 3 Sundays, as they word it in their Pagan Dialect; at 12d per day.

10 ♄ No. 239. Jno Milton, Paradise lost. 8° [1667].

25 ☉ No. 240. Ric: Mercer, Further Discovery &c. 4° [1651].

Nov. 16 ☽ No. 241. [Henry Danvers] Theopolis, The City of God &c. 8° [1672].

Dec. 12 ♄ & 14 ☽ Encomium Genesews [*sic*] Patris. chiefly Astrological; & concise.⁹

1686

Jan. 8 ♀ No. 242. The Alcoran of Mahomet, with [Alexander] Rosse's Caveat, & the Life of Mahomet. 8° [1649].

ditto About 6h p.m. Going out of my Garret my Candle being almost out, I set my foot part off & part on upon the Garret floor which

---

⁹ Now Selmes MS 51; printed in the elder Jeake's *Λογιστικηλολία* (London, 1696), sig. b2, and in Smart, pp. 74–5.

by a merciful providence slipped down thence on the uppermost stair, without any staggering or stumbling; whereas if I had stumbled (as it was almost a wonder I did not) my forehead had been dasht against a great beam that lay opposite, & thence I had tumbled down the stairs.

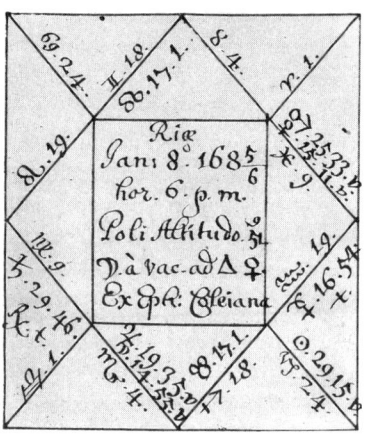

Saturn & Mars seem unconcern'd in this Scheme, And I would therefore referr the accident to the opposition of Mercury out of an airy sign both to the Radical & Transiting Ascendant & the square of Jupiter to them & Mercury. And I do think a certain concurrency of so many Planets happening at the same time to be on the Cusps of malefique houses might all together contribute to the effect, which the solitary positure of any one would not have produced, as the Sun on the 6th the Moon on the 4th Mercury on the 7th & Venus on the 8th & the rather because the positure of the houses is much the same with the Radix.

Jan. 10 ☉ No. 243. Jno Preston, Life Eternal, or of the Attributes. 4° [1631].

23 ♄ About 8h 30′ a.m. Took horse for London, being subpena'd as a witness to some bills of sale in a Cause depending at Guildhall London. The weather frosty & pretty Cold, else fine riding, came to Lamberhurst about 2h p.m., went thence an houre after; & about 5h 30′ p.m. riding in the forrest between Woodsgate & Tunbridge in the moonshine the tracks were so bad &

uneven, that I with another of my Company lost them, & the ground being so rugged & full of holes freezed; I thought best to alight & lead my horse; when another of the Company having lighted on a pretty good track, I led my horse thither, & got him into the track; & being about to mount him, the track being very low with rugged ground freezed on either side & holes of Ice between, & my horse having a trick not to stand still, when my foot was in the stirrop, he moved so much that my other foot slipp'd & I could not recover my self, but fell & slid down with both my legs under the horse's belly, still holding the Reins of the bridle in my hand. but it pleased God that the horse stood perfectly still when I lay under him; for if he had kept going as he did before though but 2 steps, he had trod either upon my belly, or my legs, & kill'd me or broke my limbs in that hollow track. But standing still, I recovered my self, & got up without further trouble. Which eminent preservation I shall always remember with thankfulness. After wards I came to Sevenoke at 8h 30′ p.m. where staid till Munday morning.

The Sun at the time of this Accident was in the 15th degree of Aquarius which is supposed to signify the legs, opposite partilly to my radical Ascendant, & was newly set in that positure, Saturn being in the last degree of Virgo, opposite to the Cusp of the 9th in my Radix. & Mars in the 7th degree of Aries just on the Cusp of the 9th in the Transit; both which seem to intimate perill in a Journey. Other Causes I find not.

25 ☽ About 8h a.m. Rode to London & came thither a little past 1 a clock in the afternoon having fine weather & little wind; found my Father in good health.

Feb. 4 ♃ The Tryall came on. but the Cause being given over for lost by the Evidence of Abrah: Wilde & Wm Goodyear, I was not called.[1]

8 ☽ Having been paid for my Charges £5 I returned from London about 9h 15′ a.m. & came to Sevenoke 2h p.m. & after an hours stay to Lamberhurst that night 8h p.m. The weather now open, not cold, no wind, cloudy; & very dark from Woodsgate to Lamberhurst & exceeding bad ways & dangerous riding.

1686 [1] William Goodyear was a Rye mariner, as evidently was Abraham Wilde: a document survives enquiring whether he was Master of the *Fellowship* at Rye in June–Aug. 1679. RYE 2/4; FRE 5257.

Feb. 9 ♂ About 8h a.m. Rode from Lamberhurst & came to Rye 30′ p.m. fine weather, Cloudy but very little wind, & not cold.

21 ☉ No. 244. T.L. Voice out of the Wilderness. 8° [1651].

Mar. 7 ☉ No. 245. N.S. Epistle dated 30th 11th month 1659. 4°.[2]

22 ☽ About 7h a.m. Rode to the Assizes at East Grinstead, subpena'd to prove a Lease to which I was witness. The weather very rainy & windy for the 1st 6 or 7 mile then left raining; came to Wadhurst about 11h 30′ a.m. Thence about 1h p.m. for Grinstead. having by the way 2 smart showers, one with hail: came to Grinsted 5h 30′ p.m.

24 ☿ The Tryal came on in the forenoon, but the defendants confessing the Lease I was not examined. After the Tryall it rained all day & the wind high; so tarried there that night, & next day came home.

25 ♃ About 8h a.m. Returned from Grinstead, & came to Rye about 8h p.m. having very good weather only the wind pretty high.

Apr. 5 ☽ No. 246. Jo: Cotton, The pouring out of the 7 vials. 4° [1642].

This day or the next I was nominated one of the overseers of the poor for the Parish of Rye, & the warrant to serve it sent me soon after; so I served it this year; but had no great trouble therein.

8 ♃ Having a bill of £43 15s return'd me protested, I rode this day to Romney about 1h p.m. to get either the money or security, coming thither at 8h p.m. I effected the latter, & had the money afterwards paid me at long run, yet without loss of Interest. Returned next morning 9h a.m. & came home 4h 30′ p.m. had indifferent good weather over head, only some sprinklings of rain sometimes & the wind brisk.

16 ♀ About 11h p.m. Took 1 scruple Pill Aureae in 2 Pills & next morning about 4h 30′ a.m. 1 scruple 5 gr[ains] more, gave 2 stools in the morning & 11 after taking broth; had done working by 1h p.m. & it agreed very well with my body; for which reason I mention the Dose.

19 ☽ Received a letter from Jno Mackley to lend him £75 more; which answered negatively.

---

[2] This item has not been identified.

21 ☿ About 11h p.m. After we were gone to bed one of my maid-servants falling asleep in the Kitchin with a Candle on a shelf neer her in woodden Candlestick. it burnt the Candlestick, & some Linen lying by it, & a past board box with the things in it, & had begun burnt the shelf to a Coal: when by God's Providence my Mother in law smelling burnt Linen as she lay in her bed, arose & came down; thereby preventing the maid & the house from being burnt.

About the beginning of May wrote to Mr. *Tournay about the money I let him have in the contests.*

May 16 ☉ No. 247. Jno Tillinghast, 8 last Sermons. 8° [1655].

23 ☉ In the evening received a letter from my Father in the behalf of Jno Mackley to lend him £50 & 25 ♂ sent a bill to ditto Mackley to receive said summe of Mr. Tho: Miller: which lent & lost.

June 20 ☉ No. 248. Jno Preston, Of the New Covenant &c. 4° [1629].

July 16 ♀ I wrote to my Father to return to Rye this Summer if he thought fit; the persecution declining, & the Excommunication being taken off by the late Kings General pardon &c. But by his Answer of the 27th he was not inclin'd to come this summer.

Aug. 22 ☉ Received advise that a bill I had lately negotiated on Mr. Serrarier[3] was protested; whereupon 23 ☽ I went over to Guldford[4] & got security for it without loss.

27 ♀ Weighed 1 pack of wooll bought 2 or 3 days before; & from that time fell on buying of wooll so that before December 25 I had bought about 89 Packs.

This Moneth I began to trade again (the Persecution being now over) & had a multitude of Business in August September October & November negotiating bills, buying wooll & Hops.

30 ☽ Mr. *Tournay's letter dated that he would refer the difference between us to my* C[ousin] *and* Mr. *Scot.*

Sept. 3 ♀ I wrote again to my Father about his return to Rye before winter; Mr. Stretton being last election put out from Town clerk & Darrington chosen in his room; who not understanding his

---

[3] Possibly Charles Serrier, whose son was admitted to Trinity College, Cambridge in 1698. Venn.

[4] i.e. East Guldeford.

place: had applied himself to me to assist him.[5] My Father's answer dated the 18th not being inclin'd to come this winter.

Sept. 11 ♄ Having bought about 12 packs of wooll of Mr. Jno Smith & this day prepared a note for him to sign, but neglecting it for some days by reason of business, wooll rising, he afterwards refused to let me have my bargain which was to my damage of £7.[6]

5 ☉ About 4h p.m. Taken with a fit of an ague, very moderate; went off with a feaver[;] pain of the head & sweat in the night.

7 ♂ About 5h p.m. A fit of a feaver for 4 or 5 hours; ending with a pain in the head & sweat in the night; but very moderate.

8 ☿ or thereabouts Received Mr. Scot's Letter, that he would pay in his Mortgage of £350.

21 ♂ or thereabouts. A letter having been sent from Mr. Edw: Cross of Exon to Mr. Tho: Miller directed to Rye (he not knowing of Mr. Miller's removal) to buy a Cargo of hops; the letter was brought to me & I sent it per post to Mr. Tho: Miller at London: who by his Answer of the 23th Instant offered to recommend me to Mr. Cross for that purpose, And also to go ½ in 20 or 24 bags to be bought between us. Both which I accepted of & the 25th I wrote to Mr. Cross, which Mr. Miller enclosed & sent to him; & he gave me order to buy 40 bags by Letter dated October 2 next.

Oct. 4 ☽ Bought 4 bags hops of Thos: Hayward between Mr. Miller & myself at £4 5s per hundred which were the first hops I ever bought.[7]

7 ♃ Having received this Wednesday's post Mr. Crosse's order I proceeded to serve him, buying some Hops this week & riding to Robertsbridge where Ro: Grove appointed to meet me at Battell market next Tuesday to sell me a quantity by Sample.

10 ☉ No. 249. Tobias Crisp, Christ alone exalted. Vol. 1 in 14 sermons. 8° [1643].

---

[5] Henry Darrington had been clerk of the trained band in Rye, and occupied a messuage belonging to the younger Jeake in 1698. On Samuel Stretton see 30.1.82 and Introduction, sect. 4. RYE 1/17, p. 69; 19/51; PAB 1.

[6] John Smith was a farmer from Maidstone, possibly the testator described as a husbandman in his will proved in 1727. KAO PRC/32/60: 307; see also 19.5.99.

[7] Thomas Hayward was probably the testator of that name from Udimore, who left £20 each to his two daughters in 1699. LAWR 44, p. 24.

12 ♂ I rode to Battel market & bought there 24 bags of Hops of Robt Grove for Mr. Cross at £4 5s & £4 7s per hundred which proved well, as did all I bought this year: for they rose.

14 ♃ In the afternoon, a fit of a Tertian ague very moderate. But I had had a grievous Cough for about a week before.

16 ♄ At noon or soon after a 2d fit more tedious with vomiting & loosness in the Cold fit: a feaver & pain after till 10 h p.m. then sweat.

18 ☽ At noon, a 3d fit, the worst of all, vomiting &c. as before, & a very violent feaver after till till 6h p.m. then a great pain in my head & a little breathing sweat.

20 ☿ About noon a 4th fit, not much cold yet vomited &c. a feaver from 2h p.m. till midnight pretty violent[.] Took some Venice Treacle at night, sweat & slept indifferent.

21 ♃ Robt. Grove brought in his hops, weigh'd next morning, came to £235 9s 6d for which gave him bill for £100 in London; & paid the rest in money to his Messenger November 6.

ditto Bought Anth: Fullers hops 8 bags between Mr. Miller & me at £4 5s & a Guiney brokerage, sold next spring to profit.[8]

22 ♀ About noon & a little after instead of my Ague I had 6 stools & somewhat more indisposed then ordinary.

30 ♄ Mr. Elhanan Tucker sent me £350 to be return'd to London, which I drew all in one bill 3 days sight, having from August to the end of the year a great Trade of Negotiating bills.[9]

Nov. 1 ☽ Shipped Mr. Crosses hops in Rob: Barthol[omew] for Exon 39 bags 1 end.[10] Invoice amounting to £419 1s 11d whereof Commission £8 4s 4d.

6 ♄ I sold Wm Baker 60 packs of wool at £7 10s per pack & 2 Guineys over, by which got about £47. The same day I bought 5 packs more the 8th 12 packs & the 9th at Battell market 20 packs all at £7 per pack. For 30 packs whereof being at Romney the 11th ♃ I was offered £7 10s per pack but refus'd it, & after

---

[8] Anthony Fuller was a yeoman from Brede. SAU 145; LAWR 43, p. 86.

[9] Elhanan Tucker was a gentleman from Tenterden, Kent, who married Ann File (see 22.1.77). Cowper, p. 583.

[10] Robert Bartholomew was a Rye mariner. Jeake also had dealings with his cousin, of the same name, who lived in Hastings. Both Jeakes witnessed his will. RYE 145/11; LAWR 39, p. 39.

in December was offered £8 per pack which refusing it fell presently so that about January 24 I sold it for but £7 5s per pack & fain to stay a pretty while for payment.

In November being over much harass'd with business I had a very violent Cough which continued ever since the beginning of October & was excessive November 11 at Romney.

Dec. 7 ♂ My Father's letter dated; acquainting me that Mr. Scot was so ill, that he could not consider the Controversy referr'd to him by Mr. Tournay & me: And soon after he died viz. the 17th Instant.

28 ♂ Wrote to Mr. Miller about my intentions of dealing to Morlaix, which prosecuted next Spring.

1687

Jan. 1 ♄ Upon the balancing of my Liedger for the year past. Computed about £67 clear profit.

16 ☉ In the evening, taken with a Quartan ague; this first fit very little.

19 ☿ About 6h p.m. the 2d fit, exceeding gentle, first a shivering, & at last a little feaverish heat.

22 ♄ About 5h p.m. the 3d fit; worse, shivering for 2 hours with pain in the head; hot after.

23 ☉ In the Evening or next day morning, advise of my Father's illness at London of an ague, the Cold fit whereof lasted for 24 hours. Upon which advise fearing I should have occasion to go to London, I went to Romney & sold 30 packs of wooll: Soon after which viz. by next post I heard my Father was amended. And soon after the price of wooll advanc'd.

25 ♂ About 5h p.m. the 4th fit of my Ague at New Romney; rather better than the former.

26 ☿ This day I sold my 30 packs of wooll unhappily for £7 5s per pack being the best I had: Losing thereby neer £30 of what I had been offered before; & might also have had if I had kept longer.

28 ♀ About 4h p.m. the 5th fit, somewhat worse than the former.

31 ☽ About 3h p.m. the 6th fit; very little of the cold [;] most feaver & pain in the head, sweat exceeding much.

Feb. 3 ♃ About 3h p.m. the 7th fit, more cold & long, but not so hot, nor so much sweat in the night; & then sick in my stomach.

6 ☉ About 3h 30′ p.m. the 8th fit, much like the former.

9 ☿ About 3h 15′ p.m. the 9th fit, more moderate; yet sweat more in the night.

12 ♄ About 5h p.m. the 10th & last fit, Exceeding moderate without sweat. This day received advice of 5 ballots Dowlas shipped for me by Mr. Miller at London, cost £98 9s 11d.

20 ☉ No. 250. Jno Owen, Exercitations on the Epistle to the Hebrews, & concerning the Messiah. And an Exposition on the 2 first Chapters of the Epistle. Folio [1668].

Mar. 23 ☿ or next morning advise per post of Dr. Nichols his payment of £350 into Mr. Miller's hands for an assignment of one of my Mortgages upon Mr. Scot's estate: which according to his desire I assigned & sent up to him soon after.[1] News also per Gazette of somethings preparatory to the Declaration for Liberty of Conscience. News per letter that hops began to rise.

27 ☉ No. 251. Jos: Caryll, Exposition on the 3 first Chapters of Job. 4° [1643].

28 ☽ Advise per Mr. Millers letter of the 26th that all the hops between us were now sold at £5 4s per hundred.

Apr. 11 ☽ Advise per his Letter of the 7th Instant that he had shipt 14 ballots Linens which I bought of him for £217 6s 3¾d in Kirby's hoy for Rye, which arrived safe in 7 days or less. Enclosed also in his Letter I received King James's Declaration for Liberty of Conscience.

28 ♃ Arbitration at Romney about Mr. Tournay's business. but never got anything. Providence having seem'd to deny it by Mr. Scot's death just before he was to have ended it. Return'd home at night.

30 ♄ I wrote to Morlaix per Jos: Martin for the value of 1700L french in Linens & paper: & sent in money by him May 3 ♂ 1524L 10s & soon after he went to sea, & arrived safe there.

May 2 ☽ No. 252. Frid. Spanhemii, Dubia Evangelica. Vol. 1. 4° [1634].

1687 [1] Dr Nichols may have been related to the Thomas Nicholls of Folkestone, surgeon, who with his wife Elizabeth sold a marsh at Brensett to James Lamb of Rye in 1740. PAB 226–8.

About this time received my Father's letter of the 29th April: consenting to return to Rye.

May 11 ☿ About 2h 30′ p.m. I took horse for London to accompany my Father from thence down to Rye, came that night to Lamberhurst having good weather; next day rode to London in a mighty storm of wind but without rain: found my Father in good health; & had good success in my journey.

22 ☉ At London I was taken with the Shingles on my left side; which were very troublesome after I got to Rye; especially from 29 ☉ to June 2 ♃ when they decreased in pain sensibly by the use of salt, oyl & vinegar beaten together & anointing them; not quite gone till the week after.

23 ☽ About 8h 15′ a.m. My Father after his long absence returned for Rye in the Tunbridge Coach accompanied with Mr. Tho: Miller And about 9h a.m. I departed from London on horsback with Mr. Jos: Smith who with Mr. Miller accompanied us throughout to Rye.[2] We all came safe to Tunbridge that night; & the next day all on horsback to Rye, when through mercy we arrived safe about 6h p.m. having very good weather, neither wind nor rain, nor intemperate heat.

---

[2] No information has been found on Joseph Smith.

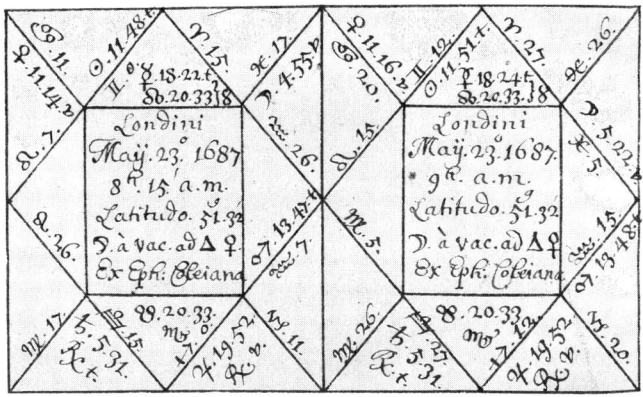

29 ⊙ About 2h p.m. We held our meeting again publiquely at Rye; my Father now first speaking therein after his Return. Of which I gave notice to the Maior the night before.

June 8 ☿ as I remember Jos: Martin returned safe from Morlaix with 6 Ballots Linens & 2 bales Paper for me costing 1712L 8s french, Landed the goods in a day or 2 after.

28 ♂ I weigh'd some wooll lately bought; & kept on buying so that by November 23th following I had bought 115 packs.

July 5 ♂ From this day inclusive till July 4th 1688 viz. for the space of one whole year, I kept a perfect Diary of all the material Accidents befalling me all receipts & payments of money, buying & selling of goods, journeys, sicknesses &c in order to the making Astrological Experiments.[3] So that being registred there I shall not here transcribe so prolix & unnecessary an Enumeration of them but only select such particulars as may seem pertinent to my present design; viz.

ditto 9h a.m. Bought 14 packs of wooll of Edward Wilmshurst. 10h a.m. Bought Tho: Odiarn's wooll about 8 packs. 8h p.m. Bought John Frenches wooll about 10 packs, all at £8 per pack.[4]

---

[3] Jeake here refers to *AEE*. See Introduction, sects. 2 and 3.

[4] Edward Wilmshurst was a grazier living at Cadborough, Rye parish (presumably related to Stephen: see 8.12.82). Thomas Odiarn was probably the Rye jurat of the same name, an opponent of the dissenters; Jeake sold Odiarn lockrams at this time. John French was a husbandman from Eastbourne who also borrowed money from Jeake. PAB 4; Smart, p. 65; ESRO D 516/22; LAWR 46, p. 27; 43, p. 121; RYE 145/11.

July 6 ☿ About 8h p.m. Bought Charles Crouch's wooll about 20 packs, at £8 per pack.[5]

18 ☽ 11h a.m. News per post of the Proclamation concerning Wooll; whence it was concluded that the price would fall; at which concern'd having bought a great quantity dear. At 2h p.m. Took a journey with my Wife, & two friends in Company to Canterbury for diversion & came that night to Chart, next day to Canterbury.

21 ♃ Returned to Chart, & 23 ♄ to Rye at 4h p.m. having good weather in our journey.

Aug. 10 ☿ At 4h p.m. Bought Tho: Cruttenden's wooll 18 packs at £7 15s per pack.

16 ♂ At 8h a.m. Rode to Robertsbridge with Cousin Frebody. Thence to Bodiham to my wife came thither 1h p.m. & next day came home in the forenoon in wet misling weather.

Sept. 5 ☽ 1h p.m. Took horse for Romney to assign over Tho: Smith's Mortgage, for which Mr. Wm Finch had procured me a Chapman[;] came thither at 5h 30' p.m. bad weather much wind & severall showers of Rain.

6 ♂ Received £103 2s 4d & assigned the mortgage at 5h p.m. & 7 ☿ 8h 15' a.m.; Return'd & came to Rye 1h 45' p.m. having very good weather & little wind.

About this time much business negotiating of Bills which continued a good part of the year.

12 ☽ A swelling in my left Ear & very painfull next day, soon after discussed of it self, & with such kind of Tumours I was troubled at times for a year or more.

24 ♄ Vain Efforts to buy Hops: they rising so fast & being now £9 10s & in a few days £10 per hundred I bought none upon my own account this year.

26 ☽ Having this morning an order from Mr. Edw: Cross of Exon to buy 30 bags of Hops for him. I rode out for that purpose at 9h 15' a.m. but had no great success they being Caught up at £9 10s 2 days before, met with but 4 bags: & next day in another

---

[5] Charles Crouch was a Rye jurat, and probably related to Thomas Crouch (see Appendix 3). RYE 19/52.

journey but 2 bags 1 end & in some space of time & with great difficulty made up about 20 bags.

Oct. 1 ♄ Bills brought me for £267 4s 6d to negotiate. Borrowed £160 for part & put off the residue to a friend; being out of Cash. Offered £8 per pack for my wooll; but refus'd it.

11 ♂ Rode to severall places to buy Hops as far as Battell; but not worth my trouble[;] came home about 7h p.m. Cloudy & a little Rain, but no wind.

19 ☿ About 11′ past 4 a Clock in the morning Brother Hartshorn's Eldest Daughter named Barbara was born at London.

25 ♂ About 9h a.m. Advice that the price of wooll was advanced & above £8 per pack given I having now a great quantity by me.

29 ♄ News about 9h a.m. that wooll was £8 5s per pack.

31 ☽ I was offered £8 2s 6d per pack for wooll: but refused to sell under £8 5s.

Nov. 7 ☽ About 6h p.m. A Chapman came to buy wooll: sold him 14 packs at £8 5s per pack &c.

11 ♀ About 2h p.m. Advise that wooll was sold at £8 8s per pack. And 4h p.m. precisely advise per W.F.[6] that £8 10s per pack had really been offered to weigh & pay by December 25 next; which advise was of Great use in directing me to insist upon such a price for mine, & to take the opportunity of selling it; it being the Top price it came to that year, & not holding up scarce a month neither.

14 ☽ About this time severall discourses about new modelling of Corporations & putting in Dissenters: but having no great edge to it at Rye, our proceedings in complying were so dilatory, & our refusall to grant the King the choice of one Member in Parliament was so disagreeable to the then Court relish, that we happily escaped the New Modell.

17 ♃ *About this night but once c*[arnal?] *c*[opulation?]*; after which terms descend* Monday *next.*

19 ♄ About noon Another Chapman came to buy some wooll; appointed to meet at the Tavern, 1h 45′ p.m. we met & continued treating till 4h 30′ p.m. & then with much adoe sold him

---

[6] Probably William Finch. See Appendix 3.

all my wooll remaining, viz. about 103 packs, at £8 10s per pack only I to find 30 Cloths, to weigh & pay & clear all by March 25 next. But it was a good while after before all of it was weigh'd & paid for, viz: above a year: yet I may count it happily sold for the price fell next spring to £6 per pack.

Nov. 28 ☽ Ordered per Mr. Cross to hire a vessel on purpose to send his hops, sent to Hasting about it.

Dec. 7 ☿ About 7h p.m. Treated with Ro: Fellows of Hasting to carry Mr. Crosses hops, & after 3 hours tarriance agreed, & shipped them next morning.[7]

13 ♄ Upon Balance of the Liedger, clear profit for the year past was £40 15s 2d.

1688

Jan. 3 ♂ *About this time wife being with child as guessed it proved a son.*

4 ☿ Busy in the forenoon considering what Quantity & sorts of Cloth to send for to Morlaix: & next day finished, & wrote to Procter & Sedgwick of Morlaix to send me the value of 2000 Crowns in 4 ships. ordering them to draw 1000 crowns presently, & per same post ordering Mr. Tho: Miller to remitt them £200 sterling from London.

11 ☿ Wrote to Mr. James Le Griel of Dieppe to draw 400 Crowns upon me & send me the value thereof in Canvas.

14 ♄ About 5h 50′ p.m. precisely, Sent for by 2 masters of Ships, one of which had 3000 Deals to sell, & the other 14 packs of wooll; but fearfull to buy because they were strangers, put them off till Monday.

16 ☽ About 11h a.m. sent for by them again; About noon, narrowly miss'd hitting my head against a door that stood a jar in an Entry hit my shoulder but without hurt. Saturn & Mars being then opposite on the Cusps of the 12th & 6th in Aries & Libra, Gemini Ascending & Venus opposite thereto[:] most of the Planets on the Cusps of malefique houses. Jupiter & Mercury neer the Cusp of the 8th in opposition to the Radical place of Mars &c.

[7] Robert Fellows was a mariner from Hastings, and brother-in-law of William Oake (see 28.1.89). LAWR 49, p. 230.

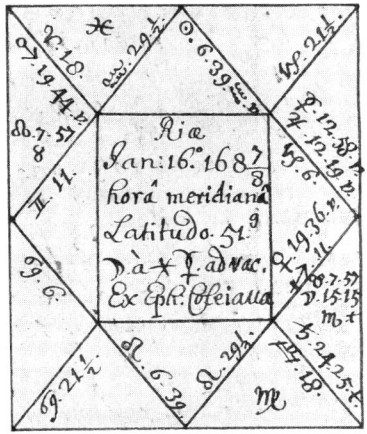

About 2h 15′ p.m. I went aboard the ships with Mr. Nic: Shinner & about 4h p.m. bought the wooll for £6 5s per pack whereof he was to have 4 packs & I the rest. The Deals we bought equally between us at £3 9s per hundred. came ashore about 8h p.m.

19 ♃ About 3h p.m. went aboard one of the ships & saw the Malt which Theoph: Gleed one of the masters had aboard his vessell about 350 Quarters, which he offered for 14s per quarter. but I durst not venture having no Experience in it, & fearing it would not sell.

21 ♄ About 8h a.m. Th: Gleed came to know my final resolves about the Malt, & by 9h a.m. concluded & bought it at 12s 6d per quarter. offered Nic: Shinner ¼ part which he accepted: It sold well & speedily, most out of the vessell so that we landed little; the profit for my ¾ was £30. By the Deals there was also profit but we were some years in selling them. By the wooll I lost above £12 it falling & I refusing to take money when well offered. viz. February 1 ☿ next when I was proffered for it & 4 or 5 packs of this Country wool £7 10s per pack by a good Chapman; my refusing to take which offer was the greatest Error I committed that year in my affairs; for after a years keeping I was fain to sell for £5 10s.

Feb. 13 ☽ 10h a.m. Sold 15 packs of wooll among which was the wooll last mentioned, but the Chapman proving insolvent never weighed of but 3 packs at £7 18s per pack & for 2 packs of that I was very much troubled to get my money: & fain to sue for it.

Feb. 16 ♃ Two Bales of Canvas from Dieppe in Alex: White arrived safe upon my Account in Rye harbour, Invoice 1001L 19s french. News thereof 10h a.m. Entry the same day. Goods landed the next.

18 ♄ Symptoms of my wife's abortion, but it passed over. About 30′ p.m. News that W[illiam] B[aker] who had been sick for some time was now relapsed & very ill so that his recovery was questioned. At which I was troubled he owing me £225 for wooll, besides a great deal more that he had bought & was to draw & pay for. And if he had died then I might probably have lost all my money. But it pleased God that he recovered & lived to pay me all my money; so that I was thoroughly clear of him; & soon after that he died, & his widow cheated most of the Creditors of their moneys.

21 ♂ About 9h a.m. wrote to Mr. Griel for 2 bales Canvas more & 8 packets Normandy to be sent per Rob: Bartholomew.

25 ♄ About 1h p.m. News from Robt Fellows his wife who had £12 on Bottomarie that he had not been heard of since he went from Topsham about 7 weeks & she feared was lost, & after this it was so long before he was heard of that I had quite given him over.[1]

Mar. 2 ♀ A Morlaix ship Tho: Urry Master having on board 10 ballots & packets of Linens for me amounting to 1827L 17s french, going for London was providentially by contrary winds put into Rye harbour; where I took out 8 but the other 2 we could not find, so they were fain to be carried to London.

4 ☉ No. 253. Peter Jurieu, Accomplishment of the Prophecies. 8° [1687].

6 ♂ Hitherto I was pretty well paid for the wooll I delivered which I had sold in November last[.] But this morning about 8h a.m. delivering 7 packs more of it, I was much troubled to get my money, & to get the residue off my hands according to the bargain.

7 ☿ About 4h p.m. News that it was confidently reported that Robt. Fellows was foundred at Sea, by one that pretended to see it.

1688 [1] On Fellows see 7.12.87.

8 ♃ About 10h a.m. Rode a Circular Journey to get Customers for Cloth & enquire about an Apprentice; succeeded in the former, but not in the latter. Lodged at Hasting that night[.] Next day went to Battell Robertsbridge & Cranbrook, where lodged that night.

10 ♄ Returned home by the way of Tenterden. about 3h p.m. came to Rye. Two great Bales of Canvas with 7 or 8 parcels Normandy costing at Dieppe neer 1300L french arrived safe in my absence at Rye per Robt Bartholomew[2] & were landed & at my house when I came home. News also at my Return that W[illiam] B[aker] who bought my wooll had lost 17 packs at sea & was like to come in trouble: & desired me to sell the remaining wooll, & he would bear the loss of it; for he could not fetch it. Received of him by bill in part of what he owed £131 16s.

12 ☽ About 7h 45' a.m. News per post certain that Robt. Fellows was well at his Port, after he had so long been given over for lost. Jupiter neer the Cusp of Medium Coeli & Venus of the 11th.

13 ♂ *Wife quick with child which proved a son.*

15 ♃ About 10h a.m. News per post that 5 ballots & 6 packets of Linens amounting to 1847L 9s french laden at Morlaix in Ralph Myers for my account were arrived safe at London, & also 1 ballot & 1 packet in Urry.[3]

17 ♄ About 2h 30' p.m. Taken with a little aguish fit, ending in an headach.

19 ☽ About 11h a.m. A 2d fit, worse.

21 ☿ About 10h a.m. A 3d fit, worse with vomiting, & ill all day. But afterwards had no more of it.

26 ☽ About 9h a.m. News per post of the safe arrival of 7 ballots Linens costing at Morlaix 1726L 12s french in J. Hacker, at London for my account. And also of the arrival of 5 ballots & 1 packet more from thence in Wm Spriggs.[4] 1613L 16s french.

27 ♂ News that W[illiam] B[aker] who owed me still a great deal of money was searched for to be carried to Dovor Castle; & it was thought would be ruin'd by the troubles in which he was involved. But it proved otherwise as abovementioned.

[2] See 1.11.86.
[3] No further information has been found on the mariner Ralph Myers. On Urry, see 2.3.88.
[4] Hacker and Spriggs are two further unidentified shipowners.

Apr. 10 ♂ *About 6h p.m. my wife being rebuked by my C[ousin] for letting the child go into rude company, took it very ill; which much offended at, and he displeased, and I was extremely vexed about this all night.*

14 ♄ About 10h a.m. News per post of the Contents of the last Proclamation against Transportation of wooll ordering the Abettors to be punished. About 11h a.m. sent for to a Circular Messenger which came from the Commissioners for regulation of Corporations to take the names of Dissenters & others that they pretended to put in. About 6h p.m. sent for again to him; & he took a list of several names. Tarried till 9h p.m. and sitting without a fire, the weather being very cold: I took a most grievous Cold, which was very troublesome all next week.

16 ☽ Brother Nath: Hartshorn with his wife & Child came to my house from London. tarrying till June 4 ☽ when they went to houskeeping.

19 ♃ 11h a.m. precisely News that Alex: White was well arrived at Rye with 13 ballots & packets of the Morlaix Linens from London. Note Mercury exactly culminating, & neer the Radical Medium Coeli.

20 ♀ About 8h a.m. Received the Linens home. About 3h p.m. Taken ill & my Cold much increased. but next day it abated. 25 ☿ being out in the Air in the Evening renewed it & next day very bad, & sweat much in the night, continuing very bad & much after the same sort till May 5 ♄ & then it began to abate.

29 ☉ & 30 ☽ Troubled with a soreness in the lower part of my forehead about the Eyebrows: an effect of my Cold & May 1 ♂ my head much out of order with it.

May 4 ♀ My Mouth & Tongue began to be sore, which were somewhat troublesome 4 or 5 days.

9 ☿ About 8h a.m. I was taken with a strange Vertigo or swimming in the head, & presently after with a sick fit in the Stomach like to vomit, which brought a sweat; but went off immediately. The Moon opposite to the Ascendant in square to Saturn.

10 ♃ About 11h a.m. News of Cosin Mackley's being lately arrested & of his insolvency; at which much troubled severall houres. About 5h p.m. Notice from Tho: Cruttenden that I must come & weigh the wooll I had formerly bought of him to morrow.

11 ♀ About 6h a.m. Went to the Castle farme[5] with men to weigh it, being 18 packs, and brought it in a Lighter to Rye about 4h p.m. & had it all in by 7h p.m. but did not unpack it.

15 ♂ About 5h 30' p.m. precisely News that a vessell was coming into Rye harbour supposed to be Wm Kirby with 13 ballots Linens for me from London worth above £300 sterling. This confirmed at 9h p.m. & next day about 5h p.m. received them home.

18 ♀ Resolved to go to London next week to see if I could secure Jno Mackley's debt.

23 ☿ About 30' p.m. Set forward for London going by Guldford ferry to Lydd & Romney about some business there; but in-effectual: thence to Tenterden where lodged that night & next day rode to London, arriving there about 9h p.m. having very fine weather and not hot.

26 ♄ About 11h a.m. spake to Jno Mackley, but could get no money, nor promise of any unless he could get an Apprentice, which never came to pass.

June 1 ♀ Having laid out in this Journey for Cloths & furniture for a Chamber about £24 and bought a small parcell of Linens for a Tryall of the sort, I returned from London this day about 1h p.m. & by 6h p.m. got to Sevenoke, having very good weather.

2 ♄ About 7h 15' a.m. went thence by way of Wadhurst, & arrived at Rye about 6h p.m. had good weather only somewhat hot; and weary. Melancholy all this journey by reason of disappoint-ments about selling my wooll & about the aforesaid Debt: & next day also ill with the journey especially toward Evening.

4 ☽ About 7h p.m. News per Corn: Peadle a journeyman shoomaker[6] that the Customehouse Officers of Rye intended to come & seize the 18 packs of wooll that I bought of Tho: Cruttenden because I had not unpackt them: but he would not tell me who gave him the Intelligence[.] I seemed to slight him, & he went away; but returned within ½ an houre & said they would certainly seize it. After his first departure I took care to have it unpackt betimes

---

[5] i.e. the farm adjacent to Camber Castle on the Rye levels.

[6] Cornelius Peadle was probably related to the numerous Rye Peadles, several of whom had also been shoemakers. See 21.4.56, 8.8.82.

next morning, which accordingly was effected, beginning the work at 4h 30′ a.m. & finishing by 10h a.m.

June 14 ♃ About 10h a.m. News per post of the death of Cousin Rich: Freebody, leaving his wife and Two Children in a very poor Condition.

15 ♀ About 8 h a.m. News of the arrival of the goods I bought at London in Alex: White's vessell at Rye; part of them landed this evening & the rest next morning. Some of the Japan furniture dented & battered, about which I was excessively vexed all the day.

Aug. 13 ☽ About 7h a.m. Theoph: Gleed came to me to buy a Cargo of Malt which he had now brought into Rye harbour; went aboard with him to see it, & about noon bought it at 12s 10d per quarter, & he to lye 14 working days to deliver.[7] By this I got about £12 with very much difficulty, making a Circular journey soon after to Hasting Battell & Robertsbridge to sell it, which succeeded at Hasting to the sale of almost 100 quarters. So that most was sold out of the vessell (the whole quantity being about 260 quarters).

ditto At 11h 49′ p.m. exactly (allowing 10′ that the Sun sets at Rye before he comes to the Levell of the Horizon, for the watch was set by the Sun's setting) my wife was safely delivered of a Son; which I named Manasseh; hoping that God had now made me forget all my Toile &c.[8]

Oct. 1 ☽ News by King James's Proclamation of the Invasion expected from Holland; & of the General pardon extending to all except Otes & 12 others.

About this time I began to be troubled with a white pertinacious Thrush in the upper Jaw within side in the Mouth, which gradually slowly encreased, & all means I used proved ineffectuall. I could never be cured of it; but it was without pain, & not very much till 4 or 5 years after.

16 ♂ Begun my Book called Astrologicall Experiments Exemplified, in a complete Systeme of Solar Revolutional Directions attended on by their respectively proportionable Effects during the space of one whole year. & occupied my self therein at spare hours till June 15 ☿ 1692. When finished it, & afterwards

---

[7] See 19.1.88.   [8] On Manasseh see 23.5.73.

transcribed it fair, & carried it to London in April 1694. where it was perused by Coley. It consisted of 20 sheets in 4°.[9]

Nov. 6 ♂ & 7 ☿   Weighed to W[illiam] B[aker] 16 packs wooll which was of that bought formerly of Tho: Cruttenden[;] delivered it on trust as formerly sold at £8 10s per pack, but he paid me for it in a short time, though I ran a great venture in trusting.

7 ☿ Advice from Mr. Miller per post dated 6th Instant that that Evening King James received an Express that the Dutch were landing at Torbay; the Prince of Orange being with them. As I remember the Saturday before at night we heard of it by a stragling vessell of that fleet that was put into our harbour.

Dec. 11 ♂ This morning at 3 a clock King James went away privately from Whitehall[.] News thereof per post the 12th ☿.

26 ☿ Advice per post dated 25th Instant at London. That it was thought there would be a speedy war with France.

1689

Jan. 10 ♃ At this time I had so great a Trade of negotiating Bills of Exchange; that from this day to February 8 inclusive I negotiated bills for £1299 4s 10d sterling. But afterwards it decreased & the war coming on I gave it over.

28 ☽ Sent a letter to Mr. Griel to send me a Quantity of Canvas per Wm Oake,[1] who was sent over to Dieppe by severall for goods before the war broke out. But he sent me none. To Morlaix we sent not; for fear the war should break out before we could have a Return.

Feb. 9 ♄ Delivered 13 packs wooll sold J.H.[2] at £5 10s per pack so that now I had clear'd my self of all.

12 ♂ Received the last Bottomarie profit: & the war coming on I gave over that Trade.

13 ☿ The Prince & Princess of Orange proclaimed King & Queen. 14 ♃ advise thereof dated & received the 15 ♀ per post. So that now through the mercifull Providence of God, we were freed from the fears of Popery & Persecution.

[9] i.e. *AEE*. On Henry Coley, the London astrologer, see *DNB* and Introduction, sect. 2.

1689 [1] A Rye mariner. The Oakes were a long-established family of Rye fishermen. LAWR 48, p. 89.

[2] Probably the mariner John Hacker. See 26.3.88.

Feb. 18 ☽ Finished my Proposal for managing the Trade of French Linens at Rye; and transcribed it fair the 19th ♂ taking up 1 sheet of Paper.

Mar. 1 ♀ No. 254. Frid: Spanhemij Dubia Evangelica; pars 2da. 4° [1639].

11 ☽ News per post from London dated the 9 Instant concerning the Parliaments address to the King & his Answer; by which was gathered a war with France would follow.

22 ♀ Having received a Letter from Mr. Le Griel: sent again to him & Mr. Le Grand for Canvas but received none; the Shallop not coming again.[3]

Apr. 16 ♂ I rode to Heathfield to view a parcell of Land to buy it; but liked it not on the view. This day I received £120 of Robert Grove & gave bill for it on Mr. Tho: Miller in London; & moreover a Letter of Credit for him to furnish the said Grove with £50 or £60 more upon Return if he wanted it.

17 ☿ Returned home from Heathfield having pretty good weather, only some rain yesterday but not much.

Advise per post dated yesterday, that there would be a speedy war with France.

29 ☽ Advise per post that Robt Grove had taken up £50 of Mr. Miller in London of my money per my order & left a bill of his hand for the same to be paid me at Rye at his Return. But he desiring to keep it a while upon Interest & I consenting; & not taking Bond for the money: he soon after died of the Measells and being much in debt which I knew not; all his personal estate did but little more then pay the Bonds & all the Debts almost upon simple Contract were lost; except mine which with much difficulty & the labour of 13 or 14 journeys to Robertsbridge I secured for the most part, not losing £10. But the vexation & pains I took was more worth then the £50 and had it been now to do, I would sooner have lost my debt.

May 1 ☿ Advice, dated 30th past, of the Proclamation forbidding the Importation of French goods after May 16th.

3 ♀ Bought Lime for the Buildings I intended this Summer; viz: to Build a Storehouse, make a Brewhouse, trim up a woodhouse, &

[3] No more information is available concerning Mr Le Grand.

to repair all the foreside of my dwelling house. About which I laid out in all between £290 & £300 of which most this year: & finished next viz: by July 4th 1690.

6 ☽ I bought a piece of Ground of Robt Browne over against my dwelling house to build a Storehouse upon for £3 10s Paid him the money & had possession delivered 14 ♂.

13 ☽ Advice of the Proclamation of the war with France by Letter dated 11th Instant enclosing the same. Whereby lost my Trade with France.

22 ☿ Advice per post dated 21 instant that the Bill for Toleration of Protestant Dissenters had passed the house of Commons; which soon after passed the house of Lords & the Royal Assent. So that now we were freed from the fears of Persecution.

26 ☉ About 2h p.m. A very little fit of an Ague. Venus then culminating on the Radical place of Mars. The Moon opposite to the Cusp of Medium Coeli. Saturn opposite to the Cusp of the 8th & Mars opposite to the Cusp of the 12th.

28 ♂ About 1h p.m. A 2d fit: a little shivering, after hot sweating & head ach: pretty well off by 10h p.m.

30 ♃ About 1h p.m. A 3d fit, more moderate then the former; pretty well off before night.

June 13 ♃ Exactly at Noon, the foundation of my storehouse was laid; the first stone by my self under this positure of heaven.

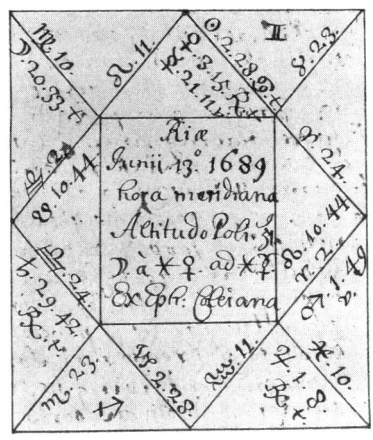

This time was elected only for Experiment sake & not out of any Confidence I had that the influence of heaven signified any thing to Artificials. In building this Storehouse I consumed £230: the walls which were of Stone; & the Roof were finished this yeare before winter; but the boarding staires, glasing & finishing work, next spring & summer, all being done by July 4th 1690.[4]

July 13 ♄ Robert Grove died. heard of it the week following & 19 ♀ wrote to Mr. Finch for his advise about securing my debt of £50 soon after rode to Robertsbridge thereabouts.

Aug. 16 ♀ Cosin Mackley's Letter dated: that he was broke, & in the Mint:[5] whereby I lost that debt being about £74.

29 ♃ A meeting of Grove's Creditors at Robertsbridge whither I also went; & the next day Mrs. Abigail Grove (Robert Grove's mother) agreed that I should administer & gave me Bond that for my trouble therein she would secure my debt.

Sept. 6 ♀ Edw: Miller's Letter dated, with more news of Cosin Mackley's insolvency & being in the Mint.[6] Note that all this summer Saturn by transite was opposite to my Radical Medium Coeli.

Oct. 3 ♃ Mrs. Grove having since the last agreement altered her mind & taken Administration herself; came yesterday to a new agreement with me that I should do the business as her Attorney, sell the goods & receive the debts, & she would engage to secure my debt: to which purpose Articles being sealed this day between us I proceeded therein.

8 ♂ I wrote to the Creditors at London to act for them in contriving to sue the heire at Law for the debts on bond that so the personal estate might be applied to the payment of Simple Contracts.

9 ☿ or 10 ♃. Received a letter from Mr. Edw: Cross of Exon dated 5th Instant to buy him a Cargo of hops, which I effected

---

[4] This building survives today in Mermaid Street, Rye, converted to residential use and called 'Jeake's House'. It still has a copy of this horoscope inscribed on a stone let into its façade.

[5] An area in Southwark named after a long-demolished mint established by Henry VIII, which was a recognized sanctuary for debtors.

[6] Edward Miller was the younger brother of Thomas (see Appendix 3), under whose care he was left by his mother Dorothy in her will, to be educated until he was apprenticed at 16. He was evidently living in London in the 1680s. LAWR 34, p. 82.

& shipped them November 19 following, & they went safe: but by his Letter of the 14th December he complained they were course.

14 ☽ This morning I received an answer from the London Creditors that they would stand to what I should do for them in Grove's business. And rode to Robertsbridge to a meeting appointed there with the Creditors on specialty[.] And calling Mr. Spiller their Lawyer[7] aside & shewing him my Letter & promising him the management of the suite; it had this effect that ye Creditors consented the money for the Shop (which they had clogg'd with Declaration's on Hicks[8] that took it as well as the Administratrix) should be lodged by the Administratrix in my hands paying interest to thém the said Creditors on specialty till the suites with the heir were prosecuted to bring him to a Composition: & accordingly it was next day paid into my hands being £412 4s.

26 ♄ This day I got clear of Wm Baker; receiving the full of the money due to me from him: which was a happy Providence, he dying not long after and most of his Creditors being cheated.

Nov. 27 ☿ I cast up what I had expended already in buildings this year, & found it about £250. the rest was laid out next Spring.

Dec. 6 ♀ No. 255. Fr. Spanhemii, Dubia Evangelica: pars 3tio. 4° [1639].

7 ♄ Received the legacy given me by Nic: Shinners will as overseer thereof 40s.

30 ☽ No. 256. T. Beverly, Scripture line of Time. 4° [1684].

1690

Jan. 9 ♃ I carried the money I received about Grove's business to Robertsbridge: Mrs. Grove being now weary of her last agreement; & desirous to have the money out of my hands; & the Creditors on specialty appointing to meet there 10 ♀ to receive their debts: there being so many severall partyes & divisions that nothing came to any good effect. So January 10 ♀ Mrs. Grove signing me an order, I paid on Bond debts about £400 of the £446 13s 8¾d I then had of Grove's estate in my hands & January 11 ♄ delivered Mrs. Grove in her bond of £1000 which she had

---

[7] Robert Spiller of Burwash was a gentleman and attorney who had chambers at Staple Inn. SAU 1189; AMS 5744/197–8; FRE 4951–2, 5212.
[8] Presumably William Hicks of Robertsbridge, mercer. AMS 5744/102–4.

upon her marriage & was in my Custody to sue the heir upon it; she giving me a Receit to testify she had received the said bond uncancelled. She demanded all the residue of the money out of my hands, & threatned to sue me in Chancery if I would not part with it; But I resolved (it being her fault to dissolve the agreement) to secure what I had in my hands towards the payment of the debt due to me. And so I came from Robertsbridge January 11 ♄ a little after noon as I remember & home to Rye about 5h p.m. having indifferent good weather. But after I came home the wind rose to that height that I do not remember in all my life to have known so dreadfull a storm of wind as was that night.

Jan. 14 ♂ I wrote to Mr. Sam: Durrant, Mrs. Grove's Attorney[1] according as I promised when I was at Robertsbridge with my finall result that I would not part with the money in my hands unless she would allow my debt, but would rather venture a Chancery suite. January 18 ♄ Mr. Durrant wrote a threatning Letter to me (not having received mine) & January 24 ♀ Another to the same effect to fright me to part with the money.

Feb. 6 ♃ No. 257. Enthusiasmus Triumphatus, Observations upon Anthroposophia Theomagica. Antidote against Atheisme. Conjectura Cabbalistica & several other pieces of Henry More. 8° [1653–6].

13 ♃ No. 258. Tho: Sprat, History of the Royal Society. 4° [1667].

18 ♂ This day by my Father's advice I rode to Robertsbridge, to see if Mrs. Grove would make an end quietly of the business between her & me: for I had heard nothing since Mr. Durrants' letters. When I came, I providentially met Mr. Durrant there; & offered him to give baile or appearance to any action of Mrs. Grove's if she would sue me: went with him to Mrs. Grove, who scolded out her mind. & said she would fetch the money out of my hands by Course of Law & I on the contrary refusing to part with it, because she had taken the trust out of my hands without my default; & having sent for the Letter of Administration out of my hands refus'd to return it to me, without which I could not sue for the recovery of the book debts according to the Articles. But we agreeing on nothing I went to my Inne vexed &

1690 ¹ Possibly a mercer of Waldron who left a will in 1708. LAWR 48, p. 221.

200

discontented; when soon after she sent a Shoomaker (in whose house she lodged at that time & who by her order had not long before received the letter of Administration out of my hands) to demand whether I would pay the money that was in my hands or no, which when I had refused as before; meer Providence put it into my mind to ask this Fellow by what authority he came for the Letter of Administration from me & did not restore it upon my demand then made; & I threatned to sue him & trouble him therefore, because I could not go forward in executing my trust for want of it. I do believe the fellow was perfectly frighted; he excused himself & went away; & not long after came again, telling me Mrs. Grove would speak with me, I refused to goe at first, telling him I did not care to hear her scolding; but he importun'd me telling me she was inclinable to agree, & Mr. Durrant was not with her. So I went with him: & to my great Admiration, found her in so perfect a calm & serene temper, that without the least hesitation or objection she agreed to allow me all my £50 upon Condition I would take 5 bags of hops which were already in my Custody at Rye at 28s per hundred which was some small matter above the then market price; & by which the price falling lower I lost about £5 afterwards. I resolved not to slip this Opportunity, lest her mind should have changed by morning; & therefore immediately I drew a Release which she sealed presently viz. about 9h p.m. therein acknowledging she had received an Account from me of all the moneys received by me & had allowed it & discharged me thereof. And next day I read over the Account & delivered it to her with the bonds & receits for the moneys I had paid, in the presence of Mr. Sam: Durrant her Attorney. And promising at her request to make one journey more to assist Mr. Durrant in making up her Account as Administratrix of her son's goods, I returned home with an Easy mind after all this vexatious business.

25 ♂ About 5h p.m. my daughter Betty fell down & bruised her face just under her right Eye; which swelled up & made all the Region about the Eye black.

26 ☿ No. 259. Jo: Bapt: van Helmont, Ternary of Paradoxes; translated &c by Walt: Charlton. 4° [1650].

28 ♀ This day the Articles between Mrs. Grove & me were

exchanged: & receits in full given; & this was the last journey & trouble I had about it.

Apr. 2 ☿ No. 260. [Peter Heylyn] France painted to the Life. 8° [1656].

9 ☿ No. 261. [Marin Cureau] De la Chambre, Discourse of the Knowledge of Beasts. 8° [Eng. trans., 1657].

May 12 ☽ My Father went to London, being summoned by Sir Jno Austen about Mr. Gott's Petition against him as unduely elected Burgess for Rye.[2] In which Journey he was taken ill, and came home so; & hardly ever well afterward.

21 ☿ No. 262. Jacobus Kimedoncius, Of the Redemption of Mankind; & of God's Predestination. 4° [trans. Hugh Ince, 1598].

29 ♃ I wrote to Sir Jno Austen's son; my Father to Sir Jno to use their Interest in procuring for me the Expenditor's place of the Levells vacant by the death of Mr. Elhanan Tucker. Answered in obliging words, but no more.[3]

June 14 ♄ I bought Mr. Geo: Tilden's wooll at £6 per pack; at which, when weighd, it came to £80 11s.[4]

About this time Jos: Martin broke in my debt for Lockrams between £11 & £12. But recover'd it with some trouble by attaching his goods; & then proposing to abate and compound, was the means of setting him free.

20 ♀ I bought Mr. Tho: Cruttenden's wooll, at £6 per pack which came to £75 7s 6d besides some small parcells I bought afterwards at £5 10s.

26 ♃ In the morning or night before my Father was taken ill with an intolerable pain in the last joynt of the middle finger of his right hand, occasioned as he thought by a little thorn which run into it before as he was weeding in the Garden, but did not then pain him. But now it became so excessive that it inflamed the whole arme, & the joynt Gangrened in a days time: but then it pleas'd

[2] Sir John Austen, who had been elected MP for Rye in 1667 but did not stand during the Exclusion Crisis, was seated in the Convention Parliament on petition. The 'Mr Gott' who challenged him was presumably Peter Gott, High Sheriff of Sussex and later MP for Hastings. Henning, i. 573, ii. 421; *CSP Dom.* 1689–90, p. 125.

[3] This was the expenditorship of the Upper Levels. Jeake's father had earlier been expenditor of the lower, Wittersham Level. As noted, Jeake's suit was unsuccessful: Tucker was succeeded in June 1690 by John Mantell and Thomas Marshall. On Tucker see 30.10.86. ESRO D 496 (Upper Levels Decree and Order Book, 9).

[4] George Tilden was a jurat of Tenterden, Kent. Hull, p. 532.

God, the Gangrene stopt & went no further; but the swelling broke in his hand in severall places, & a great deale of purulent matter issued out of it for severall days; he lost 2 joynts of the middle finger with the Gangrene & the finger & hand were but just cured up when he died viz: October 3 following. Note that Mars at this time was by Transit on my Radical Ascendant. The Sun on the place of Mars, Venus of Saturn.

30 ☽ My Father was taken with an Hiccough which lasted till July 7 ☽ following, which was succeeded by other illnesses till his Death, The brief narration of which I shall here deferr; on purpose to summ them up all together in the Relation of his Death.

July   1 ♂ News came to Town that the English Fleet was beaten by the French off of Beachy,[5] which being not far off, put the Towne in some apprehensions of danger.

2 ☿ This day I was made a Freeman of the Corporation of Rye; claiming by the usual Custome or Priviledge there, viz: of Birth And took the usual Oath in these words following. I Samuel Jeake shall faith bear unto our Soveraign Lord & Lady, King William & Queen Mary, & to the Maior Jurats & Commonalty of this Towne of Rye; & the Charters, Libertyes, Franchises, Customes, & Usages of the Cinque Ports Two Ancient Townes, & their Members, & especially of the said Towne of Rye to my power shall maintain & shall not consent to hurt them or to break them. And my scots & lots of my goods & chattells to the aforesaid Commonalty shall well and truly pay when I shall be thereunto scotted or lotted, so help me God.

The same day, afterwards was a great Consternation about the French Fleet's coming toward us & chasing the English.

3 ♃ News that the French Fleet had set Hasting on Fire; which though false yet occasioned a great hurry at Rye; whereupon this afternoon I sent my Mother in law, Wife & Children out of Towne, 3 mile; my Father being unable to remove because of his illness. My Writings I sent away also, & what Money I had by me I secured otherwise.

4 ♀ The English Fleet pass'd by Rye in sight of the Towne moving towards the Downes before the French who were not yet come in sight. My Storehouse compleatly finished this day just at

---

[5] i.e. Beachy Head.

Sunset, or 4′ after. Immediately upon it News that the French were shooting to beat down Hasting; & they did indeed shoot some bullets into the Towne, & killed a man or two; but without much other damage.

July   5 ♄ Sent for my Mother, Wife & Children back to Rye; being perswaded by some Seamen that there was no danger of the French's coming into the harbour to injure the Town. But they were no sooner come home which was about noon; but that the French Fleet began to appear in the Bay, and soon after the Captain of the Anne, having ran her on shore yesterday in sight of the Town, now set her on fire;[6] & before evening the French Fleet were most of them up in the Bay full in sight of the Towne.

6 ☉ In the morning about 6h a.m. A terrible alarm in the Towne of Rye of the Frenches coming to land; they having sent 3 small shallops to sound the depths at the coming in to the harbour; which we supposed to be either to come in this Tide, it being then neer full Sea; or to prepare against next, & that their intentions were to burn the Fireships that were then put into our harbour and to fire & plunder the Towne. Upon this an intolerable hurry all day, the trained band up in Arms with the Soldiers and Seamen of the Anne who were then in Town: sending out into the Country for more men, & planting Guns on the Beach with a Breastwork of Dealboards to make a shew at the mouth of the harbour. Nothing seen but fears & consternations; sending of goods out of Towne in Wagons & on horses & the like confusions usuall at such times. I sent my mother in law & daughter out of Towne again about 2h p.m. & with them my writings & gold; the rest of my money sent afterwards, & my wife's Cloths in the Evening. But she went not out of Towne because my little Boy was this morning taken sick of a feaver, & very bad, so that he could not be carried without danger of his Life; & therefore we had two poor women provided ready to have carried him in a Flasket if the French had landed; and my Father being very ill also concluded not to leave the Towne unless it were certain that the French did actually enter the harbour. But through mercy there was no attempt made by them to do any mischief to the Towne.

---

[6] The captain of the *Anne* was John Tyrrell. The burnt-out remains of the ship still survive. Peter Le Fevre, 'John Tyrrell (1646–92)', *Mariner's Mirror*, 70 (1984), 149–60.

Behold the face of heaven when the news was first brought me
in the morning, as I lay in bed, wherein this Remarkable is to be
observed that the houses of heaven are disposed as in the Radix,
& the Planet Mars on the Cusp of the Ascendant, the Sun as
radically in the 12th &c.

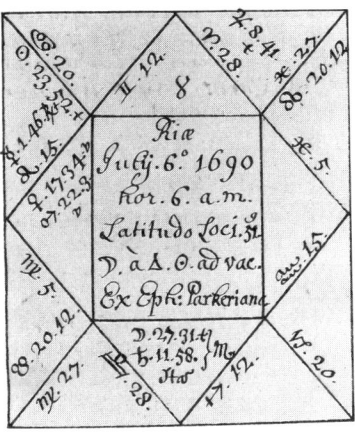

ditto   No. 263. Drue Cressener, The Judgments of God upon the
        Roman Catholick Church. 4° [1689].

7 ☽ This day I was offered a Cargo of 4000 deals by which I then
     supposed I might have got probably £80 but being still under
     fears of the Frenches burning the Towne; & my family full of
     troubles, I missed it, though I bid to the full value that could be
     affoorded; others giving more & buying them next morning, at
     which somewhat concern'd. but afterwards it appeared well
     enough that I went without them; they being bought too dear, &
     not being all sold till 4 years after, so that I believe no profit
     worth while accrued to the buyers.

     My Child's Feaver with which he was taken yesterday con-
     tinued & increased & was accompanied with a violent lasque &
     craving incessantly for beer, so Tuesday & Wednesday & as long
     as he had any Strength left, the feaver never intermitting. From
     Wednesday to Saturday night he lay very neer death, even to
     despair of his Life; & then the signs of death appearing he grew

worse & lay drawing on all Lord's day & till next Munday morning when he died.

This day as I remember we had the news of King William's Victory at the Boyn in Ireland but hardly believed till

July   9 ☿ We had it per post from London, per advise dated 8th Instant. Which somewhat heartned us in our troubles about the French.

     14 ☽ About 10h a.m. My dear & only son Manasseh Jeake died of the Feaver abovementioned. The Sun Lord of my Radical Ascendant now exactly on the Radical place of Saturn. The Moon on the Cusp of the 8th.

     30 ☿ Mr. Finches letter dated with which he sent me Peckham's debt: thought desperate.[7]

In August being first put upon it by some of the Freemen I made an Essay for the place of Townclerk to be conferr'd upon my Father & so I to act as his Deputy, because of the Test: but their Courage failing them to chuse a Dissenter slurr'd it; & Brother Hartshorne was put up, whom I assisted in opposition to Mr. Tournay; & he carried it & kept it in the succeeding elections till his death.

Sept. 17 ☿ or 18 ♃.   Received a Letter from Mr. Tho: Miller dated 16th Instant which encouraged me to buy hops at 40 or 45s per hundred. But they fell at London this 18 ♃ & rose not afterward all that year; & he neglecting to advise me by Thursday or Saterday's post of their fall & I not hearing of it otherwise, Unfortunately rode out on 23 ♂ & bought about £160 worth of Hops; & 2 or 3 bags were bought by my wife in my absence. Which was in all as it afterwards proved to my loss & prejudice of £17. The same night I rode to Hasting & heard of the fall of Hops. Returned to Rye as I remember on 24 ☿ or 25 ♃.

Oct.   3 ♀ About 8h p.m. My dear Father Samuel Jeake senior died (being 67 years of Age lacking but 6 days) after a languishing of above 3 moneths, being first taken ill June 25 last in the night with the pain in his finger above mentioned, which Gangrened as above related; Then with the Hiccough June 30 ☽ which was almost continuall, & at last joyned with a Convulsion of the Stomach so great that it was like to set his breath; this lasted till July 7 ☽ when just after dinner, he had a most violent fit of it; & then of a

---

[7] Probably the Thomas Peckham who bought wool from Jeake in 1688. RYE 145/11.

sudden it totally ceased, & he had no more of it. Not long after (assoon as the Inflammation of his hand & arm began to abate, & to run excessively with digested matter from severall holes in the hand) he was taken with the Gout first in one foot, & then in the other; in which condition he continued about a moneth; Then appeared some hopes of his recovery, & he went abroad at the Election of Maior August 25 ☽ and next Lords day viz. August 31 went to the meeting place & spake from that Text Gal. 6. 15. For in Christ Jesus neither Circumcision availeth any thing nor uncircumcision, but a new Creature; which was the last time he taught in publick. September 2 ♂ he went out to Mr. Steed's Funerall,[8] which was the last time he was abroad; for next day, viz. September 3 ☿ about 5h p.m. he was taken with a Tertian Ague; of which he had 4 or 5 fits with a vomiting and lasque, which decay'd his spirits. After those fits he seemed to be all alike: & then again had 2 or 3 more aguish fits. But on September 26 ♀ in the Night he was taken with an Erysipelas in the face; which encreased, & removed from one place to another till he dyed; beginning on the right side of his face, & going over to the left & swelling up his Eyes & Throat; and he having such abundance of Phlegm, which at last he could not bring up; his mouth parched with drought & all over sore with a Thrush or white scurf. All which dying symptoms still encreased till at last his speech failing him October 3 about noon, (his sense continuing till the last) & about 8h p.m. having no breath left, he quietly slept in the Lord. In all this long time of Sickness he never had the least murmuring expression against the Conduct of Providence towards him. But severall times in the Evening when I signifyed to him my fear that he would not live till morning; his usuall Answer was, What God will: and that with a vigour in the Expression. October 2 about 8h p.m. I took my leave of him, not knowing how soon he might dye: and told him I doubted not but he was going to a better place; & that I was glad he died in peace, in his habitation, not withstanding the malice of his Enemies: & that God had restored the Liberty of the Gospel before he died; & that we were not driven from our dwellings by

---

[8] Mr Steed must either have been the 'late cousin Mr. William Steed', to whose two sons Thomas Markwick (see Appendix 3) left £20 each in 1694, or Theophilus Steed, vintner, of Cripplegate, London, whose will was proved in 1691, and who asked his two brothers, Thomas and Robert Steed, to act as executors. PCC PROB 11/406 1691: 150, PROB 11/419 1694: 82.

forrain Invasion. He replied, I die the Common death of all men. And to others that spake of his departure; he said I go to my Father; lifting up his hand. At the time before mentioned, he would have me take out his watch & put it into his hand; which being done, he delivered it to me again, & said, I deliver you this in name of possession of all that I have which I had not given you before so that you may be in posssession actually of it & need not take Administration. When I said farewell Dear Father, & kist his dying lips; he answered; Farewell my Dear Lamb, The Lord bless thee, & prosper all that thou undertakest.

Though I was actually possessed of all that my Father had long before his death; he putting it into my hands about 9 years agoe in the presecuting times; yet I still esteemed him as proprietor of such part thereof as he gave me not before or upon my Marriage; but would have kept in his own hands had he not been forced from Rye; returning the profits of it or what he desired me to send him to London &c. So that what he left me at his death though already in possession was by computation about £540.

After my Father's death Mr. Tho: Markwick spake in our meeting for some time[.] And about Two Moneths after I began to expound the Scriptures, first some occasional Texts & soon after the Revelation beginning at the 9th Chapter where I left off before; & speaking, at first once a fortnight & after more constantly & weekly till I had some more assistance which I took care to supply. My Method being first to explain the Scope of the Prophecy, & then proceed to Doctrine & Use.

Oct. 9 ♃ or thereabouts Received an order from Mr. Cross of Exon to buy him a Cargo of hops. Next week rode out for that purpose; & having made them ready: shipt part of them, with 10 bags wooll qt⁹ each 9 Tods in Alex: White the 30 ♃ And

Nov. 7 ♀ There being a terrible storm at South East in the Noon Tide; White's vessell broke loose & ran against a Rock amongst the Barham's Rocks in the harbour: & broke a hole in her side, whereby the Hops were damnified to the value of above £40. News brought me thereof in the beginning of the afternoon with which Extremely concern'd; & had a deal of trouble in unship-

⁹ Perhaps @. Cf. 19.11.90.

ping the goods next day & saving the wet hops from the dry, & new drying some of the wet &c. The wooll I opened not but reshipt it again wet as it was & the vessell going safe (though without Convoy) the wooll being sold soon after arrivall at Exon, was not complained off for that part of it that was wet. Advised Mr. Cross of this disaster by Letter of the 8th ♄. Conjunction of the Sun and Saturn.

19 ☿ Mr. Walter Pemble sent me his Letter that he would send his wooll to Exon & give me Commission for shipping it & ordering the sale & remitting the money. So soon after he sent 25 bags, which the latter end of this month I shipt in Jno Parker together with 14 bags hops for Mr. Cross & 14 bags wooll qt 9 tods each for my self & December 1 at night he went to sea, & through God's Providence soon after arrived safe at Topsham, although he had no Convoy.[10]

1691

Feb. 5 ♃ Mr. Pemble sent 10 bags of wooll more to go to Exon by Parker, which I shipped: together with 7 bags for my self: consigning them all to Mr. Cross by Bills of Lading dated the 10th Instant & through mercy all went safe.

14 ♄ Mr. Crosse's letter dated wherein he advises that the 10 bags of my wooll that were wet in White; & had lain so ever since, were now sold at as good a price as the Rest.

Apr. 15 ☿ Mr. Crosse's Letter dated with advise of Parker's safe arrival at Exon.

May 4 ☽ No. 264. Bar: Keckerman, Systema Theologiae. 8º [1602].

8 ♀ Mr. Crosse's Letter dated, wherein he advises me that he had remitted according to order £107 10s 2d to Mr. Jno Wase at London for Mr. Pemble's use. Which said Wase as soon as he had received the money broke; & Mr. Pemble being a loser thereby, examined critically how I followed his orders in remitting the money[,] but having it under his hand, he could take no advantage of me. At long run he got £60 of Wase & I believe most part if not all the residue afterwards.[1]

---

[10] Walter Pemble was a gentleman of Ebony, Kent. John Parker was a mariner living in Rye. KAO PRC/32/56: 259; Burchall, p. 107; LAWR 45, p. 262.

1691 [1] John Wase was a gentleman of London, possibly related to gentry of the same name originating from Norfolk. Venn.

May 11 ☽ About 6h a.m. or a little after, I rode with my Wife for London; having good weather both in our journey thither, stay there, & return home. Came to Tunbridge at night, & 12 ♂ in the Stage Coach to London about 7h p.m. & to Mr. Miller's house where we lodged all the time.

16 ♄ Had the first advise of the bill of £107 10s 2d remitted to Wase as abovementioned.

21 ♃ No. 265. Tho: Burnet, Theory of the Earth. Parts 1 & 2. Fol. [Eng. trans., 1684].

27 ☿ No. 266. Tho: Burnet, Theory of the Earth. Parts 3 & 4. with the Review & Answer to Objections. Fol: [Eng. trans., 1690].

29 ♀ About 8h a.m. came from London in the Stage Coach to Tunbridge. & 30 ♄ On horsback to Rye, where we arrived 3h p.m.

Sept. 12 ♄ Mr. Crosses letter dated. & received about the 17th wherein he order's me to buy him 40 bags of Hops; which I performed soon after & advised him by Letter dated the 10th of October that they were bought from 20 to 23s per hundred & a very good parcell.

18 ♀ No. 267. Finished the reading over of a Manuscript of my Father's entituled A Chronological Speculum consisting of 200 Sheets in a very large Folio, & close wrote; & yet extending but to 150 years after Christ's Incarnation. The Rest of the work being left unfinished by my Father at his death.[2]

19 ♄ About 4h p.m. I was taken ill with

---

[2] Presumably Selmes MS 8, which meets this description except that it is an ordinary-sized folio.

a little fit of an Ague & Feaver: sweat in the night. From this time I was never well til the 11th of March following. In the figure of heaven, the Sun is on the Cusp of the 8th[,] the Moon on that of the 12th opposite to the Radical place of Mars & squared by the Sun in Cardinal signs & inimical in my Nativity: the Radical ascendant here descending &c.

21 ☽ About noon. Taken with a 2d fit, which now declared it self a Tertian; like the former, but worse, lasted till next morning, yet moderate.

23 ☿ About 9h a.m. Taken with a 3d fit very bad, with vomiting &c.: the feaver lasted till next morning.

25 ♀ About noon, Taken with a 4th fit, very bad with vomiting & 2 or 3 stools: yet no so bad as last fit: the feaver went off about 10h p.m.

28 ☽ I wrote to Mr. Sam: James to go partners in Hops; whereto he agreed by Letter of the 1st October: & after I had bought Mr. Crosse's hops; I bought 50 bags between Mr. James & my self, & about 37 packs wooll also.

About this time, assoon as I was rid of my Feaver, the Itch bred upon me: or else I caught it by lying in infected sheets in a journey to Warhorn in August last; or otherwise I know not how. At first not apprehended what it was, but by October 5 ☽ it fully discovered itselfe.

Oct. 6 ♂ By a Journey, which I made to buy Hops it was exceedingly exasperated & very troublesome. *about the scrotum once.*

9 ♀ At night put on a Mercurial Girdle, for cure of it.

10 ♄ Weigh'd the first Hops between Mr. James & me.

14 ☿ About 4h p.m. I was taken ill again with a Feaver which lasted all night, & after a days intermission began again the 15th ♃ at night & lasted all night; Then it began again in the 16th ♀ at noon & lasted till the next morning. Besides this, on the 13th ♂ I began to be troubled with a Catarrh[,] Excessive Rheum, & very sore mouth which continued extraordinary bad so that I could neither eat nor drink without intolerable pain till the 22th ♃ After which it began to amend, though very slowly. Whether it were an effect of my Feaver or the Mercurial Girdle I know not. From October 14 to the 19th I had scarcely any sleep in the nights: but afterward it began to come to me again.

Nov. 4 ☿ About 3h p.m. I was taken ill the Third time with a fit of an Ague & the Feaver following: with sweat in the night & headach.

6 ♀ About noon. A 2d fit of an Ague & Feaver following, vomited twice about 3h p.m. & one stool: sweat & headach in the night.

7 ♄ About 9h p.m. A 3d fit, all Feaver, held all night; ending with sweat.

8 ☉ About 2h p.m. A 4th fit of an Ague & Feaver, lasting most part of the night; ending in sweat & headach; but not so bad as the last fit.

9 ☽ Sent 4 packs wooll by Land to London to Mr. James for a tryall, which he received the 19th Instant & sold to 11 or 12s per pack profit which encouraged us to buy more by which we got nothing.

In the night. A 5th fit, all Feaver; like that on the 7th ♄.

10 ♂ A 6th fit, ill & aguish, but not much Feaver in the night: after mended sensibly till 18 ☿.

18 ☿ In the night I was taken ill the Fourth time, aguish & feaverish, moderately; but continued ill next day.

19 ♃ Aguish after dinner till night, Then a 2d & bad fit of a Feaver continuing all night without sweat; & my mouth grew worse again.

20 ♀ Very ill all day; & in the night a 3d & bad fit of a Feaver: not off till 10 a Clock in the forenoon next day; & then

21 ♄ Very ill all day. At night fell into a great sweat naturally, continuing all the night; which did me through mercy a great deal of good. For 22 ☉ I perceived my self very much amended: & that night I sweat again, but not so much as the night before & next morning I was better & my Mouth much mended, & continued to amend. But when my Feaver left me, there bred upon me 3 or 4 sore boyls: Two especially; under each Armhole one which were very large & sore, as big as walnuts & continued about 3 weeks. I dressed them with Diachylon cum Gummis & they were discussed without breaking. Afterwards I had some little ones; & the Itch returned though not so violently as at first; yet so much, that I had a 2d Mercurial Girdle, which drave it quite away; & in the use thereof I had no soreness in my Mouth.

24 ♂ My Letter to Mr. James dated that the hops & wooll were Shipping, which was done this week & next in Kirby & Petter.[3]

28 ♄ Bill of Lading dated for goods shipt in Kirby for London, in partnership between Sam: James & me. viz. 44 bags 6 ends hops; 12½ packs wooll. All bought Cheap, the hops none above 22s per hundred nor wooll above £5 10s per pack.

Dec. 2 ☿ Mr. Crosse's Letter dated, received about the 7th wherein he advises me that he had sold all the wooll remaining; & would remit the balance of Accompt before he receiv'd it; being in sure hands.

8 ♂ Bill of Lading dated, for goods shipt in Petter for London, in partnership between Sam: James & me, viz. 2 bags hops & 21 packs Wooll; bought cheap as before.

9 ☿ About 8h p.m. I was taken ill the Fifth time with a small fit of an Ague and Feaver, which was very inconsiderable. But after this a kind of griping Lasque & much wind for a fortnight.

11 ♀ This day & next morning I shipped Mr. Crosse's goods aboard Ben: Meadow.[4] 40 bags & 3 ends of Hops & 11 packs wooll. Bill of Lading dated the 12th.

21 ☽ Bill of Lading of 4 packs wooll more laden in Meadow to fill him up, on Mr. Crosses Accompt for Exon.

ditto I was taken ill the Sixth time with a Cough, which had crept upon me insensibly & began now to grow troublesome with a Cold; both which increased all this week, the Cough very bad in the nights with shortness of breath, feaverishness, & sweating all night.

26 ♄ Mr. James's letter dated with advise that Kirby & Petter were safe arrived the 25th Instant at London. Received the Letter 27th or 28th.

29 ♂ About 11h a.m. News that Mr. Richard Naldread of Hasting died last Lord's day in the Evening: who by his will gave me in money & Land, Legacies, to the value of about £300.

---

[3] George Petter was a Rye mariner. RYE 2/4. On Kirby, see Appendix 3.

[4] Ben Meadow was a Rye mariner, possibly the son of the jurat and mariner Robert Meadow. Robert bought some land in company with James Wightman, the husband of Jeake's first cousin Ann (see 25.6.85) in 1680. RYE 19/177; ESRO D 516/25.

In this positure of heaven, I observe these Remarkables. 1st That the Radical place of Jupiter culminates, & that Jupiter is here in the Ascendant in trine to the Cusp of Medium Coeli and in trine to the Radical places of himself, Venus & the 2d house. 2dly That here is a Congeries of good Planets in the 11th house the house of friendship; whereof the Sun, who always signifyes something publique is conspicuously posited on the very Cusp in trine of the Moon. 3dly That the 11th house & all the Planets therein, as also the Medium Coeli are wholly under the dominion of Saturn whose place is on the Cusp of the 8th & is there thought to signify Legacyes or estate arising by the death of persons, which are here determin'd to be friends, & not of the Kindred by the dominion of Saturn in the 11th. 4thly That Venus & Mercury out of the 11th cast their partil trine to the Cusp of the 2d the house of Riches.

All this week till Saterday night which was January 2 I had the Feaver every night, taking me about 4h p.m. with shortness of breath, Coughing & sweat.

Dec. 31 ♃ I rode to Mr. Naldread's funerall & returned January 2 ♄ had excellent calm & sunshine weather both going & coming; which fitted me exceedingly being so ill with my Cough & feaver.

From the time that I returned from Mr. Naldread's funeral till February 3 following I was never free from the Ague & Feaver every other night: beginning most commonly about 5h p.m. and lasting till about midnight; with much sweat afterwards; the last fit was February 2 ♂. After which an intermission of 4 days viz. till February 6 ♄.

1692

Jan. 11 ☽ Ben: Meadow went to sea with Mr. Crosses hops & wooll; & arrived safe at Topsham in few days of which Mr. Crosse advised me by Letter dated the 18th Instant.

21 ♃ Mr. James's Letter dated (& received a day or two after) wherein he advises me that he had sold all our hops to Mr. Cox, for 31s per hundred by which we got about £22 a piece.

Feb. 1 ☽ or thereabouts. No. 268. Tho: Fuller, Good Thoughts in bad times. 16° [1645].

3 ☿ No. 269. John Cotton, Treatise of the New Covenant, Queries of accommodation; Civil Magistrates power in Matters of Religion. Nature and power of Synods. 12° [1655].

6 ♄ I was taken ill the Seventh time: with a Tertian Ague & feaver: about 3h p.m. it began, & was of the same nature with my last which I had all January, but this was the worst.

8 ☽ A 2d fit which took me earlier & was worse.

10 ☿ About noon a 3d fit. which shook me about 3h p.m. a very bad fit & violent feaver in which I talked idly some hours.

12 ♀ Before noon, a 4th fit. with which I shook about 3h p.m. & then went to bed: where had a very violent Feaver; this being the worst fit of all: my breath very short; & delirious. sweat excessively in all these fits, so that I were shifted twice in a night.

14 ☉ About noon, a 5th fit. much after the same Method as formerly; but not so bad as the last: yet I talked idly; and sweat much.

16 ♂ About 2h p.m. a 6th fit, very little, or scarce sensible. but sweat much in the night. And it pleased God that this was the last fit.

Mar. 3 ♃ About 4h p.m. Taken ill the Eighth time: of a Tertian ague, succeeded by a Feaver & sweat in the night: but the fit not very bad.

5 ♄ About 3h p.m. A 2d fit; worse than the former, but after the same manner.

7 ☽ About 3h p.m. A 3d fit, like the 2d.

9 ☿ About 3h p.m. A 4th fit: but gentle.

Mar. 11 ♀ About 4h p.m. Some small remembrance of it, not worth speaking of. And after this time it pleased God to restore my health.

ditto   No. 270. Jo: Arrowsmith, Tactica Sacra Orationes 3. 4° [1657].

19 ♄ I passed my accompt with Mr. Walter Pemble[1] about his wooll, & had my Commission-money & a Receipt in full.

May 16 ☽ About this time, we were under some Apprehensions of an Invasion from France An Army being drawn to the Sea-Coast of Normandy about Dieppe & Havre de grace; & the late King James with them. But it pleased God to free us from this fear in less than a week's time, by means of the Victory obtained by the English under Admiral Russell over the French Fleet in the Channell: wherein 16 or 20 of the best ships of the French were burnt & sunk; & the English rendred entirely masters of the Sea.[2] Advise of this Victory by Letters from London dated the 21th Instant.

June 27 ☽ Rode to Hasting to assist Mrs. Naldread about the payment of a Legacy of £100 given by his will to Eliz: Lasher, and returned home that night.[3]

July 4 ☽ No. 271. Sam: Crook, Divine Characters. Fol: [1658].

ditto   I wrote to Mr. Jno Kendal a Schoolmaster & Astrologer at Colchester for his opinion about Partridge & Bishops new way of direction in Nativityes, & about the Measure of Time. & July 5 ♂ wrote to Hen: Coley about the same Subjects. Received answer from the last dated 16 Instant & from the former dated as I remember the 27th and received August 12 following or thereabouts, consisting of 1½ sheet of paper curiously & close wrote; & advancing a new Hypothesis of the Effects to proceed from Transits & not from directions. To which I reply'd with my Exceptions September 7 but never received answer.[4]

1692 [1] See 19.11.90.

[2] Jeake here refers to the Battle off Cape Barfleur in May 1692.

[3] Mrs Elizabeth Naldread was the executrix of the will of her late husband, Richard (see Appendix 3). He said in his will that he had made a written promise to his late brother-in-law, Joshua Lasher of London, to leave £100 to his daughter Elizabeth.

[4] John Kendal of Colchester was the author of Χρονομετρία (1684), which dealt with the issue of the Measure of Time and which had been published with a foreword by the London astrologer, Coley (on whom see 16.10.88). For the views of Bishop and Partridge see Richard Kirby and John Bishop, *The Marrow of Astrology* (1687), pt. 2, and John Partridge, *Opus Reformatum* (1693), though it is puzzling that this work was not published till the following year. On the Measure of Time, see Introduction, sect. 2.

In July, I bought about 33 packs of wooll; some at £6 10s per pack but most at £7 which sold not long after for about £10 profit. August 4 I wrote to Sam: Jobson a Stapler at London first about buying it.

Aug. 8 ☽ Received advise from Mr. Miller of his intentions of coming to Rye this month with his wife, & Mr. Grace & his family, coming with them.[5]

16 ♂ About noon, they came to Rye. Mr. Miller & his wife to my house & Mr. Grace &c to his farme at Pelsham. the 18th ♃ all dined at my house & staid with me till next day afternoon. Then Mr. Grace & his return'd to Pelsham & 22 ☽ Mr. Miller & his wife went thither & next day all return'd by Coach & horsback for London.

Sept. 8 ♃ Received a letter from Jobson, that he would have my wooll at the price he offered when at Rye in the End of August last which was £7 5s per pack & 1 Guinea over. Whereto return'd answer this day, accepting it.

ditto This day about 2h p.m. was a Trembling of the Earth under the Town of Rye; so as to make the houses shake; & houshold stuff move on the Shelves, but lasted not a minute. No wind stirring at the time. This Earthquake as we heard by the Gazette & Letters afterward was felt throughout England France Belgium & part of Germany as far as Frankford.

19 ☽ Received a letter from Jobson wherein he refuses to accept a bill I drew on him though he gave me leave before to draw what I had occasion for; & afterwards I had many quarrels & much trouble with him, he neither keeping time in weighing the wooll, nor paying the money[:] for whereas by the bargain, it was to have been weighd by Michaelmas, weigh & pay; he came not to weigh it till October 14 & then brought no Cloths; & all my money I could not get till the end of December; & then he abated me above 20s which I was forced to comply with to get the money out of his fingers.

20 ♂ No. 272. Daniel Dyke, The Deceitfulness of man's heart. 4° [1615].

22 ♃ About 3 or 4 a Clock in the morning Mr. David Barham died of

---

[5] Mr Grace may have been related to Michael and Robert Grace, esquires, who lived at Icklesham, Sussex, in the mid 18th century. AMS 5737/1.

the Small pocks; which occasioned me a great deal of trouble; he having put me in Overseer of his will, with a Legacy of 5 Guinea's.[6] His wife being with Child & not having had the small pocks, was out of the house. So that the whole trouble of his funeral &c lay upon me: Then she obstinately returning into the house again and having the Shop opened; his Brother was afterward taken with that distemper & likewise died thereof, so that she was fain to remove again, & to lye in at another house; about which businesses I had much more trouble; besides all that which accrued by making the Inventory, which took up 3 whole days, it being shop goods; & then by assisting her in paying all the Creditors at London[,] remitting moneys & preparing discharges & moreover in severall treatyes about putting off the Shop. So that I was not free from the trouble in half a years time.

Sept. 23 ♀ No. 273. Vulgar Latine Translation of the Bible. 4° (omitting the Apocrypha & appurtenances) [Basle edn., 1578].

Oct. 6 ♃ I bought 150 Quarters of wheat of Captain Jno Edwards a Privateer, out of a Prize already condemned in the Admiralty, called the Prophet Samuel: lying in Rye harbour; at 36s per Quarter.[7] And 40 Quarters thereof were landed & put in my Storehouse next day. And not many days afterward I treated with him about a Quantity of Sugar Candy in the same Ship, but his price being too dear I bought it not. And Edwards finding that wheat was rising, first neglected to deliver the rest of the wheat & made a journey to London, & at his return positively refused to deliver the Residue, alleaging impudent lyes & impertinencies.

  11 ♀ I wrote to Mr. Edw: Cross of Exon, but he died the 12th ☿ as I heard soon after by Mr. Nic: Broking's Letter:[8] by his death I lost a good friend & Correspondent there. *My letter to him was about the restitution of £12 1s which I could not be satisfied till I had allowed him out of the cost of the hops in the year 1690. Which I bought at first for my self and though I put them in to him at the very same price, as I could not buy [. . .] at that time, yet because I*

---

[6] David Barham was a woollen draper of Rye. His very short will includes the bequest of 5 guineas to his overseer 'my loving friend Samuel Jeake of Rye'. LAWR 41, p. 47.

[7] On John Edwards, a Rye fisherman and privateer, see Burchall, p. 107; AMS 4881.

[8] Probably Nicholas Brooking, a prominent Exeter dissenter in the Restoration period. Allan Brockett, *Nonconformity in Exeter, 1650–1875* (Manchester, 1962), 13.

acquainted him not that they were mine, and because they declined in price after this, I could not be so satisfied till I had made a restitution of some much [sic] in value as I thought I might have bought for if I had not bought any at all, or had stayed a while longer after I received his order, though I did put them in then at the price I could then buy at: for I went out in the country to buy after his order came, and could get none cheaper nor hardly so cheap as I put them in to him at. I disguised the cause of my restitution in my letter for my reputation; and circumstance so ordered it that he dying before he received my letter, could make no inquiry about it. About this time again I critically [examined?] if I had wronged any person in dealing and made restitution [completely?] to my apprehensions, the whole coming to about £20.

24 ☽ No. 274. Hen: Ainsworth, Communion of Saints. 8° [1607].

25 ♂ My letter to Jobson with the account of what the wooll he bought of me came to viz. £239 11s 6d being all now weigh'd.

Nov. 2 ☿ I took out a warrant against Captain Edwards because he refused to let me have the wheat I bought, & got him arrested same day; & then he comply'd that I should have it; & I let fall the Action.

3 ♃ Having cry'd the wheat at 5s per bushell I sold about 95 quarters this day & next, & on Munday morning, & then landed the rest.

8 ♂ About 3h p.m. My wife after having been very ill some days, miscarried of a Male child: being about 2 moneths gone.

ditto Captain Edwards being so hasty that he would not give a days time for payment of the money for his wheat, I paid him £230 which with £40 I had paid last week made up £270 & I had his receipt in full for 150 quarters at 36s per quarter.

12 ♄ I arrested Edwards again: for after I had paid him for the wheat he did not pay the Custome as he was obliged by his bargain by reason of a Contest that was between the Collector & him; whereupon the Collector came & forbid me to sell it; threatning to seize it for the Custome. Edwards being a very litigious person sent all about the Towne to get baile; which if he could have obtained he would have held me in suite & hindred my sale of the Corn: but by a mercifull Providence for me; No body would baile him; which when he saw he sent for the Collector & paid

the Custome presently. Whereupon I discharged him & paid the Charge of the arrest & tendance about 13s being very glad it was ended without more adoe. By this bargain I got about £49 part presently by what was sold out of the vessell & the rest in the winter & spring after where most was sold that was landed at 6s per bushel & fetcht away when once it stirr'd in 2 or 3 days time.

Dec. 17 ♄ Mrs. Crosses letter dated, advising of her husbands death.[9] *and that she was executrix and desiring to know how the £12 is came due, and advising that she had written a bill for it payable in Rye, which I paid & by mine of the 29th returned answer to it enough to satisfy her.*

1693

Jan. 3 ♂ This day I lent Mr. Wm. Curteis £50 & concluded to lend him £350 more at Lady day next & then to take a Mortgage for the whole £400 at 5 per cent.

ditto About 1h p.m. A difference arose between Mr. Mannooch Maior of Rye & me about 2 pictures, which not knowing that he had a mind to, I enquired casually after at the sale of Wm Pack's goods, and my wife afterwards getting the pictures of Pack's wife; so offended the Maior, that on 6th ♀ he sent the Sergeant to demand them; & threatned to have them by force.[1]

9 ☽ I was made Surveyor for the highways in the parish of Rye for the year ensuing, by warrant of the Justices in the Town, with which office I had a great deal of trouble in Collecting the money by a Tax in the year ensuing.

Feb. 5 ☉ In my Morning sleep I was taken with a Crick in my neck, which was very painfull all day, toward night it abated; but not through well in a week.

9 ♃ No. 275. J. Howe, Blessedness of the Righteous & Vanity of Man as Mortal. 8° [1673].

[9] Marie Cross was wife of Edward (see Appendix 3).

1693 [1] Nicholas Mannooch, gentleman, had been master of Rye grammar school before he was chosen jurat. His wife Mary was sister-in-law to Jeake's close friend Thomas Markwick (see Appendix 3), who left her some land in his will. No information has been found on the identity of the Packs. William Curteis was also a friend of Markwick, who left him a small bequest; he was also a cousin of Thomas Miller, who had lent him money in the 1680s. RYE 19/41; PCC PROB 11/419 1694: 82; FRE 5209.

Mar. 18 ♄ In the night Brother Nath: Hartshorn died after about a fort-nights illness. At his death I was much troubled. he was buried the 22th ☿ .

27 ☽ I lent Mr. Wm. Curteis £350 more, & giving in his bond of £50 took a Mortgage for the whole £400 for 1 year at 5 per cent.

Apr. 10 ☽ No. 276. Chr: Love, Treatise of Effectual Calling & Election. 4° [1653].

12 ☿ Sent 3 Quaere's to the Athenian Society about the Earth's Motion; Answered by them about a Moneth after.²

May 12 ♀ or Next day Advise by Cosin Wagon's Letter of the 10th Instant of the death of Cosin William Hartridge & his giving all his estate by will to Dorothy Ferrall his Kinswoman; and desiring me to come up to his funeral, & to joyn with the rest of the Kindred to see to recover the estate from her: because he was hardly Compos mentis.³ But I refused to go or to meddle there-in. Esteeming him so much Compos mentis that if he had given me his estate by will I should have defended it; & therefore I should not have done as I would be done to, if I had en-deavoured to have taken it from another.

13 ♄ No. 277. Walter Marshall; The Gospel Mystery of Sanctifica-tion, with a Sermon of Justification. 8° [1692].

June 5 ☽ · About 7h a.m. Rode with my wife from Rye to London, came to Tunbridge about 5h p.m. & next day in the Stage Coach to London & to Mr. Tho: Miller's house about 6h 30′ p.m. where we lodged during our stay. Had extraordinary good weather, not very hot, no rain nor dust nor dirt, nor any disaster. But whilst we staid at London the weather was very rainy. During my being at London had order from Mr. Nathan: Pitman to buy him some wooll by Commission.

14 ☿ No. 278. Nehemiah Cox, The last Hours of Dr. Andrew Rivet, with an Appendix. 12°.⁴

15 ♃ About 5h 30′ p.m. I presented my Father's Folio Manuscript of

---

² See Introduction, sect. 6.

³ William Hartridge, clerk, of Goudhurst, Kent, left all his lands and goods to 'my loving kinswoman Dorothy Ferrall, wife of Stephen Ferrall of Southwark, Innholder'. He was the son of John Hartridge, yeoman, also of Goudhurst, and had been admitted to St John's College, Cambridge, in 1647. On 'Cosin Wagon' see 5.7.93. PCC PROB 11/414 1693: 81; Venn.

⁴ Conceivably a reprint by Cox of *The Last Houres, Of . . . Andrew Rivet*, translated by G. L. (The Hague, 1652), an octavo, but if so not otherwise recorded.

Arithmetick, to the Royal Society for their approbation of the printing it.

June 21 ☿ About 6h p.m. Received the Manuscript back again from the Royal Society; Sir Robt Southwell President, with this Answer That they had committed it to one that had viewed it all over & found it to be a very good Collection & that might be usefull to the Publique; That they wisht me good success in the printing of it; & if it were printed several of the Society that were that way inclined might buy of them as they had occasion.[5]

July 5 ☿ About 8h a.m. Returned from London per Coach to Tunbridge, where we arrived at 7h p.m. And thence on horsback to the Wells to Cosin Sam: Wagon's where came at 9h 30′ p.m.[6] And next morning about 9h a.m. departed thence & got to Stone Crouch at noon. went thence about 3h p.m. & came home to Rye about 9h p.m. having very good weather without heat or wind. Found my family in health & without any disaster. Things fitted very well for pleasure this Journey: but expensive, I furnishing my self with a great deal of Cloths, wherein & with other Expences laid out neer £40.

17 ☽ News of the miscarriage of the Turkey fleet by Letters dated the 15th which put a great Stop to Trade; & Mr. Pitman countermanded his order to buy wooll. But in a week after he ordered me to buy 3 packs, & by another Letter dated August 1 to buy 3 packs more; & by a third dated August 5 to buy 5 or 6 packs more. Which I did accordingly at £8 per pack, & sent them soon after to London per land as he ordered.

Aug. 2 ☿ News per post of the Fight in Flanders wherein the Confederates were worsted; which also put a stop to Trade.

11 ♀ About 7h a.m. My friend Mr. Thomas Markwicke died; who by will gave me £100 &c. and made me his Executor. By reason of his death I was much harassed with business for about 8 months after: viz: selling the houshold goods, putting off the Shop, paying his debts & Legacies, he owing about £700 & giving Legacies to the value of £700 or more by will. Besides the trouble of

---

[5] See Introduction, sect. 6.

[6] Samuel Wagon or Waghorne was a cousin of Samuel Jeake, and probably the bricklayer from Speldhurst, near Tunbridge Wells, Kent, whose will was proved in 1738. He and his brother John (see 25.6.85) were the sons of a Speldhurst yeoman. KAO DRa/PW8, DRb/PWr/ 25: 42.

receiving the debts due to him, being most book debts & many
desperate &c. By his death I was put in a Capacity to print my
Fathers Book of Arithmetick; half the Charge of which he
offered to have gone in his lifetime; & desired if he dyed before
me & left me his Executor that I would print it out of what he
gave me; which was houses & land for his personall estate
amounted not to pay his debts & legacies.[7] At his Death the
Heavens were

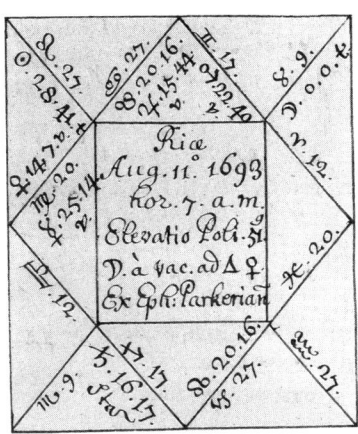

thus disposed. Which I describe only for Experiment sake; and
therein Q[uestion] whether an access of Estate & increase of
Figure were not justly signifyed by Mercury Lord of Medium
Coeli posited neer the Cusp of the Horoscope in House, Exaltation, & other fortifications; by Venus Lady of the 2d neer the
Cusp of the Ascendant in her Triplicity: by the Moon Lady of
the 11th in her Exaltation on the Cusp of the Radical Medium
Coeli & here in the 8th in trine to the Sun. Which posture
seems directly to note a Legacy by the death of a Friend: &
lastly by Jupiter in his Exaltation in Medium Coeli in the sign of
the 11th & in sextile to Venus. And secondly Q[uestion]
whether Saturn stationary in exact opposition to the Cusp of

---

[7] The elder Jeake's *Λογιστικηλογία or Arithmetick Surveighed and Reviewed* was published
in London in 1696. See 18.4.94.

Medium Coeli did not signify the perpetual Regret & Enmity of many Persons to me upon this Occasion; & the Sun on the Cusp of the 12th the Envy of a Magistrate; & Mars neer the Cusp of Medium Coeli in square to Mercury & opposition to Saturn the numerous Labours & Quarrels I went through in the management of this Executorship.

Aug. 14 ☽ Mr. Markwick was buried. And from the funeral I sent to Mr. Joseph Tucker (who just before Mr. Markwick's Death had some thoughts of settling himselfe at Rye) that he might if he pleas'd, have the refusal of the House & Shop-goods before I would treat with any one else. Which he comply'd with; & in less than a fortnight's time we agreed on these terms; that he should take the house at £9 per annum from Michaelmas and take the Shop-goods all; & such Houshold-stuff as he had occasion for, as they should be apprised by two indifferent persons; one to be chosen by either party.

16 ☿ Coming by night out of the Butchery towards my own house;[8] it being very dark; I was in great danger of falling over a Load of Wood which lay out in the Middlestreet, which being just in my way, I was within Two Steps of stumbling upon, not seeing it. But it pleased God to send a Flash of that Lightning which was very frequent that Evening; just at that very Instant: to shew me my danger & prevent it. Which wonderfull Providence I shall never decline to acknowledge. For had not the Air been inlightned at the Critical moment, that so I made a suddain stop; I had immediately stumbled against a great Log, & the inclination of my body which would consequently have ensued, had dasht my head against other great logs & sticks that lay endlong or athwart over the other, just at such a distance as they had probably run directly into my Eyes & Brain. After wards the same Evening going back again that way (it being out of my mind) I fell over the other side of that parcell of wood, & broke the skin off one of my shins, but had no further hurt; the wood on that side not lying so as to hurt my head or do me any further injury, as I observed next morning. When I view'd both sides of it to contemplate the mercy of that Providence that delivered me.

---

[8] The butchery is marked on Jeake's 1667 map of Rye. See 10.1.67.

30 ☿ The Inventory of Mr. Markwick's goods all except the shop goods was made. And from hence to the 7th of September I was busied in selling houshold goods &c.

Sept. 5 ♂ I wrote to Mr. Samuel James to go partner in buying of Hops: which by his Answer of the 9th Instant he agreed to: but advised not to be too hasty in buying, which spoil'd the business, for now they might have been bought for 26s per hundred & under, but by delaying, they rise about the 18th Instant & I being busy about Mr. Markwick's shop all that week, neglected to go out to buy. However with much difficulty I bought about 63 Bags in this month & October some at 23 28 & 30s per hundred but the most I was fain to give 33s per hundred for. Yet we got about £20 a piece by them.

7 ♃ Mr. Pitman's letter dated wherein he ordered me to buy 10 packs wooll more. This day, or the next I went to Hasting to get an Appriser for Mr. Markwick's shop; but could not by reason of their being at London.

10 ☉ No. 279. Jos: Symonds, The Case & Cure of a deserted Soule. 8° [1639].

18 ☽ Mr. John Leigh of Cranbrook came to apprise Mr. Markwick's shop; & I being disappointed of an Appriser: we agreed that he should value the goods indifferently between Mr. Tucker & me.⁹ So he began this afternoon, & ended 21th ♃ in the afternoon. The Totall of the Shop-goods with some few houshold goods that Mr. Tucker took afterwards came to £831 8s. Whereof £201 8s by agreement was to be paid down & which I received all before November 14 next. For £300 I had bond of Mr. Tucker & his Father paiable March 25th 1694. For £200 like bond paiable September 29th 1694 & for £130 like bond paiable March 25 1695. The Two first bonds were punctually paid: the last not due at the writing hereof, but I have no Reason to be solicitous about it.

22 ♀ About 5h p.m. I was taken ill with a little fit of a Quartan Ague: sweat in the night: & not well all the 23th 24th & 25th Instant.

---

⁹ John Leigh was a mercer. RYE 116/18–19.

Saturn newly past the Meridian. The Moon neer the Cusp of the 8th. else little malignity. Jupiter governing the Angles Exalted in trine to the Ascendant & the Moon, & exactly on the Radical place of the Sun. inclines to a Speedy recovery.

Sept. 25 ☽ At even, a 2d fit: but very moderate.

27 ☿ No. 280. Chr: Love, The Natural Man's Case stated. 8° [1652].

28 ♃ About 5h p.m. The 3d fit of my ague: gentle.

29 ♀ I rode to Robertsbridge to lend Tho: Ransom £120 on a Mortgage of his Copihold land.[10] By the way I met Tho: Cruttenden & bought his Wooll for Mr. Pitman. Then went to some places to buy hops but could not agree, got to Robertsbridge about Sunset, being very wet with a hard Rain continuing for the last 4 or 5 mile riding. all the day having been wettish.

30 ♄ In the Forenoon received Ransom's Surrender in the Court Baron: & lent him the money.[11] Towards evening returned home: and by the way about 6h 30′ p.m. in a dark lane riding cross a descent made by a Rivulet of water the Girth being Loose, my Saddle for want of a Cruppier ran forward on the horse's neck; & I was twice like to be thrown off into the water where being alone in the night, I might either have been

[10] Thomas Ransom was one of the witnesses to the will of John Weeks (see Appendix 3).

[11] A Court Baron was the assembly of freehold tenants of a manor under the presidency of the Lord or his steward; what Jeake refers to is the registration of the transaction in the manorial records.

drowned or trod underfoot by my horse, or at least have been all wet. But the good hand of God directed me to stop & retire before I was quite off, & the horse being very gentle did not impede it. The Figure of Heaven for this Moment is as followeth.

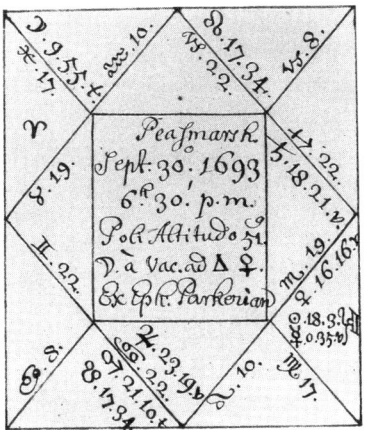

Wherein are Several Circumstances very remarkable. 1st. Saturn Lord of Medium Coeli just on the Cusp of the house of Death. 2dly Jupiter & Mars on the Radical place of the Sun in conjunction in a watry sign & exact opposition to the Cusp of Medium Coeli. 3dly the Moon neer the Cusp of the 12th in a Watry sign, & on the Cusp of the house of Death in the Radix. 4thly Venus in a watry sign in opposition to the Ascendent. 5thly the Sun in square to Jupiter Mars Medium Coeli & the 4th house. The Danger of falling I conceive from the opposition of Jupiter & Mars to Medium Coeli principally: of water from so many Planets in Watry Signs, specificating the nature of the accident. Not that I think this Positure of Heaven sufficient to have caused such an Accident without a due disposition of the Subject (as I hinted before). For if I had been sitting at home at that time I believe no such Accident could have been caused by force of those Influences: but being then on horsback, & passing the Rivulet at that very juncture of Time; subjected me to the danger of those malefique Rays.

Oct.   1 ☉ About 4h p.m. A 4th fit of my Ague.

Oct.　4　☿ About 5h p.m. The 5th & last fit: gentle.

　　　7　♄ I shipt about 20 Bags of the Hops I bought, in Wm Dan for London, which through mercy arrived safe there next week.[12]

　　23　☽ No. 281. Charles Molloy, De Jure Maritimo et Navali. 8° [1676].

　　24　♂ I weigh'd the wooll which I bought 29th past of Tho: Crutten-den for Mr. Pitman being 10 packs 3 draughts at £8 per pack, coming to £86 had it down to Rye the same day; & afterwards sent it by the Carrier to London.

Nov.　3　♀ I began to be troubled with a Cold which increased for 3 days after.

　　　4　♄ About 6h p.m. Taken Aguish; a Feaver in the night & sweat much.

　　　5　☉ Worse & feaverish all night, & so 6 ☽ and continued ill all the week; but mending toward the latter end: by the use of Canary.[13]

　　　6　☽ Shipped the rest of the Hops being 40 bags 6 ends in Wm Kirby for London.

　　18　♄ Mr. James's letter dated with advise of Kirby's safe arrivall at London.

1694

Jan.　21　☉ News of Sir John Darrell's death: & 24　☿ in the Evening con-trived with Mr. Jno Spain & Fra: Young to chuse Mr. Frewen Burgess for Rye in his stead; which was effected in about a week after.[1]

　　25　♃ Mr. James's letter dated, with advise that he had sold all our hops to Mr. Cox, at 37s 6d per hundred whereby we got about £20 a piece as abovementioned.

[12] William Dan was a Rye mariner and freeman. The Dans were a long-established family of Rye fishermen. RYE 1/17, preface, 137/53; Burchall, p. 107.

[13] i.e. Canary wine.

1694 [1] John Spain was a Rye jurat and member of the nonconformist faction; possibly the baker of the same name living in Rye in 1679. Francis Young was a Rye jurat and mariner, married to the daughter of Thomas Crouch senior (see Appendix 3). Jeake witnessed his will. Frewen (on whom and Darrell see 10.3.81) had been unseated in 1689 on petition by Sir John Austen (see 12.5.90). He did indeed sit again in 1694. Burchall, p. 102; LAWR 30, p. 171; 42, p. 66; 45, p. 264; RYE 1/17, preface, 2/1, 19/89; Henning, i. 499–500.

Feb. 1 ♃ About 5h p.m. I spake to Mr. Spain the Maior & some of the Jurats of Rye, about a proposition for clearing the Town's mortgage.[2]

5 ☽ No. 282. John Goad, Astrometeorologica, or Aphorisms & Discourses of the bodies Coelestial. Fol: [1686].

ditto This day & next I distributed the £10 given by Mr. Markwick's will to the poor of Rye.

12 ☽ Proposed to give £60 towards the clearing of the Mortgage on the Town of Rye's land; by Letter which I carried up to the Assembly & having there read, delivered it to the Maior, purporting the payment of said Summe at Midsommer 1695. Vide Copy on the File.

27 ♂ I rode to Wadhurst to see the Land left me by Mr. Markwick, & to distribute the £10 given by his will to the poor of that parish; had good weather & good success in the journey. Came home March 1 ♃ at night (having distributed the £10 that morning) & at my Return found Mr. Geo: Children (Mr. Markwick's half Brother) at my house; being come to receive the £250 given to his Children by the Will: & with him Geo: Smith an Uncle of Mr. Markwick's to see if any thing were given to him; & one that had married one of Simon Smith's daughters, to whom was given £10. Next day I paid Mr. Children the £250 & to S. Smith's daughter's husband the £10 aforesaid.[3] And had good success in getting the money in; part in debts due to me, & part I borrowed: all being dispatched & discharges sealed in a day's time.

Mar. 4 ☉ No. 283. Robt. Bolton, Discourse of True Happiness: & General Directions for a Comfortable Walking with God. 4° [1611].

14 ☿ About this time had advise from Mr. James that he had paid to several of Mr. Markwick's Creditors according to my order the full of their debts; the totall of what he paid the 28th past being

---

[2] See Introduction, sects. 4 and 8.

[3] Although Jeake refers to George Smith as an uncle of Thomas Markwick, the latter calls him 'my loving friend' in his will, leaving him a token bequest (see Appendix 3). On Simon Smith, Markwick's uncle, to each of whose children Markwick left £10 in his will, see 27.2.85. He may have been the 'Simon Smith, esquire' who was living in Buckhurst in the 1670s, and had apparently moved to Westminster by the 1680s. ESRO DLW 268–9; AMS 533; PCC PROB 11/419 1694: 82.

£69 1s 1od. And after on the 26th Instant he paid £60 13s 6d more.

Apr. 9 ☽ About 8h a.m. I began my Journey to pay several of the Legacyes given by Mr. Markwick's will, & to prove the will, & pay
the rest of his debts yet remaining unpaid at London. Rode first
to Ashford, & thence to Wye that night to pay the Legacy of £10
given to the Poor there. Had good weather over head, only cold
& pretty much wind in the morning. But dreadful & dangerous
ways from Appledoor to Ashford; yet it pleased God that I went
safe; though by reason of the badness of the ways it was neer 3 a
Clock in the afternoon before I got to Ashford. Afterwards I had
very good ways.

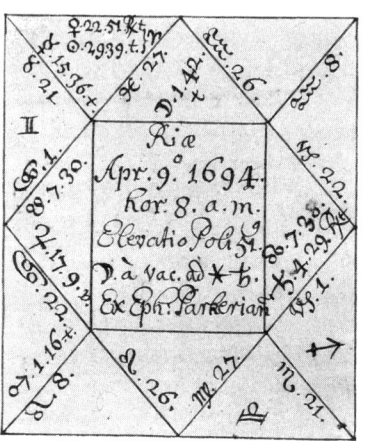

I propose not this Scheme, as if I made any Election of the
Time to begin my Journey; for I went when it best suited with
my Conveniency. But only for Experiment sake; & therein I observe the Moon Lady of the Ascendant neer the Cusp of
Medium Coeli in her Triplicity, Reception of House with
Jupiter & partil trine to the Ascendant. Saturn & Jupiter the
Lords of Medium Coeli one in his own house, the other exalted,
& both in good houses of Heaven. These Considerations seemed
to presage Health, Prosperity, Credit, Repute & Employment
advantagious, in this Journey. The Radical place of Mercury
ascending. Jupiter Lord of Medium Coeli neer the Cusp of the

2d in his Exaltation; & the Moon Lady of the 2d neer the Cusp of Medium Coeli well posited as above mentioned seem to signify some encrease of Estate by means of this Journey. But the radical place of the Sun on the Cusp of the 2d & Mars in the 2d in square to the Sun note Expences. Saturn on the Cusp of the house of publique Enemies in opposition to the Ascendant, fitly denotes the many Quarrels & Controversies I had with the Legatees at London. And the Cauda Draconis in the Ascendent Scandals and Reflections.

10 ♂ Having in the morning distributed the £10 to the Poor at Wye, I went thence about 9h a.m. for Lenham; came thither about noon, & having from thence sent a Letter to one of the Legatees to meet me at Maidstone, I went thither about 1h p.m. having small Rain for the last 8 miles riding. Came to Maidstone about 3h 30′ p.m.

11 ☿ After dinner, went from Maidstone to Town Malling to distribute £10 given to the Poor of that parish, & £10 to the Poor of Ryersh. Had good weather.

12 ♃ In the morning having distributed the Legacies of £10 a piece to the Poor of the parishes of Town Malling & Ryersh & paid Fra: Smith one of the Legatees £10[4] I departed from Town Malling at 10h a.m. in Company of Two Citizens which I met there going for London, & having baited at Farmingham, came thanks be to God safe to London in good weather about 6h p.m.

13 ♀ I went in the forenoon to Doctors Commons to prove Mr. Markwick's will: but Mr. Dew whom I intended to imploy about it being out of Town my business was retarded for some hours.[5] But about 2h p.m. Mrs. Dew directed me to another Proctor Mr. Sam: Boheme, who went with me & I took the Oath of Executor, which was administred to me in these words as I Remember. You do believe this to be the last Will & Testament of Thomas Markwicke; you shall well & truly pay his debts & legacies, so far as the estate shall amount to & the Law charge you: & you shall exhibit a true Inventory, & give a true account unto the Court when you shall be thereunto required: So help you God. Then I left the Will with Mr. Boheme, & appointed

---

[4] Francis Smith was an uncle of Thomas Markwick. PCC PROB 11/419 1694: 82.

[5] Mr Dew was probably William Dew, son of William, of London, who was admitted to Trinity College, Cambridge, in 1687, and received his LLB from Trinity Hall in 1693. Venn.

next Tuesday forenoon to call for the Copy of that & the Inventory. Afterwards I went into Southwark to present a bill of £240 & another of £30 which I brought up with me: And having gotten them accepted I gave notice to severall Creditors & Legatees, that I appointed to pay them next Tuesday at 3h p.m. at the Hoop Tavern on Fish-street hill.

Last night at my coming to London, I was acquainted by Mr. Miller at whose house I lodged that the Act for the Million Adventure filled apace & that he intended to put in £400 & would have wrote to me to have known whether I would have put in any; but that knowing of my coming to London; he deferred the acquainting me by writing. Upon which having considered this day I resolved to put in £100 if I could get money in London upon return to do it. Looking upon it Providential that I should come at this time: for had I staid at Rye I believe I should have put none in; for want of being animated by the Example of the Londoners. And I did not indeed think of putting any in at all till the Friday or Saturday before I came from Rye. And this being not a Lusory but a Civil Lot: & the putting the Act in Execution (when once made) being now become necessary for the support of the Government in the War against France, I was the better satisfied to be concerned in it; & after many deliberate Reflections with my self at Leisure times after my return to Rye, I concluded this might be lawfull. Though I always was & still am an utter Enemy to the practice of all Lusory Lots: & all those Sales of goods by Lot & money Lotteries, which about this time swarmed at London. Notwithstanding that, in this Journey I purposely bought Gataker's book of the Nature & Use of Lotts, which I carefully read over & considered after I came home. All whose Allegations for the lawfulness of Lusorious & needless Lots did not at all alter my Judgment, Dr. Ames in his Marrow of Divinity & Cases of Conscience speaking more sense in 2 or 3 pages against them; than Gataker in all his Book can for them.[6]

Apr. 14 ♄ I got a promise of £50 upon Return & after a promise of £20 more of the Fishmongers Cox & Ferris, to be paid at my Return

[6] See Thomas Gataker, *Of the Nature and Use of Lots* (1619) and, on his dispute with Ames, K. L. Sprunger, *The Learned Doctor William Ames* (Urbana and Chicago, 1972), 175–6. On lotteries in London in the 1690s see Ewen, *Lotteries and Sweepstakes* (see Introduction, sect. 8 n. 37), 123 ff., and Dickson, *Financial Revolution* (see Introduction, sect. 8 n. 35), 45.

to Rye.[7] And in the Evening I wrote to my Wife to borrow money for me against my Return. I having put my self out of money & borrowed neer £300 before; to fit my self to pay the debts & legacies of Mr. Markwick: till I could raise money out of his estate.

16 ☽ Several Projects about this time began to run in my mind, to venture & try to advance my Income, the war having spoiled all my Trade at Rye & I making but 5 per cent of my money at Interest upon Mortgages & Bonds, upon which I could but barely maintain my family. The Projections that I thought upon, were putting into this Million Adventure, Buying of Blank Tickets therein after the drawing, Selling of Tickets before the drawing, Putting in moneys upon the other Act of Parliament then coming out viz: that of 8 per cent perpetual Interest in the Bank of England, & on the Lives at 14 per cent one Life 12 per cent 2 lives & 10 per cent 3 lives: And buying Stock in the East India Company whose actions were now fallen to 82 per cent & probably supposed to fall lower.

17 ♂ In the forenoon I went & fetched the Copy of Mr. Markwicks will under Seal of the Prerogative Court, & the Inventory from my Proctor Mr. Boheme. And in the afternoon about 3h p.m. went to the Hoop Tavern, where till 6h p.m. I was busied in paying debts & legacies of Mr. Markwicke's viz. about £130 debts, & £70 legacies. viz. those to Rich: Pope & Mr. Steeds 2 sons. But with Mrs. Fosters daughters & their husbands Haskins & Cramphorn; & with Jno Hills one of her Grandchildren I had much quarrelling. They refusing to seal the Releases I had made, there being this clause in them to quit their Interest in the personall estate: though no more was given to them than what I offered to pay them. The Daughters moreover quarrelling because I had not brought money to pay their Children though Minor's their Legacies.[8] So we parted in discontent, and appointed to meet again on Thursday morning next.

18 ☿ In the morning I paid John Hills his Legacy of £20 and contented my self to take such a Release as he agreed to: Then paid

---

[7] For Jeake's dealings with Cox and Ferris in 1699 see FRE 5325–6, 5330–1. See also Appendix 3.

[8] Richard Pope lived in Southwark, and Mrs Foster was an aunt of Thomas Markwick (see Appendix 3) who had lived in Maidstone and was dead by 1694. Markwick left £20 to each of her children and grandchildren. On Mr Steed see 3.10.90. PCC PROB 11/419 1694: 82.

2 debts more about £23. In the Afternoon I spake with Two Printers, Richardson & Darby about the Printing my Fathers Folio Manuscript of Arithmetick next year, the Totall charge whereof I had computed to be about £270.⁹ In the evening Haskins & Cramphorn who had this day been chosen Guardians at Doctors Commons for [*written twice*] 4 of their Children Minors, came to me & demanded their Legacyes. Concluded to pay them the money, & to meet them To morrow at 4h p.m. beside Doctors Commons, & to have my Proctor with me to advise about my safe paying it.

Apr. 19 ♃ In the forenoon I received £70 of Mr. Cox the Fishmonger upon return; which with £25 that Mr. Sam: James promised this day to lend me, supplied my Occasions with money enough to buy 10 Tickets in the Million Lottery. At 3h p.m. I went to Doctors Commons, met with Mr. Dew & Mr. Boheme the Proctors, who advised me to pay the Legacies due to the Grand-children of Mrs. Foster that were yet in their Minoritie into Court, as the safest way, & so to let Haskins & Cramphorn their Guardians give Bond to the Court & take the money out thence. So met them according to appointment at 4h p.m. & after much quarrelling because I would not pay it to them & take their bonds & such security as they brought; it was at last concluded between us, that I should suffer an Action against me by Con-sent & so pay the money into the Prerogative Court where they were chosen Guardians, & that I should allow 40s towards the Charge: & should remitt up the £80 due to the Minors to be paid into Court as soon as I could get returns from Rye. But the legacies of £20 apiece due to the wives of Haskins and Cram-phorn I brought with me & paid them at the same time; taking Releases made by their Proctor & sealed by them & their wives.

20 ♀ About 10h a.m. I received the £25 which Mr. James lent me to make up my money for 10 Tickets in the Million Adventure[.] And then I went to R. Smith's at the Grashopper in Lombard-street, one of the receivers appointed by the Act.¹⁰ Came thither

⁹ Evidently John Richardson of Fenchurch Street and John Darby of Bartholomew Close; Richardson had printed the 1685 edition of Cocker's *Arithmetic*. H. R. Plomer, *A Dictionary of Printers and Booksellers . . . 1668–1725* (Oxford, 1922), 97, 253.

¹⁰ Lombard Street was a well-known centre of goldsmiths and bankers, and the grasshopper sign, which still survives, was famous. Nothing further has been found on R. Smith.

about 11h a.m. About 11h 30′ a.m. I paid £93 16s 7d for 10 Tickets. And just at noon I received the Tickets.

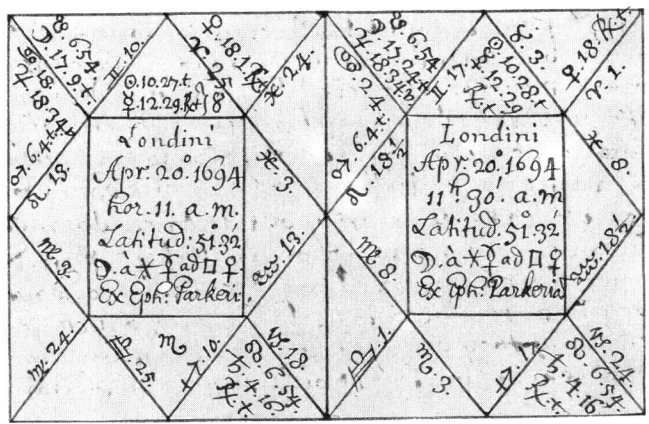

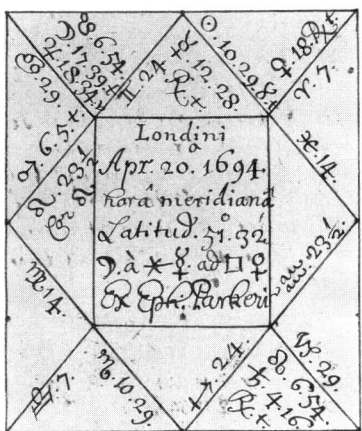

Note that I made no Election of the Time: but went assoon as I had procured money, & had Leisure to go. The Numbers of my Tickets were from 44 M 461 to 44 M 470 Inclusive.

About 1h p.m. I received the Citation from the Prerogative Court by Consent about the Legacyes.

In the Afternoon, I went to see Mrs. Savage who had lately the Miracle wrought on her of the Cure of her lame hand & side; the Relation whereof I had seen before in print, with the Affidavits' taken before the Lord Maior.[11] I met with her husband & her self both at home & had the truth thereof confirmed by their own Mouths.

Apr. 21 ♄ In the forenoon I went to Dr. Prichard's to see after a debt of £5 which his Brother owed me.[12] And about 10h 30' a.m. Going through his Brewhouse after him, or rather by his side it being darkish I stept with my Foot into one of those Tuns or Fats where they put wort or Liquor; & fell down with my whole Body into the place. But through God's wonderful Providence I had no hurt, neither was there any Beer or Liquor at that time in the Tun so as to wet me. For which great Providence I desire to be for ever thankfull; for I might have easily broke my Brains against the sides of the Tun in my fall or if not so might have broke a leg or an Arm. The Heavens at this time were disposed as followeth.

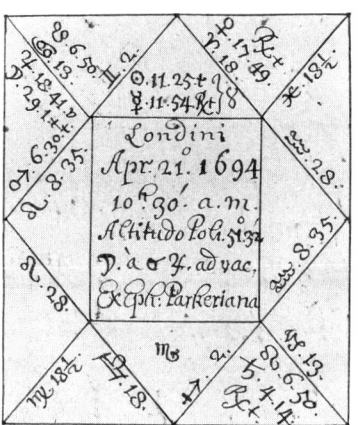

Wherein note that Mars is just risen, & Venus culminating. The former according to the Providential disposing of secondary Causes seeming to signify the fall; & the latter the escaping

[11] See Introduction, sect. 6 n. 25.
[12] Nothing further has been found on Dr Prichard.

without hurt. Nor does this Consideration diminish the Glory of the God of Nature in the admirably miraculous Textures of his Providential dispositions: which when I contemplate, it makes me cry out, as related in the Prophecy of Exekiel. Chap 10. 13 O Wheel: that is O wonderful Providence.

23 ☽ About 9h a.m. I came from London & lodged that night at Mr Children's in Tunbridge parish. And assayed in that parish to take up £500 on Mortgage, to make use of in those ways that came into my mind at London; & which my Resolutions continued to prosecute. But I could not speed there.

24 ♂ About 7h a.m. Went thence for Rye & by the way spake to Mr. John Robins & Mr. Rich: Holman at Beckley to pay in £405 which they owed me upon three Mortgages.[13] I came home exactly at sun set. & found my Family all well at my Return. And through the good hand of God upon me all things succeeded well in this Journey & I did many businesses much to my satisfaction. Note that yesterday & to day the weather was excessively hot as if it had been the heat of summer in July or August: hotter than ever I knew it at this time of year. which made my riding somewhat uneasy.

27 ♀ Borrowed £100 of Nic: Stone which was procured by my wife against my Return with part whereof I paid the £70 I had of Mr. Cox upon Return.[14] And now all my Care was to borrow money that I might not be disappointed of my intentions of putting in more in the Million Lottery, & of putting in upon Lives & in the Bank. For I could not possibly get in the debts owing me on the suddain.

30 ☽ I sent up a box to London per Carrier with some unnecessary Plate & Dollars to the value of £19 5s to be put in the Million Lottery. And £64 in Gold of my Mother's which she intended to put in.

May 1 ♂ Mr. Miller's Letter dated, advising me that the Act was passed

---

[13] Richard Holman was probably related to John Holman of Beckley, clerk. He may also have been related to Jeake's mother-in-law, Barbara Hartshorne, whose first husband was John Holman, and who had been living in Beckley in 1648. On Robins see Appendix 3. AMS 5742/21; FRE 5237; Jeake MS 2/1, fol. 2v.

[14] Nicholas Stone was probably related to the Stones of Peasmarsh, a gentry family; a Nicholas Stone owned lands in Framfield in the 1740s. Jeake bought wool from a man of this name in the late 1680s. On Cox see Appendix 3. AMS 5742/20, 3637/8; RYE 145/11.

for 8 per cent perpetual Interest, viz. the Bank; & the fund for the Lives was in the same Act. And that E: India Stock was at 80 & 81 per cent.

May 3 ♃ I went to Winchelsea Fair to speak to severall Debtors of my own & my Mother's to pay in their debts. And to enquire if I could borrow any summes. I met with Mr. Weekes who promised to lend me £100 next week; & Tho: Hunt who said he would bring me £50 in part of the debt he owed me.[15] So as fast as I could borrow money, or gather in debts, I got returns at Rye & remitted it up to London.

7 ☽ Advise from Mr. Miller dated the 5th Instant that he had sold my Mothers Gold & bought 7 Tickets for her from Number 88 M 91 to 97 Inclusive. In one of which she had afterwards a benefit of 20 per annum at the drawing. viz. No. 88 O 93.

8 ♂ Mr. Dew's Letter dated, advising that Haskins & Cramphorn by their Proctor moved to have me excommunicated for not sending up the Legacies.[16] & advising me to send up the money; which I did soon after per Carrier; because I could not get Returns fast enough for all Occasions at that time.

ditto Mr. Miller's letter dated advising that he had bought 3 Tickets more for my Mother No. 88 M 148 to 88 M 150 Inclusive. And that E. India Stock was at 74.

11 ♀ I proposed to several of the Town of Rye to put in 20 Tickets in partnership in the Million Lottery; which was effected; my self having one of the Tickets, & because we wanted one person to make up the 20th I went ⅓ of a Ticket more. And 12 ♄ we paid the money to Dr. Wright who was hired to carry it to London next Munday. who went & on Tuesday paid it in to one of the Receivers for 20 Tickets from No. 79 M 391 to 410 Inclusive.[17]

12 ♄ In the Evening Mrs. Francis came to my house & maintained a Long Quarrell with me about her Grandson Tho: Markwick's board in his childhood & moneys she had given him; & for Nurse's wages & troubling of her house with him in his sickness when he died there of the small Pocks; which she would have

---

[15] Thomas Hunt was a yeoman from Beckley. LAWR 51, p. 54.

[16] On Mr Dew see 13.4.94. On Haskins and Cramphorn see 17.4.94.

[17] Wright appears to have had a medical practice in Rye in the 1690s. He may have been the son of Joseph Wright of Maidstone, 'practitioner of physic', who died in 1703. FRE 5301–2; KAO PRC/32/57: 291.

had me paid her out of his Father's estate.[18] Being I suppose grieved that Mr. Markwick made me Executor; & not considering the large Compensation he had made in his will to her & her Daughter & others of that family for those obsolete demands the latest of which was above 5 years agone.

14 ☽ Advise from Mr. Miller dated 12 Instant that he had received the pieces of Old Gold which I sent per Carrier the 7th Instant. & that were after sold for about £26 towards making up a summe to buy 10 Tickets more on my own Account.

ditto The same day I sent up £82 in money in an hamper to London per Carrier to pay the aforesaid legacies. Which went safe, & was paid into the Prerogative Court the 18th Instant & I had an Act of Court for my discharge.

15 ♂ Mr. Miller's letter dated advising that Dr Wright had left the 20 Tickets in partnership in his Custody, as ordered, & that the said Tickets cost just £189 11s 6d.

21 ☽ Advise from Mr. Miller dated 19th Instant that he had paid £94 19s for 10 Tickets more for me upon the Million Adventure viz. No. 94 M 1 to 10 Inclusive, bought that day.

29 ♂ Mr. Miller's letter dated advising that last Saterday he had bought 10 Tickets more for my Mother, No. 34 M 741 to 750 inclusive, which cost £95 5s that being the last day of putting in. it being all filled.

June 7 ♃ Occupied about considering the Effects of Directions in my Daughter's Nativity: the Directions being calculated by me some few days before.

9 ♄ Mr. Millers letter dated; advising, That whereas I signifyed I would put in above £100 on the Annuity for Lives if money came in (having already ordered him to pay in £100 into the Exchequer on that Account by mine of the 26th past) That he had money paid in & would let me £200 for 6 moneths at 6 per cent which I accepted of.

14 ♃ Advise from Mr. Miller dated 12th Instant That he had that day paid £100 for me into the Exchequer upon the Annuity for Lives.

[18] Mrs Francis may have been the widow from Mersham, Kent, whose will was proved in 1709. Thomas Markwick (see Appendix 3) referred to her in his will as 'my loving mother-in-law', KAO PRC/17/81: 191; PCC PROB 11/419 1694: 82.

ditto   I wrote to him to pay £200 more for me on the same Account. & desired his advise about the Bank.

June 18 ☽   Advise from Mr. Miller dated 16th Instant that he would pay for me next week £200 more into the Exchequer. And that the Bank was well thought of by the Merchants & that he intended to venture in it. And that East India Stock was at 74 & Blank Tickets at 65.

19 ♂   This day Mr. Miller paid for me £200 more into the Exchequer upon the Annuity for Lives: & advised me thereof by Letter bearing the same date. Wherein he also advis'd me that the Books for taking Subscriptions to the Bank would be laid open on Thursday the 21th Instant.

ditto   I wrote to Mr. Miller that I intended to subscribe £400 to the Bank.

22 ♀   I rode with some Company to Peasmarsh for diversion, carrying my Daughter behind me, & being nigh ½ a mile out of Town about 9h a.m. she wanted to gallop which trying a little upon

plain ground, & coming out of it again; she being unskilfull, was toss'd off from the Pillion, but did not let go her hold; being also tied; & I holding her up partly with my left hand, till Dr. Wright[19] being in Company came & set her up on the Pillion

[19] See 11.5.94.

again, The horse all the while standing very still: else if he had been unruly, she had probably been trampled under his feet or otherwise mischief'd. Which Providential preservation I desire to take notice of with thankfullness. And do observe a like positure of heaven at this Accident to that related April 21 last, Mars being here very nigh to the Cusp of the Ascendant & Venus to that of Medium Coeli.

25 ☽ About 9h 30′ or 10h a.m. Advice from Mr. Miller by Letter dated the 23th Instant. That unless I got a bill to be paid at sight or came up myself for greater certainty, I should come to late for the Bank; there having been £733000 subscribed to it since Thursday last viz. in 3 days time. When I received this News I had a Jointure to write which I had promised, & money to procure for the Bank. I went out in the Town to enquire & providentially met Robt. Brown by the Fishmarket[20] whom I went to get him to send me a Letter to Mr. Miller by the Rippier's that might be delivered next morning & asking him if he had any money to let, he readily offered me £100 for 1 year at 6 per cent which (having no time then spare to try for it cheaper) I accepted of & received it in the afternoon giving Bond. And having wrote & finished the Jointure, & dispatched such necessary businesses as required doing before I went, I made my self ready for my Journey carrying the £100 with me (whereof about ½ was in Guineas) And at 7h p.m. I took horse for London, having fine cool riding & very pleasant still weather: & about midnight I got to Lamberhurst, where I lodged that night.

26 ♂ At 6h a.m. I went from Lamberhurst & arrived at London by 4h p.m. having, thanks be to God, good weather & good success in my Journey. I met with Mr. Miller in Fenchurch street, who told me he had subscribed £200 for me yesterday, & paid down £50 the ¼ part of said subscription out of moneys he had lately received by bill I remitted him before. And now understanding that none who subscribed less than £500 could have a Vote by the Charter I resolved to subscribe £300 more to make mine up £500. And accordingly about 6h p.m. I went with Mr. Miller to Grocer's hall and at 6h 30′ p.m or thereabouts & paid down £75 & subscribed for £300 more.

---

[20] The fish market is marked on Jeake's 1667 map of Rye: see 10.1.67. On the Rye 'rippiers', who carried fresh fish to London by road, see Vidler, pp. 32,50.

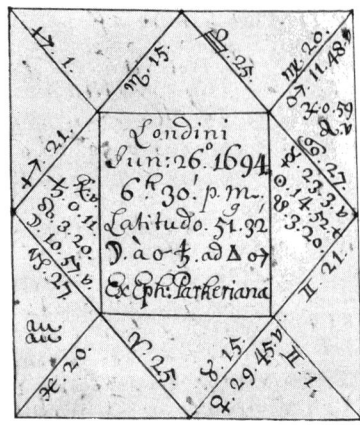

June 27 ☿ This day I spent in settling my Accompt with Mr. Miller, & informing my self about East India Stock, & visiting Friends.

28 ♃ In the morning I went to the Exchequer to see the entry in the Book, of the £300 that Mr. Miller had paid for me upon the Annuity for Lives. In the afternoon about 4h p.m. I came from London; & came to Tunbridge that night a little before 11h p.m.

29 ♀ About 6h a.m. Came from Tunbridge & stopt at several places about business; so that I came not home to Rye till about 9h p.m. had very good weather. This day the Act for Stampt Paper & Parchment began to take place.[21]

30 ♄ About 4h p.m. Edward Martin came to my house & offered me his Hops 20 bags at £3 per hundred they being now risen at London to about £4 per hundred upon a failure of the new Crop.[22] I went with him & drawed them; & about 7h p.m. bought them at £3 per hundred. And per post offered Mr. Miller the ½ he having done me many services for which I had not hitherto an opportunity to shew my gratitude.

July   4 ☿ I weighed the Hops & marked them ℞ No. 1 to 20 weighing 52 hundreds 2 quarters 6lb & gave bond for the money paiable

[21] i.e., 5 & 6 William & Mary, c. 21, a fiscal measure intended to raise money for the war.

[22] Edward Martin was possibly a miller who had been living in Rye in 1660; he might also have been related to the yeoman of the same name who was living at Twineham in 1755. Burchall, p. 107; AMS 4800.

September 4th according to agreement. In the Evening received Mr. Millers Letter dated 3d Instant accepting of my offer with great acknowledgments; &* advising that East India Stock was at 72 or 73 per cent.

* This per letter of the 7th.

About this time I had a violent Diarrhoea; which after I had been troubled with some few days; was perfectly & sensibly cured by the use of burnt Brandy twice a day.

17 ♂ A great rain which 'twas thought might bring hops somewhat forward. Cool & Cloudy weather after it. More rain on Thursday forenoon. A smart shower on Friday about 3h p.m. Hops at this time at £6 10s per hundred in London. But after this they declin'd; & though ye Rains proved to no purpose & there never was less new Hops known yet they sunk to under £6 per hundred & continued dull till the writing hereof viz. November 23th 1694 being then unsold.

18 ☿ This afternoon Mr. John Dunmoll a Londoner being at Rye came to me & offered me £5 10s per hundred for the 20 bags of hops, the money to be paid either here or at London:²³ which if I had taken there would have been £132 profit between Mr. Miller & me in fortnights time, & without disbursing any money because I bought at 2 months pay. The Sun & Jupiter were in exact conjunction to a Minute at the time of this Offer. And I was in much fluctuation whether to accept it or not. But being resolved to see & venture the utmost effect of the Rains & the result of this year's Crop, I refused it. Supposing if they failed utterly (as by what I had seen in my Journey to & from London I guess'd they would) that they must be dearer.

19 ♃ Resolved to send the Hops to London per Kirby's hoy. And being to ship them to day, it fell a raining that hindred me till the morrow. This evening wrote to Mr. Miller that I design'd to buy some E. India Stock.

20 ♀ I made ready again to ship the Hops. And one Bag being just put into the wagon at 3h p.m. it immediately fell a raining: whereupon I altered my mind; & had it took out again. The Bag was no sooner out but it fell a raining as if it had been poured out of buckets for ¼ of an hour, and rained afterwards ¼ of an

---

²³ A John Dunmoll owned land at Wadhurst, Sussex, in 1674. AMS 1678.

hour more, but that was moderate. So that if I had loaded the hops had been very much damnified.

July   21 ♄ In the morning about 6h a.m. I began again to load the hops; & it pleased God, we had then curious sunshine weather, & little wind; so that they were in the Lighter by a little past 7h a.m. and were safe put aboard the Hoy off in the harbor before 10h a.m. And next morning the Hoy went to sea.

27 ♀ In the Evening advise from Mr. Miller dated 26th That East India Stock was upon a Critical point, by reason the Dutch had 8 ships arrived; & they brought no news of 2 or 3 of ours which were expected, which if they arrived before Michaelmas, the stock would rise considerably; if not, or if they miscarried it would fall much lower then now it was being now about 71 or 72 per cent. *This day my wife had the monthly courses came* [sic], *and after they ceased she had no more, being with child in August.*

28 ♄ After a long & Fluctuating Consultation in my own thoughts, being now wholly out of Cash; at last I resolved about 2h p.m. to order £400 Stock to be bought in the East India Company: & wrote to Mr. Miller to buy it if he could have it for 70 per cent or under.

30 ☽ News in the forenoon that Kirby was safely arrived at Woolwich neer London last Saturday with the Hops.

31 ♂ Mr. Miller's letter dated with advise that the Hops were safely arrived at London.

Aug.   2 ♃ His letter dated advising that E. India Stock was risen to 76 or 77 so that he could buy none unless I enlarged my Commission: which thereupon I did to 77.

4 ♄ His letter dated, offering to pay my 2d payment into the Bank; which I accepted of my money being not yet come in.

11 ♄ His letter dated advising that E. Ind: Stock was risen to 78 so could buy none yet.

20 ☽ In the forenoon advise from him dated the 18th Instant That East India Stock was fallen to 77 last Saturday upon a Report that 2 ships were miscarried. And that if I would buy, now seemed to be the time: & that he would furnish me with all the moneys he could which might be £150 if not more. So that if I remitted the rest he would buy for me £400 Stock. But that,

what I did must be this week; for if the ships arrived it would rise to £100 per cent in one day. Whereupon I considered all this day; & resolved at last though it would be very difficult for me to compass money to effect it on the suddain: yet to indeavour it; & to proceed having so fair encouragement. And accordingly I procured bills for £53 14s which was all I could get in the Town: and 21th ♂ I sent them up to Mr. Miller with an order to buy £400 Stock if he could buy at 77 & that I would send more bills suddainly.

30 ♃ About 9h 8′ a.m. A Tile from the Eves of my woodhouse, fell down just clear of my head: so near that the dust of the Mortar that came down with it, flew upon my Hat. But the merciful Providence of God preserved me.

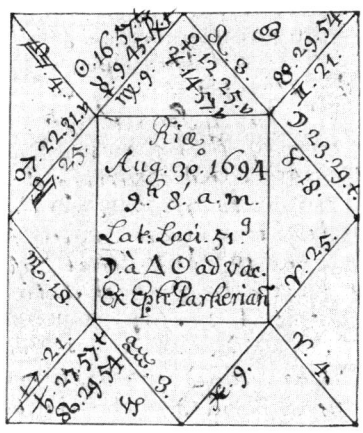

Note that Mars was just then risen; &c.

Sept. 1 ♄ This day happened a Remarkable Transit, viz. a conjunction of Jupiter & Venus in the 16th degree of Leo, the very degree Ascending in my Nativity. *About this time concluded that my wife was with child.*

ditto Mr. Millers letter dated, advising, That E.I. Stock was risen to £78 10s & so I must either enlarge my Commission; or must stay.

4 ♂ My Answer dated, ordering him to buy £400 Stock there; if not about 80 per cent.

Sept. 8 ♄ Being at a great Nonplus to pay a bill of £45 which I had taken up & sent last week to buy Stock in the E.I. Company and also to get bills for more money to be remitted in order to lye there ready to buy said stocks, And having no Cash by me. Behold as I was walking the Streets' Fra. Young[24] met me & going with him to read the Gazette, he offered me without asking £40 or £50 without Interest till Michaelmas. And to make up the rest which I wanted (besides what Mr. Miller could furnish me with) Edw. Martin[25] providentially brought me a bill of £30 & was willing to stay fortnight for the money without Interest unless I kept it longer. And Mr. Tho: Reynolds[26] came the same day with a bill of £100 which he owed my Mother to be received in London which bill I took, & so became her debtor at Interest in his stead therefore. So that now being fully supplyed, I sent up the said Bills of £30 & £100 the same night per post to London to Mr. Tho: Miller.

10 ☽ About 8h 30′ a.m. News per post from him dated 8th Instant That he had that day bought for me £400 Stock in the East India Company at 80 per cent. It being the very day wherein I had those unexpected supplyes of money. So that Providence sent me the bills very opportunely; they being this day in Mr. Millers hands in London & being on sight were ready at the transferr which was not made till the 11th Instant.

12 ☿ About 9h p.m. Advise from Mr. Miller dated the 11 Instant That he had that day paid for the £400 Stock for me £320 & for Brokerage & acceptance of the Transfer at the East India House £2 2s 6d[.] And that the same day he was offered 7 Guinea's per cent for the refusall of my said Stock for 6 moneths at 80 per cent. Which after a great fluctuation & reluctancy all that evening & next morning, I resolved to take; & accordingly I wrote to him in the forenoon the 13th Instant & sent it next post; but when he received it, he could be offered but 6 Guineas per cent. so he took them not: which proved to my advantage also; as hereafter appears at the Sale. For by his Letter of the 18th he

---

[24] See 21.1.94.
[25] See 30.6.94.
[26] Thomas Reynolds was probably related to the gentleman of the same name from Hastings who died in 1683; Jeake bought wool from a man of this name in 1686. LAWR 36, p. 123; RYE 145/11.

writes that he would wait a little longer in expectation of the Ships arrival.

17 ☽ My Wife went to Brother Holman's at Hasting, & returned Oct. 13 ♄ following.[27]

20 ♃ I wrote 4 Quaere's to Mr. Miller about E. India Stock, to inform my self the better of the nature of it. Which he answered by Letter of the 25th[.] And desired then to know my mind more fully about taking Guineas for the Refusall.

26 ☿ or 27 ♃   Advise by the same Letter of the fall of Hops at Sturbridge fair from £8 10s to £6 10s though no new hops came in: & that they were bought up & brought to London by the Salters:[28] & now between £6 & £7 at London & dull.

Oct.　2 ♂ I wrote to Mr. Miller to take 6 Guineas per cent for 6 months refusal of my E.I. Stock at 80 per cent leaving it to him.

4 ♃ His letter dated in answer, Advising that he was bid but 6 Guineas percent. And that there was a discourse on the Exchange of one East India Ship being arrived in Ireland & 3 more coming. So that he would first stay to hear whether the news were true.

6 ♄ Mr. Millers letter dated with advise that the news about the E:I. ships proved true; so that Stock was risen to 86 per cent & now he would not take Guineas. Received this letter 8 ☽ in the forenoon.

11 ♃ His letter dated, advising that the news of the 4 E.I. ships held true no further, then that they sailed from the Cape of Good Hope for Barbados May 4th last. So that Stock was fallen to 85. And that he was offered 6 Guineas for 6 months refusal at 90 per cent.

13 ♄ I sent up the Names of my Nominees upon the Annuity for Lives, to be put in at the Exchequer according to the time limited by the Act. viz. £100 at 12 per cent on the Lives of my self & daughter, £100 at 12 per cent on the Lives of my wife & daughter. & £100 at 14 per cent on the Life of my wife.

17 ☿ Received of Jno Young for the Assignment of Mr. Jno Robins's

---

[27] Richard Holman of Hastings was the son of Jeake's mother-in-law, Barbara Hartshorne, by her first marriage. LAWR 45, pp. 263–4; RYE 138/23.

[28] The identity of the Salters is unknown. Stourbridge Fair was a well-known wholesale market for agricultural goods.

Mortgage £250 & seal'd the assignment.[29] And now having received this money in, my business circulated well without having occasion to borrow any more moneys; but as I had begun to pay off: so now I proceeded.

Oct. 20 ♄ Mr. Miller's letter dated, advising me not to take Guineas for the refusal of my E.I. stock: but to wait till the ships arrived when it was thought Stock would rise to 95 or 100. & then to sell: & buy again afterwards. And advise that the Bank did very well; & that every £50 paid in was worth 54½.

23 ♂ Mine to him as I remember; with orders to take 10 9 or 8 Guineas per cent if offered for 6 months refusal of my E.I. Stock at 80 per cent or if he could sell it out right at price Currant or to that purpose at any time whin 3 months that he might so do without writing to me for orders.

25 ♃ His letter dated advising that Bank Stock was now worth 112 per cent & few sellers.

29 ☽ About 10h a.m. News per post per Mr. Miller's Letter of the 27th Instant That, that day I had a benefitted Ticket risen to me of £10 per Annum by the Million Adventure. No. 44 M 465. It's printed in No. 18 Saturday 27 October 1694.[30]

30 ♂ My letter to Mr. Miller, ordering as I remember my E.I. Stock to be sold at 85 per cent. But providentially he sold it not before 2 of the ships arriv'd.

Nov. 3 ♄ About 15h p.m. Eliz: Hartshorne youngest Daughter of Brother Nathaniel Hartshorne died at her Nurse Widow Porter's house; being aged about 3 years.[31] Buried Wednesday following, from my dwelling house.

5 ☽ Advise from Mr. Miller dated 3d Instant That at a General Court of the Bank of England held the 2d Instant The Governor had acquainted them; That with the payment of $\frac{1}{10}$ more of the several subscriptions into the Bank (which makes $\frac{3}{5}$ in all) they should be able to pay the whole into the Exchequer by the first of January; they having a great stock of money by them. So that

[29] John Young may have been related to Francis Young: see 21.1.94.

[30] The draw for the Million Lottery was announced in *The London Gazette*, no. 3014 (27.9–1.10.94); however, the place where the winning numbers were printed has not been located. Cf. 10.11.94.

[31] Widow Porter was probably Alice, the wife of John Porter, labourer. Burchall, p. 105.

now by the payment of £50 or $\frac{1}{10}$ of my subscription by the 27th Instant which made up £300 or $\frac{3}{5}$ of the total: I was at present eased from any further trouble of providing £200 more between this & the 1st of January: only giving Bond to the Governor & Company for payment of said £200 20 days after demand.

10 ♄ About 9h 30′ a.m. News per post per Mr. Miller's Letter of the 8th Instant. That that day my Mother in Law Mrs. Barbara Hartshorne had a benefitted Ticket risen to her of £20 per Annum by the Million Adventure, No. 88 M 93. It's printed in No. 26 Thursday Nov. 8 1694.

14 ☿ This Evening I received advise by Mr. Edw: Miller's letter of the 13th Instant[32] That News came that day to London of the arrival of 2 East India Ships at Plimouth, viz. the Charles the 2d & the Sampson. And that Stock was thereupon risen to £98 per cent. I received the Letter about 9h p.m. Jupiter being then in 25.46′ Leo on the Cusp of the 2d[:] Mars in Sagittarius in trine to Medium Coeli. The Sun in Sagittarius in trine to the Ascendant.

15 ♃ Upon this News, I wrote to Mr. Tho: Miller to sell my East India Stock at price Currant. For it pleased God so to order it; that though many endeavours had been used to sell it; yet it was not disposed of till the ships arrived.

17 ♄ Mr. Miller's answer dated, advising that he had not sold my stock; being in hopes to have gotten 100 by Reason that there were 2 more E.I. ships expected every day; & thinking to sell when they came in; but they not coming, stock was now fallen to 95.

24 ♄ News that the Million Lottery ended last Thursday. And that there were no Benefits arisen to our 20 Tickets in Company.

26 ☽ About 10h a.m. Advise from Mr. Miller dated the 24th That (having waited all that week for the arrivall of the 2 remaining E.I. ships & they not coming so that it was feared they might be lost) he had that Evening sold my East India Stock at 92 per cent (which he bought for me at 80 per cent no longer agone that September 8 last.) & was to have it Transferr'd & receive the money this day. Saturn & Mercury rising in Capricorn on Jupiter's radical place.

---

[32] On Edward Miller see 6.9.89.

ditto   My Mouth very sore with a Cancerous humor; which brake out somewhat violently this week; having eaten away part of the Gum; & was very painfull. But it pleased God somewhat to asswage the pain in 3 or 4 days.

Nov. 29 ♃ This Evening I finished the present Diary to this Instant 29th of November 1694.

APPENDICES

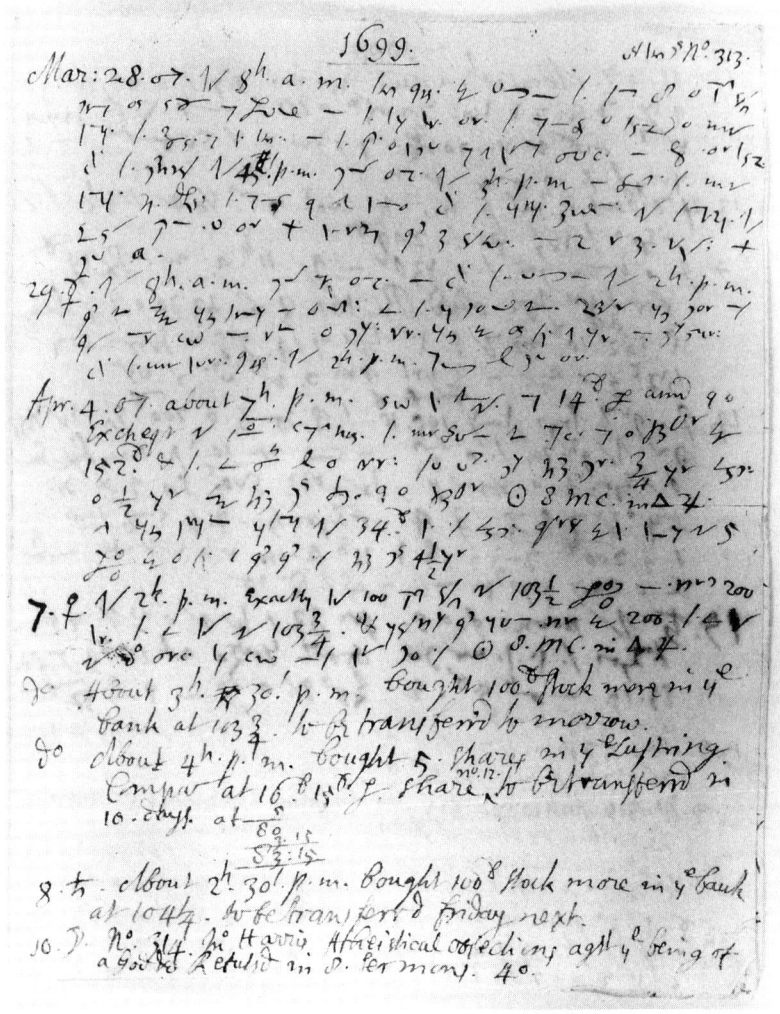

FIG. 2. The first page of Jeake's shorthand diary for 1699 (Rye Museum Selmes MS 57)

JEAKE'S SHORTHAND DIARY FOR 1699

R Y E Museum Selmes MS 57 comprises a journal which Jeake kept from 28 March to 19 October 1699. It is written on two sheets of paper folded to form a quarto paperbook of four leaves, of which the last is blank except for the word 'Diary' on its verso.

The original is almost entirely in shorthand, which has here been transliterated. It is often hastily written, and its quality deteriorates after the first page, reproduced here as fig. 2. Since the manuscript has no punctuation apart from full stops after numerals, this has been silently added, and the spelling, which is mostly phonetic, has been standardized. The sections which appear in longhand in the original have been distinguished by being printed in italics, except for times of day, the title 'Mr.', the dates in the margin, and quantities, which are always in longhand. As in the main diary, Jeake's astrological notes use standard symbols, which have here been transliterated.

At the top right-hand corner of the first leaf of the manuscript is the shorthand note 'Last book was N°. 313' (see fig. 2).

For memoranda relating to the years between 1694 and 1699 see Introduction, sec. 3 n. 5.

Mar. 28 ♂ About 8h a.m. took horse for London to tend on the bank stock during this session of Parliament and to buy more there, to finish the business with Mr. Benge, to dispose it, buy books, and to take the model of a meeting place and per[form] other business. Came to Wadhurst about 45′ p.m., went thence about 3h p.m. and spake to Mr. Benge.[1] He promised to finish in a month. Came to George Children's at Tunbridge about sunset. Taken ill there after my riding; had 3 stools and 2 or 3 vomits; after well again.

    29 ☿ About 8h a.m. went from thence and came to London about 2h p.m. Had an indifferent good journey and thanks be to G[od] without any disaster. Good weather not hot nor cold, no rain,

---

[1] Jeake had sold land at Wadhurst in 1697, and this may have been the source of the trouble with Benge, on whom see Appendix 3. FRE 5321.

the ways very good for the time of year; no way dangerous. Came to Mr. Miller's house about 2h p.m., found all well there.

Apr.   4 ♂ *about* 7h p.m. sold my annuity of £14 per *annum* in the *Exchequer* at Jonathan's Coffee House to Mr. Skelton, an officer of the Exchequer, for £152; & to be paid all the arrears till Lady Day, which were ¾ year besides the ½ year before which was ready in the Exchequer.[2] The Sun upon *Medium Coeli in* trine to Jupiter. A good bargain getting about £34 by it, besides interest for my money at 5 per cent for the time I had had it, which was 4½ years.

7 ♀ About 2h p.m. *exactly* I bought 100 bank stock at 103½ per cent and ordered 200 more to be bought at 103¾. & yesterday had given order for 200 to be bought at that [?] price but could not meet with it. The Sun on *Medium Coeli in* trine to Jupiter.

ditto   *About 3h 30' p.m. bought £100 stock more in the bank at 103¾ to be transferred tomorrow.*

ditto   *About 4h p.m. bought 5 shares in the Lustring Company at £16 15s per share; no. 12 to be transferred in 10 days at*

$$\frac{s}{80}$$
$$\underline{3.15}$$
$$\overline{83:15}$$

8 ♄ *About 2h 30' p.m. bought £100 stock more in the bank at 104¼ to be transferred Friday next.*

10 ☽ *No. 314. Jno. Harris, Atheistical Objections against the being of a God &c. Refuted in 8 Sermons. 4° [1698].*

11 ♂ *About* 10h a.m. moved Mr. Onley[3] to be at £20 charge in buying of some of my books of arithmetic, the better to enable me to build a meeting place at Rye; with promise if I could do it conveniently, then to give it to the poor at Rye.

13 ♃ *About 3h 15' p.m. bought 200s of bank stock at 104½ to be transferred tomorrow; comes to £209.*

*   *In* the forenoon went to the Exchequer, and about 11h a.m. received £19 *for* ½ years annuity. *And* received 16l. 8. 6, which

---

[2] Jonathans was a celebrated London coffee-house which, from 1697–8, was the chief centre of dealing in stocks and shares.

[3] Perhaps William Onley, printer, of Little Britain and Bond's Stables, near Chancery Lane. Plomer, *Dictionary* (above, 1694 n. 9), 224.

with the guineas received before, made £162 10s *in* full for my annuity of 14 per cent and reversion, being £152 for the annuity and ¾ year's arrears due at Lady Day last.

14 ♀ Having borrowed money £195 10s to make up for the £200 stock bought yesterday, went about 9h 30′ to the bank, and soon after 10h p.m. received all the transfers for the stock I had bought: *viz.* £500 stock in all; which being bought of 8 persons had 4 transfers for 3 for single 100's and two for £200. Finished all by 11h a.m. or a little after and paid all the money in bank bills, notes and Sh[illings] to make up.

15 ♄ About *noon* had the 5 shares which I bought at the Lustring Company transferred to me by Mr. Will. Sheppard, Gold-smith,[4] at 16. 15 per share, 83. 15, and paid 5s for admission into the company. In all £84. Sun near the radical trine of Jupiter.

17 ☽ *About* 8h 30′ p.m. but not exactly Mr. Roberts sent to me to come to him tomorrow night at 7h p.m. about setting up a lecture at Rye.[5]

24 ☽ *No. 315. Antisozzo, sive Sherlocismus Enervatus. 8°.* supposed to be written by Vincent Alsop [1675].

ditto About 11h a.m. news of the French having an army at Dunkirk in transport ships, on which bank stock fell from 105 to 104, but next day by evening rose up to 105 again.

26 ☿ About 8h p.m. took leave of Edw. Miller, being to go for Venice next day.[6]

May 3 ☿ About 7h 15′ p.m. news of the K[ing] of Spain's death but not thoroughly credited; ill news for me because of the fall of bank stock which came to 103—this indifferent; but not confirmed next day. 4 ♃ The Parliament's prorogued; glad of that.

11 ♃ *About* 7h p.m. but not exactly news by Mr. Short[7] that Mr. Benge could not pay me the money for the loan and that he was very weak and kept his bed mostly, though he thought not dangerous at present; his illness occasioned by steel[?] unguent he used indiscreetly for the itch. *Also* danger if he should die that I

---

4 William Sheppard was evidently a dealer, from whom Jeake also purchased bank stock. Bank of England Archive, Bank Stock Ledger, 1, fol. 145. See also ibid., fols. 392, 407, 427.

5 Nothing is otherwise known of this plan by Mr Roberts.

6 On Edward Miller see 6.9.89.

7 Possibly Darell Short of Wadhurst, gentleman. AMS 2104.

must refund the money and take the loan again; somewhat troubled about this, but very little by spies[?] being otherwise composed. Square Sun & Saturn this day and the Sun very near to conjunct Mars. Saturn 1 Pisces opposite to the 2d house. *This* business but[?] had stayed in London to finish this fortnight, and now I must tarry fortnight longer till Mr. Short writes to him and sees if anything can be done.

May 16 ♂ About 5h p.m. news by Mr. Short from Mr. Benge that he could not pay the money, but if we could contrive it any way he would consent to any thing; so he concluded to persuade Mr. Barham to let down the money as soon as he returns to Wadhurst, and I concluded to return for Rye this week if I could.[8] Trine of Jupiter and Venus on Medium Coeli.

17 ☿ About 10h a.m. I had £700 stock transferred to me by Mr. Miller which he bought for me in January last. Venus on *Medium Coeli in* trine to Jupiter.

About 6h p.m. news per Mr. Short that Mr. Benge's goods were served with an execution; troubled at this because I forced to hold; he's a great deal of trouble about that business.

18 ♃ Dined at Mr. Bristow's this day per invitation.[9] Venus in trine to Jupiter on Medium Coeli. Tomorrow invited to *Sir* R. Ashton's but went not because I went out of town.[10]

About 6h 30′ p.m. news per Mr. Short that Mr. Gott[11] was inclinable to finish the business about Mr. Benge, and he would take care to perfect it when he went down to Wadhurst, which would be next week, so that it would signify nothing for me to stay; whereat resolved to go down this week and get a horse of the carrier. *Lustring* 18½ per share.

19 ♀ About 11h 30′ a.m. came from London and arrived at Maidstone a little before 9h p.m. Good ways and weather. 20 ♄. Spoke to Mr. John Smith, the great hop merchant of Maidstone,[12] to get some acquaintance with him and advice about

---

[8] Mr Barham may have been related to David Barham: see 22.9.92.

[9] Robert Bristow was a merchant, director of the Bank of England and landowner in the Winchelsea area. Romney Sedgwick, *The House of Commons, 1715–54* (3 vols., London, 1970), i. 488.

[10] This was probably Sir Ralph Assheton, second baronet and a Lancashire MP. Henning, i. 562–3.

[11] Conceivably Peter Gott: see 12.5.90.

[12] See 11.9.86.

hops, which he promised to give me if I wrote to him about the new crop; after spoke to Mr. Knight about the price of flaxseed; by inquiry he satisfied me it was not sold above 36s per quarter at London last year.[13]

21 ☉ In the afternoon spoke in the Baptist Meeting at old Dr. Wright's house from 1 Corinthians 1. 23. 24, having no preparation before but meditation on this Lord's Day, and pleased G[od] to carry me through the doubt.[14]

22 ☽ About 9h 30' a.m. but not exactly remembered; came from Maidstone with cousin[?] Betty Wightman[15] and arrived at Rye safe, thanks be to G[od], at 9h p.m., having very good ways and weather; by the way spoke to Mr. Knight to give me advice how hops came forward, which he promised.

29 ☽ About 11h a.m. advice from Mr. Miller dated 27 that the committee of the Lustring Company last Thursday agreed to make a dividend of £4 per share if the G[eneral] court will agree to it, which they have called to meet next Thursday at 10 of the clock; and he doubted not but they would approve of what the committee had done. *This* good news for me because of those Lustring Shares I bought so lately, and it was likely would make it rise so that I might sell out. *Advice* of bank $103\frac{3}{4}$; *E. India New* fallen to $62\frac{1}{2}$.[16]

30 ♂ Wrote to Mr. Miller to sell my 5 Lustring shares if he could sell them for £22 or upwards.

June   5 ☽ About 9h a.m. advice from Mr. Miller dated 3 instant that the Lustring Company had ordered a dividend of £4 per share paying any time after the 11th instant which would be £20 to me. *This* day I wrote a letter of attorney for Mr. Miller to sell me 5 shares in the Lustring Company after he had received this dividend. *Bank* $103\frac{1}{2}$; *New E.I.Co.* fallen much.

10 ♄ About 8h p.m. wrote to Mr. Miller that after he had received my dividend to sell my 5 Lustring shares between this and midsummer at £15 per share if he could get no more.

---

[13] Mr Knight may have been the Thomas Knight of Lydd who caused Jeake financial problems in the 1680s: see 8.12.82.

[14] On Dr Wright see 11.5.94.

[15] Probably a relative of Jeake's cousin, Ann Wightman, who also lived at Maidstone: see 25.6.85.

[16] On the New East India Company see Introduction, sect. 8.

June 11 ☉ About 7h 30' p.m. but not exactly news per letter from Mr.
Short that Mr. Benge was gone off and would agree to nothing
as yet in order to finish my business; and that there was talks of a
statute of bankrupt would be granted against him so that he
could not get anybody to buy the farm; and that his opinion was
it was my best way at present to get possession of the loan, by
getting J.P. the tenant to attourn to me, which I had resolved on
before, and designed to go 13th ♂ in order to see after it.[17]

12 ☽ *About 1h p.m. bought the house adjoyning to mine of Rbt. Hambledon for £27.*[18]

13 ♂ *about* 6h 30' a.m. but not exactly took a journey to get possession
again of my farm at Wadhurst after Mr. Benge broke; came to
Wadhurst that evening but Mr. Short could not be spoke to till
I were going to bed. *Next* day after waiting for him till my
pair[?] was quite tired *viz.* till 2h p.m. he came, and we went to
the farm, and the tenant, though somewhat unwilling, attourned
to me and paid me 6d *in* token thereof. Then rode to Mayfield to
inquire about hops and after to Burwash, where lodged that
night & 15 ♃. Fain to tarry there all day because it rained
almost all the day there; made some more inquiry about hops
and learned several[?] things about it.

16 ♀ About 6h 30' a.m. came from Burwash and called at Robertsbridge to inquire about hops, and then came home about noon;
had a little rain about 2 mile from Rye but not much. Found my
daughter Betty very ill at my return, which troubled me extremely. *The Thursday after Midsummer* she went to board at
Mrs. Brewer's at £20 per annum.[19]

24 ♄ In the forenoon advice from Mr. Miller that he had received
£20 for my dividend at the Lustring.

ditto *No. 316. Francis Potter, An Interpretation of the Number 666. 4°*
[1642].

21 ♀ My wife with child.

30 ☉ About 5h p.m. but not exactly taken with an aguish fit, but very
moderate; sweat in the night.

[17] J.P., Benge's tenant, has not been identified.
[18] For the conveyance of this property to Jeake from Robert Hambledon of Rye and his wife
Mary, daughter of John Jacob junior, mariner, see ESRO SAS/C 293.
[19] Jeake wrote to his daughter at 'Madam Brewers, Fowlers, Hawkhurst' on 5 Sept. 1699.
FRE 5359.

31 ☽ Advice from Mr. Miller dated 29th that he could not sell my Lustring shares for £14 per share, there being no buyers at all.

Aug. 2 ☿ Having bought a house to build a meeting place in Rye this day, the writing was sealed and the fine levied, the recovery to be finished after this.

3 ♃ *About* 9h 30′ a.m. or if any mistake then a little before, I bought a hopgarden of Mr. Bishop at £8 per hundred.[20] He offered it me as I walked in the streets. Jupiter 19 Sagittarius in trine to the Sun in Leo 21. Mercury about 9 Virgo on the radical place of Venus. Hops fell very soon after & by the 4th of *September* advice from Maidstone that they were there at £5 per hundred, and twice thought they would come to 4, so that here was already almost £40 less by this bargain. I was much troubled and melancholy about it after I had bought them, and all this month indisposed with this and my daughter Betty's being so ill of the greensickness at Hawkhurst. The bank kept rising all this month till it came to 110.

Sept. 4 ☽ Advice that the bank was at 112¼ per cent.

6 ☿ My son SM[21] taken with a quotidian ague and very was very [*sic*] bad, Thursday, Friday, Saturday, Sunday, Monday and Tuesday, but through m[ercy] somewhat abating on Monday.

7 ♃ Rode to Udimer and Beckley about getting my hops shipt.

11 ☽ Advice that bank was 114½ Friday last.

12 ♂ Shipped 6 bags of hops for Exeter in Henry Coaker value £100.[22]

21 ♃ Advice from Mr. Miller dated 19 instant that hops were risen to £6 10s fine and that bank was at 119 per cent with the dividend included.

This day SM lost his ague.

Oct. 19 ♃ Advice from Mr. Miller dated 17 instant that he had sold my bag and end of hops to Mr. Cox for £5 5s per hundred, by which I lost about £11.

---

[20] Mr Bishop was probably George Bishop of Northiam, gentleman, who had been elected town clerk of Rye in 1681. RYE 1/17, p. 57, 19/36.

[21] i.e. Jeake's son, Samuel, who was two years old, and one of the three of his children who survived to adulthood. Smart, p. 78.

[22] Nothing further is known about Henry Coaker, although he might have been related to the yeoman of the same name living in Rye in 1607. PCC PROB 11/110 1607: 39.

APPENDIX 2 (i)

SOME ASTROLOGICAL TERMS AND CONCEPTS

READERS' appreciation of the astrological component of the text may be enhanced by a brief introduction to the doctrines according to which Jeake drew up the horoscopes in the diary and commented on the astrological circumstances of events. Only those astrological complexities which are essential to an understanding of Jeake's concerns in the diary will here be dealt with, but these notes should at least help to make sense of Jeake's terminology and of the basic rationale of his astrology.

The astrological principles that Jeake used were essentially those condified by the second-century writer, Ptolemy, in his *Tetrabiblos*. These depended on the presumption that the heavens had a direct bearing on events on earth. They took for granted a highly qualitative view of the planets, each of which was supposed to have a distinct character which was made manifest in its terrestrial correlation: thus while Venus and Jupiter were on the whole benign, Saturn and Mars were harmful. In addition, the angular relations between the positions of the planets in the heavens at any time, called *aspects*, were deemed to be significant. The principal such aspects were an *opposition* (180°), a *trine* (120°), a *quartile* (90°), a *sextile* (60°), and a *conjunction* (when two planets were close together). Some aspects were more favourable than others: whereas an opposition was the worst possible aspect, a trine was highly beneficial, a quartile was moderately bad, a sextile moderately good, and a conjunction neutral. These mutual relations were balanced against the character of the planets involved: thus the influence of a bad planet could be modified by friendly aspects.

Also fundamental was the notion that the *ecliptic*—the Sun's path in its apparent orbit around the Earth—could be subjected to a twelve-part division into the *zodiac*, each part governed by a *sign* with a distinct character, in each of which the Sun spent about thirty days a year. These zodiac signs could be seen in consecutive groups of three, corresponding to the seasons and known as *quadrants*: within these, the sign marking the start of each season was known as the *cardinal sign*. Alternatively, the signs could be grouped into four *triplicities*, arranged in a equilateral triangle to each other in the heavens, the signs in each being associated with one of the Aristotelian elements, earth, air, fire, and water.

Both the zodiac signs and the planets and their positions had significance in themselves, but the relationship between the two was important, since certain planets were deemed to have a special relationship with certain signs, and were called their *ruler*. There being twelve signs to allocate among seven planets, the Sun and Moon had one each and the other five two each as their *mansions*, each planet gaining strength when placed in its own sign. Conversely, a planet was said to be *in detriment* when it was in a sign opposite its mansion, while a further—slightly more arbitrary—relationship was that of *exaltation*, which linked planets with a specific degree of certain zodiac signs.

Since the position of the planets in relation to one another and to the different parts of the zodiac was believed to have a crucial effect on events on earth, practical astrology was concerned with the elucidation of this influence on the weather, on general events, and on the affairs of individual people.

The principal means by which this was done was by drawing up a *horoscope* to ascertain the state of the heavens at a particular time for a specific location. This was a chart which gave a schematic view of the heavens and on which could be plotted the positions of the planets, the zodiac signs, and any other celestial phenomena such as comets. To some extent, the position of the planets could be ascertained by observation, but—particularly for astrology as precise as Jeake's—this might be supplemented by the use of printed *ephemerides* in which the positions of the planets were more exactly and completely given. Jeake's endorsements to his horoscopes show that he derived the data for them from William Lilly's *Merlini Anglici Ephemeris* up to 1681 and from the version of it produced by Lilly's disciple Henry Coley, first under Lilly's name and then under his own, from 1682 to 1690, when he changed overnight to the newly accurate tables compiled by George Parker, first issued in that year.

Apart from the source of his data, Jeake also noted on each horoscope first, the place for which it was cast—Rye, London, or wherever—and its latitude (sometimes expressed as 'Latitudo Loci' or 'Latitudine', sometimes as 'Poli Elevatione' or 'Poli Altitudo', the altitude of the elevated, i.e. north, pole); secondly, the exact date and time (sometimes given as ante- or postmeridian, but sometimes going up to twenty-four hours postmeridian); and thirdly, a note of the aspects of the Moon at the moment in question, which were frequently included in ephemerides and which it was standard practice to include in charts for specific events. The latter have not been transliterated, but a key to the astrological symbolism used is given in the second part of this Appendix: Jeake notes both the Moon's immediately previous aspect and also that towards which it was moving, stating 'ab' or 'ad vac[ua cursi]', i.e. void of course, if it had had no previous aspect or was not about to enter one.

The horoscope was divided into twelve *houses*, each representing a part of the heavens, six above the horizon and six below. In a modern horoscope these would be presented as segments of a circle; in a seventeenth-century one they were normally represented by a diagram divided into triangles by a series of concentric boxes. But the numbering of the houses was the same, going anticlockwise from left to right. The first house, lying just beneath the eastern horizon, was known as the *ascendant*, since planets in this house were shortly to rise above the horizon. The sequence then passed through the second to sixth houses, lying out of sight below the horizon, coming back into view again with the seventh, the *descendant*, and then continuing round to the twelfth. The *medium coeli*, or *mid-heaven*, was the centre of the visible

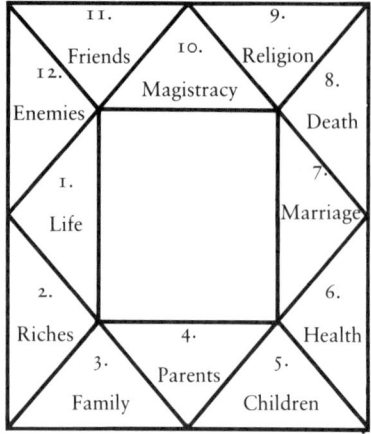

Fig. 3. The horoscopic houses

part of the heavens, in other words the tenth house, midway between the seventh and the first. Opposite it was the *imum coeli*, the fourth house. The beginning or edge of each of the houses was known as the *cusp*. It was especially significant for a planet to be on or near the ascendant or medium coeli, or, to a lesser extent, on a cusp.

From the point of view of interpretation, different horoscopic houses were deemed to have significance for specific topics, as is set out in Fig. 3. With the positions of the planets and zodiac signs entered on the horoscope, conclusions could be drawn from the whereabouts of the planets in relation to each other, to the signs of the zodiac, and to the horoscopic houses. The character of the planets was crucial, but interpretation also had to take into account such further complications as the direction and speed at which a planet was moving, particularly a planet which had just risen above the horizon. Lastly, the fixed stars could be entered in the horoscope and conclusions drawn from their location.

To some extent, the positions and mutual relationships of the planets at any moment had a significance in themselves, applicable to anyone. But in addition—and especially in Ptolemaic astrology—such dispositions might have a particular import for a specific individual due to what might be called the astrological character that he or she had acquired from the state of the heavens at the moment at which he or she was born. The horoscope cast for this moment was known as the *radix* or radical horoscope, and many of Jeake's astrological comments in the diary contain cross-references to his radix.

Despite these allusions, Jeake's natal horoscope is not given in the diary, evidently due to the extent to which this work was an arsenal of data for Jeake's further astrological studies. Instead, his radix is reproduced here from p. 5 of his earlier work, *Astrological Experiments Exemplified*.

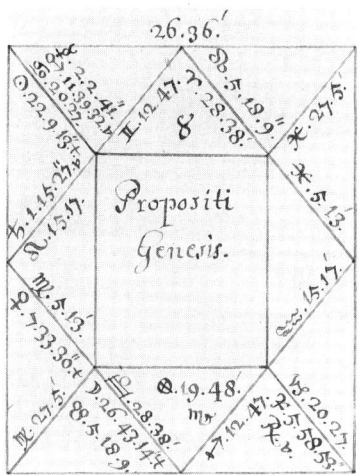

Fig. 4. Jeake's natal chart (William Andrews Clark Memorial Library MS J43M3/ A859, p. 5)

It must be left to practising astrologers to give a full assessment of Jeake's personality on the basis of this chart, but a few of its leading characteristics may be noted here. Perhaps its most prominent feature is the position and mutual relationship of two benign planets, Venus and Jupiter, which are in trine to one another, a very beneficial aspect. Both are in earthy signs, Capricorn and Virgo, while Venus is in the second house of the horoscope, the house of riches. In addition, however, Jupiter is in opposition to Mercury in the eleventh house, an inauspicious aspect, while the Sun and Saturn share the twelfth house, thus signifying the likely malice of enemies. Also unfortunate was the square of the luminaries, the Sun and Moon, while a further striking feature is a group of three planets in the sign Cancer—Mercury, Mars, and the Sun: this suggests a timidity which goes some way to neutralize the boldness which might have been predicted from the influence of the sign in the ascendant, Leo (the ruler of which was the Sun: cf. Jeake's comment in his entry on 1 November 1678).

To some extent it was as if certain planets or zodiac signs were 'lucky' for Jeake in different aspects of his affairs because of their position in his radix. At a more advanced level, however, the disposition of the planets in the natal horoscope could form the basis for precise conclusions about future significant events in the individual's life. This involved the doctrine of *directions*, a type of astrology which was of particular interest to Jeake. Directions were arithmetical calculations of the times at which incidents might be expected to occur from the relationship in the horoscope between the *promittor* and the *significator* (Jeake sometimes uses the form *significatrix* for feminine planets such as the Moon or Venus). The most important significators were the Sun and Moon, though significance might also be attached to other planets and the signs of which they were ruler, while the other planets also acted as promittors. In addition, a horoscope might be cast for the *revolution*—the time in each year of an individual's life when the Sun returned to its position in the radix—and directions in this revolutional chart might also be deemed significant. A further related doctrine was that of *transits*, according to which meaning could be found in the moment at which a planet crossed a house, and particularly the cusp of a house, in the radical horoscope: this was thought to produce good or evil according to the nature of the planet concerned and of the place transited.

These notes should at least identify Jeake's terms and give some indication of the highly complex lore according to which interpretations were reached. Jeake's piecemeal astrological comments in the diary illustrate the latter further, as, for instance, when he noted that Saturn, a malevolent planet, was rising in a watery zodiac sign at a time when he fell up to his middle in water in a well (16.6.70), or when he linked his inclination to study geometry with a direction of Mercury—the planet traditionally associated with ingenuity—with the Sun, the ruler of the ascendant in his nativity (11.12.73). A complete account of this interpretative superstructure cannot be attempted here, however, since it would take a volume in itself. Interested readers may pursue it further in an astrological handbook much used by Jeake, William Lilly's *Christian Astrology* (1647), which has recently been reprinted, while a lucid exposition of astrological principles will also be found in J. C. Eade's *The Forgotten Sky: A Guide to Astrology in English Literature* (Oxford, 1984).

KEY TO THE SYMBOLS USED IN JEAKE'S HOROSCOPES

The planets

☉	Sun	♂	Mars
☽	Moon	♀	Venus
♄	Saturn	☿	Mercury
♃	Jupiter		

The signs of the zodiac

♈	Aries	♎	Libra
♉	Taurus	♏	Scorpio
♊	Gemini	♐	Sagittarius
♋	Cancer	♑	Capricorn
♌	Leo	♒	Aquarius
♍	Virgo	♓	Pisces

Aspects etc.

☌	Conjunction	△	Trine (120°)
☍	Opposition	*	Sextile (60°)
□	Square (90°)		

☊ Caput Draconis, the Dragon's Head
☋ Cauda Draconis, the Dragon's Tail

℞ Retrograde

BIOGRAPHICAL GUIDE

THE following notes on persons mentioned frequently in the diary give occupation, place of residence, relationship to Jeake (or to others mentioned in the diary), and any other relevant information. Those who are mentioned only briefly are identified in footnotes at the relevant point in the text. Since a high proportion of those dealt with here also appear in the Introduction, no cross-references have been given.

BAKER, WILLIAM. Gentleman from Stone, Isle of Oxney, Kent, with whom Jeake had various transactions in the 1680s. PCC PROB 11/403 1689: 21; RYE 145/11.

BENGE, MR. William Benge was a gentleman from Wadhurst, Sussex. AMS 5729/102.

BROWNE, ROBERT. Mariner, and one of the richer inhabitants of Rye. He had various transactions with Jeake in the 1680s. LAWR 45, p. 339; RYE 145/11; FRE 5117–8, 5122, 5129.

CHILDREN, GEORGE. Half-brother of Thomas Markwick (see below), living at Tonbridge. In his will, Markwick left £100 to Children's son named Markwick, and £50 to each of the other children. PCC PROB 11/419 1694: 82; KAO DRb/PWr/25: 23.

COX, MR. A fishmonger, evidently from London, to whom Jeake sold hops on several occasions.

CROSS, EDWARD. A rich merchant of Exeter who employed Jeake to buy hops and wool for him and ship them to Exeter. PCC PROB 1/412 1692: 199.

CROUCH, THOMAS. Rye jurat and opponent of the nonconformists. The Crouches were a long-established Rye family, most of whom had been butchers (see 6.7.87 for a reference to Charles Crouch). LAWR 36, p. 121; RYE 2/2.

CRUTTENDEN, THOMAS. An apothecary from Cranbrook, Kent, who sold Jeake wool on several occasions. AMS 5729/53; KAO PRC/17/80: 199.

FINCH, WILLIAM. Gentleman from New Romney and solicitor for the Cinque Ports in the early 1690s. Jeake had commercial dealings with him in the 1680s. SAU 353; Hull, pp. 544, 547; RYE 145/11; FRE 5124, 5128.

FREEBODY, RICHARD. Husband of Jeake's first cousin Sarah Key (see family trees), and a gentleman from Udimore. He was probably the testator of the same name from East Grinstead, whose will was proved in 1689, but neither of the Jeakes nor their close relatives are mentioned. His widow moved to London after his death. Smart, p. 78; PCC PROB 11/397 1689: 154; AMS 4617; LAWR 41, p. 2.

GILLART, LEWIS (senior and junior). Both were Rye merchants, and the elder was referred to in 1660 as an alien, while the younger later served as jurat in Rye and engaged in joint trading ventures with Jeake. Burchall, p. 97; RYE 1/17, *passim*.

GROVE, ABIGAIL. Mother and executrix of the will of her son Robert (see below); from Coldwaltham, Sussex. PCC PROB 11/404 1691: 80.

GROVE, ROBERT. Draper from Robertsbridge, Sussex. He had issued a halfpenny token in 1667, and had various dealings with Jeake in the 1680s. J. S. Smallfield and Ernest Ellman, 'Sussex Tradesmens' Tokens of the 17th century', *SAC* 24 (1872), 133; AMS 5729/53; RYE 145/11.

HARTSHORNE, MRS BARBARA. Jeake's mother-in-law, widow of Richard, who had been master of Rye grammar school and a jurat. She had been married twice before, to John Holman and George Harding. FRE 5264, 5269, 5271; Burchall, p. 103; RYE 19/16 and 2/1.

HARTSHORNE, ELIZABETH. Daughter of the above; married to Jeake in 1681. She later married Joseph Tucker (see below).

HARTSHORNE, NATHANIEL. Jeake's brother-in-law, son of Barbara, whose various adventures are recounted in the diary.

JAMES, SAMUEL. A business partner of Jeake's; no further information has been found on him.

JAYE, JOHN. An apothecary of Fenchurch Street, London, who was married to Jeake's cousin, Mary Key, and who acted as a London correspondent for Jeake. Smart, p. 78; FRE 5063 ff., *passim*.

KIRBY, WILLIAM. Rye mariner. RYE 2/4; LAWR 50, p. 199.

LE GRIELL, JAMES. A merchant from Dieppe, who sold Jeake canvas etc. FRE 4847, 4849

MACKLEY, JOHN. London tallow chandler, and husband of Jeake's first cousin Elizabeth Key. Mackley was Jeake's chief London contact in the 1670s, but later went bankrupt. Smart p. 78; FRE 4867 ff., *passim*.

MARKWICK, THOMAS. Rye woollen draper and a close friend of Jeake, who acted as his executor. One of the Rye nonconformists, he appears to have served an apprenticeship with Thomas Miller (either Jeake's friend, see below, or an older man of the same name). PCC PROB 11/419 1694: 82; RYE 113/5 and 2/5; Burchall, p. 105.

MARTIN, JOSEPH. Rye mariner. RYE 2/5.

MILLER, THOMAS. Rye merchant and nonconformist, and Jeake's main partner in his early ventures; later, his chief London contact. Richard Naldread and Thomas Marshall (see below and 29.10.69) both referred to him as a kinsman. LAWR 34, p. 82; 41, p. 2; PCC PROB 11/332 1670: 38.

NALDREAD, RICHARD. Gentleman from Hastings who left £100 and land in Hastings in 1690 'to my loving friend' Samuel Jeake, and £5 to the poor people who belonged to the 'Meeting of Protestant Dissenters in Rye'. He refers to a deceased

Rye jurat, Allen Grebell, as his brother (see 27.6.92 for a note on his widow and executrix). LAWR 41, p. 2.

PITMAN, NATHANIEL. A gentleman who employed Jeake to buy wool for him; probably from London.

PROCTER & SEDGWICK. Merchants at Morlaix.

RADFORD, JOSEPH. Possibly the saddler of the same name who had been living in Rye in 1660; he was a jurat in the 1680s and one of the dissenters' major opponents. The Radfords were a long-established Rye family, most of whom had been shoe-makers in the sixteenth century. Burchall, p. 103; LAWR 44, p. 130.

ROBINS, JOHN. Jeake·bought wool from him; he was probably the gentleman of the same name who was living in London in the 1680s, and had previously lived in Hawkhurst, Sussex. AMS 5729/53.

SCOT, EDWARD. Gentleman and nonconformist from Lyminge who moved to Stepney, London. His wife Mary was the daughter of Sir John Honeywood. Berry, p. 169.

SKINNER/SHINNER, NICHOLAS. Merchant and business associate of Jeake's, living in Rye. Nephew of Thomas Marshall (see above). Jeake acted as overseer of Skinner's will and was left £2 for his pains. PCC PROB 11/397 1689: 165; Burchall, p. 103.

SMITH, THOMAS. Possibly the chapman who was living in Rye in 1660. He had various transactions with Jeake in the 1680s and wrote to him from Lydd. Burchall, p. 102; RYE 145/11; FRE 4954, 5022-3, 5156.

TOURNAY, THOMAS. Town clerk and jurat at Rye, and the leader of the country party in the town in the period of the Exclusion Crisis. RYE 1/17, *passim*; 19/15.

TUCKER, JOSEPH. Gentleman from Buxted, Sussex, who settled in Rye and later married Jeake's widow Elizabeth. AMS 3167, 5742/20; Smart, p. 78; Cowper, p. 584.

WEEKS, JOHN senior and MRS. Gentlefolk from Westfield, and close friends of Jeake's. Samuel Hylands (see 25.6.85) was probably a son-in-law of the Weeks's, and Jeake had hoped to marry their other daughter Mary (see below). PCC PROB 11/363 1680: 123.

WEEKS, JOHN. Son and only male heir of the above. PAB 202; AMS 3703.

WEEKS, MARY. Daughter of John Weeks senior, who left her £900 and a mortgage worth £100 in his will. PCC PROB 11/363 1680: 123.

WHITE, ALEXANDER. Rye mariner (and possibly the 'yeoman' from Playden who left a will in 1704). The Whites were a long-established family of Rye fishermen and 'feeters' (fish wholesalers). RYE 2/5; LAWR 45, p. 240.

WIGHTMAN, HENRY. Husband of Jeake's first cousin Ann (née Dallet). MS Jeake 2/3, fol. IV.

Family Trees of Jeake and Related Families

1 The Jeake Family

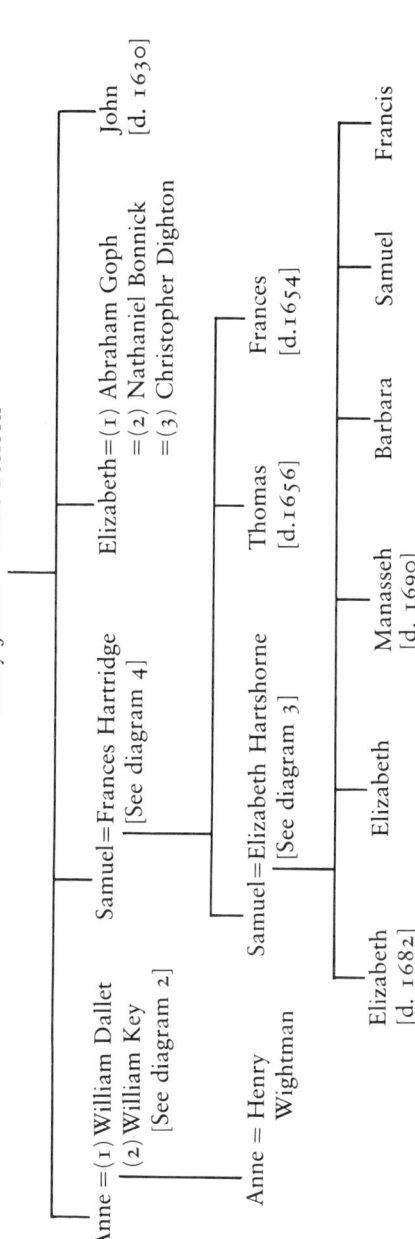

Henry Jeake = Anne Peerson

Anne = (1) William Dallet
    (2) William Key
    [See diagram 2]

Samuel = Frances Hartridge
    [See diagram 4]

Elizabeth = (1) Abraham Goph
    = (2) Nathaniel Bonnick
    = (3) Christopher Dighton

John
[d. 1630]

Anne = Henry Wightman

Samuel = Elizabeth Hartshorne
    [See diagram 3]

Thomas
[d.1656]

Frances
[d.1654]

Elizabeth
[d. 1682]

Elizabeth

Manasseh
[d. 1690]

Barbara

Samuel

Francis

For fuller information on some of the people mentioned here see Smart, pp. 78–9.

All spouses and children from Jeake's immediate family have been included in this diagram (with date of death if they died in childhood). More distant kin have only been included in the family trees if they have immediate relevance for the diary.

2. The Key Family

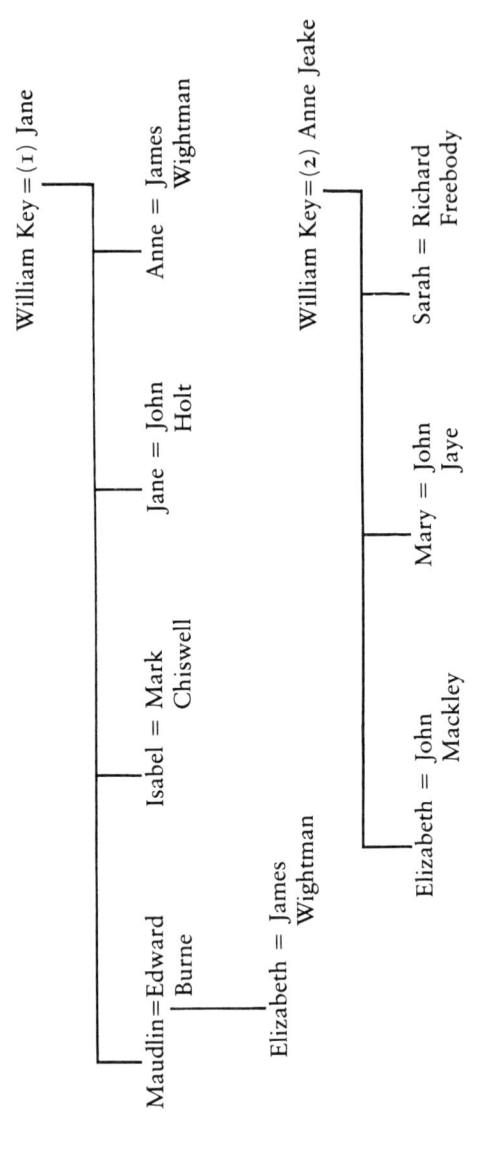

William Key = (1) Jane

Maudlin = Edward Burne

Elizabeth = James Wightman

Isabel = Mark Chiswell

Jane = John Holt

Anne = James Wightman

William Key = (2) Anne Jeake

Elizabeth = John Mackley

Mary = John Jaye

Sarah = Richard Freebody

3. The Hartshorne Family

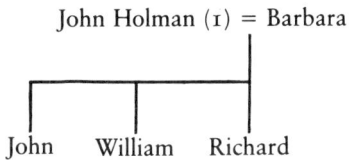

John Holman (1) = Barbara

John   William   Richard

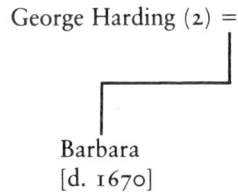

George Harding (2) =

Barbara
[d. 1670]

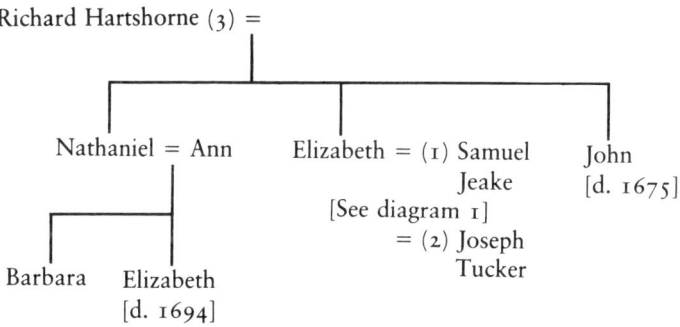

Richard Hartshorne (3) =

Nathaniel = Ann   Elizabeth = (1) Samuel   John
                                       Jeake   [d. 1675]
                              [See diagram 1]
                                = (2) Joseph
Barbara   Elizabeth   Tucker
           [d. 1694]

4. The Hartridge Family

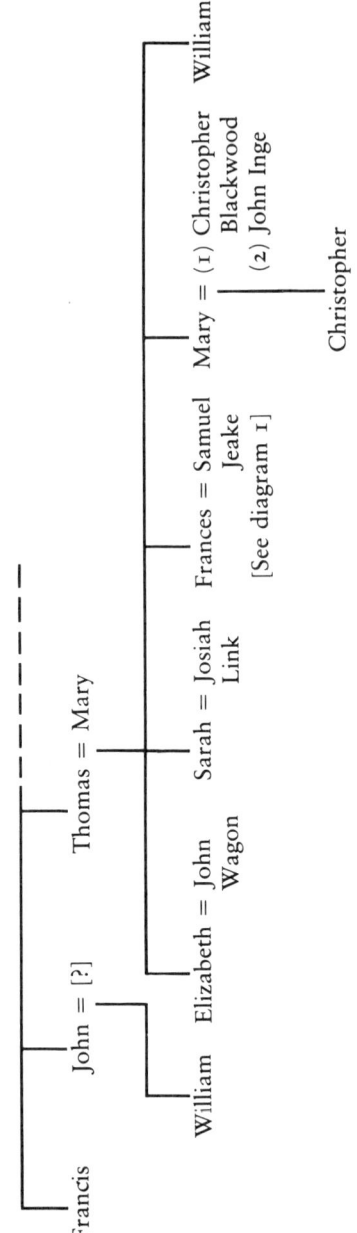

GLOSSARY OF TECHNICAL TERMS AND OBSOLETE WORDS

ACTION. A share in a joint-stock company.

AEGYLOPS. An ulcer in the inner angle of the eye.

ALOEPHANGINAE, PILULAE. Aromatical pills made from aloe, used for their cleansing effect.

ALTERATIVE. Medicine intended to reduce the processes of nutrition to healthy action.

ANDROMEDA. A constellation of the Northern Hemisphere.

ANGLES. The four cardinal points of the horoscope, namely the Ascendant, the Imum Coeli, the Descendant, and the Medium Coeli.

AQUA THERIACALIS. A compound water recommended for use in fevers.

ASCENDANT. The first cusp of the horoscope, where the ecliptic is cut by the eastern horizon.

ASCENDING. Used by Jeake to describe signs etc. in the ascendant.

ASPECT. An angular relationship between the planets in the heavens.

ATTACHMENT. A writ commanding arrest for contempt of court.

AUREAE, PILULAE. A strong purgative made from aloes, diagrydium, etc.

BAIT, TO. To stop for refreshments while travelling.

BEDSTAFF. A stick used in the structure of a bed.

BILL OF LADING. The official detailed receipt given by the master of a vessel to a person consigning goods to it.

BODAR. The officer of the courts at Dover Castle: from 'bode', Middle English for 'command' (Hull, p. 316 n.)

BOTTOMRY. A type of mortgage whereby a shipowner borrowed money at an agreed rate of interest for the duration of a voyage, pledging his ship as security, the lender taking the risk that if the ship were lost, so would his money be.

CADENT. Falling from an angle, i.e. the third, sixth, ninth, and twelfth houses of the horoscope.

CAPIAS. A writ ordering an officer to arrest a person.

CARDINAL SIGNS. Aries, Cancer, Libra, and Capricorn, i.e. the signs of the zodiac marking the start of each season.

CATAPLASM. A poultice or plaster.

CHOLER, YELLOW. Bile, the discharge associated with the choleric humour.

CONGERIES. A collection of things heaped together.

COPARCENER. One who shares equally with others in the inheritance of the real estate of a common ancestor.

COSTIVE. Constipated.

CROCUS METALLORUM. An antimony-based compound medicine.

CROWN OFFICE. The office at which the business of the King's Bench was transacted.

CRUPPER. Leather strap buckled to the saddle and passing under the horse's tail to keep the saddle from slipping forward.

CULMINATE. To arrive at the Medium Coeli.

CURTESY. 'Tenure by the courtesy of England' described a husband's right to life tenure of his deceased wife's real property.

CUSP. The beginning or edge of a horoscopic house.

DEPENDING. Archaic usage for 'pending'.

DESCENDANT. The seventh cusp of the horoscope.

DETRIFIED. In detriment: a planet in the sign opposite the sign of which it is ruler.

DIACHYLON CUM GUMMIS. Yellow diachylon, an emollient plaster composed of the juice of herbs.

DIALLING. The art of constructing and using sundials.

DIASCORDIUM. A sedative made from cassia, cinnamon, tormentil, opium, water germander, etc.

DISCUSS. To dissipate, dispel (humours etc.).

DOCTORS COMMONS. The buildings occupied by the Association or College of Doctors of Civil Law in London, where Prerogative Court wills were registered.

DOLLAR. English name for a German thaler or Spanish piece of eight.

DOUBLE SHALLOP. A large, heavy boat with two masts.

DOWLAS. A coarse type of linen.

DRAGON'S HEAD/TAIL, CAPUT/CAUDA DRACONIS. The point where the Moon's orbit crosses the ecliptic going north and going south.

ECLIPTIC. The Sun's path in its apparent orbit around the earth.

ERYSIPELAS. A febrile disease involving inflammation of the skin.

EXALTATION. See Appendix 2 (i).

EXTRACTUM RUDII. Pills of this compound, made of colocynth and other ingredients, were recommended in pharmacopoeia of the day for their cleansing effect.

FACTORY. Activity as a factor or agent.

FINITOR. The horizon.

FLASKET. A long shallow basket.

FLEGM, PHLEGM. Mucus, the discharge associated with the phlegmatic humour.

FONTINELL, or fontanelle. An artificial ulcer for the discharge of humours.

GRAVEL(L). Aggregation of crystals found in the urine.

GRAND JURY. The presenting jury at the local assizes.

GREEN SICKNESS. An iron deficiency anaemia affecting young women of the age of puberty.

GUTTA SERENA. 'When the sight is gone, and no fault appears in the Eyes'. (Riverius, *Practice of Physick*, trans. Culpeper (London, 1655), 62).

HOUSE(S). Used by Jeake either for the twelve-fold division of the local sky, or, more loosely, as a synonym for 'sign'.

HOY. A small vessel, usually rigged as a sloop, employed to carry passengers and goods, especially on short distances along the sea-coast.

IMUM COELI. The fourth cusp of the horoscope.

INFORTUNES, THE. The malevolent planets Saturn and Mars.

INTERNAL. A medicine taken internally.

JOINTURE. The holding of property to the joint use of husband and wife for life or in tail, as provision to the latter in the event of widowhood.

JURAT. A municipal officer of the Cinque Ports: comparable to the office of alderman elsewhere.

KENTING. A kind of fine linen cloth.

KING'S BENCH. The supreme court of Common Law.

LASQUE. Looseness of the bowels, diarrhoea.

LOCKRAM. A type of linen fabric made in Brittany.

LUMINARIES, THE. The Sun and Moon.

MEDIUM COELI. The mid-heaven, the tenth cusp of the horoscope.

MELANCHOLY. See Introduction, sect. 7.

MERCURIAL GIRDLE. A belt-like bandage dabbed with mercurial ointment or salve, used for treating skin diseases.

MERIDIAN. A circle crossing the equator (from the poles) at right angles.

MILLION ADVENTURE. See Introduction, sect. 8.

MISLING. Slight rain, drizzle.

NOYALL. Cloth manufactured at Noyal, in the *département* Ille-et-Vilaine, France.

OXFORD ACT. The Five Mile Act of 1665, passed while Parliament was sitting at Oxford during the Great Plague.

PARTILE ASPECT. An exact aspect in a multiple of 30°. (See platique).

PECCANT. Unhealthy, corrupt.

PHLEGM. See flegm.

PLATIQUE. An angular relation between the planets which is not quite the multiple of 30° required for a partile aspect (q.v.).

PREROGATIVE COURT. The court of the Archbishop of Canterbury for the probate of wills and trial of testamentary and other civil causes in which effects to the value of £5 had been left in each of two or more ecclesiastical jurisdictions.

QUARTAN. A type of ague: see Introduction, sect. 7.

QUEVÉ, KNOTS À LA. A calligraphic term from the French 'queue' describing the elaborate tail-like flourishes that were appended to the ends of words.

QUOTIDIAN. A type of ague: see Introduction, sect. 7.

RADIX. The natal horoscope.

RECEPTION. Two planets being positioned in each other's signs.

RETROCESSION, IN. i.e. retrograde: the apparent backward movement of a planet in relation to the fixed stars at certain points in its passage along the ecliptic.

RHEUM. Mucous discharge caused by catching cold; catarrh.

ROAD. In maritime parlance, a sheltered piece of water near the shore where vessels can safely anchor.

SCORBUTICK. Symptomatic of, or proceeding from, scurvy.

SHALLOP. A large and heavy boat with one or more masts.

SIGN. The twelve-fold division of the Sun's path in its apparent orbit around the earth.

SPECIALTY, ON. By special sealed contract.

STAPLER. A merchant of the Staple, the London market where wool was sold.

STATIONARY. The point in a planet's orbit when it enters or leaves a state of retrocession (q.v.).

STOMACHLESS. Having no appetite.

STRUMOUS. Pertaining to a struma, a scrofulous swelling or tumour.

SUBPENA, or subpoena. Writ issued by Chancery commanding the presence of a defendant to answer a matter alleged against him.

SUFFUSION. The defluxion of a fluid over part of a body; in the case of the eye, a cataract.

SULPHUR PER CAMPANUM. Sulphuric acid, so named because of the bell-shaped receptacle in which it was distilled.

SYROPUS CARYOPHULLATUS. A compound made from cloves.

TERTIAN. A type of ague: see Introduction, sect. 7.

TEST. The oaths or declarations prescribed by the Test Act of 1673.

THERIACA ANDROMACHI. A further general medication, the term 'theriac' being given to several confections, especially of an alexipharmic kind.

THRUSH. A disease characterized by white bladder-like specks on the inside of the mouth and tongue, caused by a parasitic fungus.

TILT BOAT. A large rowing boat with a tilt or awning, used on the Thames, especially between London and Gravesend.

TOPICAL. Medicines outwardly applied to the affected part of the body.

UNGUENT. An ointment or salve.

UNGUENTUM NUTRITUM. A compound of oil of roses, litharge of gold, etc., recommended in the pharmacopoeia of the day as cooling and drying and good for itches etc.

UVULA. Conical fleshy lobe hanging from the palate.

VENICE TREACLE. A celebrated remedy concocted from a range of ingredients. See Introduction, sect. 7.

VERTIGINOUS. Affected with vertigo or giddiness.

VESICATORY. An ointment or plaster applied to raise blisters in the skin, in which fluids collected and could then be discharged.

VOLATILE SALT OF VIPERS. Volatile salts were made by boiling a substance—in this case evidently the flesh of vipers, a common ingredient in medical compounds—with a large quantity of water and then allowing the salt to crystallize.

WORT, or liquor. Infusion of malt for beer-making.

APPENDIX 4 (ii)

QUANTITIES AND MEASURES

BAG (wheat, hops). Approximately 300 pounds.

BALLOT (cloth). 70 to 120 pounds.

BARREL (herrings). 32 gallons.

BUSHEL (wheat etc.). 8 gallons.

DRAUGHT (wool). 61 pounds.

LOAD (corn). 5 quarters.

LOAD (timber). 50 cubic feet.

PACK (wool). 240 pounds.

PUNCHEON (liquids). Approximately 100 gallons.

QUARTER (wheat etc.). 8 bushels.

TOD (wool). 28 pounds, or 2 stone.

APPENDIX 5

JEAKE'S SHORTHAND

THE following notes give a brief summary of the system of shorthand set out in 1645 by Samuel Jeake senior in his manual *Veni et vide. Brevity abbreviated* (Selmes MS 1). It was this that his son used, with minor variations, in his diary. This efficient method is similar to that presented in several contemporary printed manuals, but most closely resembles that of Edmond Willis in his *An Abreviation of Writing by Character* (1618), one of the earliest phonetic shorthands. Most of the shorthand alphabet and many of the shortforms are the same as those used by Willis. For references to some other contemporary shorthand manuals see E. H. Butler, *The Story of British Shorthand* (London, 1951).

The Alphabet

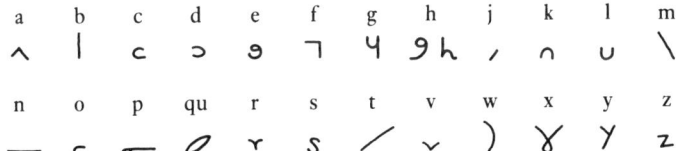

The symbols for vowels in Jeake senior's alphabet were not often used by his son, who preferred to indicate vowels at the start and end of words by a tick or dot. Diphthongs were also indicated by a tick. Vowels which occurred in between consonants were indicated by the position of the second consonant, as in most systems of shorthand in this period:

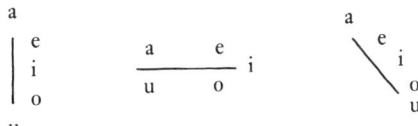

Examples

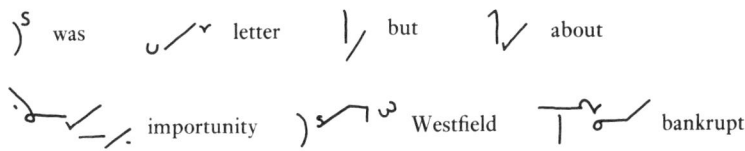

279

Jeake senior included many shortforms for whole words or parts of words in his manual. His son used only a few of these, and added some of his own. Those most commonly found in the diary are listed below, with his father's version given in brackets if there were differences. The meaning of those in the second list has been guessed from the context in which they were used in the diary, or from shorthand drafts of letters and sermon notes (see above, Introduction, sect. 3 n. 11).

Shortforms taken from Jeake senior's manual

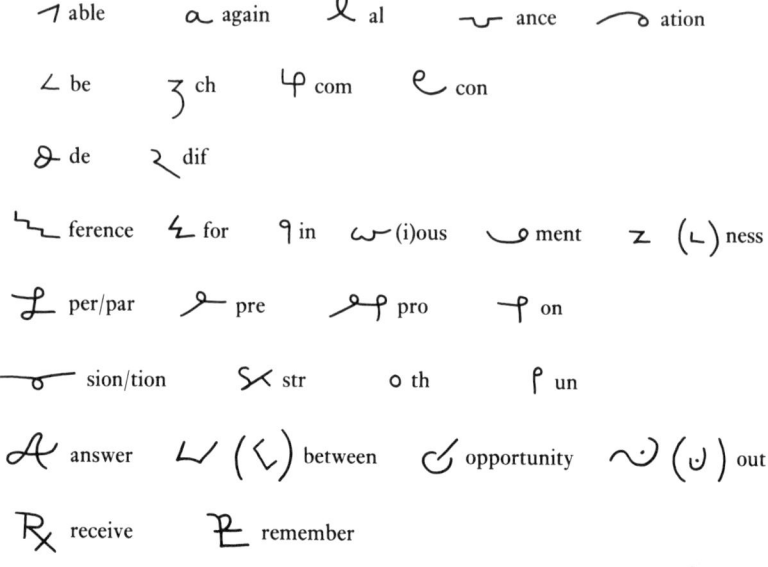

Shortforms introduced by Jeake junior

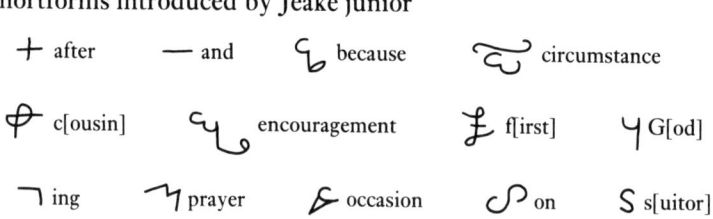

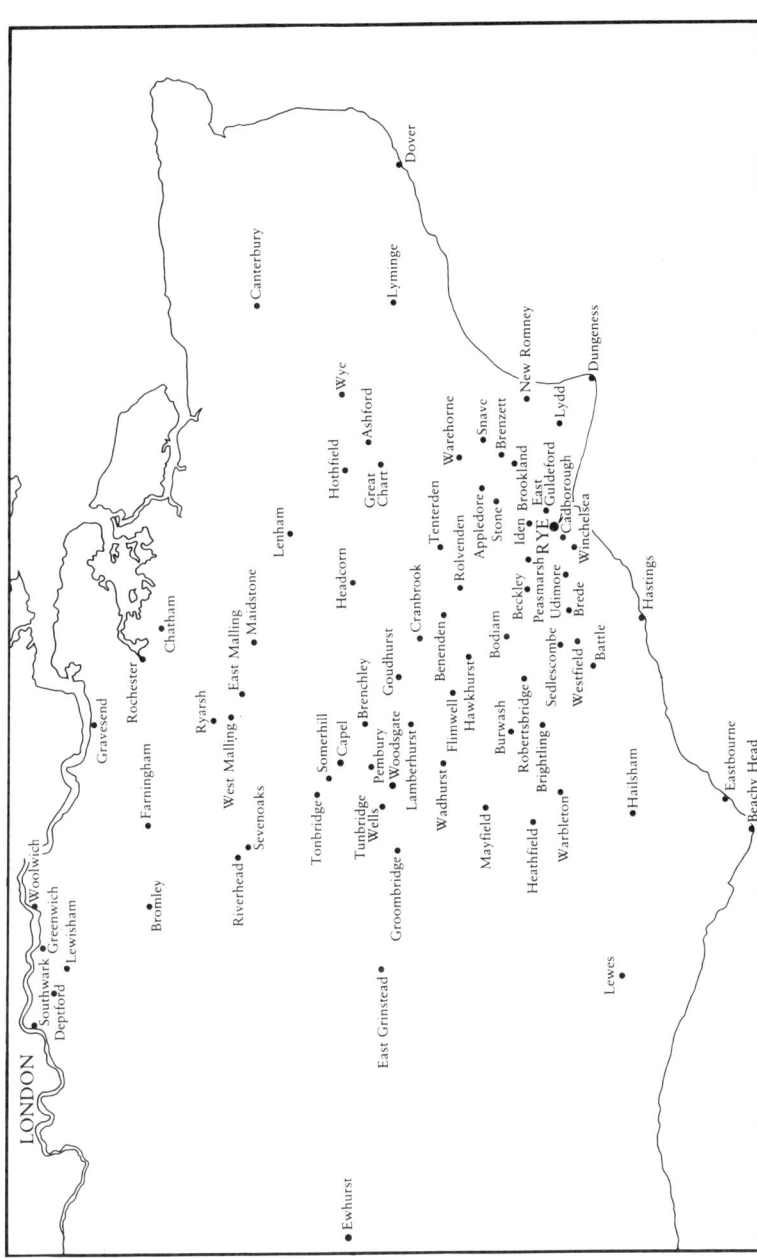

Places in south-east England referred to in the diary

INDEX